EVERY WOMAN'S GUIDE TO
LOOKING GOOD

CU00717629

Colin McDowell is the fashion editor of *Country Life* magazine, and has extensive experience of the fashion world. After spending several years in Rome designing *haute couture* and ready-to-wear and working as a fashion editor for a trade magazine, Colin McDowell returned to London to write. He is a regular contributor to the style pages of the *Guardian*, has written for many publications including the *Observer*, *Tatler*, *Mail on Sunday*, *Good Housekeeping* and many foreign newspapers and journals as well as being a regular broadcaster on radio and television. He is the author of two successful books, *McDowell's Directory of Fashion* and *A Hundred Years of Royal Style*, both of which were published to great critical acclaim, and have established him as a major writer on the fashion scene.

McDOWELL'S DIRECTORY OF TWENTIETH CENTURY FASHION

"At last the essential book for anybody interested in fashion design and all that is associated with it has been published . . . I find this book fascinating and only wish that it had been written ten years ago . . . anybody interested in fashion, from the serious student to the ardent clothes buyer, will find this book an extremely good read and a bargain for twenty quid."

Jasper Conran, *The Literary Review*

ISBN 0 584 11070-7   £20.00

A HUNDRED YEARS OF ROYAL STYLE

A fascinating record of royal style scanning a century and covering four queens – Alexandra, Mary, Elizabeth and Elizabeth II – as well as Wallis Simpson, who became the Duchess of Windsor, and the Queen-to-be, Princess Diana. McDowell probes behind the royal image, giving details about the royal designers and suppliers, protocol, public relations, state occasions, travelling abroad and the Royal Year. Illustrated with a marvellous selection of colour and black and white photographs together with original drawings by Colin McDowell.

ISBN 0 584 11071-5   £14.95

EVERY WOMAN'S GUIDE TO
LOOKING GOOD

COLIN McDOWELL

Muller, Blond & White

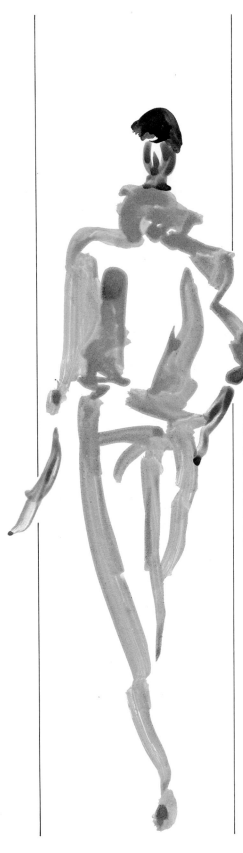

First published in 1986 by Muller, Blond & White Limited,
55 Great Ormond Street, London WC1N 3HZ.

British Library Cataloguing in Publication Data
McDowell, Colin
   Everywoman's guide to looking
   good.
   1. Clothing and dress
   I. Title
   646'. 34   TX340

   ISBN 0-584-11115-0

Contents

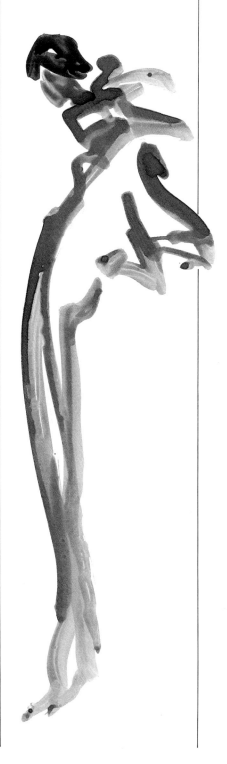

chapter 1

Taking stock

Are you nervous about fashion? Do you feel slightly intimidated when you look at the images of female perfection in the glossy magazines and compare them to your own form? Do you feel that there is a fashion mystique and you are out in the cold? Don't worry, so do thousands of other women.

I have written this book because after several years in the fashion world as a designer, writer and journalist, I feel that the average woman needs just a little help to develop her own self-confidence so that she chooses clothes and wears them in a way that pleases her. Style does not require an exclusive and separate frame of mind. Any woman can train her style sense so that she can make her clothes work for her — and that includes you.

I believe that every woman can be better dressed. All that is needed is confidence and that is what I have tried to give in this book. I have swept away the mystique and mumbo-jumbo to take the reader back to basics.

Are you perfectly happy with your appearance? Do you feel totally in charge when you walk into a room? Do you feel at ease with the latest fashions? If not, this is the book for you. In its pages you will not find information about fashion as something requiring an exclusive and separate attitude of mind. You will find advice on training your fashion intelligence so that you can choose clothes that work for you.

Getting it right

I hope that it will give you the confidence not to be over-awed by fashion. The assured woman knows how to read a fashion magazine for what she is looking for. She knows how to choose clothes without being intimidated by an over-bearing saleswoman. She achieves what she wants by knowledge. She must have fashion knowledge and self-knowledge if she is to

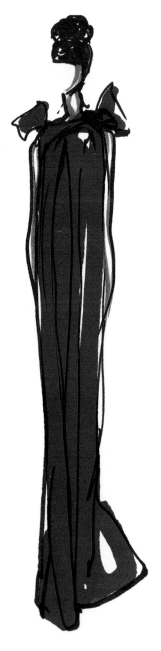

Making the best of yourself often means not being frightened of colour. The successful dresser makes colour work for her. It can express a mood or create a lasting image of your personality. A striking effect can be created by ruthlessly excluding all details, avoiding distracting accessories, and allowing a column of pure colour to speak for you — if you have the confidence.

avoid becoming a fashion victim. Self-awareness is the key to getting it right. As the legendary Diana Vreeland once said to me,'' When I am paying they have to get it right — and that means right for me, not them.''

At any time there is a popular image of what is the fashionable look for that moment. Subconsciously we all recognise it and respond to it. The big shoulders, short skirts and clumpy shoes of the forties appear old-fashioned even to someone who has never looked at a fashion magazine in his life. Why? Because they are so totally different from the current received image of female appearance which is seen every day on the streets, in newspapers and on television.

What is style?

Style is being yourself, but it has to be a little more than that. I you try too hard, you might look smart or chic but you will never look stylish. This is why women who work in fashion rarely have style. Their appearance is too carefully thought ou colour coordinated and all of a piece in the current fashion to allow the individual to come through.

Ignoring fashion

Remember that style is individuality. Never let current fashion swamp your personality. The most stylish women I know are self-absorbed and self-involved. They know what works for them and say to hell with what fashion might be doing. For instance, whenever I see the *Grand Dame* of fashion, Diana Vreeland, she always looks the same. Short hair severely scraped back, scarlet lipstick and a little cashmere sweater and pants, normally black and usually from Yves Saint Lauren or Givenchy. The factor that changes, and gives her real fashion clout, is her superbly barbaric jewelry. This is her strong statement and it carries her look. She wears a simple but powerful neck ornament and lots of huge bracelets and somehow manages to make them almost like animate objects. Last time I spoke to her she was wearing grey cashmere from Givenchy. She had put the sweater on back to front because she found it more flattering that way. Her bangles and bracelets were used almost as an extension of her voice as they clashed and clattered with each dramatic arm movement And none of it was accidental. She was achieving the effect she wanted with the maximum of style.

Sadly there is only one Vreeland and no other woman on earth has her style — except perhaps the members of certain

frican tribes who have more natural style than all of Paris put
ogether.

ow do you achieve style?

ne Vreeland way is by knowing so much about the roots of
ashion that you have forgotten more than most women will
ver know. Diana Vreeland is so steeped in fashion that she
an now largely ignore current trends and still be uniquely
tylish. Another way is to be so totally unconcerned with
ashion trends that your clothes are completely original and
ossibly even eccentric — Dame Freya Starke, the traveller, is
 supreme example of this. No one can wear a cotton sun
onnet with her style and authority.

   You, of course, have to steer somewhere between these
vo. You do so, as I have said, by making the effort to become
formed whilst resisting the temptation to become *enslaved* by
ashion. You read magazines intelligently but do not rush out to
uy the top-to-tail look seen in the photograph. That will merely
ake you look fashionable — you want to look unique.

Vho influences you?

believe that everyone cares deeply about how she looks, even
 she is not interested in fashion, hates shopping, has few
lothes and little money to spend on them. After all, everyone
as to buy clothes, and you choose them either to align
ourself socially with a group or perhaps to deliberately
istance yourself from one or many groups. It is impossible to
ake an abstract choice without reference (consciously or
ubconsciously) to the way you see other people and fashions.

he fashion photograph

he reference most commonly relied upon is the fashion
hotograph. There are very few women who do not read one or
ther of the magazines published to service their special
terests. All these magazines have some degree of fashion
ontent and, of that, ninety per cent is visual. In many cases,
ne hundred per cent of the fashion information is given in
nages, not words. We can only perceive fashion through the
yes of the interpreters. Designers create clothes, fashion
ditors create fashion — the accepted received image of how
o wear the clothes at any one time. Fashion editors are the
eople who define fashion. Their interpretation of how to wear
ne current season's clothes affects not only the man and
voman in the street, but also next season's designs because

*If you **are** confident enough, colours which clash can be used to great effect — but do not be tempted to go over-the-top. This scheme works because the two strong and hot contrast colours are cooled and controlled by the basic black of the dress. Remember that sharp and bold colours should be used in small doses if they are to keep their effect — which is to make you look stunning, not stunned.*

*Do not be afraid of colour. It can be used in many different ways. A pillar-box red jacket can be cut on classic lines and worn in a very traditional way as it is here but, because it is a **strong** colour, it makes a statement and can never look dull. Obviously . . .*

designers are influenced by the way their clothes are worn thi season.

Clothes maketh man

The social force of clothes cannot be over-estimated. We lear a great deal from people's clothes — about their personality and attitudes, their wealth and social position. Clothes may conceal the naked body, but in all other respects they reveal us to our fellows. The fashion historian James Laver called clothes "the furniture of the mind made visible" and certainly our attitudes, personalities and even intelligence are communicated, wittingly or unwittingly, by what we wear. This is why looking at ourselves in relation to our clothes is not a frivolous waste of time, but a serious and worthwhile occupation.

Clothes guides — dangerous fantasy

No one, unless she is completely mad, is going to spend time "recreating" her personality by dressing in response to the sort of nonsense that says, "Do you have long straight hair? Do you dream of wide open spaces? Do you love rich, natural colours? Then the American Indian look is the one for you." Get out there and do it yourself — only then will you feel at ease with the way you look.

Who am I and what am I?

Before reading any fashion magazine or clothes article, befor visiting any shop, even before looking in the window, look at yourself. Only you have the chance to really know yourself an your lifestyle and most of us don't until we consciously think about it. Only you can hope to dress yourself successfully, an remember, success with clothes could lead to success in life. How we dress is important to just about every aspect of our lives — career, romance and social wellbeing. You can be as attractive and successful as any other person provided you start from the basis of honest self-assessment. After all, who knows you better than yourself?

The naked truth

Tell yourself the truth and begin by accepting that there are limits to what you can alter in your appearance.

The body unbeautiful

If your breasts are large, dreaming is not going to reduce thei size. If you have thick ankles, the chances are that they will g nicker. If it is your hips that first show that you have put on weight, this is not going to change. But don't despair. Disguise and camouflage can work wonders. So, surprisingly, can the blatant highlighting of a figure "fault". It all depends on the clothes you choose and how your wear them.

Look at yourself critically and privately. Take off all your clothes and, without holding in your stomach or consciously pushing back your shoulders, stand normally and then slowly turn round in front of a mirror, preferably a full-length one. You will probably be shocked but don't despair — ninety-nine percent of people doing the same thing would have the same reaction.

Complacency from lack of challenge

We too soon become accustomed to ourselves and allow our self-critical faculty to be lulled. We need a shock to wake us up from our complacency. Who has not caught sight of a dishevelled, wind-swept woman in her middle years battling down the high street, and recoiled in horror on realising that the woman is herself reflected in a shop window!

Most of us wear the same sort of clothes, maybe actually the same favourite garments, more or less all the time because they are so comfortable and unchallenging. We can put them on and forget about them. But all this has to change when we are confronted by a special occasion which snaps us out of our normal complacency. Suddenly we have to step out of our normal routine of dressing. It could be for a wedding, a special dinner dance or a holiday. We are forced to look at ourselves in a way that our normal lives and clothes for that life never demand of us.

Realisation — too late

Now the "if only" feelings rush in, the dissatisfaction and despair. How easy it is to forget the way the pounds are creeping on until the thought of summer beaches brings us face to face with the realities of those revealing swimsuits! Perhaps it is only when thinking about a smart outfit for a wedding that we realise we have neglected our shoes which have gone too far to be smartened up for the occasion. The long dress that fitted just last Christmas will not zip up now that it is needed for the office dance.

Be positive

There is no need to feel desperate just because the body in the

. . . bold colour is crisp, fresh and youthful — but you do not have to be young to get away with it. Red is a marvellous flatterer for the older woman. It "goes" with greying hair and, provided you make-up in a way that counteracts its strength it can help you to look wonderful.

mirror is not perfect. Whose is? Admittedly a handful of lucky girls have the makings of a perfect body and a few of them succeed in developing their potential so that they do have very beautiful bodies. But remember, they have worked very hard to achieve them and they let them dominate their lives because they make their living from them. Model girls, actresses and entertainers are at an advantage in their worlds if their bodies are beautiful and in peak condition. You are not a model girl, you don't have to strive for this sort of perfection. What you should do is make the best of what you have and not waste time crying for the moon.

Basic body shapes

Ideas of what is considered beautiful or sexy in the female body constantly change. The Minoans and some Medieval courts considered it perfectly acceptable for women to bare their breasts but insisted that they wore long skirts because to show the ankle was the height of immodesty. It was not until this century that it became acceptable for women to wear trousers and they began to show their legs by wearing skirts which stopped higher than at any time in Western civilisation. Eastern women may wear diaphanous gowns, but they modestly cover their faces.

 Similarly, the desirable shape and size of a body has changed over the centuries. We all know that the women painted by Rubens were distinctly fat — a slim Edwardian woman was considered a poor thing at that time but a large, pouter-pigeon bust was the height of desirability. The same bust was cause for concern in the twenties when the young and fashionable wanted to be as flat-chested as young boys.

Body shape can be roughly divided into three categories.

The ectomorph, or gazelle type

The flapper had the classic ectomorph figure as did Katherine Hepburn in the thirties, Audrey Hepburn in the fifties and, the most extreme example of all, Twiggy in the sixties. In the eighties the current ideal of the ectomorph woman is embodied in the Princess of Wales and Princess Michael of Kent.

Fashion editors love ectomorphs as they have no bumps to spoil the line of the clothes in photographs but whether men find these adolescent boy figures so exciting is a different story. Like gazelles, these figure types look marvellous when young, but tend to be too gaunt and stringy as they age.

Collections may seem so varied that you do not know which look is going to work for you. The best way to overcome this problem is to follow a leader — either a designer or a mass-market manufacturer — whose clothes appeal to you. Stick with him and learn why he designs and cuts in a certain way.

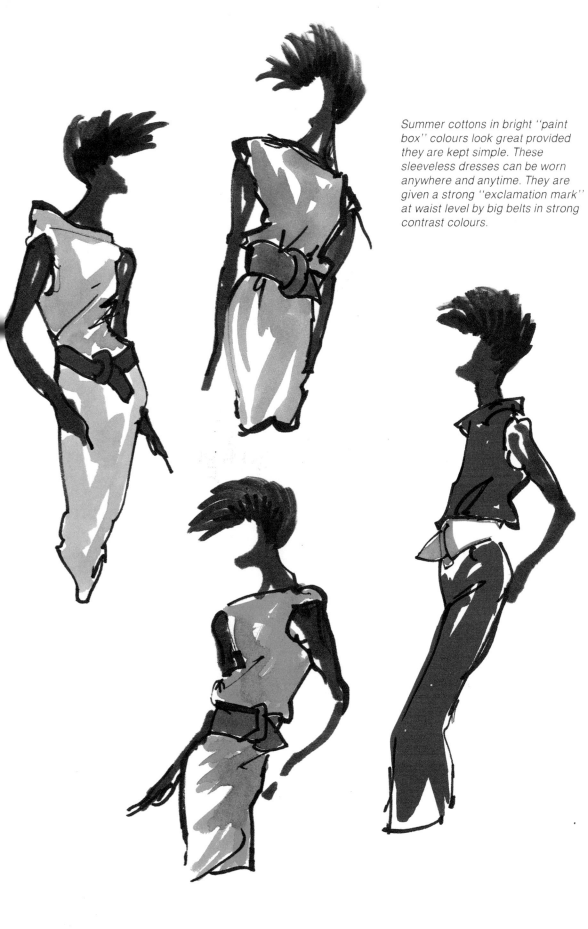

Summer cottons in bright "paint box" colours look great provided they are kept simple. These sleeveless dresses can be worn anywhere and anytime. They are given a strong "exclamation mark" at waist level by big belts in strong contrast colours.

Silk is the great flatterer for all figure types. This loose (but not shapeless) smock in a strong colour and bold patterns is the sort of thing which, when worn with plain silk pants, suits most women: pregnant, young, old, slim and not-so-slim. If you can't afford silk there are plenty of substitutes which will give you the same sort of effect.

The mesomorph, or tiger type

The mesomorph is the figure you often have as a teenager, or the one you end up with if you work at making your body super-fit as an adult. It is the perfectly efficient shape. Fat, muscle and linearity are about equal and the body is not especially thin. This tiger type is best exemplified by Marie Helvin or Jane Fonda as the leaders in a very large pack of media women and fashionable figures including Raquel Welch.

The endomorph

The Rubenesque woman was the endomorph type and although this is now the least fashionably acceptable figure, there are still plenty of them around. They are not necessarily the least sexy either. Just as Rubens and the men of his time were turned on by endomorph women, so Mae West, Liz Taylor and Dolly Parton prove that this figure type is still considered an archetype of female sexuality in this century. The secret, if you are in this group, is to keep your figure as curvaceous as those three ladies have rather than letting it spread all over as Mama Cass or Sophie Tucker did. Think of yourself as a cuddly koala bear and you will be okay — you are in trouble when you spread like a rhinoceros.

The endomorphic figure type tends to get overweight and has little muscle and very limited linearity. However, many women with endomorph characteristics are not really endomorphs — if they were thin in their teens and twenties then they are more likely to be in the commonest of the three sub-divisions.

The endomorphic mesomorph

The standard figure that has run to fat because the woman has "let herself go". Very common in the Western world.

The ectomorphic endomorph

The prevalent "feminine" figure with a good bust and ample curves but not much excess fat.

The ectomorphic mesomorph

Here is the muscular and athletic woman, often with a long frame and long legs that can frequently disguise the fact that a certain amount of extra fat is being carried.

That honest look at yourself in the mirror will tell you which basic shape you fit into.

Body presentation

Just as ideals of figure type change in the constantly shifting sands of what is beautiful, so does presentation — not only in an obvious way as with the Edwardian determination to corset and cajole breasts into a solid monobosom, but in the much more subtle but equally telling area of deportment. The way you stand, sit and walk are a reflection of two things, your figure type and your clothes.

Dictates of fashion

Very early fourteenth-century paintings show women with thei stomachs thrust out and their shoulders slumped forward in what was clearly the very latest fashionable pose. It was a stance affected by the fact that the very full long skirts of the time had to be pulled forward and held across the stomach to enable the wearer to walk.

Edwardian women stood and sat bolt upright because their very heavy tight corsets made it impossible for them to do otherwise. They also walked slowly for the same reason — an the fact that their clothes weighed a ton. Also their complicated hair arrangments and enormous hats were alway precariously perched and speed might easily dislodge them both — so a measured pace was *de rigeur*.

A taste of freedom

In the twenties the freedom that short skirts and light material gave to women enabled them at last to take real strides instead of mincing steps. The loosening of corsetry also enabled them to stand and sit in the relaxed way that men did. Trousers, worn by women for the first time in history, meant that women could sit comfortably with their legs splayed out – something which had never been possible before.

Restriction returns

Modesty, the bane of women throughout the ages and largely imposed by men, returned in the thirties and came to its high-point of twentieth-century artificiality in the fifties. To look elegant the fifties' woman had to have a certain stance with head and hips thrust forward (rather like a chic tortoise) so tha the clothes fell in the way the designer had planned. At its mos extreme, in fashion shows and magazine photographs, the position taken up by models was as unnatural and awkward looking as that in the early fourteenth-century paintings.

When you are looking at catwalk shots of the Collections, remember that the clothes have been picked out for theatrical effect with eye-catching and often outrageous accessories which are never meant to be worn on the street. Train your eye to strip away the candy floss and get down to the line, shape and proportion of the garment.

Freedom back for good

The sixties swung right away from this artificiality. Youth was the thing every woman was chasing. Wearing the briefest clothes possible made for carefree and careless movement. Even though skirts were tiny, modesty was not a problem due to the advent of tights which helped to solve the perennial problem of things showing.

After the total confusion and uncertainty of the seventies, the eighties have produced our own woman who combines the best of previous generations. She is as free as her twenties' forerunners and as poised as any woman in the thirties. She has cast aside the twin artificialities of the fifties superchic and the sixties baby doll whilst using the strides they took towards the creation of that uniquely eighties female — the poised, natural woman who is mistress of her own space.

Make the best of yourself

Within the norms of stance and deportment in response to clothes types and society's expectations, your individuality will be reflected by the way you stand and move.

Know your good points and highlight them in your dress and in your movements. The powerful American fashion magazine "W" deplores the Princess of Wales's tendency to try to disguise her height by stooping forward. What they call the "Di Slouch" does not make her look shorter — it merely destroys a superb advantage nature gave her. Tall girls should walk tall with long, healthy strides, with their heads held high.

I have a very dear friend who, although over fifty and rather overweight, has legs like Betty Grable. Her mother, who is in her eighties, goes one better — she has legs like Deitrich. My friend highlights her perfect calves and ankles by wearing very high heeled shoes whilst her mother, whose legs are totally without blemish, always sits as if she were on the Shanghai Express. She positions her legs in an elegant, thirties' way, slightly tucked in, parallel and close together, which shows them off to the very best advantage. She knows they are her strong point and draws attention to them by invariably wearing straight skirts which stop just at the knee.

Face up to your body

No matter what your figure type or size, convince yourself that by facing up to what you physically have or do not have, you can make the most of your body to such a degree that you can

Women have never enjoyed as much freedom as they do in this century. A brightly coloured or boldly patterned length of material wrapped around the body and casually tied can be worn, with or without anything underneath, anywhere the sun shines hot, and even after sundown. A large hat, fake earrings and dark glasses create a look which is glamorous, mysterious and fun, but which costs next-to-nothing.

transform yourself. Of course your overall appearance and attractiveness comes from many more things than your physical shape — not least your personality. A caring, considerate and humorous person is going to be loved much more than a cynical, self-centred one — regardless of figure type or style of dress. And this brings us to the basic question — what do we want our clothes to do for us? What aspect of our personality do we wish them to project?

Mind made visible

If you are a career woman working hard in a man's world, you probably use your clothes to accentuate your efficiency and clear thinking. A designer, on the other hand, will possibly use her clothes to show her flair and originality. A schoolteacher might dress to demonstrate her dependability and integrity — consciously or subconsciously. No matter what aspect of your style you are aiming to project, your success rate will depend on clear thinking. Familiarise yourself with your physical strengths and weaknesses. Analyse why you dress in a certain way and why certain things appeal whilst others don't. Your clothes are a reflection of your personality. Through them you tell people about the sort of person you are. As you meet people their reaction to you is like your mirror reflection. It tells you how successful you are at creating your image.

Dressing for your lifestyle

This book is written for real women living real lives who have only a limited amount of time and energy to spend on their clothes. They have better things to do with their time than transform a boy's shirt by adding antique shell buttons before going out!

Fashion journalism

"Clothes for the life you lead" is a common enough headline in magazine and newspaper fashion articles, but what does it really mean? The high glossies might, at first, seem to be dealing with a lifestyle far removed from yours. After all, how many women really buy grand ball dresses costing over a thousand pounds, regularly give formal dinner parties requiring long dresses or wear designer-label outfits costing many hundreds of pounds? Obviously very few. But before you toss these magazines aside as being totally irrelevant, ask yourself, "What can I learn from them?"

Visual training

Remember that fashion magazines are your barometer of what is really fashionable at the moment and, more importantly, they are your early-warning system of the looks to come. Their policy of showing the very best design regardless of country or cost gives you an invaluable visual training which works as a yardstick for your own more modest purchases. The expertise shown in accessorising the clothes they have chosen gives you a guide for putting together your accessories and has often led to a look so strong that at street level it is more powerful than the individual clothes.

These magazines are not to be ignored. Flick through them at the newstand, read them in the hairdressers or buy your own copy depending on your budget. The International Collections issues are certainly not cheap, but it would be worth investing in these twice a year. Quite a number of newspapers also give full, written reports about the looks to come, particularly around Collection time.

Study the experts carefully

The majority of magazines do not feature the high fashion end of the market but concentrate instead on clothes that are easily available to their readers around the country at prices they can afford. This does not, of course, mean that their offerings are dowdy, second best or boring. The fashion teams who have chosen the clothes to show you have the same high level of expertise as their colleagues on the glossies. They have also been to the top fashion shows of the world, and have just as well-developed and finely honed a fashion sense. They choose their fashion page items in the full knowledge of what the top designers are doing.

They take their knowledge and give it practical form in the clothes they feature at prices they feel their readers can afford. They are the direct link between the salon and the high street and as such are invaluable to you. Which of the many different magazines appeals to you is only found by trial and error, but if you wish to be an informed clothes buyer, it is important to read at least one on a regular basis.

Reading fashion magazines will not turn you into a fashion freak or anything as pathetic as that. It will, however, considerably enhance your chances of buying soundly and not making expensive mistakes.

If you are feeling a little unsure about how to put together a look, it is not cheating to buy exactly the combination of clothes displayed in the window. It won't express your personality, but you will at least have the comfort of knowing that your appearance has been created by the fashion expertise of a highly trained display person.

In the last few seasons fashion designers have rediscovered the body. Tight skirts, waist emphasis and big shoulders are now the current look. Some of the younger designers in Paris go a little wild in their attempt to put the message across. Here a leather jacket, animal print skirt and several layers of lace are teamed with leather boots to deliberately break the rules of taste. Although looking like this is amusing it is only for the very assured extravert.

Fashion journalists

A newspaper fashion report is a distillation of hard work, intuition and wisdom and it is important that you use it to help you plan how you will be dressing in the months to come.

Their lifestyle

One of the major problems for fashion journalists is keeping a grip on the reality of clothes in terms of their readers. The journalists themselves are so often surrounded by fantasy. Consider the sort of life they actually lead and the problems become clear. The job of the fashion journalist is to bring her readers the latest news about clothes, the latest breakthrough with a look and the latest and most exciting examples of good design. At the same time she has to try to be aware of the sort of lives her readers live, the amount of money they have to spend on their appearance, and the sort of information that will be of interest and value to them. She might, or might not, share their attitudes, but she ignores them at her peril.

Her problem is further complicated by the fact that innovation costs money, so new ideas almost always spring from individual designers whose clothes are almost certainly beyond her reader's price range. High Street clothes are exceedingly difficult to photograph in such a way that they appear exciting because, by their nature, their designers must play safe and, too often, their creations are dull.

All of the people all of the time

The journalists' lives seem glamorous and desirable to most women who have an interest in clothes. Indeed they are glamorous and desirable in many respects but also very difficult.

A good fashion journalist requires considerable critical and physical stamina and needs a head that is not easily turned by flashy razzmatazz. The fashion journalist must be able to look behind all the PR hype which fashion is given these days. In addition she has to please an editor who has an ever-anxious eye on the advertising revenue. She cannot risk her fashion department jeopardising her newspaper or magazine's production budget by displeasing key advertisers. Innocent readers would be surprised to know how important this is considered by some of the most prestigious magazines in the world whose editors often insist that keeping advertisers happy is more vital than keeping readers informed. Articles and features are cut and altered without qualm in order to retain an advertiser's good will.

Seasonal fashion shows

Twice a year the fashion journalist is under seige. Eyes, ears and brain are bombarded with things proclaiming themselves "new" and designers shrieking "LOOK AT ME!" Fashion editors are always working a season (six months) in advance of their readers' buying pattern. It is very hard to sustain enthusiasm for six months. What was exciting and new in March in its original designer's form, seems tired and weakened by September when the look has to be featured again. In addition, the job of covering the international fashion shows is not nearly as glamorous as it sounds.

Glamour and pressure don't go together and fashion journalists are highly pressurised and working flat out at this time. The idea that they go to elegant little fashion shows, drink a glass of champagne and watch beautiful clothes gently paraded before them in cloistered calm is a total myth. The reality demands that they are as tough as stormtroopers, as alert as gun dogs and as persistant as insurance agents. What do they go through in Paris, Milan, London and New York that requires such characteristics?

The Collections

The showings of the new fashions are called the Collections and each city usually requires a week in which to fit all its designers. The journalists from all over the world jet in the day before Collections Week begins, book into their hotels and immediately start work. They find a pile of invitations to fashion shows waiting for them at their hotels. They must check these against the timetable and if any tickets are not there, they must telephone or go in person to the fashion houses concerned to obtain them.

Shows come thick and fast — as many as eight a day. The battle and crush to get in, even with a ticket, is continued inside with frequent disputes over seats and fights for various places. Added to this is the fact that if the French and Italian officials want to be difficult (and they frequently do) they can hide behind the language barrier and you have a situation of extreme tension which can lead horribly easily to frustration and nervous exhaustion.

Even after the shows are over for the day there are frequently parties at which the journalists, notwithstanding

Ethnic looks are a constant fashion fad — as are clothes based on workwear, highlighted with male accessories like waistcoats and flat caps. The Asian coolie look of tunic and narrow cotton pants is adapted here to look young, casual and very flattering.

migraines and swollen ankles, must be seen to sip yet another glass of warm champagne. Many leave these parties to go back to their hotels to write their articles before collapsing into bed. They will have arranged an early call so that they can be ready for the next gruelling day. Under all of this pressure they still have to look at clothes critically and constructively to make a story for their readers.

Day in the life

"But it's work," she protests as she sets off for the Bahamas on a cold January day. "It's so complicated," she moans as she arranges an all-expenses paid trip to Mexico. And she is right, but of course, so are those who gaze at the fashion editor's lot with envy seeing only the glamour.

What does a fashion editor actually do all day?

This is a question I am frequently asked. The answer depends on the time of year, the nature of the publication and, of course, the personality and predelictions of the individual. I work for a weekly publication which is unique in that it is also a glossy magazine aimed at the non-specialist reader with a wide range of general interests. The number of fashion pages varies but normally I have three to fill each week. My editor believes, as do I, that there is a need for good fashion writing so I produce copy in the way that newspaper fashion editors do in addition to the photographs which glossies nearly always use instead of writing. I work two to three weeks ahead of publication date. This is longer than newspaper editors have and shorter than monthly magazines which often work three months ahead. I thus have an almost unique flexibility over what I feature and when I do so, but I have less time than some of my colleagues.

Getting the story

The old newspaper adage that the only way to get a story is to get on your feet and go out and find it is very true of fashion journalism. The good fashion journalist spends much more time out than in the office, talking to PRs, designers and buyers, looking around the shops and generally keeping an eye out for little developments and movements on street level.

The fashion editor lives a life totally dominated by diary, address book and telephone. I can take a couple of random pages from my diary to show how days typically develop.

9.30 am

telephone my secretary from home to confirm that none of my appointments have been altered, tell her what she should arrange during my absence from the office and hear if anything important has come in the mail.

9.45 am

take the first taxi of the day to an appointment with a PR in the Marylebone Road. She has taken on an interesting young couple of designers specialising in highly individual novelty knitwear. Over the first of many cups of indifferent coffee the PR, who happens to be one of the highly professional and intelligent ones, tells me about the designers and how she sees their work developing. We then go through the racks together and I note what interests me. These particular designers fall into a very common category. Although I cannot personally use their work yet, they are worth watching and also telling colleagues about, so although not immediately productive, my appointment has not been in vain.

10.20 am

Another taxi, this time to Knightsbridge where a well-known shoe shop is giving a presentation of an Italian designer's shoes, with the designer present. Here I am joined by my assistant, who has also already had one appointment in another part of town, and we are offered that second standard fashion beverage, non-vintage chamgpagne, as an alternative to coffee. The PRs are nervous, the Italian's English is only so-so, and he is known to be unpredictable. Things are not helped by his voluble young Italian friend who talks a great deal but speaks no English. However, the shoes are beautiful and my assistant makes arrangements for samples to be ear-marked for a photographic session in a couple of weeks' time whilst I phone my secretary to keep in touch, and get her to phone to warn our next appointment that we will be late.

11.10 am

We arrive, ten minutes late, at the press office of a very famous Knightsbridge store where we are greeted kindly and offered more coffee. We are here to choose samples from their Spring ready-to-wear range for a big colour shoot we are doing abroad. The PRs talk us through the racks ensuring that we see everything and then we start to group the possible choices into stories — either of shape, pattern or colour.

There is much swapping before my assistant and I are

It is all too easy to begin to wonder if you are reading the wrong magazines — all the fashions seem so young. But remember that fashion models are always young and blessed with perfect bodies. That does not mean that the clothes they are wearing are only suitable for young people. Having said this I must add that the young/old barrier is much more flexible than many women imagine. The real barrier is often a psychological one — you are terrified of looking like mutton dressed as lamb. For example, I think that colour has no conscious age — start by being bolder with the colours you choose and the colours you combine and work from there.

satisfied that we have the basis of our stories. The clothes we have chosen will be called in to the office to be racked with choices from other sources before editing down to what we are actually likely to shoot abroad. This is not quick work.

12.40 pm

We are out on the streets again and looking for taxis. I am off to lunch in Soho with a PR who is arranging an interview with an American designer who is launching a new line in London next Spring. I hope to meet him and see the clothes when I am in New York.

My assistant's lunch is a sandwich snatched on the way to choose belts needed for a shoot tomorrow before being back in the office to see three models who have brought in their composites, as their photographic cards are called. Ideally, I should see them personally, but time is tight and I trust the cards — and my assistant's judgement.

3.15 pm

Back in my office, my assistant is busily telephoning, arranging and confirming models, photographers and clothes. My secretary comes in with a pile of mail, including lots of invitations to be fitted into the diary, and a list of people I should call back. On my desk are the latest photographs with a query from the art department about where they are to be cropped (or cut). My subbed copy for the next issue is there with a note saying that it is too long and must be cut by three inches. An agonised note from the photographer says that tomorrow's girl has cancelled due to flu, so we quickly need a replacement. His suggestion is such and such and could my assistant confirm with the agency if that model is free.

3.30 pm

I have an editorial meeting which is mercifully uneventful although its outcome means more work for my department as we are to be involved in shooting an advertorial. This, as the name implies, is an advertisement arranged in such a way as to appear almost like part of the editorial of a magazine. I am not sure of the ethics of this but know that advertorials, although involving lots of hard work and tedious negotiations, do work for both sides.

4.10 pm

After a couple of phone calls and a quick briefing from my assistant I begin to edit my copy (which must go down by five o'clock) to the background of endlessly ringing phones.

4.30 pm

I am in the art department working with the art director on the layout of photographs for an evening dress story. Should we bleed two, crop the others and have them as drop-ins? How long is the copy? What's the headline? The typeface? All of this takes time as once the decisions have been set up at the printers, it costs a lot of money to change them. I find it fascinating and exciting to lay out pages and can hardly tear myself away to look on the light box at the colour transparencies of a beauty shot we did a few days ago.

5.20 pm

Back in my office to dictate letters to my secretary so that she can type them tomorrow morning whilst I am out.

5.30 pm

I collect press handouts and publicity material to read at home tonight. I confirm arrangements with my assistant for tomorrow's shoot and leave for a beauty launch cocktail party. I leave relunctantly as I have much work to clear and normally would stay in my office for at least another hour. My assistant also leaves for a press show. On this particular day we have been invited to four press launches at six o'clock — a very common occurrence.

6.10 pm

In a West End hotel, being offered champagne and canapes, glossy publicity material and a beautifully packed presentation of the new product, taking the opportunity to chat to colleagues and already worrying about the evening to come.

6.30 pm

I take a taxi home, check the answer phone before a quick shower prior to changing into a dinner jacket and running out for another taxi.

7.0 pm

I am in a grand hotel on the Embankment for drinks before the fashion show arranged by an up-market fashion chain to show us its new range. The show, scheduled for 7.45 is half an hour late, ends at 8.50 and is followed by a formal dinner.

11.20 pm

I finally manage to leave.

11.45 pm

I am in bed reading press handouts.

Every wardrobe needs a plain coloured short coat. It will repay its cost many times over whether it is flared from broad shoulders or semi-fitted and tailored with set-in sleeves. Choose a pale colour for glamour and flattery. It can be worn over dresses, skirts or pants in plain or patterned fabrics.

A day on location

7.0 am

I stagger out to my car and set off for a small village near Tunbridge Wells where I am to meet my assistant and the crew. They have travelled down in a location van for the outdoor shoot of country clothes which we are doing in the woods using dogs provided by friends. The crew consists of the photographer and her assistant, the model and the make-up girl, who will also look after the hair (in a studio a separate hair stylist would be included but for outdoor shots this is not necessary).

9.15 am

The make-up girl and the model are ready for the first outfit, to be photographed with an enormous and rather frisky Irish wolfhound. My assistant helps to dress the model whilst I check the locations which the photographer and I have chosen. Whilst she and her assistant are setting up cameras, checking lights etc, I am talking to the owners of the dog and learning about her personality and behaviour.

9.45 am

We begin. About ten minutes are spent in getting the camera ready and taking test polaroids before we are ready for the dog and the real shoot. By now the dog is excited and bounds around like a pony dragging the model along. Whilst I shout ''Marvellous!'' my assistant, who has to return the clothes and face the PR, shrieks ''Don't let the coat drag in the mud!''

Two rolls of film are exposed and the photographer is sure that she has what she needs. The model changes, her make-up is freshened and we discover we have been sent two left feet for the special boots we wished to feature.

10.50 am

Nevertheless, we are now ready for the second shot to be done with our Irish wolfhound who is by now thoroughly overexcited because the next lot of dogs, a retriever and a cocker spaniel, have arrived and are taking a very active interest. Amidst a flurry of anxious owners, barking dogs and intertwined leads, we manage to photograph the next outfit. The rest of the morning passes in much the same way. We photograph five outfits, thank owners and dogs for their patience and cooperation and finally break for lunch.

12.30 pm
A sandwich and mineral water outdoor picnic in December is not the ideal lunch, but my assistant has organised it admirably, spirits are high, the sun has come out and we are trying to forget that our feet are like blocks of ice.

1.15 pm
We move to a new location, decide on likely spots and set up the camera for the first shot, which is of winter woollens. The model's make-up and hair have been completely changed as these photographs are for a different issue and we hope to give the illusion that we have not used the same girl. As the temperature has dropped considerably and we are not shooting coats, the model becomes progressively colder as she shivers in her woollies but manages to look relaxed and happy for the camera even whilst turning grey with cold.

3.30 pm
The light is going, the last shot is being taken whilst my assistant tries to create some order from the pile of clothes hastily torn off after each shot and thrown into the van. When she has made space, everyone piles into the van and it heads off to London. I drive behind. We are frozen and tired but feel that we have had a good day's work.

5.45 pm
We arrive in London. I go to my office to check things there, my assistant to her home where she packs and labels everything for collection and return tomorrow morning.

7.0 pm
I set off for home having decided to miss the launch of a new range of luxury luggage as I am simply too tired.

Why do we do it?
Because it is a life which has a great deal of glamour as well as hard work and worry. The fashion editor's role is a crucial one as a go-between linking designers and trade with customers. Ultimately we know that we are working for you and our satisfaction comes from doing it well so that our readers are informed and aware of what the clothes world has to offer.

But magazines are not the only area of the media that has an influence on your choice of style. Let us look at the other great influence that has emerged over the last thirty years.

A perfect no-nonsense approach for evening is this one by an Italian designer who puts a large deeply-coloured T-shirt with a simple straight skirt to create a very sophisticated outfit. You can do the same. Notice how a small sliver of white from the vest beneath is allowed to show at the neck as a flattery factor. For extra glamour a "Chanel" bow in satin or velvet, tops off this soignée look.

"Fashion is the acceptance of the ridiculous." *Jean Cocteau*

The music business

When Mick Jagger first appeared on stage wearing a frock he made a more powerful fashion statement than any designer could hope to, no matter what he put on the runway. When David Bowie first appeared in make-up he began the movement for cosmetics for non-gay men which continues today with the popular "It looks even better on a girl" make-up campaigns. And he did it in a way that no beauty house could hope to.

The stage is mightier than the salon

Because they were megastars of the pop music world, Jagger and Bowie made cross-dressing acceptable and unisexual attitudes part of the philosophy of most people under thirty.

Maximum exposure

It is a question of exposure just as much as adulation. A television appearance by a top group will be seen by millions — and so will their clothes. No fashion magazine can compete with these figures. So, naturally, designers are only too happy to kit out the superstars, often without payment. A "look" seen on television has more impact than the same look photographed for a magazine — and if it really captures the attention of the viewer it will be tracked down, even though no clue is given on television as to who designed it.

The image makers

By and large, pop stars choose clothes to project an image that will reinforce the impact of their songs. Their stage appearance is usually a heightened and more theatrical version of their off-stage choice of clothes. Viewers see the full-strength version and so become used to over-the-top looks, copy them and thus strengthen street fashion until it is a very powerful statement of shape, colour and texture and is called London Street fashion. This in turn encourages the designers to be bolder — old-fashioned concepts of taste are chucked out of the window, fancy dress prevails and anarchy ensues. This has happened recently in London, to the delight of foreigners, but for how long?

The stylists

So, is the pop music influence benevolent or malign? My view is that it is a very good thing that our eyes have become accustomed to good strong colours and bold textures as a result of television, but it must be remembered that often what we see on our screens is not true fashion at all. Although Bowie, Jagger *et al* pop in to Paul Smith of Covent Garden, or Scot Crolla in Mayfair to buy their gear, few clothes by the top designers are worn by the stars on our screens. Most of them use one-off young designers or avant-garde stylists to make clothes which show them off to the best possible advantage. Pop stars make attractive clothes horses for the young designers because their clothes can be outrageously theatrical and yet still acceptable. Remember Gary Glitter and Adam Ant? They were packaged to just the right level of exuberance by their stylists — and it took some time for the High Street to catch up. Now theatricality is the High Street — so someone like Prince could look almost normal wearing his stage clothes in the cold light of day.

Female singers

Conversely, female singers have less impact on fashion than male singers do — for two reasons. Firstly, female attitudes to fashion are already much more diverse and open than male, largely because most women read at least one magazine that has a highly expert fashion content, whereas men do not. In fact, there is no mass market male equivalent to *Company, Elle* or *Cosmopolitan,* although whether this reflects the demand from men or the timidity of publishers is debatable.

The second reason grows from the first — female singers tend to wear fashion that is already on the street, although which street varies! So it is much harder for them to shock or make an impact with their appearance than it is for men.

Not just for teenagers

Although pop music is largely aimed at teenagers, the effects of its packaging are seen in a much higher age range. Miss Selfridge and Warehouse obtain a high proportion of their customers from the twenty-plus age range and their looks appeal (quite rightly too) to women in their thirties.

Oriental influences

In the eighteenth century the cultural effect of Japan and China on interiors, furniture and pottery was considerable and it has lasted, as the popularity of the willow pattern proves. In the last decade, Japanese influences have had a similar effect on fashion and, in my opinion, they will continue to for just as long.

New wave designers

Designers like Rei Kawakubo of Comme des Garçons, Yohji Yamamoto and Issey Miyake, although too expensive for most pockets, have been copied and adapted at all levels of the fashion trade, and so their influence has spread.

What is the influence?

Layered, asymmetric and unstructured clothes which are so undemanding to wear, all come from the Japanese. "Poor" materials that crush and crease were popularised by the Japanese. Abstract patterns and unusual "off" colours used in several combinations on one garment were brought to prominence by the Japanese. Above all, the Japanese philosphy of design (and one does exist) based on non-status, non-sexual dressing has found an answering chord in thousands of young women.

Soaping up

At quite the opposite end of the scale we now have *Dynasty* dressing which would have been inconceivable five years ago — but now it seems an attractively super-feminine alternative for more and more women bored with loose, unsexy clothes. The influence of the televison soaps is seen increasingly in the streets.

Female form is back

Body conscious cuts, draping and judicious gathers are used to highlight the femininity of the body with emphasis on the waist and bottom. The time is right for this sort of clothing and the Paris giants Azzedine Alaïa, Claude Montana and Thierry Mugler, who exert a considerable influence on the rag trade, are all working with structured cuts to emphasise the body.

At your service

With so many influences pushing themselves at you from every direction you have to put your trust in the fashion journalists. Once you have learned from them to train your eye and your brain you are in a much stronger position to dress wisely for your sort of life. The next step is to identify exactly what that life really is.

There is nothing wrong in feeling secure in classic, traditional shapes. After all, they have become classics simply because they work so well for so many women. Often, a traditional look is based on things borrowed from the male wardrobe. Here the checked shirt, lambswool pullover and tweed trousers are all male items of clothing but the wearer does not look at all masculine.

Many women are afraid of checks but they have no reason to be. Checks are lively, give movement and always look fresh and clean-cut. Here, as you can see, they can be made to do different things according to their scale and the scale of the garment. They look equally as good on a large or a close-fitting jacket but remember to keep things under control by using solid, plain colours for everything else. Another word of warning — check pants look young and fun but only if they are not distorted by over-generous contours. Look especially closely at your back view before you buy.

A controlled approach to colour in your wardrobe always pays dividends. You should aim to give yourself maximum flexibility by being able to interchange items in colours which work together. Ther is absolutely nothing wrong in having a short informal coat, such as the duffle coat here, in the sam colour as your full-length coat. It means that accessories and the clothes you wear them with will go with both outdoor garments.

One of the most invigorating and releasing movements in fashion over the last ten years has been the increased acceptability of what the Americans call "sweats" and we call "jogging outfits". In cotton generously cut, they are the ideal clothing for anything involving active movement. They are just as much at home on the beach and around the house as in the gym.

chapter 2

Finding your style

Nowadays, women don't talk about fashion, they talk about style, and really it is this that I am trying to help you develop. Success with clothes depends on evolving your sense of style and individuality.

What is style?

It is, in fashion terms, an attitude of mind which develops an approach to putting clothes together to suit your personality. It is being able to take an inexpensive T-shirt, for example, and throw it together with second-hand or cheap chain-store clothes for a totally individual look. It is using every resource available to you, instead of going into an off-the-peg store and choosing a complete 'processed' look.

Fashion is old-fashioned

What attracted you to this book? Obviously you are interested in fashion but do you know that the term itself is out of date now? Fashion is also out of date. The thing the woman of the eighties is looking for is style, and that is a much more difficult thing to achieve than being fashionable. In the past there was something called fashion. It was dictated by the great designers, usually in Paris, but sometimes in London as well, and it consisted of a line, colour and shape which everyone wore. The classic example of this, and the most famous, was Dior's New Look. It had such impact that fashion journalists who were covering the show were, by the end of it, actually trying to pull down their hemlines to make themselves look more fashionable. Everything that had gone before suddenly became unfashionable and by the next season all women were wearing longer, fuller skirts. This sort of hysterical reaction to the dictates of one or two fashion designers is now long gone. The modern women says "fashion is dead, long live clothes."

Couturiers reigned supreme
If you look back at old fashion magazines of the forties and fifties you will see that (with the exception of Dior's New Look bombshell which was completely different from the fashion of the moment) most designers were in agreement. This was not because they copied one another, or because they were telepathic — they were following the Logic of Fashion. Each season's new trends grew from and developed the strong lines of last season's fashion. So fashion was a rhythmic movement Within the logical development of the fashion there was plenty of scope for originality, but the designer did not waste his time looking for instant novelty.

Advent of the sixties
Ready-to-wear designers became the powerful source of ideas in the late fifties and the couture (high fashion) influence on each season slowly faded.

The problem with ready-to-wear is that, like television, it gobbles up ideas and spreads them wide very quickly, so novelty is at a premium. During the sixties marvellous fashion ideas were thrown off by designers in an amazing display of fashion fireworks. By the early seventies chaos reigned and fashion had lost its way. Women began, in the phrase of the time, to "do their own thing". There were fewer and fewer followers and so the need for leaders diminished. Women had changed. The pill, equal opportunities and woman's liberation had given them the courage to be independent — and the new attitudes included a changed approach to how they dressed.

Prisoners of fashion
Perfectly-turned out products of a fifties' couturier, the sort of women that models like Barbara Goalen were impersonating, might well have looked the height of glacial chic and distant "don't touch" elegance but the reality was different. They were prisoners — if not behind bars, certainly in a straight jacket — and the thing that was imprisoning them was their clothes. The clothes they wore were there to gratify the fantasy of male dress designers who put appearance before the person.

Fantastic fashion — fantastic prices
The vast amounts of money that designers charged meant that

their clients were almost always "kept" women whose clothes were paid for by husbands or lovers. The reason was simple — women who worked for their living were unlikely to make the huge amounts required to pay the bill for couture clothes and, if they did, they wished to spend it on more permanent possessions. Also, if they worked they were unlikely to have the time to spare for lengthy fittings. Remember that buying a couture wardrobe in Paris would keep you in the city for at least three weeks every season and the days would be full with fittings and choices, endless decisions over lining, colours or button shapes, as well as the organisation of all the accessories.

It was a busy round for the mondaine customers of the great couturiers — milliners, furriers and shoemakers had to be consulted about which of their designs would be suitable for the new look, and perhaps most importantly of all, hours were spent at the corsetieres. If the underpinning was not perfect, everything failed.

The modern woman

Modern women have turned their backs on much of this. They are simply too busy to give up hours of their lives to fittings. They work too hard to squander a sizeable portion of their wages on something frivolous like a hat. Their lifestyle follows the trend towards speed and informality. Most modern women want to slip on a pair of briefs, a sweatshirt and some jeans, brush their hair, maybe dab on a little lipstick and be off, as carefree as their men. And they are right.

A price to pay

But women, like everyone else, pay a price for freedom. As fashion is no longer dictated to her, the modern woman has to learn to think about her clothes and herself in order to create her style.

There is no way to avoid the self-commitment that this involves. If you are interested in how you dress and you care about how you present yourself to the world, then you have to devote a certain amount of time to it. If you cannot be bothered to make the effort then admit it — buy a pair of Crimplene slacks and an anorak and forget about your appearance. The paradox is that when you forget about making an impression, you often achieve a really stylish appearance. Think of poor mad Virginia Woolf whose clothes were frequently pinned together, but who always looked immensely stylish.

Traditional patterns and styles rarely remain as static as we imagine. Here a classic tweed is used on a shape based on a Victorian man's overcoat (complete with velvet collar) but it doesn't look at all old-fashioned.

Being casual does not mean looking scruffy. A cotton sweatshirt one size too big can be twisted and pulled into the shape that you want. Put it with a contrasting colour in jogging pants or a skirt and you have created the look which is uniquely yours.

The two-edged sword

Although the new approach to fashion gives you a great deal more freedom to do what you want to do, it is much more difficult and much more dangerous. It is always harder to get it right when there are no hard and fast rules. It was very much easier in the old days when there was a look and you dressed in the fashion from head to toe. You knew that you were secure because that was the way you were supposed to look.

Complete looks — a cop-out

This attitude has gone now for the majority of women although if you are very rich and somewhat lacking in imagination, you can still go to top designers and get a head to toe look. This is still quite easy. If you are lazy or insecure, the shop assistant will tell you exactly how to wear the look, how to put on the clothes properly, how to accessorise them and will make you a sort of fashion plate. You are likely to look very boring. The clothes are not going to suit your personality and you will feel awkward and unnatural wearing them. Onlookers will know at a glance that this just isn't you.

This approach also lacks imagination and ensures that you will never look individual, original or different. You have to work on this business of getting style. You must know yourself and know what suits you. Then you have to develop a sense of flair and learn to be a little bold.

Heed warning signs

But be careful. For example, if the details on a garment are over-emphasised or exaggerated, this spells danger because it usually means that there has been some uncertainty at the design stage which has led to over-designing. An example illustrates this.

A few years ago the Italian designer Armani produced beautiful blousons for men and women. In the first season they were very simple in outline, very classic in scale and very strong. In the second season he exaggerated them slightly and added a little more detail. This brought them to the notice of everybody and suddenly all the cheap manufacturer were copying the Armani blouson. But they did not have his skill, his brilliant sense of scale and superb taste to know when to stop decorating. So the result, especially for men, was very over-designed, over-emphasised shapes with far too much detail. The imitation Armani blousons were a million miles away from he purity, style and class of the original design. So, when you are buying clothes consider whether the thing is well-designed or over-designed.

Style is knowing the difference

You can tell by looking at the proportion, the balance, the rhythm of a garment whether it is well-styled or not. A good sense of proportion requires a designer to relate all parts to one another in size, length and volume. Balance is achieved when the designer creates equal degrees of interest in either direction from the natural centre. Rhythm is created so that the eye moves smoothly and easily, connecting the points of interest without jerking from point to point. Remember these three things — proportion, balance and rhythm. When you look at a garment actively consider where the point of strongest focus is. Decide how the garment is structured. It may be tailored and severe with a lot of padding and interfacing, or it may be soft.

Your proportions

Decide whether the garment is suitable for your scale, your shape, your size because your body has its own proportion, balance and rhythm as well and if this fights with your clothes you have a disaster situation. The line of both the fabric and the garment design provides valuable illusions of height and length if you use it correctly. Line can also give the illusion of diminishing you if you are over tall, or feel large. Whenever you look at clothes you must say to yourself "Where do I fit in?" but strive at the same time to remain individual.

Judging off the peg

Remember when you are shopping, things sometimes look unpromising on the hanger. A young fashion editor I know takes a belt with her when she goes shopping and she plays around on a seemingly unpromising basic garment to assess its potential. You can try this — find a way of wearing the garment which is completely different to the way it is presented in the shop. You often discover that in fact an unpromising shape is actually something that will work for you. You should teach yourself to look honestly and subjectively at clothes in relation to yourself. You have to analyse the components of the garments that you are looking at and, of course, you have also to analyse the composition of the various approaches to fashion that you see in different designs, in different shops and different magazines.

Sophistication is an attitude of mind. You do not have to wear slinky black dresses, stiletto heels and diamond necklaces to look sophisticated. Real sophistication comes from following the adage "less is more" and keeping your appearance simple and uncluttered whilst controlling your use of colour.

Do not be afraid of bold colour or uncompromising shapes. As long as you are controlling them, and not them you, they are the most direct way to create your own fashion statement. You do not have to be formally fashionable. All of these looks could be recreated easily. Look at their ingredients: the shapes, patterns and colours. See what you have in your wardrobe which is similar or could be augmented with one or two new purchases to create your own strongly individual look.

Sharp colours with white are a sure-fire way of looking good in summer. They will highlight your tan without cramping your style.

The elements of style

Not so long ago the important thing in any garment was its length. Hemlines were the yardstick of what was fashionable and what was not. Nowadays this is not the case. Much more emphasis is put on the shapes and the proportions. It is the shapes and proportions that make the garment currently stylis or give it a dowdy, old-fashioned image. The thing you are hoping to do with anything you purchase is improve upon and strengthen your existing wardrobe. Remember also that the kind of wardrobe that works best is based on clothes that link in shape and colour. To find just one colour that suits you and stick to it year in year out is totally lacking in imagination. Don't be narrow-minded — experiment and reassess your taste. Don't overdo one colour because you may end up with that deadly over-coordinated look where everything is so carefully worked out that you look boring. You must avoid being too careful.

Pocket Venus

If you are a short person, dress to maximise everything you have. You must aim for a long line, and you can do this by keeping everything in more or less the same tone. Elevate yourself by having shoes and stockings in the same tone as th rest of the outfit. Don't have violent and strong contrasts from top to bottom.

Fit budget to lifestyle

The way you spend your clothes' money depends on your way of life. If you are a working mum, probably the majority of you money will go on good, sturdy, practical long-lasting day clothes. If you work in an office where you are on display all the time, probably quite a lot of your budget will go on accessories. If you are a woman who spends much of her time at home, possibly your accessories bill will be very small. So how you apportion the money you have to spend depends very much on the way you live.

Trousers — aim high

There is one area where I think money should be spent a little more freely and this is on trousers. Men have looked great in trousers for years, but men are a completely different shape to women. Trousers must be designed for the female figure and they have to fit in more directions than any other garment you wear.

If you are buying trousers or jeans, get the best you can afford. Go for cut. For example, the best trousers in the world are cut by Yves Saint Laurent. Anyone who can afford Yves Saint Laurant's sort of prices is not wasting money by buying a pair of his trousers. Of course, very few people can afford this level of dressing, but the basic idea is correct — go for excellence in cut.

Your wardrobe

The way your build up your wardrobe depends on your way of life and your personal tastes, but you should always ask the question of any potential new acquisition — will it earn its keep? The answer could well surprise you. Many of the items of clothing that we buy from habit and replace because we have always had one, are not really necessary in our lives. For example, twenty years ago few women would have considered their wardrobe complete without a dress. Now, thousands of women, especially the young, do not possess one. In a quick straw poll of working girls under thirty I discovered that not one owned a dress for daywear and only one had an evening dress.

Woman in a suitcase

An interesting game to play is to imagine that you have been invited for a three week holiday in America with the man of your dreams. The only stipulation he makes is that your luggage, containing clothes you already have, must pack into one hand case small enough to fit under Concorde's seats. What items from your wardrobe would you choose that would ensure you were well dressed for any occasion? Would your wardrobe enable you to join him, or would it let you down because too many items in it were bought for one specialised purpose? Except under very special circumstances all these types of garments should be regarded as bad buys.

Clothes that work for your wardrobe must be wearable in different and varied combinations. This is obviously economic sense and that is why more and more women turn to separates. They give them flexibility of choice without the need for a wardrobe bursting with rarely-worn clothes.

The things you choose for your basic wardrobe (and the number of items it contains) depends on you, but most women will choose some of the following.

Jackets

The suit as the all-purpose item of a wardrobe has been joined

Try and sit down in the changing room to see how a garment behaves. Move your arms around and lift them above your head watching in the mirror to see how the material moves. Don't be embarrassed!

by the jacket and separate skirt or trousers. For the woman who prefers the formality of a suit the best bet could still be th Chanel style suit of soft, textured tweed consisting of a collarless cardigan-type jacket and a straight, loose skirt. If th sort of look appeals to you, it will last you for years.

A more business-like suit with a collared jacket and straight skirt will provide similar value. The number of jackets you decide are necessary for you is variable, but for an efficient wardrobe, two is probably the minimum. One should be useful for the day and one should be adaptable for evening wear.

First-choice jacket

Your first choice could be a single-breasted jacket, a classic o modern dressing, or a double-breasted one which is often mor sporty. If you want a blazer look, a good bet is a navy wool gabardine. Another valuable all-rounder is a woollen jacket in grey or beige. If this fits the rest of your wardrobe the garmen can give you a great deal of fashion mileage. Remember, the more neutral the fabric, the more versatile the garment and th greater the flexibility.

Waterproof jackets

If you live in the country or have to wait in town for buses, it could well be that a waterproof or reversible jacket might be your most practical bet. However, there are dangers here. I personally feel that it is almost impossible to look good in padded waterproof anoraks unless you are very young and very slim. Why they are bought in such quantities I cannot understand — they have become a blot on our High Streets. There are those who think Barbour jackets should be kept for rolling hills and long meadows — where others won't see you!

The blouson

Blousons, of cotton or denim, can look very good and are extremely practical, but remember that a blouson will tend to highlight your hips and bottom, so if these are broad, it is probably best to avoid this style.

Dual-purpose jacket

The sort of jacket you choose for your second one is again dependant on your lifestyle. Perhaps you need a cover-up for glamorous evening occasions which are not all-out dressy affairs — a jacket is your answer. Anything is better than thos dowdy shawls and stoles! But make it earn its keep, choose a velvet one in a dark colour and it will be useful during the day as well.

Beautiful skins

If you decide not to look for a dual-purpose jacket, then your second choice could be a good quality suede or leather. If looked after and properly cleaned, skins will give you many years of value. It is worth waiting and saving up until you can buy good quality skin. The thing to look for is malleability. Good skins should be soft and liquid in the hand, You should be able to scrunch them up and yet immediately they should resume their original shape. The cheaper, stiff, hard suede and leather garments are not worth buying. Go for the best skins — thin and flowing as wool. Keep them soft by having them professionally cleaned even if that means expensively cleaned. Cheap, harsh chemicals can turn soft suede and leather into inflexible lumps and make them as stiff as boards.

If you do treat to yourself to a suede jacket, remember to carry an umbrella because with our uncertain climate a sudden rain shower could mark and stiffen the suede and ruin the jacket.

Beware over-designed leather

Leather and suede, especially blousons, seem to attract inexperienced and self-indulgent designers who enjoy putting on as many little extras as possible. These over-designed and fussy items date very quickly. Avoid exaggerated scale, any inset of leather on suede or vice-versa, any two or three colour trimmings and all gimmicks with epaulettes, pockets and zips if you want your expensive blouson to give you service for the years it is capable of. What looks more tired than the distressed leather or the huge shoulders and aggressive zips of a few seasons ago? Bad taste roisters along the racks of leather and suede clothes more than anything else in the shop — so be on your guard.

Singing in the rain

Do you need a raincoat? Perhaps you can get away with a raincoat instead of paying more money on a winter coat. If you have to wait at windy bus-stops you will probably answer the first question with a heartfelt yes. However, if you spend most of your time popping in and out of a car you might well decide that a windcheater or waterproof blouson is more suitable. I

Classic pants, a silk scarf and a big sweatshirt still represent one of the sexiest ways of looking casual without any of the packaging for the opposite sex which more structured ways of dressing sometimes suggest.

always thought a raincoat an unavoidable item until mine was stolen over ten years ago. I couldn't afford to replace it at the time and I have not done so since — I don't seem to get soaked more often than before.

Go classic
Thousands of women feel that a good quality raincoat from somewhere like Aquascutum or Burberry is a better buy than a coat — and so it can be if it is a classic design. It can last a lifetime and never go out of fashion.

Lining chic
I have to say that lining chic is one of the things I cannot bear and it has affected raincoats more than anything else. It is ridiculous that a garment can become a status symbol because of what's on the inside, but that is what has happened to the classic English raincoat — and now the over-insistent checks are found on scarves, umbrellas, luggage and even hats! So, humble items have become vulgarised into status symbols but, thanks to their very high prices, the backs they are seen on are more often foreign than British.

Separates

The separates mentality has grown in the last thirty years and has permanently changed the face of fashion. The blouse or jumper and skirt was for a long time the homely alternative to the dress. Designers did not include such items in their shows and in fact rarely designed them. Up to the late fifties the couturiers, who led fashion, created frocks for afternoon wear and suits for the morning. Skirts did not have a life separate from a suit jacket except in very informal circumstances. Most women of fashion would have a grey woollen skirt for wearing with the twin set and pearls at home or a tweed one to team with a jumper or cardigan for wearing in the country, but for going out they hardly existed.

Increasing importance
With the emphasis on ease and youth, the ready-to-wear designers, who were becoming increasingly important, saw skirts, shirts, sweaters and tops as the perfect way to create the informal rlaxed and flexible looks increasingly in demand. Whether they could imagine that the movement would end in the banality of huge T-shirts bearing simplistic slogans being

promulgated as fashion is doubtful, but they certainly destroyed the absolute rule of the frock — probably forever. It is now possible to see complete fashion shows of work from top designers which contain no day dresses at all. That is the extent of the separates revolution and you will of course be part of it. So what do you need?

The T-shirt

Every woman, regardless of size or age, should have a stock of T-shirts. These normally short-sleeved, cotton jersey wonders with round V-necks are so easy to wear, so simple to wash and so quick to dry that many women I know wear no other tops and spend months of summmer relaxation with no worries at all.

Have some white and some coloured and use them as a second skin. Some women can create a very sexy evening look with well-cut jeans, a white T-shirt, some large costume jewelry and a tan. They look marvellous whether they are on holiday in Brighton, Blackpool, Nice or Miami.

It needs hardly be said that T-shirts lose everything if they are too tight. Depending on your style they should fit like a glove or be one or two sizes too big — never too small.

The shirt

The blouse is an endangered fashion species. It is rapidly being ousted by its more amenable counterpart, the shirt.

What is the difference? It is all in the cut. A shirt is much more relaxed and roomy than a blouse and herein lies its popularity — it is so easy to wear a shirt. Good shirts are cut like a man's, with or without a shoulder yoke, and normally look their best if they are slightly over-sized. For the last few seasons young fashion followers have bought huge shirts — often directly from men's shops — and have made the over-sized aspect their fashion statement. They look very good and there is something irresistably vulnerable and sexy about girls in clothes that look as if they have been filched from their boyfriends' wardrobes — which sharp girls often raid!

How many shirts do you need? As many as you can afford. They are true staples of your capsule wardrobe whether plain, striped, checked or patterned, cotton, wool or a something in between. And don't forget that the best shirt value is often to be found in the menswear department. For a rather more formal look, for example, think about a man's evening shirt. The pleated or frilled-front ones can look terrific with a

Buying a blouse or shirt can be a problem. When standing very straight in the fitting room (as we all do no matter how much we slouch normally) everything looks fine. When you get it home and return to your normal stance, the trouble begins. All too often the blouse that seemed perfect in the shop gapes at the bust when you sit down. This is almost always because the manufacturer has skimped the cut to save the cost. You can solve the problem either by choosing more expensive garments, or by going one size up.

The "loving hands at home" image of knitting as a cottage craft producing garments no woman of taste would be seen dead in is way out of date. Sophisticated yarns, colours and shapes have brought knitting into the world of high fashion . . .

diamante bow tie or a coloured silk scarf tied like a riding stock, especially with a decorative pin.

Necks without collars

A clean, collarless neckline always looks marvelous in fashion shots but in fact, it is a very difficult line to carry off. Young model girls with twig-thin necks and perfect jawlines look stunning without a collar, but are you sure they will have the same effect on you?

A collar softens, frames and flatters the face, it takes attention from wrinkled necks and dowager's humps. Without you are very exposed. I am not saying that you should avoid collarless necklines altogether, but I do think that you should look at yourself very critically before buying — especially if you are over thirty, over-weight or over-thin.

The straight skirt

The skirt you choose will depend upon your figure. A straight skirt is the most flattering all-purpose style. It can be quite plain, or can have a kick pleat in the front for ease. A rear or side slit is another device for walking ease but be careful that is not too deep — if too much leg is revealed you will look vulgar.

The dirndl skirt

Dirndl-style skirts are gathered at the waist and can hide a lot of figure problems. They are especially flattering to the woman who is very thin or has not got a pronounced waist. Paradoxically, a dirndl can also look good on the woman who is carrying rather more weight than she should. The hip fullness of a dirndl makes it the least formal and most casual skirt.

The A-line skirt

The slightly flared or A-line skirt is the useful compromise between the straight and dirndl styles. It suits all women — easy fitting and slimming to the hips, it can be worn all day for any occasion.

Features to look for

When buying a skirt remember that front buttoning ones are easy and informal. Pleats help movement but can make the skirt bulky. A lined wool or tweed suit will retain its shape and not seat in the way an unlined one might

Be careful over length. The scale of a skirt in relation to your height is vital and it changes with your heel height of course. Also the balance of top and bottom has to be considered when putting together your skirt and top. A long straight skirt takes some carrying off. If you have style it can look very sophisticated, if not it can end up by looking dowdy and gauche, or old-fashioned and ageing. If in doubt, do not go longer than mid-calf length. Full skirts can always be worn longer but again, bear in mind your figure. If you are short, a full skirt which is too long will make you look dumpy.

Culottes

In my opinion, divided skirts and culottes nearly always look dreadful unless they have been designed by a genius in the field such as Amani. However, most are particularly unfortunate from the back even on someone who is slim — on anyone of a more robust build the effect is most alarming. Avoid them unless you are very sure.

Sweaters and jumpers

These are staples of your wardrobe. The more you own the more flexibility your dressing will have.

The choice of wools is enormously wide — smooth lambswool and cashmere, Aran, Fair Isle, Shetland and cotton knit. The range of necklines includes turtle, cowl, crew, polo, round and V-shaped. You can choose from cardigans, boleros, short-sleeved jumpers and gilets and chunky cable knits. Add to this the vast range of colours made available by modern dyeing techniques, and you know why you must have as many examples as possible in your wardrobe. The versatility of sweaters is almost infinite.

Casual knits

For day your choice is between classic and casual. Both types look good with skirts, although casual chunky knits scale best with trousers.

One word of warning. The softness and colours of knitwear makes it easy to be lured into buying individual items without really thinking how they will fit in with the rest of your wardrobe. All too soon you can have drawers full of white — or blue, green, and multicoloured — elephants that only work with one other item.

With knits, it is essential to coordinate, and if bought wisely they can give enormous range and versality to even the

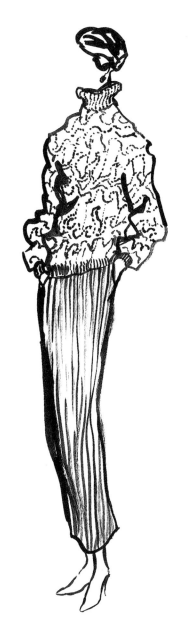

. . . a beautifully patterned sweater can now be dressed up to look as sophisticated as any other item in your wardrobe. Balance its bulk with a longer skirt — in tweed, velvet or wool.

smallest wardrobe. Don't forget cotton knits for summer. Also keep an eye on the menswear deparments. Sweaters from Marks and Spencer's men's range have been staples of fashionable girls for some years now.

Basic black
Every wardrobe should contain a black polo or rollneck sweater. It can be in cotton, wool, cashmere or silk, with long or short sleeves. You will soon find it is so useful that you will buy duplicates in different materials. To go with it, get yourself some black ski-pants or close-cut straight legged trousers. You won't look like a Juliette Greco existentialist left over from the fifties because you will wear it with a brightly coloured or strongly checked jacket or blazer and you will make-up a little more strongly to counteract the draining effect that black can sometimes have.

Cashmere or lambswool?
What about cashmere? This super soft wool is, of course, the height of luxury and is priced accordingly but is it worth it?

I believe that cashmere is always worth the money, but like real silk, it is an expense that can be avoided without much deprivation. Your life is not going to be blighted nor your fashion potential reduced by not owning a cashmere.

Buy good lambswool in a subtle shade and you are spending much less money more wisely. The finest cashmere is very delicate and is not created to be worn regularly day in, day out — if you buy sweaters to get real wear from them, avoid it. Lambswool is much tougher. Ultimately, good pure and subtle colour is more important for fashion impact in knits than texture and that is where money should be spend. Having said that let me confess to a hatred of one knit texture — I dislike angora.

Evening knits
Don't forget that knits can look extremely dressy and are good for evening. American women know how to exploit the chic possibilities of an evening look based on the simplest ingredients. A formal black lambswool or cashmere classic sweater, and a black skirt and pants, enlivened with an elaborate belt or a simply stunning sculptural necklace is the standard party look for American journalists covering the European fashion shows.

Trousers

If you are buying trousers and jeans, buy the very best you can afford. In my experience the most reliable cut in jeans for women is by Levi's and Gloria Vanderbilt. For trousers, go to upper market fashion chains with a name for good cutting. Look for a snug fit over the hips and make sure that they are not too tight across the bottom. The most versatile and practical cut is straight-legged and these will remain acceptable longer than other styles even though flares are trying to make a comeback. But remember the poet's warning.

> *"Sure deck your lower limbs in pants*
> *Yours are the limbs my sweeting*
> *You look divine as you advance*
> *Have you seen yourself retreating?"*

This is an object lesson for every women. It is of vital importance that you buy trousers and jeans with the most critical eye possible. Really look at yourself hard — do not listen to the saleswomen or the well-meaning friend. Look at yourself from every angle in a multi-faceted mirror, and if you have any doubt at all, don't buy.

Make absolutely certain

I have to admit that I think a great number of women look terrible in trousers and should avoid them at all costs. It is much better to buy a really good skirt or a dress than to wear jeans or trousers just because they are labelled casual, fun, young, sexy or whatever, because if you haven't got the right figure they won't look any of those things on you — they will make you look dreadful.

Coats

I wonder if these are really necessary for a large number of women. So many of us only brave the elements long enough to dash from the house to the car, or from the tube station to the office. For many women an overcoat is an expensive and cumbersome article of clothing easily replaced by a warm, roomy jacket.

However, if you consider that your way of life requires a coat, what should you be looking for? It is possible to buy one for under sixty pounds and quite easy to pay well over two hundred pounds for one. Most women settle for a price somewhere between the two.

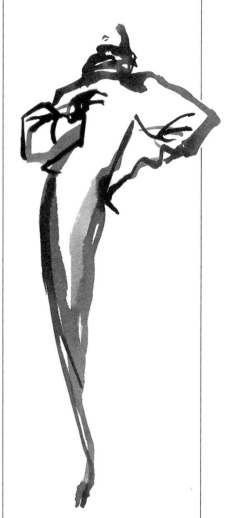

Glamour is much more than the clothes you wear. How you wear them, how you stand and how you move are the bases of style.

*The long, narrow tube of material, draped and perfectly hung, has been the evening look favoured by top Paris couturiers for the last two seasons. If this is a look which you can wear (and you don't need me to tell you that it does **not** work if there are any prominent bumps) then remember . . .*

Long-distance styles

The two things you need in a coat are flexibility and timelessness — after all, it is an item that you will wear for at least six months of the year and you will probably expect it to last for two or more seasons. Be wise and go for a simple classic style cut on generously full lines, understated but with balanced proportions. Wool, tweed or a cashmere mix are the best fabrics and large checks should be avoided if you do not have alternative coats.

Dresses

Whether or not you bother with these is a matter of personal taste. One of the most fashionable women I know is now twenty-eight and I have never seen her wearing a dress and yet she is a designer and always looks fabulous. Having said this, Textile Market Studies figures for British sales still puts dresses at the top of the list, so someone must be buying them! If it is you then you no doubt view them as absolute wardrobe staples, and of course, for many women they are.

The shirtwaist dress

A classic shirtwaist dress can be worn virtually anywhere at any time of day and is amenable to all sorts of dressing up to give it maximum fashion flexibility. The addition of a jacket makes it a sophisticated all-in-one statement whereas with flat shoes and no jewelry it can look casual and sporty. Wrap-over, tie belt styles are extremely flattering as are straight cut ones like lengthened T-shirts. When buying dresses think about not only of the style but also the colour and pattern.

Checking colour and print

Don't forget that if you are covering your whole body with one colour or print you have to get it right. Walk briskly around the showroom and notice what happens to the print when it is moving. Look in all the mirrors. A print that works well at the front of a dress might have been badly matched at the back so that it looks awkward from behind.

Evening wear

If your social pattern justifies buying wardrobe items for evening wear, you should aim for maximum flexibility and this means choosing separates. The big, important ballgown is only important once or twice. Its impact diminishes in proportion to

the drama of its initial effect. The more superb it is the more
memorable it is and the sooner everyone, including you, will
tire of it. After all, we tend to go to dances with more or less
the same group of friends most of the time. Much better to be
understated and choose tops to wear with long skirts or
evening trousers. Lacy knit evening sweaters can look very
feminine with straight evening skirts.

Maximum exposure

Glamour for evening is often created by a degree of
nakedness. This is why simple camisole tops with slender
straps look so good. They can look very elegant with a long
skirt or a strictly tailored classic suit in black velvet or fine
wool. The sleeveless, perfectly plain silk T-shirt with a deeply
scooped neckline is another marvellous no-fuss item for
sophisticated dressing. Again, an over-size silk shirt worn with
the top buttons undone and the full cut sleeves casually rolled
up looks especially good in a strong clear colour or a pattern of
paisley or Madras.

Going short

You may well decide that your social whirl is best catered for
by going short. At most evening affairs short dresses are now
the norm. The secret is to keep it simple. Satin, silk and velvet
will make a short dress look very formal, whereas cotton will
be less dressy but will look good on all but the most formal
occasions. A chemise is an excellent shape for a short evening
dress especially with a low-cut back. With all short evening
dresses a degree of thought is needed about accessories. You
don't want to overwhelm an elegantly simple dress with tons of
costume jewelry, glitter stoles or fussy boleros. A good gold
chain necklace, a perfectly plain gold metallic belt and gold
sandals are all you need.

For an alternative try silver. If the dress is very straight and
totally undecorated and you feel that your waist is your best
feature, pull all the attention to it by an ornate sculptural belt
— but if you do keep your necklace and earrings very discrete
or you will look like a Christmas decoration.

One night stands

More and more women are facing the fact that spending a
great deal of money on an evening dress which is worn for a
limited number of occasions is not the best way of using their
clothes budget. I think they are right. I agree with many of my

. . . keep everything as simple as possible for maximum impact.

friends who now hire a dress for the night. Whether it is for the once-a-year ball or twice-a-month dance, it makes good sense to hire. If a dance dress is hanging in your wardrobe it is not earning its keep and if it is regularly being worn, you and your partner will soon become tired of it.

Most large cities have dress-hire shops and some of them stock original models which have only been worn a very few times. Others will design and make an exclusive dress for a fraction of the cost of a standard designer gown provided it is returned to their stock of gowns for future clients. If there is one near you, make a habit of popping in to see what new things they have. Do not be snobbish about wearing second-hand clothes — all the garments are dry-cleaned after use. Remember also that you can normally buy from these shops and you can frequently pick up amazing bargains. They do not stock only evening wear of course. You can hire clothes for any occasion from them.

Fur or fake

I find real fur coats totally unacceptable, regardless of whether or not they are made from the pelts of endangered species. Mink farms are as distasteful to me as battery hen farms. Having said this I must admit that a dark wild mink or Russian sable coat is a very beautiful thing aesthetically if not ethically. I suppose everyone must make an individual decision over this.

If you decide against real fur, what is the fake scene like? Well, no fake fur will have the movement or sheen of a top quality real pelt, but it can nevertheless be a reasonable substitute if you are prepared to pay a few hundred pounds.

Fun furs

At the other end of the spectrum you can have a lot of fun with the frankly fake furs that make no attempts to pretend that they are the real thing. Fantastically patterned, brightly coloured (even dayglo) they are fashion's equivalent of Disneyland so think carefully about your personality before buying.

Track suit culture

Jane Fonda made it smart for women to be fit. Lisa Lyon made it chic for women to develop their bodies. Whether getting fit or getting muscle, the little black dress of the gymnasium is the tracksuit. A few years ago this utilitarian garment, previously made in drab or neutral colours, suddenly began to be styled. It started in Southern California, home of American sports and leisure wear, and fanned out across the world. The rag trade realised it was on to a good thing. By producing tracksuits cut to flatter the form and dyeing them in fashion colours, especially pastels, manufacturers realised that they could give the tracksuit a life outside the gym.

Not just for sport

In no time at all, tracksuits were worn for relaxing at home, doing the housework or gardening and increasingly for going out and about. It is not surprising as they are the most relaxed and undemanding of all items of clothing. They form the second beach-head of the informal leisure revolution begun by jeans and, like them, they are here to stay — as you would expect of garments suitable for both sexes, all ages and most figures apart from the very fat.

The thing I find encouraging about the tracksuit revolution is that they exemplify the modern philosophy of dressing for comfort, not for effect.

Sporting shorts

Hot weather brings out the daring in all of us, but how brave do you have to be to wear boxer shorts — certainly not as daring as the beauties on the beaches of the Riviera who wear nothing *but* silk boxer shorts!

You don't necessarily need to be a teenager to wear shorts but you need a pretty youthful figure — as you do if you are to look anything other than grotesque in a mini. Cellulite thighs are the problem in both cases.

I have said elsewhere that I feel that trousers, shorts and jeans are tricky and only a few women can wear them. Do a test of your own — look at ten of your girlfriends. I should be very surprised if you can say that more than two of them look better in trousers than a skirt, and even more surprised if you do not conclude that at least half of them look much worse. So, if you can honestly say that you are in good condition, try shorts. But remember that the High Street is not the beach so show a little restraint. Pop on a tracksuit bottom before you set off for the supermarket. If you do wear them and look good be ready for some male chauvinist hassle. Pathetic as it is, it is almost unavoidable.

Jumping off

Jumpsuits and dungerees are classless, ageless and

If your bust is best described as matronly — beware. Never buy anything cut on the tight side. Avoid decorations such as lace ruffles which will make you look bigger but use ties and stocks which will minimalise your size. Remember, as the famous American designer Donna Karan said to me, ''If you wear broad shoulders you automatically make your bust look smaller — it's obvious.'' Neckline interest can also help to reduce your bust's visual impact. Unless you want to look like Barbara Windsor avoid tightly belted waists.

seasonless. There is a place for them in everyone's wardrobe. They can be totally informal in cotton or denim or quite dressy in silk or velvet. You can play them up with lots of jewelry or dress them down by wearing them unbuttoned over a cotton T-shirt, with their sleeves and legs casually rolled up.

Wear them in an informal way for lounging around and relaxing though a friend of mine has a dark green velvet jumpsuit which she wears with gold jewelry for formal dinners and she looks absolutely stunning in it.

Camouflage

Large, loose shapes are frequently recommended for big girls but I am not sure that the flowing smock or all-enveloping kaftan necessarily presents the best solution to the problem. The old saying about a ship in full sail comes to mind!

Keep it neat
I think that large women always look neater and smarter in fitted clothes. I certainly feel that they need to wear belts to define their waists and cut down that impression of acres of fabric floating all over the place.

Save it for skinnies
Where I think large, over-sized looks do come into their own is with girls who are inclined to be skinny. Fitted clothes accentuate their thinness, over-sized garments can make them look very sexy.

The borrowers

When Rex Harrison sang ''Why can't a woman be more like a man?'' he was thinking about their heads — in fact nowadays women take more and more of their looks from traditional men's clothes, often with stunning effect. Quite apart from designs based on a male original, such as trouser suits or tuxedos, it has long been obvious that women look good in clothes made for men.

Cross-dress
Fashion conscious girls have worn men's shirts and sweaters for many years. The braver ones borrow men's ties, hats and even their long Johns. Long may it continue because this

cross-dressing can produce a very sexy and attractive appearance.

Dressed for combat

Safari jackets, army surplus and combat clothes have all rather gone into an eclipse and I am personally not too upset about this. The overall combat look which was popular some time ago was generally rather drab, but individual items such as American army officer shirts, or British army drill trousers can look very good teamed with more traditional feminine items. Non-military second hand clothes, especially those originally designed for men or boys, can look stunning. Smart girls have been raiding Hackett for men's cricket sweaters and boots, flannel shirts, Tattersall waistcoats and tweed sports coats for some time now and, by skillfully combining them with existing items in their wardrobes, they have created masculine/feminine outfits of great charm.

Mathematics of style

Every item in your wardrobe should fit into your dressing equation. It should be amenable to many permutations. Each item must be adaptable to earn its keep. For example, a shirt is only valuable if it can be fitted into several equations. You should be able to multiply it across many outfits. A suit should allow both jacket and skirt to work separately with separate items. Adding and subtracting to and from your basic items is also part of your individual fashion equation. It is instructive to do a plus, minus, multiply and divide against a list of major items in your wardrobe to see how useful your clothes really are.

Geometric equations

When you are buying clothes or when you are dressing for any occasion you should always be aware of the shape and silhouette you create as you stand, move or sit. It is a question of geometry. Sophisticated women know very well that shoulder pads are the most flattering aids, regardless of figure type. Paris has recently gone overboard for the Hollywood forties look of very broad, built-up shoulders to accentuate the femininity of the figure and although many shoulders are now grotesquely over-padded, you can follow suit with caution. Emphasized shoulders will always help you.

Figure-emphasising clothes are **the** *fashion story of the moment. The elements to look for if you want this look are broad shoulders and tight skirts. Highlight your waist with a big belt. Remember that the jacket should be cut full so that you have a generous amount of material in the peplum to make your waist look smaller.*

Plan but be bold

How well your wardrobe works depends on how much thought you give it before you go shopping. Be strong-willed and stick to your plan of what you intend to buy. Obviously you will wish to break away from the safe and sure for some of your purchases and yours would be a very dull wardrobe indeed if it did not have some surprises and excitements. Crack your stylistic mould every now and then. Choose a colour which is new for you. Buy a garment which you have not previously had in your wardrobe. Select a shape or proportion which is different from your normal look.

chapter 3

Colour, pattern and texture

The psychological effect

According to psychologists, colours mean different things to different people and the way we react to a particular colour varies according to our psychological state at the time. A colour that seems exciting when we are in a buoyant mood can be menacing when we are less confidant; a shade that soothes us at one time can bore us at another. Whatever colour does, whether it stimulates, excites, soothes, irritates or depresses, it can never be ignored.

The psychological effect

According to psychologists, colours mean different things to different people and the way we react to a particular colour varies according to our psychological state at the time. A colour that seems exciting when we are in a buoyant mood can be menacing when we are less confidant; a shade that soothes us at one time can bore us at another. Whatever colour does, whether it stimulates, excites, soothes, irritates or depresses, it can never be ignored.

What is colour?

The dictionary definition of colour is that it is the sensation caused by light of various wavelengths on the eyes. Our reactions to colour are affected by its hue, brightness and saturation.

There is no limit to what you can achieve with pattern and colour, provided you are in charge and don't let it all run away with you. Whether you choose a pattern that is small (even tiny polka dots) or large, the principles are the same. Unless you are very confident avoid mixing patterns in an outfit. Strong, plain colour or neutrals always look best with a patterned fabric — whether it is a tiny overall floral, something stronger and larger-scale or . . .

. . . very large and bold. These sort of patterns are so strong that they need nothing fussy to weaken their impact. The silk pyjamas are for very sophisticated summer evenings; the cotton pants and p.v.c. duffle coat would brighten any day, anywhere and the printed cotton rain coat would defy any weather.

Metabolic changes

Psychologists have experimented with colour under laboratory conditions and their results have been convincing. Warm colours such as red and orange can be used to raise a person's temperature and blood pressure in a way that justifies their being called hot colours. Just as red can make the heart beat faster, cool colours such as blue and green can apparently slow it down.

Coloured emotions

It seems therefore that there is some actual basis for expressing our emotions through colour. When we talk about seeing red, we mean that for a split second we almost lost control and our temper was as hot as the colour. Our temper had the same effect on our psyche as has red. And what about having the blues? Blue slows the heartbeat and we think of it as a cold colour. Some people find still blue water depressing, others find a completely blue room has a chilly atmosphere however warm the air temperature.

Arousing colours

You don't have to be a Van Gogh to see that colour can be used to stimulate emotion and obtain certain reactions. Red with its high saturation and low brightness has always been associated with seduction and arousal but red is also the colour of danger and it arouses quite different feelings of high anxiety under different circumstances.

Colour contradictions

The style of clothes can completely change the effect of their colour. Let us look at a few examples of the way style alters one's reaction to colour.

Daring red, classic red

The shiny red dress has been an archetype of seductive dressing for a very long time whether in the Can-Can dancer's costume or the slinky side-slit skirt worn by the lady of the night. But imagine a woollen dress in soft, warm red with a cowl neck and a classic piece of jewelry — nothing could be more sophisticated and elegant.

If you were going for an interview, would you wear red? Well, you would probably avoid a vulgar, trashy scarlet outfit because this would subliminally effect the interviewers

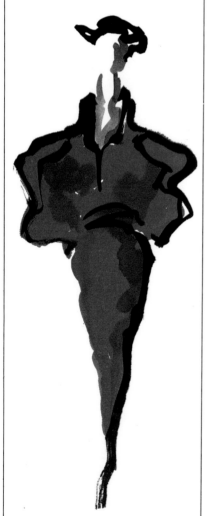

Femme fatale or sophisticated lady? Red can be worn in either way. It can pin-point areas of your personality and send out signals which are unmistakeable.

reaction to you — they may think you are flighty and superficial — but your sophisticated red wool suit could have a different strong effect on the interview board — it could tell the interviewers that here is a confident but reliable woman.

Sombre black, sexy black

Black is not in fact a colour, it is the absence of colour, and over the centuries it has received a lot of bad publicity. It is associated with sobriety and sombreness and is the colour of mourning which tells other people that you have put aside the frivolous side of life.

But black is also a very sophisticated colour. It has a strong effect on people, and nothing is as smart as a crisp black suit with a dash of colour in the accessories. Here black says you are a serious and stylish person, and sorrow plays no part in the effect you create.

Let's change the style again and put black on a woman with a buxom figure, change the outfit to a skin-tight dress in shimmering black with a side slit revealing black, fish-net stockings and the personality that is projected is totally different. It is neither sad nor sober — it is as trashy and sexy as red can be.

Conditioned reaction

The dividing line between the different reactions caused by colour is a fine one. Clearly not everyone responds to a particular colour in the same way. Often one's response has less to do with the effect the colour is really having than the pre-empted reaction caused by early training and education in one's response. If as a child you were brought up to think that bright red was common that attitude may persist in adult life and you may think it vulgar to wear such a colour.

Food illustrates this conditioned reaction very clearly. Badly presented food can be as unappetising as badly cooked food. A plate of white chicken, mashed potatoes and parsnips may taste just as good as the same chicken served with bright green peas and crispy roast potatoes, but the pallor of the first promises less flavour than the contrasts of the second.

Colour placement

Painters knew that the value of certain colours can be changed by placing other colours next to them. A mark of pure yellow on a white canvas will have a value in relation to the white background. A scarlet mark next to the yellow immediately

changes the effect. If the painter places another yellow mark on a canvas and puts a blue mark next to it, he will find that he has created another colour value. White, red and blue will each make the yellow appear different to the viewer's eye and provoke a different mental reaction. It is important to understand how colours affect each other and remember their interactions when you ar putting together an outfit. Time spent on colour planning is never time wasted.

Personal colours

You must also realise that it is dangerous to emulate others. You must get to know your colours and not be tempted to buy a pink top simply because your girlfriend looks great in it. All too often you find that when the excitement has died down and you really look at yourself in that colour, it looks awful.

Creating an effect

Colours can be combined to blend together or to contrast with each other to bring out their opposite strengths. As a general rule of thumb, if you blend tones together the final result is elegant, restrained and sophisticated. Using strong contrasts creates a dramatic and exciting effect which can also be very witty. How you choose your colour depends largely on the effect you wish to create. Teaming a beige dress with pale pink or grey accessories is clearly going to be more restful and refined than livening it up with peacock blue or purple — although of course these colours would work perfectly well together.

Classic colour blends

Over the years certain blends have developed and they always look stunningly elegant. Grey and white have worked beautifully with each other since the thirties when they became a popular combination in Paris. Beige and brown, known in the fifties as coffee and cream, are warmly sophisticated together. Cream and dusty pink are almost guaranteed to produce a gently glamorous look.

Classic colour contrasts

These have proved to be enduring in the same way. Black and white always looks striking, cream and navy has the same impact but is less brash. Bright red with white, navy, black or beige is a strong and perennial look. You can go for blends or

Pastel shades and sugared almond colours can be mixed indiscriminately without ever clashing. They will always give an impression of fresh prettiness provided that you send them to the cleaners regularly — they look terribly grubby if not kept spotlessly clean.

Draped and cinched fullness is the fashion story for the sophisticated woman. It looks its best for day in a short jacket worn with a straight skirt and . . . .

contrasts, but remember, the disposition and the balance of colour areas is crucial.

Popular colours

There are rules of colour which have been developed for good reasons and normally these are automatically obeyed because they seem naturally right to our eyes. But they can be ignored very successfully provided you know exactly what you are doing.

Blue

There are more sales of blue clothes than any other colour apart from black. This fact reflects the exceptional range of tones which blue can have. From its palest shades through baby blue to deep and dramatic electric blue, there is a tone for every skin type and hair colouring and it can be worn by women of every colour and nationality. What other colour can look as good on a blond Nordic type as it does on a dark Spanish person?

I recently conducted an experiment at the Sales. I went to the Marble Arch branch of Marks and Spencer, which attracts buyers of every nationality under the sun, and watched the buying pattern which emerged in the sale of men's and women's knitwear. Initially the reds and blues consistently attracted the buyers, but four times out of six it was the blue which was taken to the cash desk. The favourite was a rich royal blue.

When I visited Estée Lauder's hospitality suite at the top of the General Motors skyscraper in New York overlooking the whole of the city, I was struck by how restful it was. She had chosen different blues to use throughout — along with mahogany furniture. The effect was powerful but friendly.

Red

Blue is a comfortable and undemanding colour for most of us. Only its most strident deep shades might present problems for some colour types. Red is a much trickier shade but again can be marvellous on the right person.

I have always warned against cheap reds. The colour most women need is a soft red — either with a good amount of yellow in it or tending towards pink. I get very excited about all colours but nothing is as thrilling as playing, as I used to when I

was designing in Italy, with different shades of red. The range
is so wide — from near orange to almost burgundy.

The most exciting flat I have every been in is Diana
Vreeland's on Park Avenue in New York. Everything in it is red.
The doors are a glossy scarlet, the red sofas are piled with
multi-patterned red cushions and the carpets are also
predominantly red. The effect is stunning but, at the same
time, restful. This reflects Ms Vreeland's perfectly sure hand.
What could have been a restless nightmare of colour is not,
because every red is strong but soft and every one blends with
the others. There are no crude tones introduced for cheap
dramatic effect. The lesson for using this most exciting colour
in your clothes is obvious. Remember, only little children like
the most glaring colours and if properly chosen even strong
colour need not dominate. Think how perfectly London's red
buses work visually with the city.

Yellow

In certain parts of the world yellow is considered a colour only
suitable for whores. I am sure that this has presented protocol
problems for the Queen when she and her advisers have been
deciding her wardrobe for her foreign tours. Her colouring is
such that she can wear yellow with great success and this is
rare in a woman of her age. Normally yellow is a colour for the
young. Nothing looks nicer than a tanned young girl in a
sunshine yellow jogging suit or a lemon yellow T-shirt and white
jeans.

Nevertheless, yellow can be treacherous and you need to
look at yourself very critically before deciding. If you do not tan
easily or darkly, you should perhaps avoid it. Certainly, for the
average Anglo-Saxon colouring yellow bathing suits should be
eschewed as should yellow evening dresses. In both cases the
tone of yellow is crucial but, nine time out of ten, it picks up the
sunlight to such an extent that your skin tones seem to turn
grey. Artificial light has the same effect of bleaching the
wearer's skin as it picks up the glow of the yellow.

This is obviously true of the rich, golden yellow range, but
also often applies to the paler and more manageable tones.
For most women, it is safer to keep yellow in small, highlight
doses so that you can then control it instead of it dominating
you. A safe rule of thumb is to always choose the paler shades
if you want to cover a sizeable portion of your body in yellow
— but don't be afraid. A good yellow cotton sweater or T-shirt
can electrify an otherwise tame colour scheme.

*. . . for evening in a short ruched
and draped skirt tied with a bow at
the side. A skirt like this in a plain
coloured taffeta silk can be worn
with a variety of different tops
according to the formality of the
occasion.*

*Colours that might be expected to clash very often do not. If they are part of the same colour family (the reds, the yellows or the purples for example) and are merely different tones from different ends of the family they will tone with each other very well **provided** that they are complimentary, as this fuschia and purple are here.*

Green

Green is the cinderella of colour. Many women feel uneasy with it and in fact have superstitious fears that it is unlucky. This is a pity as it is a very subtle colour with a shade to flatter any type of colouring. Redheads have known about the flattery of green for a long time but its appeal should not be exclusively for them.

Actually, far too may redheads over-rely on green. I recently visited Spain where several times I met a redheaded English woman who, as expatriates tend to do, had become frozen in her fashion sense. Her clothes reflected the old-fashioned concept of refinement achieved by all-over colour. Unfortunately, she had chosen green as her shade. She favoured jade and a very deep spruce green. Both were marvellous colours but used all over (including eye shadow) the effect was deadening and depressing. Her companion wore only black. Drinks with them was a real downer but they thought that their boringly funereal choice of colours was tasteful.

In a sense, that was the problem. Too much good taste kills everything. If the green had been enlivened by a strong flash of fuchsia and the black with some shiny electric blue, these women would have looked marvellously dramatic instead of dowdy.

Green is a colour that works exceptionally well under artificial lights. The emerald and jade shades can look stunning for evening — especially in irridescent or glossy fabrics such as shot taffeta or fine layered fabrics such as chiffon. For day, green velvet worn with grey, beige or white has an unbeatable sense of understated class. Green is a colour that rewards a bit of thought and some experimenting.

Orange

What a loss of dignity this colour has suffered over the last few years! The crudest, sharpest day-glo tones have been eagerly used by designers and stylists desperate to be new and now. It is a great pity because, in its rich golden tones, or paler peachy range, orange can be subtle and flattering.

It is also a colour that works very well with other colours in stripes, patterns or checks as well as solids. Like yellow, it must be approached with discretion. Those cheap orange sundresses in the colour's most strident saturation that appear every summer are just that — cheap and strident. Avoid them.

Instead, look to wear orange in stripes with cooling colours

— grey, white or pale blue, or make it dramatic by using it in small amounts together with black, winter green or even navy. Unless you are very confident about your skills in make-up you would be wiser to avoid orange near your face. It can have an even more greying effect on your skin than can yellow. Having said this, I remember last Christmas having drinks in the country and our hostess, whose hair was grey, wore a deep apricot cashmere high-necked jumper, which was almost orange, and looked terrific. Her make-up picked up the orangey glow of her jumper and her lipstick was golden-orange. The whole effect worked marvellously.

Fuchsia

Like orange, this colour has suffered some indignities recently. It can be softly flattering if it tends towards the cooler mauve tones but can be vulgar and almost impossible to wear when it veers towards the shocking pink range. Of course, it is the latter which the rag trade likes. It is cheap and cheerful and looks arresting in the windows of Oxford Street. Only one woman in a thousand can really carry it off. Others look hot, uncomfortable, vulgar and as if they are about to join a circus act.

Fuchsia's strength is as a mixer. It is the angostura bitters of the colur story — used sparingly it can make an outfit, but it is impossible at full strength.

I think that the most stunning use of fuchsia I have ever seen was by Yves Saint Laurent. He tied a wide fuchsia strip of taffeta around a simple black velvet evening gown, pulled it into a huge bow at the back — and left it. The effect was simple, direct and classic, with a Japanese purity. Again, Chanel and the great tweed weavers of Scotland have always known how beautifully a strong fuchsia can work as an accent in woven wools when by itself it would be overwhelming.

Purple

Everything that applies to fuchsia also applies to purple. It can look rich and regal, or crude and sharp. The difference normally depends on the price you pay. Even with today's modern dyeing techniques manufacturers seem to have difficulty in producing a good tone which can be sold cheaply. Purple has always been associated with kings, or mourning but even then only for the most impressive moments of ceremony.

Modern dressers should view it in the same way. For day wear it is tricky, but can look marvellous in the evening. The subtlety of shot fabrics an velvet in purples can be hard to beat, especially for women with light-coloured hair under artificial lighting. Remember that at its finest purple is lightened by ermine — you can achieve the same effect with silver or diamonds, either artificial or real.

Breuer and The Bauhaus

Marcel Breuer, famous furniture designer, architect and teacher at the German design school, The Bauhaus, said this of furnishing schemes but it also applies to the colours of the clothes we wear.

"A complete scheme is no arbitary composition . . . it must be able to serve both those needs which remain constant and those which vary. This variation is possible only if the very simplest and most straightforward pieces are used: otherwise changing will mean buying new pieces."

Colour and your wardrobe

Rationalising your approach to colour is part of the process of having a wardrobe that really works for you. Remember, whether your wardrobe is extensive or small, it will only be successful if you have a controlled colour scheme based on colours that suit you and work together. Three or four main colours are the essential foundation of your wardrobe.

Mains and secondaries

A preplanned approach to colour is important. All it requires is an understanding that in your wardrobe you need main and secondary colours. Your main colours should be neutrals like grey, beige, navy and white. Your secondary colour choice is limitless.

Anything goes

One of the assumptions often made about colour is that there is a limit to the number of colours that suit an individual. This is much less true than is generally thought. Think of model girls who have to wear and look good in virtually any colour that is handed to them. They make-up to the colours that they are wearing and you can do the same thing.

What to wear with what

Although there is often a dominant shade each season (such as the blacks and greys of recent winters) and strong accessory colours (like day-glo orange, pink and green a couple of seasons ago) you do not have to wear them. Experiment with colour and find out which ones are right for you. Looking fashionable is no substitute for looking good.

Grey
Here is a good winter colour. Main accessory colours with grey can be white, soft or sharp yellow and any red from scarlet to cherry. Violet and brown also work with grey. Use these colours predominantly but highlight them with accessory colours. Sub- secondaries to be used sharply could be orange, peacock, purple, black, peppermint or grass green.

Beige
This works well in a winter wardrobe too. First secondaries also include white, but beige blends well with cream and contrasts beautifully with violet, black and even orange. Sub-secondaries could be dark brown, navy, a subtle blend with coral or a sophisticated touch of spruce green.

Navy
Navy is often used as a summer colour and main accessory colours range from gentle beige and pale greys and pinks to contrasting white. Pick this up with splashes of scarlet or violet, strong yellows and oranges, spicy peppermint and gentle sky blue.

White
The most popular summer colour of all is again not really a colour but the absence of colour at the other end of the light spectrum. Pastel colours blend beautifully with white — greys, beiges and dusty pinks look cool and sophisticated, navy makes a smart contrast colour. Second choice secondary colours can be any strong or sharp colours.

Brown
This colour looks most glamorous with cream, pale grey or black as first accessory colours. Electric blue, orange and violet can be used as second accessory highlights but be careful. You have to have precisely the right shades. Browns and oranges for example can look stunning if they are the right tones but awful if they are not. This is an area where the experienced and trained eye gets it right and the less knowledgeable should tread carefully and experiment, so get

Even quite good clothes can look nothing on the hanger. Often very expensive clothes which are soft and flattering on the body look limp and uninspiring on the rack unless you know how to look beyond the rather depressing droopiness. Notice the details, the scale, the workmanship and finish after you have checked out the colour that initially attracted you. If they seem to be alright swing the garment on its hanger to see how much rhythm and poise it has. If it seems half-way interesting, try it on. It only takes a couple of minutes.

All that you have ever read about the dangers of stripes is perfectly true but you shouldn't let it frighten you off completely. If you are very thin avoid going vertically, if you are overweight be careful of them horizontally.

out those glossies and make sure you know absolutely what you are doing.

Burgundy
Cream, pink and beige work well as first secondaries and cobalt, gold and black are strong sub-secondary colours.

Jade
Jade is a colour that is sadly neglected. It can look stunning with beige and certain shades of grey whilst black, violet and orange work well as sub-secondaries.

Be brave
Far too many women are timid with colour and feel that they must stick to the known way. This is a pity. Of course, it is comforting to feel the security of having colours in your wardrobe which you know really work for you. However, it is very limiting if you never move outside their range. It is not easy to make a major investment in a colour about which you are not sure. If your hunch is wrong and it doesn't work then a lot of money has been thrown away. Keep your basic wardrobe to those colours that have been tried and have proved themselves, or stick to neutrals. For experiments try a new colour in a scarf, a sweater or perhaps a short-term inexpensive dress. Play with the new colour. Use it with other colours in your wardrobe — both the obvious ones and the unexpected. If the results are a little disappointing and you still want to make the colour work for you, adjust your make-up. Suddenly an incompatible colour might suit you.

Breaking rules
Any rule can be broken but you must know what you are doing. The famous Italian designer Emilio Pucci caused a sensation in the fifties by using cerise, purple and turquoise together. He was the first to do so but the combination was so right for its time that it swept the world. The colour revolution continued in the sixties with psychedelic purple, yellow and red being combined and amazingly working together very well. The saturation and degree of strength of the colours has a big influence on whether they work together.

How many colours?
The number of colours you use is just as important as which colours you combine together. In this, as in many areas of

dress, the younger you are the more you can get away with. Vibrant primary colours mixed together can zing with excitment and look fabulous on a woman in her twenties but would be hard for a forty-year-old to carry off. Fun, excitement and youth are all symbolised by strong colours boldly mixed but for most women a limited number of colours works best.

Stylish combinations

Stylishness is normally achieved by mixing no more than three colours in one outfit. Having said this it should be added that one-colour outfits rarely work. If garments and accessories are all in the same shade the result looks too contrived and oppressive. A red dress with matching red shoes, handbag and jewelry is not nearly as effective as it would be if white or black were used to highlight and lift the red.

Strong or crude

It is important to differentiate between strong colour and crude colour. Some colours are treacherous and can be so bold as to work against the wearer. Red is a good example. A good red with depth and strength can be very powerful and work exceedingly well. A cheap, crude red robs the complexion of its colour and, especially when the sun shines, can dazzle to such an extent as to almost turn the wearer's face into a photographic negative. Navy and black can also drain you of your colour if you are not careful, but women with white or blond hair can look marvelous in navy.

Make a safety area

As a general rule, avoid black and navy next to the face if you are not in the first bloom of youth. Create a safety area for your face by wearing white, cream or pastel shades at neck level. Strengthen your make-up and a wear a light collar or a piece of reflective jewelry. If you wish to wear these colours right through middle and old-age you can but you must fight back a little. If you do the rewards are there. They are classic colours which always give a touch of style. They are also very slimming and figure flattering.

Dark for slim

The darker the colour the slimmer the appearance because dark, rich colours make any area look smaller than it actually is. Light, pale colours give an illusion of space. You know this from interior decorating experiments in your home. The

You can break all the rules if you are tall and slim and manage to look stunning whether (as opposite) you go for the drama of very broad stripes or as here, you choose a finer form.

principle, based on valid scientific precepts, is just as sound when the area to be covered is not a room but you.

This does not mean that to look slim you must walk around like a crow dressed in black from head to toe. Far from it. What you should remember is that any colour is more slimming in its darker tones than in its lighter versions. So, if you want to look slimmer, go for the darker tones.

White with care

It is a fact that even model girls look less slim in white than when wearing black — and they are carrying no extra weight! Remember that pure white clothes are beloved of designers and fashion editors because they photograph stunningly. They never look so good in reality and it is wise to avoid their glare by choosing off-white, cream or very pale pastels to achieve the same effect except for the very young who can get away with it.

Be particularly careful with white footwear if your feet are over a size five. White shoes can make you look like Minnie Mouse!

Coordinate throughout

When you are wearing pale colours, especially in lightweight summer outfits, check them for transparency and organise your underwear accordingly. Nothing looks worse than a dark bra and pants showing through a white or pastel dress. The rule is simple enough. If you are wearing pale colours on the outside wear pale colours on the inside — skin tones are better still.

Placing colours

Everyone has favourite colours and most of us tend to have preconceived ideas about what colour goes with what. This thinking can act like a straight-jacket as far as fashion is concerned. Try two experiements to find out if you are a straight-jacket thinker.

Experiment one

First of all lay out your three favourite outfits as you would wear them. For example, dress, jacket, tights, shoes and bag; or jumper, skirt, tights and shoes; or T-shirt, trousers, tights and shoes. How close in colour are they and how colour-interchangeable are they? My guess is that, if you haven't

An unbeatable combination — a striped sweater or sweat-shirt with plain, tailored trousers or ski-pants. This sort of classic casual wear is ageless and classless. It is equally at home in town or country.

cheated over your favourites and really have chosen the clothes which you wear together most often because you think they go, the answer to both questions will be "very".

Now remove one element from each combination and replace it with something that you would never wear with the other items. For example, maybe your regular shoes for one outfit are black leather courts. What happens if you substitute your red suede loafers? Are you happy with the result? Put the outfit on, including the substitute footwear and see if it works. If you think not, are you sure or might your thinking be straight-jacketed by habit? Dressing by habit is a sure-fire way to end up looking boring and predictable, so break out of it.

You can try this experiment with all the items in your wardrobe and, by mixing things that you have never worn together before, you can perhaps extend your wardrobe possiblities without buying anything new. Only buy when you have exhausted all combinations of possibilities using your existing wardrobe.

Experiment two

Look through your wardrobe and note down the colours that are missing. In most cases you will find that there is quite a wide range of colours not represented and you must ask yourself why. Have you rejected certain colours because they have not worked in the past, and if so, how do you know that they will not work now? Have you rejected certain colours, untried, as a result of prejudice? If so, what is the basis of the prejudice?

Bearing in mind the basic broad colour stories in your wardrobe go out and buy an *activator*. By this I mean something in a sharply contrasting colour that you would never normally think of choosing. It does not need to be a crude or strong colour. It can be subtle and even subdued but it must be quite different from the colours at present in your wardrobe. Remember, you do not need to spend much money on this — a cheap scarf, a pair of gloves or plastic belt will be sufficient for the experiment. If you are feeling richer, however, the value of this exercise will be doubled or trebled if you buy two or three items of different colours — perhaps reduced in a sale.

Play with the new items by putting them with all the combinations of colour in your wardrobe. Look long and think hard about each one. In many cases you must be prepared for the new colour not to work with the others, but the value will be if at the end you can say *why* it does not. With other outfits it

In my opinion natural fibres are always superior to man-made ones — although the best of all worlds (comfort, competitive price and practicality) is probably to be found in mixtures of the two.

might work quite well but not set them alight. If you are lucky it should absolutely revitalise some of your outfits. In this way, you can extend your colour range and prevent your wardrobe becoming straight-jacketed.

Colour coordinate your wardrobe

Begin by organising your hangers into broad colour ranges. For example, have all reds, pinks and oranges together in a group.

Look for colour bands

Do you find that you have one or two strong colour bands containing several garments? If you do then you have either been buying in a planned way or you have strong colour preferences which keep coming up in your regular shopping. Both of these situations are positive and can be built upon.

Are you an impulse buyer?

If, however, you have many different groups of varying colours consisting of perhaps only one or two garments then you are buying in an uncoordinated way. This suggests a random approach with no clearly planned or logical buying pattern. Perhaps many of the things in your wardrobe were impulse buys. It would be an interesting experiment for you to sit down and list all those items on your wardrobe rail which you hardly ever wear or only wore one or two times when you first bought them. In any case, by spreading your colour story too thin you are weakening your impact and your choice when it comes to mixing and matching.

Invest in main colours

Decide which are your main colours and invest in them. Do not scatter colour indiscriminately throughout your wardrobe.

Accessory colours

When choosing accessory (or secondary) colours remember that you have a choice — you can either heighten the main colour by contrast or you can harmonise the main and secondary colours.

The contrast colours with the greatest impact are the deep and dark ones such as black or navy or, at the other end of the range, white or cream. Obviously the strongest and most dramatic schemes are achieved by taking your colours from the opposite ends of the spectrum. The greatest impact is made by the negative/positive effect of black, navy and any dark tones of other shades linked with white, cream or light tones. However, the power of sharply contrasting colours should not be forgotten. For example, navy can be sparked by emerald, dark grey spiked with purple, and of course, there is the classic combination of black and bright red. Vibrant accessory colours like these can be exceptionally effective if used sparingly and on a small scale. Too much and their advantage is lost but in the right proportions these sharp accents can have an amazing effect. Accent colours can be very bold and strong but must be brief.

Witty colour coordinations

Dressing wittily is something which we English are not very good at. Perhaps it has something to do with our understated, dry sense of humour. French women understand witty dressing. They can put articles together in an offbeat way or use an unexpected splash of colour. It is worth playing with colour to obtain this witty effect.

Classic wit

Classic witty colour combinations which amused as they shocked are purple and daffodil yellow, electric blue with lettuce green and Schiaparelli's famous shocking pink cerise with black. When you are playing with colour in this way you can have a lot of fun and also learn a great deal about colours and their effects but always remember the importance of scale.

Keep it sharp

Short, sharp bursts of bright accent colours are fine — vast areas of strident colours are not. Unless you are very assured and have convinced yourself absolutely that you are right, it is wise to avoid using more than one vibrant accent colour at a time.

Unique fashion statement

As your confidence grows you can develop a bold, original and totally unique way of presenting yourself. You can ignore the rules once you understand them and know what you are achieving by doing so. For example, a girl I know who had hated her naturally orange and very frizzy hair has stopped cringing at her reflection in the mirror, has forgotten the playground gibes of ''Carrots!'' and has made her magnificent

Before you think about colour, look closely at the shape of the garments. A softly clinging skirt is still going to remain that no matter what colour you choose; a large collarless jacket is not going to be any easier to wear in a different colour. In the fitting room, look beyond colour and pattern to the shape which you and the clothes make. If it is not flattering no colour in the world can change that.

mane of hair the starting point for all her fashion statements. She treats her hair as her dominant accessory and chooses colours to play it up instead of trying to tone it down. Her most successful look was achieved by wearing a bright orange T-shirt dress. "Orange with orange — ugh!" the experts would say and in theory they would be right. It is the wrong colour for carrot-tops. And yet the rule was broken with stunning effect. This sort of boldness can work but it requires a sure hand and a skilled eye. The girl I am talking about is a trained designer and she knew the right shade of orange to work with her hair and make-up. Had she got it wrong she would have looked dreadful. So remember — breaking rules is only for the skilled, experienced and knowledgeable dresser, but with flair you can achieve similarly memorable effects if you train your colour sense.

Colour families

Professional designers and those very clever women who arrange merchandise in shops, always think in terms of colour families. So should you. It involves taking a professional look at your wardrobe to sort out your families. But first, let me explain what a family is.

It is made up of garments that work together and are interchangeable by virtue of the actual items and the pattern and colour they are made in. For example, a designer talks of his citrus story. This will possibly mean a unit consisting of a T-shirt, a mini-skirt, a pair of peddle-pushers, a sweatshirt, a cotton scarf and cotton socks — all in a choice of at least two colours, perhaps pale orange and lemon. These colours can be combined to give the buyer considerable flexibility when purchasing. With this as a capsule, if the designer finds that sales are good, he can top up the family with other coordinated items as the season progresses. For instance, he might add a shirt and two different styles of pants in mid-season.

Tempting families

A buyer's family is arranged to make it easier for you to buy and to make you more likely to include extra items that "go", either at the initial purchase time or later in the season. Let us imagine that her family is the burgundy and grey story. She will put the items together so that your thinking has been done for you. You see a grey herringbone tweed jacket with a pair of grey flannel pants, a grey skirt and a burgundy lambswool sweater. Nothing could be easier. Then you notice a pair of grey toning pepper and salt trousers which perfectly match everything else, then a burgundy classic skirt, a herringbone skirt, burgundy pants — the family grows ever more desirable, and out comes the credit card. The buyer has done her job.

Start your own family

You should be able to lay out all of your clothes in families. If you can't then your buying pattern is wrong. If you can, you will then be able to see what purchases to make to logically extend each individual family and give it broader, more flexible life. You will inevitably have maverick items which fit nowhere, a favourite sweater that has outlived the skirt it went with for instance. Don't automatically discard it. Use it as the basis for a new family by buying a couple of new items that will work with it.

Plagiarise

One final point about colour in fashion — take your lead from the experts. They have done much of the basic thinking for you. You can see the results of their experiments free every time you look in a dress shop window.

Window shopping

Learn to read window displays. Notice how an effect is achieved by the use of certain colour combinations. Train yourself to analyse and edit what you see in shop windows. Mentally take a display apart and isolate each item not just for design, pattern and shape but also for colour. Work out why that particular blue was chosen for the belt, how that grey dress would look if the beige jacket was changed for the stone cardigan on the other figure.

Background colour

Do not forget to note the surrounding colour — the background shade has been carefully chosen to accentuate the colours of the outfits. Could you use that colour to achieve the same affect when creating your own look?

The glossies

The other training ground to use is the colour pages of fashion magazines. In the super-glossy high fashion magazines the majority of the clothes featured will almost certainly not bear any relationship to your life — nor will the prices. But before

If you are buying a short straight skirt, do not get it too tight otherwise it will ride up when you sit down. The Queen Mother often chooses generous wrap-over skirts and she is an expert at sitting down with dignity and decorum. The new wrapped sarong skirts can solve the problem, unless the manufacturer has been mean with fabric in which case the wrap-over will gape and stretch in an ugly way. Always try sitting down in a skirt before you buy it.

you cast aside that picture of a coat so extremely proportioned and priced that only a six foot four millionairess could buy it, look at how it is styled. Picture stylists for top magazines are very clever, extremely aware of how to use shape and colour and, above all, have exceptionally advanced and highly developed fashion consciousness. Use their knowledge. Notice how they accessorise a garment. Understand their use of scale and colour. Nothing is accidental in their picture — everything has been chosen as being positively the best thing to put with the rest.

Do your research

The colour training you can obtain by spending half an hour actively and analytically looking at fashion pictures can revolutionise your approach to how you dress. A random selection of three magazines should, if you are looking properly, tell you all you need to know. Don't forget that you do not need to buy three magazines. Take one and study it then pick up on the same looks and feeling whilst flicking through other magazines at the newsagent. Learn to think about colour in relation to everything in daily life.

Become an active colour analyst

It requires no special skill or training. Anyone can train herself. Wherever you are, you are surrounded by colour and it is having an effect upon you all the time. Think about colour combinations, colour proportions and colour stories in daily life. Why are certain forms of packaging more appealing to you than others? It is almost certainly as a result of the designer's choice and use of colour. When browsing why do you pick up certain magazines and not others? Why do some book jackets or greetings cards attract you more than others? Colour plays a major role.

Analyse the appearance of other women. Nine times out of ten the thing that attracts you or alarms you won't be the design of their clothes, but their colour combinations.

Analyse the soaps

Teach yourself to watch television from a colour-critical point of view. Soap operas are a particularly good training ground. The colours chosen for the heroine, the femme fatale, the dangerous woman are all carefully worked out, cleverly coordinated and finally packaged to give the viewer an instant idea of the sort of person the character is. Clearly clothes styling is also very important in this and we look at soap opera style later on but remember that a crucial aspect of one's reaction to a person is in response to the clothes that person wears. Be aware of colour and its effects in all aspects of your life and use it as a powerful force in your wardrobe.

Kandinsky and The Bauhaus

The German design school, The Bauhaus, was set up between the wars to take a new look at all aspects of design. It is no accident that the first courses involved a completely new and basic approach to colour. The famous Russian artist Kandinsky evolved a way of training the eye to understand and assess colour values and his course on colour has had far-reaching effects. The things Kandinsky said about colour and line in painting are very useful when applied to choosing clothes — colour and line have a positive effect upon both viewer and wearer.

Colour temperatures

His colour theory, derived from Goethe and Rudolf Steiner, was based on his assumption that colours have temperature and tone. His four major sounds in colour were warm and bright, warm and dark, cold and bright and cold and dark. The temperature of colour was determined by its tendency towards yellow (warmth) and blue (cold). Kandinsky felt that yellow advances aggressively and blue retreats passively. This active-passive balance is found in his other two contrasts — white and black, red and green. He believed that green, mixed as it is from the total opposites yellow and blue, creates perfect balance and harmony, being both passive and self-sufficient.

Line temperatures

Kandinsky's theory of line followed his colour theory. Verticals he said were warm, and horizontals were cold. Diagonals tended towards one or the other depending upon their position or direction.

Playing with pattern

Nothing would be duller than if we all had to wear plain woven or dyed colour with no pattern. Nothing would be more limiting either as pattern can be used to give variety and ring the changes in even quite a limited wardrobe. Bearing in mind that

Casual knitted cardigans and jackets have a place in every woman's wardrobe but they do not need to be dowdy, boring or predictable. There is a huge choice of fashion knits now. If you knit for yourself, you will know that there has never been a wider choice of patterns, yarns and dyes — so, take full advantage of them.

Remember that shops now coordinate their colours in displays to tempt you to buy a complete look. Very nice if you can afford to and need a completely new, head-to-toe look. If not, you must keep your wits about you. Buy only one item. Say you have decided on a new cardigan. Stick to your decision and, before buying, decide how many existing things in your wardrobe will go with it. In this way you won't get carried away.

statistics tell us that forty-seven percent of British women are size 14 and over it is important to know the basic do's and don'ts about pattern.

As a general rule, the smaller the pattern and the more limited the colour contrasts, the more elegant the printed fabric will look. The larger the pattern and the stronger the contrasts the more stunning and memorable the pattern will be. Again, a small pattern will have a more slimming effect than a large one although I know of at least one large lady who ignores the rule with great style and treats her shape rather like a tank to be camouflaged — which she does very effectively with large, brightly-coloured abstract patterns.

Riot of patterns

In the last ten years there has been a revolution in our thinking about pattern. Previously it was the height of vulgarity to mix scale, colour and type of pattern in one outfit. Kenzo and other dsigners in the seventies put paid to that for good. Looking back, their mixtures of colours and patterns seem quite desperate in their determination to break the rule of good taste, but things have since calmed down without losing the new ground they broke.

We can now successfully mix spots and stripes, geometric and floral prints, large and small-scale checks, the same patterns in two different colours and any number of variations on these and a hundred other ideas which would have horrified the old style couturiers. In fact the French designer, Ungaro, or the Italian, Lancetti, will use as many as five different prints in one outfit and still manage to keep them under control.

Widen your scope

I do not suggest that you go that far but, unless you have already consciously made an effort, the chances are that there is scope in your wardrobe for a much bolder approach to pattern than you have considered up to now. For years the best of taste dictated that a check jacket should have a plain skirt. We now know that the same check on a smaller or a much larger scale, can look stunning especially if everything is, for example, black and white. But what is to stop the same check jacket looking terrific with a coloured blouse in a large, overall abstract or floral pattern?

Plaids and checks

Old-fashioned ideas of taste said that checks and plaids do not mix. Kenzo also finished with that one. Punks followed his lead and in no time our eyes were used to Royal Stuart and Black Watch tartans worn with black and white houndstooth checks and black leather. Now it is a recognised part of fashion lore that tartans and checks of all sorts work well if they are put together by a sure, but not crude, hand. One of the secrets for keeping control if you are doing your own mixing is to remember that you can get away with virtually any combination provided you use colour to unify and connect them. Having said this, nothing looks more stunning than several patterns and plaids mixed in a negative/positive variation on opposites — black and white, cream and olive, red and navy or lemon and lilac. With a two-colour scheme like that you won't lose control. On the other hand, three or four variations using the same motive, for example floral prints on different scales, can work superbly as the early Laura Ashley outfits showed.

Keep it clean

A word of warning about pattern. Now that the layered look has been temporarily put to rest (although not for long I am sure) you should be aware of the dangers of mixing in a way that makes your patterns look cluttered. Obviously the bigger and bolder the pattern, either in motive or colour combination, the less need there is for the garment itself to be detailed. A big pattern makes its own statement. It does not require fussy collar details, flounces, busy sleeve treatments or layered skirts. A classic draped bust and skirt will probably always be the best look with a big pattern but as this is a rather dull and middle-aged solution all I will say is keep your shapes clean and large and carry the boldness right through.

Beware stripes

Every woman knows the dangers of stripes. Remember what happens to verticals when they have a body in them, they distort and wander. The problems with horizontals are obvious so unless you are very slim and very young stay away from them.

Textures

The safe and dull way of dressing is to wear an outfit in a uniform texture and weight of material. But by doing this you deprive yourself of a lot of excitement and stimulation. The way you put together different weights and textures of fabrics

If you are confident about your shape remember that knitted skirts can be very flattering. A chunky top and a clinging skirt make a very pleasing combination. Make sure that the skirt is lined and treat it with care if you want it to last without going limp or shapeless.

largely depends on current fashion as well as your personal needs, but it is useful to know the characteristics of certain fabrics.

Man-made fabrics

Remember that fabrics like nylon polyester or acrylic might be quick drying, light weight and crease resistant, but they do not breathe. They make you sweat. However, in a mixture with cotton where the natural fibre dominates, they can give the best of both worlds.

Silk

This is fragile but also warm and luxurious. Unfortunately it has a tendency with some women to build up a static charge which causes it to cling. This is fine if you have a body like Krystle Carrington, but tricky if you are built more like Bet Lynch.

Cotton

This is a most versatile material, lightweight and cool, it is always comfortable to wear especially in the summer. However, unless it is treated it tends to crease which is why it is normally blended with man-made fibres to give it much more wash and wear flexibility.

Linen

This has the same characteristics as cotton: it is cool, comfortable and highly absorbent. It is perfect for hot weather but it creases even more than cotton if it has not been given a special finish. Most fashion folk like the creased and crumpled look of untreated linen — I loathe it!

Wool

The most commonly used of all fabrics is very flexible, slightly water repellent and comes in an amazing variety of thicknesses and surfaces. It is warm and comfortable to wear but it is vulnerable and must be carefully treated. It will shrink if washed carelessly and can 'pill' if not treated gently. It is always prey to moths.

You can be as bold as you like with colour and pattern. For example, green and orange are both strong colours but they can work together in various strengths and proportions. They are at their most powerful (left) in their purest statement but they can be mixed with other colours and patterns to create a formal (centre) or informal (right) effect. Other colour combinations can be used in the same way.

Traditional shapes and fabrics can be used in a way that makes them new. A perfectly plain dress and coat look different because the colour tones are similar, yet contrasting; a check skirt looks fresh with a blazer in a strong colour and a large traditional check shirt worn as a coat is given new life by being teamed with boldly striped peddle-pushers.

A scarf at the neck is flattering. There are many different ways to tie it to get the effect that suits you. Plain colours (as here, black for glamour) checks or spots are probably the most flexible scarves to have in your wardrobe.

chapter 4

Shopping around

There are shops that sell clothes and there are fashion shops. Every high street has the former and they are often very good. The worthwhile ones will have a strongly individual style whether it belongs to the owner/buyer, as in a privately owned boutique, or a high-powered committee of experts. The majority of women shop at this level. However, before looking at individual shops or national chains, it is interesting to look at fashion shops.

Fashion shops

These are the shops where the highest design standards are upheld and only the very best clothes by the great designers are stocked. It is axiomatic that quality, not cost, is the criterion for merchandise in these shops.

Why Britain has so few

It is perhaps a reflection of British buying patterns that the number of true fashion shops in this country can be counted on the fingers of one hand. As any London designer will tell you he can only survive by export sales. Clothes bearing names like Jean Muir, Betty Jackson and Jasper Conran cannot fail to be expensive which means that outlets for them are limited to a handful of London shops and perhaps half a dozen in the provinces. British women, unlike their American or Italian counterparts, spend a surprisingly small proportion of their annual budget on clothes. Priority goes to home and holidays. That is why the model fashion departments of up-market stores like Harrods and Fortnum and Mason rely so heavily on foreign customers to keep them going. The same is true of London's two most famous fashion shops, Browns and Harvey Nichols.

Browns and Mrs Burstein

Browns of South Moulton Street is a testimony to the buying skill, merchandising knowledge and outstanding fashion sense of one woman — Mrs Joan Burstein. She understands fashion at all levels, can pick up a new approach or changed attitude before other shop owners are aware of it, can spot new talent with an unerring eye (she has been first to introduce more great designers than anyone else in London — often spotting them even before expert journalists) and she knows precisely how to buy.

Skillful buying

Buying is the basis of success in all fashion retailing but, with a high-profile but rather small fashion shop like Browns which carries the world's most expensive designer names, it is crucial. Mrs Burstein and her team, a highly informed band chosen and trained by her, must know exactly what items to buy from each collection. If the buying is successful a garment should excite and lead public taste whilst fitting into the overall personality of the shop. When it is remembered that many of the items in the shop cost well over a thousand pounds, it is easy to see why mistakes cannot be made too often.

International reputation

Fashion experts from all over the world shop at Browns. A look in their windows or a browse through their racks tells you immediately what were the best looks in each collection and it is worth a visit even though the prices are way beyond most pockets. What you can do however, is train your eye and develop your fashion sense using the expertise-of Mrs Burstein who has done the editing for you.

Harvey Nicks

Exactly the same thing is true of Harvey Nichols. This Knightsbridge store is the prestigious flagship of the Debenham's chain and its name is synonymous with the very best contemporary design in all fields. Clothes conscious women always keep an eye on what is going on at Harvey Nicks, as they affectionately call it. They are wise to do so.

Top international names

Like Browns, it is first in the field with the best lines from the top names from all over the world. The buyers, Claire Stubbs (sister of the actress Una) and Paul Davies, have two of the best fashion noses in the business and their highly developed fashion intelligence rarely lets them down. Paul Davies, who buys for the International Room, spends a considerable part of his year abroad, searching for the very best clothes in Europe, America or Japan. These buyers are responsible for enormous annual budgets and they use their skill, taste and formidable fashion knowledge to put together looks which have made their store one of the best fashion shops in the world. Time spent browsing in Harvey Nichols fashion departments is never time wasted.

Harrods

The whole world seems to be in love with Harrods, but behind all the hype, what is there for you? The answer is an exceptionally wide range of styles at prices from the reasonable to the scary. Harrods is so big and powerful that its team of buyers can sample and buy clothes from all over the world. They give customers a uniquely broad choice from the one-off work of the world's greatest designers to mass-produced lines chosen for competitive pricing.

Jaeger and Alexon

Shops like Browns, Harrods and Harvey Nichols lead the field but they are closely followed by groups like Jaeger and Country Casuals who have their own shops either within a store or on the High Street. They both stock only their own-label clothes and they specialise in up-market, elegant design. Country Casuals and Jaeger clothes are right not only for the more dressy country occasions but also work extremely well for city life. Both have a considerable following of loyal customers who always go there first because they have learned over the years that the clothes are well made and, although not cheap, normally represent good value as investment buys.

War in the High Street

The opposing armies are the chains like Marks and Spencer, British Home Stores, Hepworth's, Next and Burton's Principles. The fight is of vital importance to British fashion because these are the shops in which the majority of women spend their money. The influence of these big companies on taste and

Wrapped and layered effects, first introduced by the Japanese, still hold their own in fashion circles but they now follow the body lines more closely. They need a skilful eye for pattern, scale and colour if they are not to make you look like a walking jumble sale.

The "Out of Africa" safari look is very much with us at the moment but wide safari shorts of the kind worn in North Africa during World War II are perennial summer favourites. They are cool and relaxed and look equally good with light or dark T-shirts in cotton or silk. For the total look, add a safari jacket.

> "A really elegant woman never wears black in the morning."
> *French Fashion advice*

style is enormous. Just look in your own wardrobe and see how many of their labels you have. You will not be exceptional if you find that they predominate.

Marks and Spencer

There is probably no woman in Great Britain (including Royalty) who does not have some items bearing the Marks and Spencer St Michael label. The traditional M&S (and B.H.S.) fashion image has been considerably smartened up since the Next, Richards and Principles ranges began to make their impact on the High Street.

Next, Richards and Principles

All three are aiming for the same market, the young to middle-aged woman who is fashion conscious but not fashion crazy. Their customer is looking for sensible wearable clothes which are fashionable in cut and colour but which avoid all extremes. In a sense, Next and Principles are heading a High Street revolution by producing well-designed, well-cut and well-made clothes at a competitive price, without sacrificing fashion content. Their designers are highly trained fashion graduates who go to all the shows in Europe (and some in America) and comb the world for the best looks to translate into good quality clothes for Everywoman. The same is true of Richards.

These shops are a permanent addition to our High Streets.They are chains backed by a great deal of marketing knowledge and design experience. Conran's outlet, the Richards shops, are at present being given a nationwide facelift, and will certainly have a big effect on future High Street fashion.

Survival in the jungle

How can you ensure that, out of the enormous range of styles and colours available in every High Street today, you buy the right thing? Well, firstly you must keep your head, and decide how many clothes you really need.

The French approach

It is instructive to compare British and French approaches to shopping. The average English woman would be shocked if she could see how few garments a Frenchwoman's wardrobe contained. She might also be surprised to notice the difference in quality compared with British standards. A Frenchwoman is prepared to pay over the odds to have clothes which suit the life she leads and are adaptable for various functions. She wears her clothes over and over again and, far from searching for something novel for each occasion, is delighted when friends say "Oh, I am so glad you wore your blue again — you look so good in it."

Frenchwomen are tough and canny shoppers and they are prepared to spend time looking for the right article. Quality is their goal, not quantity. Having found it they expect their clothes to last a long time — and yet continue to keep their looks. Frenchwomen also know that good accessories are the open sesame of elegance. They know the importance of buying them all together so that they match or complement each other perfectly, and they look carefully at the details. Poor workmanship in never tolerated. Every Frenchwoman knows that, having chosen a pleasing shape and colour for, say a handbag, you do not buy it unless it has a well-made clasp. A Frenchwoman knows that top-quality, well-made goods last a long time and outlive three or four cheaper versions. If her clothing and accessory choices are classic they will remain in style for as long as ten years.

Shopping — high stress?

Do you enjoy shopping or is it a painful necessity? Psychologically, shopping for clothes can often be a high stress situation. Even the most successful and assured shopper is occasionally nervous. The cause of nervousness for most shoppers is three-fold. By far the biggest concern for most of us is the cost of clothes, they are expensive and become more so every season. The dread of making a mistaken, and therefore costly, decision inhibits us.

Spoilt for choice

Again, in many fashion departments the choice is so wide that uncertainty and confusion are caused by too many alternatives. In a short while the shopper can be so overwhelmed that she does not know what she wants.

Predatory shop assistants

Often she is not helped by the shop assistants who can be intimidatingly grand and insolently indifferent to the customer's plight. They also do not help rapidly evaporating confidence when you notice that they have the perfect figure, immaculate

Paris designers are interested in the return of the long skirt with gores or floating panels. They use it on formal, figure-hugging evening wear but it can create a very easy-to-wear and relaxed day look as well. An outfit like this could be in silk for evening or cotton or corduroy for day. Remember that off-beat colour can be very slimming and make you appear highly sophisticated.

In our climate dressing for the worst whilst hoping for the best is not new. So there is no real excuse for sombre rainwear. Why not soft red or pale lilac to combat a dull and dreary day?

make-up and not a hair out of place — you, on the other hand, are wet and bedraggled having flogged up and down rainswept streets. They are cool, calm and collected, perfectly relaxed in cool fine wool dresses impeccably chosen for comfort in the shop — you are sweating profusely in the sauna-bath temperature of the shop because you are wearing your winter coat. No wonder self image sinks to an all-time low.

Out of your league
It is not helped by all the clothes which you like seeming to be exclusively in small, model-girl sizes — suddenly you feel as big as an elephant. Again, the elegantly accessorised displays seem to be peddling an ordered and sophisticated lifetstyle light years away from yours.

Fight back
Do not be overwhelmed. Dress shops, especially the chic little boutiques, are fantasy places which are not meant to be taken as real life. They present the ideal but they don't only *sell* to the ideal. You and your money are the vital reality without which the whole tinselly fantasy collapses. You need a strategy to enable you to keep up your confidence and fight back all the feelings of unease and lack of confidence.

Don't become a shopping victim

Many shopping advisers suggest that the answer to uncertainty in the shop is to weigh up all the pros and cons and only then make your decision. I do not agree.

Be prepared
The real secret of successful shopping is to do your homework first. Look very carefully at your wardrobe, realise where the gap is, and decide on the sort of garment you want. Then go to the shops feeling carefree and confident of success.

Banish the dithers
If you instantly fall for something, do not have second thoughts. Buy it. The more you dither the less likely you are to make a wise choice. My belief is that clothes bought in response to instant enthusiasm are always good buys — provided you have made yourself an informed shopper before you enter the shop. You must know yourself, warts and all, and you must understand fashion. With a trained mind you can't go wrong.

What type of shopper are you?

Having said all of this, it must be admitted that our personalities are going to give us certain biases towards different types of shopping. There is nothing wrong with bias towards any of the following types provided you are aware of it and can, if you consider it necessary, guard against it to some degree.

In my experience there are two kind of shoppers — those who hate it and view time spent in a shop as a necessary penance, although not time wasted, and those who love it and are always ready for a browse around.

Shopping haters

The haters never browse. They go shopping when there is a necessity and, having filled the hole in their wardrobe, leave as soon as possible. Paradoxically, the haters are often the better shoppers. It is surprising how many women I know who have a really sound fashion sense and are always well-dressed and yet hate shopping for clothes. Another paradox is that they are often the ones who really understand fashion. They buy fashion magazines, study them and seem to have a tuned-in fashion intelligence which is uncluttered by looking at too many clothes in a shop.

Shopping lovers

However, those who love shopping and spend hours in clothes shops can build up an enormous store of fashion wisdom simply by looking at many different garments, noticing their scale, colour and detailing, and checking on how well they are made. As informed and experience shoppers, they can avoid expensive mistakes, can sort out the good quality items from the dross and are frequently able to buy a look at a fraction of the price the uneducated shopper might pay.

Shopping browsers

But the browser's path is not without dangers. If a compulsive shopper (or, more accurately, frequenter of shops) does not have a clear head and a strong fashion sense, she can soon become overwhelmed by the sheer breadth of choice. She can see so many alternatives that she cannot select the one for her. She then begins to make confused and mistaken choices. If a browser is to survive long periods of exposure to rack upon rack of clothes, then she must do her homework. I am sure that you have all had the crushing experience in large department stores of being surrounded by rails of clothing stretching as far as the eye can see. It can be paralysing. Too much choice is worse than no choice at all unless your fashion intelligence has been trained to filter what you see.

Be ruthless

You have to bear in mind what you are specifically looking for and ruthlessly disregard the rest. You also need to keep in mind your absolute upper price limit and stick to it. A friend of mine always keeps herself in check by saying, ''What would Mr James say?'' Mr James is her not always friendly local bank manager! Keep a tight hold of yourself when shopping, especially if you have had a glass or two at lunch, because the difference in mood when buying and when wearing can be so great that the garment will spend most of its life hanging in the wardrobe. Remember, you don't *have* to leave a shop with a purchase, you don't *have* to end the day buying something, no social event is so important that you really must have something new to wear. Far better revert to an old favourite wisely bought on another occasion than to buy a garment that will 'just do'.

Take time

An important rule of all clothes shopping, whether you enjoy the process or can't get it over quickly enough, is give yourself time to think. Serious shopping which is to end in purchasing today as opposed to browsing for possible buying in the future needs time and concentration so that price, style, colour, fit and eventual use can all be adequately assessed.

Active try-ons

Never buy anything without trying it on (except in shops like Marks and Spencer where there are no changing rooms) must seem like a very obvious piece of advice. But remember that there is active and passive trying on. Again the secret is to take time. I remember when I used to design clothes for the wife of the American ambassador in Rome, fittings always took a very long time. The reason was that she was an expert shopper and was, quite rightly, determined to make sure everything was right. Your approach to trying on should be just as rigorous. Do not be inhibited by the sales girls. Do you care if they consider you eccentric?

Movement and a critical eye

You must walk around, sit down, lift up your arms and move your head around when trying on. If the garment feels right through all of this, repeat it, just to be sure. Notice particularly how the hem behaves. If it hangs unevenly, dipping at the back or sides, the garment has not been properly made. Then look at your face, neck, arms, wrists, waist and legs, quite separately, and decide how they look. If you have come out shopping in flat heeled shoes and intend to wear high heels with the garment, make sure the proportions are correct when you stand on your toes. In this way you are submerging the preconceived image of how the garment should look according to magazine photographs. You are instead receiving the image of how the garment actually looks on you. You will probably learn some interesting things. For example, those collarless necklines which make the model girls look so young and vulnerable, can make a thick neck look like a tree trunk, can exaggerate a dowager's hump and are often unflattering and too exposing for women with more normal figures.

Ridding yourself of the received image to make way for the real image takes time and practice. However, it is the best way to shop if you want your purchases to give you lasting satisfaction and value.

Check labels

It is often instructive to check where the garment is made. Italian or French sounding names are no guarantee that the garment was actually made in that country. Furthermore, they are not even a guarantee that they were designed there. Many French sounding names appear on garments made in Hong Kong or Taiwan. Again, unless the label says 'Made in Italy', the very Italian-sounding name might well be the trade mark of a German firm using German designers. There is obviously nothing wrong with garments like these. No one is guilty of sharp practice and if it is an item that completely fulfils your needs, there is no reason for not buying. But knowing what it is you are buying is an important part of good shopping.

Designer labels

I am always being asked whether or not designer labels are worth the money. It is not a question that can be anwered simply. A designer becomes known through ability or by hype. Frequently, fame is a result of both. No matter how good he or

I am often asked by older women whether I think black, greys and browns are too sombre for grey hair. I cannot see why, but if they do not seem to work so well for you, remember that colour highlights are very important as you get older. Make-up to counteract the fact that your natural face and hair colour are fading. Use a contrast colour, quite a bold one, to brighten an outfit. Try to wear lighter shades near your face. In this way brown, black or any other so-called sombre colour will not make you look like some drab little Jenny Wren.

she is the name can only become a household word through a great deal of highly expensive publicity. The garments bearing his name have to pay for this publicity — which means that the purchasers of the garments bearing the name are paying for it. This is not necessarily a bad thing and, in fact, it is an inevitable part of the economics of the market place.

What's in a name?

The question for you as the buyer is, does the name mean that the garment is automatically superior to similar garments without it? And does it justify its higher price? What are you likely to get from a designer label that you won't find in cheaper labels?

Put simply, you could be getting a more generous cut, a finer quality fabric and a more subtle colour. You should be getting a very well finished, high fashion garment with a degree of exclusivity to it. A store might buy one hundred dozen identical shirts in a cheap range, but only a dozen with an expensive designer label. Designers guard their names quite jealously and they know that to be associated with sub-standard merchandise is the surest way to finish them off. A designer label is certainly a guarantee of quality but not necessarily a proof of value for money. Designer clothes are expensive and only you can determine whether or not they are worth the extra money for your way of life. But the old cliche that you are only paying for a name is rarely true in my opinion. You are paying for a name that guarantees a certain standard. Obviously a dress from Jasper Conran is going to be a lot more expensive than one labelled with a made-up name like Madame Francoise and considerably more than a rag trade, mass production number labelled Francine Exclusive. But it will look different, feel different *and* make you feel different. Well cut, good quality clothes give confidence, there is no doubt about it.

Designer patterns

When the ambitious home dressmaker proudly carries home her Paris original pattern and starts cutting out her material, she is hoping that she will get the look for which richer women have to spend a fortune. But will she?

The answer is yes and no. She will get the shape and cut of the designer's original, provided she is a good home dressmaker, but unless she is an expertly trained professional, she will be unlikely to capture the essence of the original. There is very much more to top dressmaking than merely

Top designer clothes are often too close to fantasy to have any obvious relevance to the average woman's daily life. But before you dismiss them see if there is anything in their thinking which can help you. Here, for example, an extreme look has a practical point — the flounces flatter by covering awkward areas and softening an otherwise very demanding silhouette.

cutting out and sewing. Real expertise is required to make a dress fit perfectly. It has to do with the way the seams lie, the collar sits and the sleeves are set in. They in their turn are not merely influenced by the quality of the dressmaking, they are affected by the quality of the fabric. A silk at over twenty pounds a metre is going to be very much better behaved than a sartorial upstart costing just a couple of pounds a metre. So, although through patterns you can have access to good design at a fraction of the cost of the original, do not imagine that the finished product will be as good as the original. It won't, no matter how skilled a home dressmaker you are.

Designer knitting patterns

The spin-off from designer's dressmaking patterns has been with us for some time but it is only recently that designer knitting patterns have appeared. They are the result of the upgrading of knitting when it came out of the poor relations' closet in the seventies with the amazing knits of Kenzo, Kaffe Fassett and Bill Gibb, and Edina and Lena.

New books of designer knitting patterns proliferate. What do you get for your money? If you have a knitting machine or are a really expert hand knitter the answer is very much the same article for which you could pay a small fortune if you bought it ready-knit from the desinger's boutique. After all, most designer knitwear is made by women outworkers in their homes and they are not necessarily better at it than you. Certainly, your finished knitted garment stands a much better chance of looking professional than your dress made from a designer's pattern.

The retailer's view

Whether you are shopping exclusively or in High Street chains, whether you know precisely what you want or are keeping an open mind, you will only be human if you slip into one or two of the shopping categories known to everyone involved in the retail fashion trade. In fact, many experienced saleswomen assure me that they can tell what type of shopper a woman is by the way she walks into the shop! One who has worked at all levels of retailing contends that there are six basic shopping categories which spell danger. If you recognise yourself in some of them, don't worry. You cannot change your personality when you are shopping but you can guard against the worse excesses it might lead you into. Knowing which

Glossy magazines and fashion shows always present clothes in a very idealised form. For example, they regularly show them with impressive hats and imposing gloves although they know that nine out of ten women rarely wear either these days. You must train your eye to get behind the hype and strip off those things which are irrelevant to you so that you can study the dress below.

category you incline towards may help you to shop much more soundly.

The ditherer

This is the commonest type of shopper. How many times have you seen a woman in a shop unable to make up her mind and longing for someone to make the decision for her? If this is you, the cause of the problem is usually not that you do not know what you want but that you need someone to tell you that you have made the right decision. You have a low level of self-esteem and you value anyone's opinion more than your own. You enrol the advice of an indifferent friend, a bored husband, or an uninterested shop assistant rather than make your own decision. Then you worry all night about whether you have made the right purchase and return it to the shop the next day.

Experienced shop girls swear that they know, even as they are packing the purchase, that there is at least a fifty-fifty chance that this will happen with the ditherer. The best way to break out of this situation is to force yourself to make a quick decision, entirely by yourself, and wear the garment over and over again. No one should require anyone else to make a decision for her.

The label freak

We have all met her. "That's a lovely jacket," is answered by, "Yes, it's a Jean Muir." or whatever the prestigious label says. There was a fad, mercifully diminished now, for wearing the label outside the garment. What greater proof of lack of self-worth could there be? Because this is what gaining confidence from a label is about. You do not think that you are sufficiently important to stand up by yourself. You are not able to trust your own taste so you dodge criticism by naming names. "After all," you reason, "it must be good if it is Yves Saint Laurent — who would dare to criticise my taste when it would mean criticising him?"

Hiding behind a designer's status is an expensive and thoroughly unsatisfactory approach to buying clothes. Boost your ego by learning how to spot quality regardless of the label, and if you are wearing a famous name, keep quiet and let it speak for itself.

The inverted snob

Here is the other side of a frail ego. This is the woman who thinks a bit about herself but is afraid that others will not. You live in a miasma of embarrassment and imagined slights. You are terrified of walking into smart shops because you find the elegant saleswomen intimidating and feel uncomfortable and inferior in such exclusive surroundings. So you gravitate towards chaper chain stores or mass-market department stores and end up buying clothes you don't really want simply because you are less menaced by the surroundings.

Force yourself to cross the impressive portals of the posh shops and you will find that they are not nearly as intimidating as they seem. Near where I live in London is a boutique bearing a very grand name. Whenever I passed by, it was empty apart from two rather haughty looking shop girls. I found it totally inhibiting until I had to collect some clothes to sketch for a newspaper and I discovered that they weren't haughty at all. They were desperately bored and unhappy and longing for someone to come in.

When you are faced with a situation of awe-inspiring grandeur remember that they need you much more than you need them. Walk in with confidence and they will be only too anxious to help.

The grabber

If you go into a shop and need the gratification of instantly buying something, you are what is known in the trade as the grabber. You love shopping and you have a compulsion to buy, regardless of whether you need or really want the garment.

What you are doing is overcoming feelings of inadequacy or powerlessness. Retailers love you. They carefully arrange and place displays entirely for your benefit. Just look in your wardrobe and see how many things you have which have been worn only two or three times and you will know the dangers of your attitude.

You can train yourself out of this approach only by rigorously deciding what you need to buy and buying just that one item. If a shop does not have it, do not buy something else in compensation — walk out empty handed.

The herder

Here is one of the most boring an economically unsound shoppers of all. You are the one who has to follow the herd, play safe and dress like everyone else. Your refusal to take risks means that you are spending money merely to look and feel safe — what a waste! It also means that you are always one step behind fashion. By the time the chain stores are full of

A good look to try — mix pale and bright tones of the same colour.

a look and you feel it is safe to buy, fashion has moved on.

Why do you do it? You are afraid of standing out, looking a fool or being different because you cannot bear the thought of rejection. Learn to please yourself. If you see something in a magazine or shop window that takes your fancy, buy it. Do not wait until everyone on the High Street is wearing it.

The bargain hunter

This is the final type in this broad categorisation of shoppers. I think we all fall into this category to a greater or lesser extent because we all want a bargain, but are not always sure what a bargain actually is.

A true bargain is surely something that gives value for money either by transforming your wardrobe or by lasting forever, regardless of its cost. Most of us associate bargain hunting with sales, but this is obviously only half of the picture. The most expensive item in your wardrobe might well be your greatest bargain, but before examining the true nature of bargains, let us think about sales.

The sales season

The purpose of an end of season sale is to make space for the new season's fashions. The purpose of a mid-season sale is to move clothes which have not sold as well as expected and will possibly have to be reduced to cost if they are still in the shop at the end of the season. Sale merchandise is often the result of unwise wholesale buying because of an over-optimistic commitment to a look which did not catch on. It may be the result of a buyer playing her hunch before its time and ending up with a stock of clothes that do not fit the received image.

Sale merchandise may also indicate an unexpected change in the country's economy. Few people realise that a slight rise in the mortgage rate, or an increase in the price of petrol can seriously affect buying patterns in the volatile world of fashion. Any of these things can mean that a shop has to sell off its merchandise for less profit than had been originally planned.

What's in it for you?

These are some of the reasons why goods are offered at reduced prices, but how can you turn a buyer's indiscretion to your advantage? Provided you keep you head there could be a great deal in it for you. A girl I know bought a beautiful tartan jacket at a Kenzo sale for a sixth of its original cost and it was definitely a very wise purchase; it automatically gives her a high-quality look.

You probably wonder why a famous designer like Kenzo needs to sell off his clothes and the answer lies in the fact that he is a famous designer. Everything he designs is in the forefront of fashion and every season the look must be new. Last season's clothes have to be sold off cheaply. The point is that something old-fashioned at the very top end of the fashion scene still has a very real life at High Street level. High fashion is at least a season ahead, so if you buy at a designer's sale you will be getting clothes that will remain fashionable for longer because they are clothes from the vanguard of fashion.

Designer label sales

Fashion journalists are well aware of the benefits of designer's sales. They frequently make a mental note of a garment in the designer's show at the beginning of the season and pick it up at cost price at the end of the season. They know that a perfectly proportioned, exquisitely cut overcoat in top quality cashmere which retails at almost one thousand pounds is a real bargain when offered for three hundred and fifty pounds six months later.

This is the basic formula for good bargain buying, save up so that you can pay the maximum price knowing that something which costs you hundreds of pounds in the sale very probably cost thousands a few months earlier. These sort of figures may horrify you. You may feel that any three-figure number is far too much for one garment, but if it is still stylish in ten years time, imagine the saving you will have made.

However, remember that the more uncompromisingly high fashion a garment is, the more likely it is to be reduced. If you can carry off difficult colours and demanding cuts, you can often get a spectacular bargain at the top end of the market. But be cautious. A look so extreme that it shrieks ''this season'' can often look dated in fashion circles by the end of the season or merely bizarre and eccentric in a less fashionable way of life.

High street sales

The same principles apply on a more everyday level. Department store and High Street sales should be approached with caution. Do not be tempted to buy the fashion colour of this season in a sale because if you do, you will get only a short period of wear from it before it seems very dowdy and

Colour must be controlled. A witty flash can easily degenerate into a vulgar splash. Crude colour is not the same as strong colour and knowing the difference is probably the hardest skill to acquire if you are not blessed with a natural colour sense. Do not be disheartened. One look at the colour used in cheaper lines of merchandise will convince you that so-called design experts also have difficulty in telling the difference between a witty choice of colour and a cheap and nasty one.

out of style. The clothes are on sale because shape trends are changing and the shop knows that they won't look right next season. Obviously, the safest things to buy in a sale are the neutral, classic looks. A grey skirt, a beige sweater, a navy blazer, these are not likely to be so highly styled that they will go out of fashion. They are good buys if you need them.

Seconds

If goods are offered as seconds or slightly flawed make sure that the shop girl tells you exactly what the nature of the flaw is. Look very carefully at the item. Work out if you will be able to correct the fault, disguise it or live with it. For example, an uneven hem could be remedied, but an imperfection in the leather of a shoe might soon develop into a split. The shoe would be useless and you would have no redress with the manufacturer. No matter how cheap, this could not be considered a bargain.

Investment dressing

Except for designers' sales fashionable women rarely go to the sales. Nevertheless, their wardrobes are full of bargains. For them a bargain is something which, largely independent of its price, has proved to be a valuable addition to their wardrobe. By definition a bargain is something which is chosen by a wise and informed fashion intelligence. A dress bought for twenty pounds in a sale and worn two or three times is not a bargain whereas a jacket costing five times as much but worn over and over again is a bargain even if it was not bought in the sales.

Real bargains are not restricted to money and often the best bargains have nothing to do with passing fashion. For example, a well-cut sheepskin jacket could last for twenty years, a good leather bag could last for just as long. At one end of the scale you could have a strong pair of purposeful wellingtons which last a lifetime, and at the other a piece of understated jewelery which gives you just as good mileage. In fact, if you want lasting value from your clothes and accessories it is important to avoid anything too fashionable. This approach is known as investment dressing.

Middle-of-the-road

Investment clothes are cut on traditional, classic lines in natural materials and neutral or understated colours. They are a background canvas, the mood of which can be changed and updated by the addition of the latest colours and shapes in accessories. It is what a young journalist friend described as the trenchcoat versus the fluorescent sock syndrome.

The way to success in investment dressing it to build up your wardrobe of top-quality, longlife items by making one major purchase a year. Whatever you buy as an investment must be middle-of-the-road fashion with absolutely no fashion details which can date it to a particular year. These items are your trenchcoat buys for which you pay high prices, knowing that they will last. Of course, you do not have to turn your back on the fluorescent sock. You can buy as many cheaper, up-to-the-minute fashion fad looks as you can afford to brighten your investments. But even so, remember the austere old adage, "I cannot afford to buy cheaply!" It is true if you have not taught yourself to buy wisely.

What is in this year?

I am always being asked this question and it shows a very old-fashioned concept of fashion. There are no styles that dominate fashion as they did in the days of couture but there are trends. Each season there is sufficient of a consensus amongst designers to create a look. We have recently had large cabbage rose silks for summer jackets, the equestrian look for winter, the bustle effect for evening and the widespread use of a particular colour such as fuschia last autumn but none was so sweeping as to make other ideas unfashionable as the "in" looks of the past did. And what a good thing!

Buyer beware

Public relations girls are often very clever. In the fashion world they play a vital role in bridging the gap between the trade and the press but, it must be said, they can occasionally be guilty of "hype" — and so can the press if they don't remember to listen critically.

In the exotic, hysterical world of fashion, "good" can quickly become "marvellous", and soon end up "divine". That is hype — people forget the true value and worth of a designer or garment.

Does it matter?

As far as the public is concerned, yes it does because if a label is hyped it soon becomes very expensive and the credibility gap between value and cost yawns very wide. This is when we

Despite what was said on page 118 there is no doubt that when a designer gives us the "works", complete with magnificently impractical hat, few can remain unmoved by the glamour. Underneath it all we have a very wearable and practical garment.

get the designer T-shirt costing a couple of hundred pounds — total madness!

Good cutting

Time and again I have referred to good clothes benefiting from a more generous cut, and I want to explain exactly what I mean by this.

All garments on the shop rail have started life as a sample. This is a garment made up from the original design specification and from it the production garments, often many thousands, are developed. The sample is carefully costed, taking into consideration the number of processes involved in the making, the man hours required to produce it and the amount of material used.

Nibbling down

If the garment is being made down to a price one of the easiest and most effective ways of bringing it within budget is to use less fabric. The shoulders, sleeves and bodice can all be narrowed by a fraction, the waist and skirt can be reduced a minute amount if necessary. The hem and the overlaps at the seam might also be slightly reduced. If the garment is being made to fit a size ten for example, the reduced version will still be a size ten but it will be a very close-fitting ten. This process of nibbling obviously takes place at the cheaper end of the market where costs must be kept down. As the price goes up, so does the allowance of fabric. An expensive garment will always be more generously cut with ample hems and seams.

Quick quality check

The best way to look at the quality of a garment is to turn it inside out. This may produce some quizzical looks from the shop girls, but be bold, particularly if this is going to be one of your investment buys.

You are looking for that more generous cut, but take a look at the way the seams have been finished. If they have been pinked (clipped in tiny zig-zags to prevent fraying threads) the garment will not have as long a life as one with seams that have been oversewn. Check that pocket edges have been finished correctly, and that there are no loose threads. If there is a zip, check that it runs smoothly up and down and that it has not been inserted so close to the edge that material catches in the teeth during use. It must lie flat and not pucker

The long, long coat, fitted, belted or straight, must be big and full. This is a perfect example of the scale to look for when buying your winter coat this season.

or buckle the smooth line of the seam. Have a look at the lining. Really top quality coats do not have the lining hanging free at the hem, it is properly inserted and joined at the base.

Pattern principals

Finally check the pattern. There is nothing more irritating than a bold pattern of plaid or stripes which does not match. Stripes across the body should match the stripes of the sleeves, the yoke at the back should not interrupt the run of the pattern, and if there is a patch pocket, for example, on the outside of a shirt, the pattern should match here too. Cheaper shirts get around this problem by cutting the yolk and patch pockets on the cross of the material so that the misalignment of the pattern looks like an intentional piece of design.

The fight for quality

It is obviously possible to get good or bad value at every price level but the cheaper the garment the more vigilant you have to be. In the days of exclusive couture you paid a price and bought perfection. Now you can pay the price and still not get perfectly made goods. For example, even the top designers have virtually abandoned any attempt to match and correspond stripes or checks at seams. Again, as a colleague of mine recently pointed out, you can pay a three-figure price for a designer-label silk T-shirt and still find puckered seams and loose hanging threads.

Ready-to-wear quality

I maintain that the best value for money is found at the top end of the big ready-to-wear manufacturer's ranges, where machine-work is precise and quality control has some meaning. With cheaper clothes you can still find well-made clothes but you should be aware of manufacturer's short cuts which keep the prices down by compromising the quality. For example, a skirt requires less material if it is not cut on the cross, but it can never be made to hang as well as one that is. Again a manufacturer working in thousands of garments can save a lot of material if he cuts back fractionally on the depth of the hem but the skirt will not hang as well as one with a generous hem.

Face facts

These are the rag trade facts of life and there is no point in running away from them. Cheap clothes are cheap because they use economic methods and they scrimp on quality and quantity. Nevertheless, by doing so, they bring stylish and up-to-the-minute clothes within the reach of all. I find the attitudes of these manufacturers perfectly acceptable except that there are still far too many sweatshops in the rag trade where women (usually foreign) work long, hard hours for low wages.

Unacceptable manufacturing

Unfortunately there is an increasing tendency for other clothes to be made by virtually the same methods but, with a designer label inside, sold for vastly inflated prices. These are the ones to be on your guard against.

You do not automatically get what you pay for any more — and I can prove it. I once worked for a manufacturer in Italy whose clothes sold at the top ready-to-wear price point. One batch of expensive jackets which had been made up by out-workers was sent out with two right arms and no one noticed until some (but not all) of the customers who had paid such high prices for them sent them back!

The mark up

Remember that this is enormous on some clothes. The price you pay for a designer label can mean a mark up of as much as four hundred percent. The story is clear at sales time. This is when clothes are offered at the lowest profit margin to enable the shop to clear them out but they are not giving them away — a profit is still being made. Recently in the West End I saw a three-quarter length coat on sale for £680. It had originally been offered at a full price of £1,240. This in itself is a disgraceful price for a coat, but bearing in mind that the reduced cost still provided the shop with a profit, it is obvious that anyone who bought the coat at the original price was giving the shop an obscenely large profit. The same story, with less dramamtic figures, is told every day in every shop in the land.

Fabric quality tests

Here are some simple tests that you can try on the fabric of a garment before you buy.

The pill test

Rub the fabric roughly between your fingers. A good quality fabric should leave no sign of rubbing at all.

Who says stripes and checks don't work together? Like everything else in fashion, you can happily break the rules if you know what you are doing. This combination would look stunning in navy and cream or, for a less dramatic effect, go for beige and brown.

The crease test

Scrunch the fabric tightly up in your hand for a few seconds. A practical fabric should recover quickly when you release it.

The static test

Rub the fabric between your fingers for several seconds. If the fabric sticks to your fingers the synthetic percentage is too high and the garment will cling to your body.

The slippage test

Pull a seam sharply from either side. If the fabric is poor, the threads will gape and stretch.

Recipe for success

Let's run through the essence of successful shopping. Plan ahead and shop alone. Wait until a willing friend will take the children on for a morning — nothing is more frustrating than trying on clothes knowing that a toddler is making his way relentlessly towards the immaculate window display. Differentiate between wanting and needing, but follow your hunch and never hesitate. Try on in a professional way and try to relate colour to the clothes you already have in your wardrobe. Give yourself plenty of time and above all, if you are in doubt, walk out.

Successful dressers learn how to choose a basic garment which they can wear with different items in their wardrobe to create a different look. The flexible wardrobe which we show here and overleaf consists of a large scale cotton jacket; a large cotton man's shirt; a pair of black cotton peddle pushers and a black cotton T-shirt. By putting them with different items and wearing them in different ways you can exploit their full potential. Look in your wardrobe and see how many items in there are always worn in the same way. Then experiment to see how you could change things.

Informal clothes for stepping out and enjoying yourself have never been so colourful and so accessible. A cheap solution to the problem of what you can afford to buy can be found in interchangeable pants, sweat-shirts, blousons, jackets and scarves. Half a dozen carefully toning pieces can give you a very wide choice of different looks.

chapter 5

Sheer luxury

Have you ever wondered how you would dress if you were a very rich woman? Where would you shop, which designers would you choose and which garments would you select? We could play a little fantasy and imagine that you were one of the couple of thousand of women in the world for whom cost is so immaterial that shopping is a not a matter of shops, but of fashion capitals. We could browse around the most exclusive temples of fashion in Europe and America.

The fashion capitals with clout are Paris, Milan and New York. They are closely followed by Rome, London and Los Angeles. They are important because they all have world class designers. They are the watering holes of the rich and contain the best hotels, the most exclusive shops and the top restaurants — in short, the places where the rich and privileged feel happy and relaxed and ready to spend their money. In Chapter 1, I tried to give you some idea of the hectic pressure that most fashion editors are under, but I also said that what makes the job worthwhile is the chance to visit wonderful places. I was thinking not so much about the exotic locations for fashion shoots but the sophisticated cities which I visit on a privileged basis as an insider knowing where to go and what to see.

The fashion cognoscenti

If you were super-rich you would automatically have an entree to this exclusive world. You would be aware, for example, that those in the know think less in terms of individual shops than in areas where the top shops cluster. The cognoscenti know that things are not static and once a street becomes familiar to everyone as a symbol of luxury, the style and chic have probably moved on.

The drape-and-tie skirt is fashion's newest idea. Based on a sarong, it can be either formal or casual enough for the beach, depending upon the fabric and what it is put with. These skirts are extremely flattering for most figures and, with a T-shirt and jacket, could see you through a wide variety of occasions.

If you are worried that your legs are not your strong point wear longer skirts and direct attention above your waist (left); however, if your legs are good nothing will show them off better than a well-shaped pair of pants (centre); if you feel that they are neither good nor bad then use colour and shape (even in accessories) to create an overall impression.

Which cost the least? Nine out of ten people would say the T-shirt and pants on the left, and would assume that the cocktail dress on the right would be the most expensive but it depends on the fabric and the label. The T-shirt and pants are in pure silk, they have a world-famous designer's name on their label; the tweed suit is from a top quality British ready-to-wear house and the cocktail dress is a polyester rag trade ''rip-off'' of a top designer's work. It costs half the price of the designer T-shirt and the suit costs just slightly less than the designer pants. Learning to assess quality is one of the most important steps towards becoming a wise shopper.

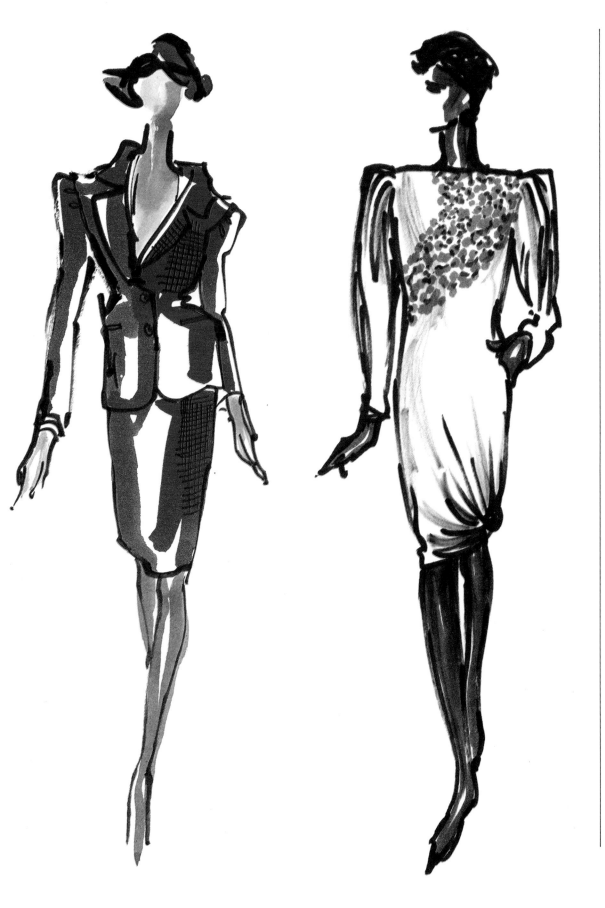

In London, Bond Street and The Burlington Arcade are good examples of this. There are very few top fashion folk other than the foreign tourists who are there to buy something from a well-known address. The stylish people are in South Molton Street, Sloane Street, Christopher Place or Knightsbridge where they can check the real pulse of London's retail fashion.

Milan

Here you would head immediately for Via Monte Napoleone and Via della Spiga. In this area are found the most sophisticated boutiques of this very fashion-conscious city — and the most sophisticated women in Europe. A female colleague once confessed that no matter how much effort she made over her appearance and no matter how elegant she felt when she started to walk down Monte Napoleone, by the time she was at the end of the street she felt a down-at-heel sloven.

Milanese women have this effect on other women. They are so perfectly turned out, so fashionably dressed and so absolutely of the moment, that they put everyone in the shade. Another colleague once wrote in shocked terms that whereas English women would faint away at the thought of buying a blouse for a price equivalent to a new dishwasher, Milanese women did it without hesitation. She was right, but rather missed the real point which is that the Milanese woman has the dishwasher as well!

These are some of the most privileged women in Europe and their position is a reflection of the unique economics of Italy which make it possible for most middle-class women to employ a maid to cook, wash and sew — something that vanished a long time ago for all but the very wealthiest in most other countries.

Rome

Shopping here is as easy as it is in Milan. There is one street, Via Condotti, off which run side streets like Via Fratina, coming out of Piazza di Spagna and above it Via Gregoriana, where the fashion house of the legendary Valentino is found, and within this area you will find every major fashion house and jeweller in the world. So let us look more closely at what Paris, Milan, London and New York have to offer.

Paris fashion spots

I always feel that the Milanese are much more chic than the Parisiennes these days. In fact, in your search for fashion's privileged in Paris, you would probably find as you walked down the Rue de Rivoli, that most of the really elegant women you met would be American, South American or Japanese tourists who had just issued forth from the Crillon Hotel.

Paris is like London in that its fashion spots are spread across the city. The boutiques and couture establishments of the great designers are found near the Champs Elysee on streets like Avenue George V or Avenue Montaigne. Many of the great international jewellers are also established in this area. But there is another, equally chic area bounded by the Rue Saint-Honore and the Rue de Rivoli and including such famous stopping-off points for the super-sophisticated rich as Place Vendome and Place Victoire.

Manhattan Island

Surely this is the most magical sounding name of all. This crowded island contains amazing contrasts — the hopeless poverty of the Bowery and the exclusive grandeur of the Upper East Side, the sophistication of Park Avenue and the squalid vulgarity of Times Square.

For luxury shoppers there is only one area — the park end of Fifth, Madison and Lexicon Avenues and 57th Street. Here are found all the great department stores which are New York's especial glory, including Saks, Lord and Taylor, Bergdorf's, Henri Bendel and everyone's favourite, Bloomingdale's. They are all delightfully conservative and peddle a line of luxury garments which are the cream of the world. One of the newest wonders is Trump Tower, a riot of marble and fountains which contains many different boutiques. Chic New Yorkers tend to sniff at its nouveau vulgarity and leave it to the tourists.

We cannot move on from Manhattan without mentioning its other unique shopping experience — a visit to its hushed and cloistered jewellers like Tiffany and Van Cleef and Arpels where everything is understated except the prices.

New York

New York is not really fashion in the European sense — it is superb styling. No new ideas seem to originate in New York, but designers there use their skills to Americanise looks already seen in Paris and, especially, Milan. They create marvellously finished and wearable clothes and their prices are sky high. Because of the New York lifestyle many of the best clothes are for evening. It has to be said also that many

For a formal look a dress and short jacket can be "tied together" by using a scarf in the same, or similar, material to the dress. It always gives a sophisticated and thought-out effect.

American designers produce clothes which seem vulgar in their extravagance to European eyes.

Los Angeles

Higher prices are demanded and paid here in the top boutiques. The shopping areas for the seriously rich are Wiltshire Boulevard and Rodeo Drive. Exclusive lines from all the great designers of the world are found in such top boutiques as that owned by Lina Lee, who comes to Europe every season and spends about six weeks in Paris and Italy sifting through everything until she has found the best.

Ultra-rich in France

Paris is as powerful as ever as a centre of fashion. Wearing something designed in Paris is still, as it always was, the dream of the majority of women. The fact is, of course, that the dream is based on a very out-of-date idea of Paris — the Paris of the fifties and early sixties. In the days of Dior, Chanel and Balenciaga the glamour and elegance of haute couture reigned and major newspapers would scrap their front page headlines to feature the latest Paris fashion headlines. It is hard for us to imagine that the creations of dress designers were ever considered front page news, but they were. Major newspapers like *The Daily Mail* and *The Daily Express* gave the Paris shows top billing.

Those days are of course gone but the power of Paris is still very potent. Clothes from the great designers of Paris still influence mass market tastes and their ideas are copied and watered-down by ready-to-wear designers all over the world.

Yves Saint Laurent

In our rich woman fantasy, where would you shop in Paris? Yves Saint Laurent would be the first on most women's list and rightly so. For over twenty years this shy and super-sensitive man, of whom his business manager once said, "Yves was born with a nervous breakdown," has been leader of the pack. His development has been steady and largely consistent although many of his collections have in the past displeased press and buyers. He is now at the peak of his powers. He has a skilled and experienced workforce, many of whom came from the great houses of Dior, Balenciaga and Chanel. They have been with him so long that they understand his design intelligence and know precisely how to interpret his wishes.

They do so superbly.

You could buy almost anything here with confidence. In my opinion, no one cuts trousers like Yves Saint Laurent and to go with them what better than one of his perfectly cut little short-waisted jackets or precisely proportioned classic blazers?

His evening wear is spectacular and not for introverts. However, it is truly magnificent if you have the style to carry it off. Swathed silks and taffetas, shirred, ruffled and flounced, are used to the maximum of theatricality. They stop just this side of vulgarity. Y.S.L.'s judgement is precise and brilliant — he knows exactly when to say ''enough''. Alas, less skilled copyists who try to recreate his look cheaply lack the taste of the master and end up with fussiness and confusion.

Karl Lagerfeld

Close behind Yves Saint Laurent (many fashion journalists would say level with) is Karl Lagerfeld. This German designer has been a powerful force in Paris for several years. He designs several different collections. He used to create super-sophisticated ultraluxurious clothes for Chloe although now he concentrates on furs for the Rome firm of Fendi (who we will look at when we jet over to Italy on our shopping spree), and he designs for Chanel. He also creates his own-name line for his own house.

He is known for his refined but often outrageous designs. A few seasons ago his expensive evening dresses were embroidered with diamante taps, showers and sprays of water! Lagerfeld's skill as a dressmaker is supreme and the wise wealthy woman would choose a slinky evening dress or cocktail outfit from his own house and one, (or two) of his perfectly updated little suits which he does with consumate tact and skill for Chanel. If she were very bold and self-assured she could pick up some original and eye-catching costume jewelry and accesories from Lagerfield — but they are always so powerfully ''now'' that she would have to throw them out at the end of the season!

Wide, softly-rounded shoulders are the look of fashion at this moment on suits, coats and jackets but be careful not to get them too extreme — they won't flatter and they will date all too soon.

Sonia Rykiel

Sonia Rykiel's clothes are some of the most wearable and flattering in Paris. Wealthy clients and knowledgeable fashion journalists choose her beautifully relaxed cashmere or silk jersey separates in fondant or off-beat brights. They give to the wearer a totally understated elegance which is right for anywhere, any time and any age.

''When a woman starts to take an interest in the linings of her coats and jackets it means that she has already become very refined.'' *French Fashion adage*

Hubert de Givenchy

One of the long established Paris houses is that of Hubert de Givenchy. Here elegance reigns supreme. Startling originality, shocking colour and outlandish shapes are mercifully missing from a Givenchy collection. His couture line especially personifies the glamour and refinement of top quality dressmaking at its best. Givenchy has dressed Audrey Hepburn for over thirty years. His clothes inspire that sort of confidence and trust — most of his customers have been with him for a long time simply because he knows how to make them feel elegantly at ease.

Jean Louis Scherrer

Jean Louis Scherrer is another house with a faithful private clientele. He first caught the eye of Madame D'Estaing, the President's wife, in the sixties and his opulently luxurious clothes, although not in the forefront of fashion, have a great appeal for the super-wealthy international woman. He swathes her in fur, lame, the finest silks and embroidered, beaded cloth of gold. For most, the mix would be indigestably rich, but many very wealthy women find it just right.

Madame Gres

For over fifty years the evening dresses of Madame Gres have been collector's items — and they still are. She takes silk jersey and, working directly on the model, drapes it with such subtlety and precision that every creation is timeless. Wealthy women queue up for them.

The hospitable city

So, in Paris, the best way to spend real money is to visit the establishements of the great designers. They are not all French — Paris has always been a hospitable city which has opened its fashion doors to people of all nationalities provided they bring real talent. This, in turn, fully uses the skills of the French artisans who, as they always have, make the best imitation flowers, the most original buttons and the wittiest trims in the world.

Super-rich in Italy

Milan is the fashion capital that causes headaches for Paris. The Milanese have the ability to produce clothes that are utterly wearable and make most women look and feel a million dollars. Although they lack the originality and daring of the

French at their best, they produce more consistently good designers than Paris does. Virtually any Milanese designer is a good bet. Even when they are less than sure of themselves, they still have style, class and pace. They know how women want to look. Milanese clothes are well-cut, wearably proportioned and subtly coloured. The Italian colour sense is legendary. The praise it receives is richly deserved whether it is exuberant or sombre. Italians mix shades and tones with skill worthy of the great artists of the Renaissance.

The big six are Armani, Ferre, Krizia, Missoni, Soprani and Versace but remember that, even outside your wealthy woman fantasy, there are houses like Basile, Complice and Max Mara who, at the top end of the ready-to-wear, always show superb collections.

Giorgio Armani

Giorgio Armani is second only to Yves Saint Laurent in the world league of fashion designers. His sense of scale, balance and proportion is faultless. He creates the perfectly cut jacket. Its shoulders have just the right amount of fullness to balance his beautifully poised collar and harmonise with the jacket body which is cut to scale perfectly. Armani does these jackets every year in subtle tweeds or his favourite Prince of Wales check and wealthy fashion-conscious women buy at least one each season.

If you like shorts and culottes, then Armani is also your man. He is the genius of the Milan designers and richly deserves the title bestowed on him by the fashion press of King George.

Mariucca Mandelli at Krizia

Knitwear has been the strength of Italian design since the early fifties and for this the wealthy woman goes to Krizia or the Missonis.

The knits at Krizia are, like the rest of this lively fashion house's clothes, designed by the founder and owner Mariucca Mandelli. An ex-schoolteacher, she has been responsible for many looks which swept the world. She loves animals and uses them on her knitwear either as creatures draped across jumpers or as patterns based on their skins. The leopard and tiger prints and knits popular a few seasons ago originated with Krizia. Her strength lies in her strong colours, her taste which enables her to break the rules and get away with it, and her wit. She is one of the few designers with the confidence to design humorous clothes.

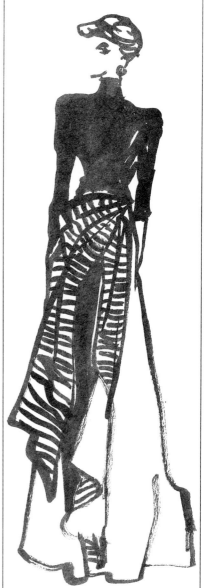

Do-it-yourself can produce some very strong effects, provided you have confidence — remember Scarlet O' Hara and the curtains! A plain black skirt and jumper can be lifted on to another plane by the careful choice of contrasting fabric, wrapped and tied to make an overskirt.

Evening glamour has a lot to do with surfaces. See-through lace and net can work marvellously with matt velvet or shiny satin for a very sophisticated evening look. They have maximum impact if the silhouette is kept clean and uncluttered.

The Missonis

The firm of Ottavio and Rosita Missoni shows the other side of Italian knitwear. Subtle, refined colours are joined in combinations which are, literally, breathtaking. In fine bands, stripes or blocks they shimmer like a Brigit Riley painting. Design shapes are kept deliberately simple because, with the Missonis, colour is all. They are probably the most original colourists in knitwear in the world so it is not surprising that their knitted jackets and jumpers were displayed at the Whitney Museum, New York as if they were abstract paintings. Few designers' work could survive this treatment but the Missoni knits did so — triumphantly.

Versace

In the autumn of 1985, Gianni Versace received a unique honour. He was invited to present his clothes at a special gala evening presided over by Prince Michael of Kent in the Victoria and Albert Museum, London. The fashion show, one of the glitziest evenings London has seen, was followed the next day by a fashion seminar, presided over by Versace. He recieved this special treatment in recognition of his supremacy as a designer of clothes for men and women. His leather wear, cut on the most generous scale, is found in the wardrobes of wealthy fashionables worldwide and his softly fluid metallic evening dresses are snapped up by costume museums as unique examples of the dressmaker's skill. If you have the money, follow their lead.

Ferre

Gianfranco Ferre is commonly considered the intellectual of Italian fashion. His clothes are constructed on the same mathematical principles as architecture or engineering. The result is that they have unique proportions, marvellous cut and totally logical details. For the women who can carry them off, his clothes have a style and presence which make her feel marvellous — but it must be said that many women find them too demanding. Certainly, Ferre creates clothes that are far too serious to be slipped on and forgotten about in the way that those of lesser designers might be.

No wealthy woman would shop in Italy and neglect to visit Rome. She would go there to buy from three designers.

Valentino

Valentino has developed his skills over the last ten years to such a degree that many fashion pundits consider that his couture is on the same level of sophisticated glamour as that of Yves Saint Laurent. Certainly he creates beautifully refined and luxurious day and evening wear which is deliciously feminine. A friend of mine who buys many of her clothes from Valentino told me, "He likes women — you can tell the moment you put anything on that he has designed. His clothes make me feel totally feminine and supremely confidant."

Expensive clothes go on. They might miss a season due to a change of length, but they come back in later seasons because the scale of good garments changes only slowly and well-designed clothes have a long life.

Fendi

The Fendi sisters have a vast fashion empire and create clothes and handbags for all occasions (every smart woman owns at least one Fendi bag) but their unique contribution to fashion is the furs which they create with the collaboration of Lagerfeld. They are unlike anything else on earth. The Fendis take mink, sable, (even rabbit) and mould it, perforate it, shave it and print on it to produce baroque creations which cost a king's ransom. No matter what one's view of the ethics involved in working with furs, one cannot help but admire the sheer skill and daring of Fendi furs.

Roberto Capucci

How many women have heard of Roberto Capucci? Outside fashion's inner circle, very few indeed I would imagine and this is not surprising. This totally original and dedicated designer creates clothes (especially evening wear) of such extreme and architectural subtlety that only the fashion connoisseur can understand them. Definitely not everyday wear and most certainly not frocks to put on and forget about, Capucci's evening designs are unlike anyone else's.

Although extreme and often impracticable, Capucci's design skills are copied and watered-down by some of the world's top designers, and so his fashion influence is wider than one would imagine. The wealthy woman who buys at Capucci is purchasing an heirloom of tomorrow — every garment is a collector's item.

Italian leather

Finally, no woman would leave Italy without investing heavily in what, for many, is the great glory of Italian fashion — leather. In addition to their outstanding colour sense, leatherwear is what keeps Italian design out in front for many women.

Butter soft, cream-liquid, the best Italian leather is unbeatable — and so is the Italian understanding of how to

There is a widely held belief that designer clothes are only likely to look right if you have a model-girl figure. This is not true. The simple rule is that the more expensive a garment, the better bred it is and its behaviour will be impeccable on any shape of body. It is a question of generosity of cut, quality of material and standard of finish. I have seen quite dumpy women try on clothes which I imagined could only look good on bean-thin six foot tall models, but they came out of the changing rooms transformed. They looked and felt radiant because the quality of the designer look has given them confidence.

work with it. They treat it as if it were the finest wool or richest silk. Their blousons are superb, so are their handbags (and you don't have to be so wealthy to buy an Enny bag which is head and shoulders above the rest for value and style) and their shoes.

Where would smart women be without the Italians?

Hyper-rich in Britain

Like New York, London is a marvellous city in which to buy clothes. Virtually every major designer in the world is represented in London's shops, boutiques and department stores. Continuing her fashion pilgrimage, which British designers would our wealthy woman invest in? London luxury design is dominated by two women.

Jean Muir

First and foremost, without question, would be a trip to Bruton Street to pick up a few of Jean Muir's classically proportioned and understated dresses in silk, wool or cashmere. Totally wearable and beautifully made, they are an investment. So are her soft suedes.

Jean Muir understands cut, proportion and colour as no one else does in London. Her clothes change very little over the seasons but they show her constantly developing and deepening design ideas. She is an evolutionary, not a revolutionary designer.

Zandra Rhodes

Zandra Rhodes creates fantasy evening dresses. Virtually any woman would like to possess at least one, if she could afford it, for those moments when she wants to feel like a delicate fairy-tale princess.

A Rhodes evening dress is a fluttering butterfly of the finest silk chiffon, delicately coloured and printed, and its hems are often embroidered or dotted with pearls. It is far removed from real-life fashion but it is absolutely beautiful — and thousands of women long for one.

Bruce Oldfield

Bruce Oldfield, favourite of the Princess of Wales and Joan Collins, creates very sophisticated, transatlantic clothes which look superbly polished and sexy on a good figure. His evening gowns are status symbols and well worth investing in, but he can also design you a beautiful day outfit using exclusive fabrics.

Jasper Conran

Another favourite of the Princess of Wales and, incidentally, one of the youngest designers in London, is Jasper Conran. His stature as a designer grows each season. There are no fireworks or show stoppers in his collections — instead he produces elegant and glamorous clothes which are utterly wearable. They are designed to flatter and do not look ridiculous on a woman over twenty-two as does so much of London's young fashion.

Joseph Ettedgui

I have already discussed the huge influence of fashion stores like Harvey Nichols and Browns but, in assessing London's contribution to the style of the rich, mention must be made of two seminal thinkers whose shops reflect their highly-tuned response to even a bat's squeak of anything new in fashion. Joseph Ettedgui has a nose for the new that is second to none. His shops in South Molton Street and Sloane Street are mecca for the filofacts folk who would rather die than not know the latest in fashions for clothes and home. Joseph does not merely cater for them — he leads them. They trot along to Joseph Tricot, Joseph bis and Joseph Pour La Maison to take in deep drafts of his original but totally laid-back approach to design.

Lucile Lewin

If Joseph has a nose for the new, Lucile Lewin of Whistles has the eye. Her taste and her uncanny ability to jump ahead of the pack makes her shop the first stop for fashion journalists hungry to be told what is new and to be given a lead for up and coming stories.Ms Lewin just knows. If you want to be in fashion's vanguard, keep an eye on Whistles.

   This ability to take clothes from various sources and weld them into a unique fashion story is London's strongest contribution to the world of clothes. This was the thinking behind street fashion, which London art school students picked up and which is now continued by key figures like Joseph and Lucile Lewin. They are much more than shopkeepers. They are inspired stylists who reflect their attitude to life by creating clothes for a lifestyle which all the fashionable seem to want.

The glamour of cashmere has captured everyone's imagination and it is now a status symbol world-wide. There is still nothing to beat it as a "throw" draped around the shoulders over a simple, slim silhouette.

To have any impact fur should be large and luxurious and worn with style — but make it artificial, if you can.

Seriously rich in America

New York is the home of super-sophisticated, big-city fashion for the seriously rich, ultra-smart and exceptionally slim. But American fashion has two sides — high style city-slickers on one side and homespun naturalism on the other — or if you like, silk and cashmere versus linen and denim. The factor all American clothes have in common, apart from being very well made, is that they can all be worn by the not-so-young which, as they are very expensive, is perhaps just as well. The wealthy woman who wants to look elegant and alluring will probably call in first on either Bill Blass or Oscar de la Renta.

Bill Blass

The secret of Bill Blass's success lies in his ability to keep fashion under control. His smart suits are popular with women who lunch in New York's fashionable restaurants and his opulent evening gowns are a cunning muxture of American taste and European high fashion. In both cases, they can be worn unselfconsciously by sophisticated women of any age.

Oscar de la Renta

De la Renta's clothes are every bit as opulent and feminine as those by Blass but they are more dramatically sensual and extrovert. Both designers also have in common prices which are only for women very confident of their bank managers. De la Renta trained with Balenciaga and worked for many years in Paris, so his clothes have a European authority to them.

Ralph Lauren

Understated and totally American, the clothes of Ralph Lauren appeal to the perfectly sophisticated women who have the confidence to dress down, not up. You won't find impressive bows or slinky grand entrance ball gowns here. Instead you try on beautifully simple cashmere sweaters, silk skirts and gaberdine pants and suddenly discover that this American understands class in clothes as few Europeans do.

Calvin Klein

Like Lauren, Calvin Klein uses the best and most undemonstrative materials to fulfil his understated All-American outdoor look. Sportswear is his forte but his cashmeres, blazers and tweeds are far from the banality of jogging suits and recall the clean healthiness of Katherine Hepburn in her thirties' comedy films with Spencer Tracy.

There is a saying that the British man gets the woman he deserves. Certainly there seems a grain of truth in this. Whereas Frenchmen see nothing effeminate in understanding women's fashion or being knowledgeable about perfumes, Englishmen are less secure and must dismiss this side of life as "women's nonsense". Their attitudes are as different as British real ale and French claret. I do not think this necessarily makes British women less sophisticated, but exotic blooms require certain soils and temperatures, and Britain does not normally provide them. Style cannot flourish in a vacuum and sadly it is more likely to be found in the fashion-conscious cities of Milan, Paris or New York than in London.

Galanos and Adolfo

Many rich American women, including Nancy Reagan and her friends, look West for their status clothes and buy in Los Angeles. Here is the couture house of James Galanos whose perfectly made, highly priced, prestige clothes are seen at all the American society bashes where the ultra-rich gather. The same is true of the clothes of Adolfo, Mrs Reagan's favourite designer, whose Chanel type suits and slinky evening looks have frequently been photographed on her back.

Designer detail

What sort of finish should you look for in a very expensive garment? If you are buying a couture dress made to your measurements by a great couturier like Givenchy you can expect (and you will get) perfection. You should demand it from the top-of-the-market, ready-to-wear model too. After all, a Lagerfeld embroidered evening dress can easily run away with a couple of thousand pounds.

Even today a couture dress from a prestige house like Yves Saint Laurent relies on very precise handwork. Basting stitches and the distance between them are exactly measured (they are half a centimetre long), pockets are hand-tacked, machine sewn and then gone over by hand.

As I have said before, you can learn a great deal about a fashion house by examining the inside of a garment. I know women who do not hesitate to turn a dress inside out to inspect the finish. Close examination shows them the level of workmanship and gives them an idea of how long their expensive purchase is likely to last.

This does not mean that they expect the dress to fall apart but it tells the real fashion experts something much more important — how long it will keep its shape. Cheap clothes can lose their shape and take on that of the wearer all too soon — expensive clothes do not. The difference comes from the quality of the fabric, the skill of the cut and the degree of support they get from inside — and this is the reason for the inspection.

Classic interfacing

A well-constructed garment produced in the classic dressmaker's way, uses a muslin interlining across the bodice and shoulders — often with rows of stitching to give it added body. Necklines and waistbands are strengthened by a bias strip of fabric. In the old days of couture, perfection of hang was achieved in a variety of ways. An inside belt of grosgrain was often added to a dress to keep it in place and stop it sliding around or riding up.

Weights and chains

Low-cut necklines and backs may be kept in position by weighting them with dressmaker's weights sewn in ribbon and attached to the point of the V or U of the line. These weights are also used to make sure that very fine, lightweight fabrics hang straight. They are placed in the hem of skirts and jackets (at the back) for the same reason but Chanel kept her suits hanging perfectly by using a fine gilt chain instead of weights with her extra light, loosely woven tweeds.

The lining

Really expensive clothes are usually fully lined and in the great couturier's heyday even blouses for suits were lined — with chiffon for a very light effect, and organza for body. Organza was used to line fine wool and heavy wools were lined with taffeta or silk. Silk dresses were always lined with silk. Further proof of perfectionism was found in the fact that not only was every cut edge of fabric inside a couture dress oversewn but also turned up edges of hems were often given a binding of narrow silk bias ribbon.

James Galanos still lines every garment with silk, either satin, chiffon or crepe. His buttonholes are handmade and all seams and hems are sewn by hand.

If you get some (or even any) of these time-consuming and therefore costly refinements on a modern garment, you are doing well. Garments made to these exacting standards keep their shape and look good for years. That is what the wealthy woman gets for her money.

Dressing for the part

This chapter has been all about luxury clothes but for most modern women the real luxury lies in being in charge of their lives and being able to choose for themselves how they will dress. This freedom usually comes from earning one's own living but the very fact of doing so tempers the actual freedom. As women take over more and more key roles, the importance of dressing for the part grows. Women need to decide how to

Suit flattery consists here of a dark jacket with wide revers and a detachable white collar worn over a plain white vest. The scale of the short jacket and wide shoulders work in a most flattering way with the knee-length skirt. This is town dressing at its most glamorous.

dress for a business meeting, to chair a committee or to make a public appearance.

For men, the solution to these problems was found a long time ago — a dark suit, white shirt and sober tie have long been the standard uniform. For women it is not so easy. For one thing, women's clothes have been linked to their sexuality for so long that they do not always know how to dress to neutralise themselves — or even if it is a good idea to attempt to do so.

For this reason, as a coda to all the luxurious super-dressing we have been looking at, I want to finish this chapter with a practical examination of how you could organise your looks for your working life.

Advantaged men

It has to be admitted, and I say it with no sense of superiority, that women are still disadvantaged in the world of work. In a sense, it is because they have been so advantaged in the field of clothes. They have always had more freedom to dress in an individual style than men have which means that the possibilities of putting a foot wrong are greatly increased.

Job interviews

Take a crucial situation like this. A man knows that he is expected to appear in the uniform we have already mentioned. It is much harder for you to make a decision about appropriate dress. You have more possibilities and less historic precedent to guide your choice. Things are further complicated by the fact that you will probably be interviewed by men, possibly older than yourself, who might have an attitude towards women's dress far removed from current fashion thinking. How far should you be prepared to compromise your fashion knowledge and your preferred style?

Dressing down or dressing up

If you live in jeans and cowboy boots and you are applying for a job, say, in television or the music business, you might just get away with turning up for an interview dressed as you normally do. But in any other situation it would be fatal. Conversely, to appear for interview in a frilly, over-feminine flounced little-girl dress, costume jewelry and over-the-top baby curls hair is not going to get you very far either.

Cheaper clothes work for only one season because the details that make them "now" are imposed, not integral. Their designers start with details. Good designers start with shape and scale.

The interview suit

You could, of course, fall back on the interview suit — just as a man would. But do not make it too severely tailored or you might look intimidating. Wear it with a simple blouse or jumper and resist the temptation to feminise it with those ghastly pussy-cat bows that Mrs Thatcher wears. They are simpering, half-hearted and institutional. Keep jewelry to a minimum. Do not teeter in on stiletto heels or in peep-toe sandals. Ensure that your hair is under control. Do not forget your finger nails — if you can't afford a manicure spend some time on them yourself. If you wear scent, apply it very lightly.

This is packaging and you might well find it distasteful — but men have done it for years.

Separates

If the very idea of wearing a suit makes you cringe then, of course, you can wear a blouse, skirt and coordinated jacket and this instantly gives you more flexibility. You can wear a flannel skirt, cotton blouse and gabardine blazer; or a fine tweed skirt, silk shirt and corduroy jacket; or a cotton skirt, blouse and linen jacket. The choice is yours and it is a very wide one. Do not imagine that you have to appear in dull grey, navy or brown to be successful, but it is probably wise to keep away from strong colour contrasts. Remember that the men interviewing you could well be inately conservative or measuring you against their wives who might dress in a very meak and mild version of good taste.

Doing the job

Once you have the job you can obviously relax a lot and wear the sort of clothes you always enjoy. If you are doing the job well, your appearance will soon be taken for granted in the nice sense of being trusted and relied on. But there are still rules which you should impose on yourself. Remember always that as a professional woman you are dressing for an audience and your clothes and your finish must be appropriate for that audience. It is a question of good manners.

Understatement always works best. It is much better to dress down for the office than over-dress. In that way you will not alienate or menace your workmates.

Severe dressing

This can be intimidating if too strong. Avoid a mannish appearance — your authority should come from your

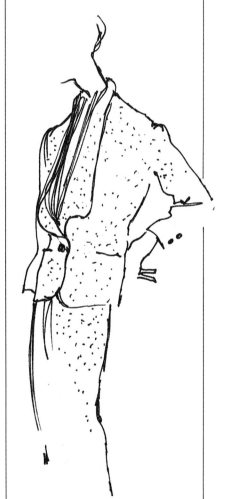

Soft country tweeds always look their best with gently draped blouses, ties or scarves — in silk if you can afford it. For the best effect, go for toning, rather than contrasting shades.

confidence in your femininity. Choose clothes that keep their cool and don't become crumpled and creased the moment you sit down. Natural fibres are almost always best able to cope with the artificial temperatures in most offices.

High profile
Do not see your working life as an opportunity for wearing out old clothes that you no longer like. In fact, as your work is your high profile exposure, your clothes should be the best you can afford but, of course, this does not mean that they have to be luxurious.

Make a conscious destinction between day and evening style (and fabrics) so that you do not find yourself unconsciously dressing unsuitably. Avoid bright colour and strongly patterned fabrics. If you wear nail varnish make sure that it is always immaculate. Chipped nails look inefficient.

Ring the changes
Build up a big enough wardrobe to be able to ring the changes and do not always wear the same blouse and skirt together. It is easy to fall into the trap of having an office uniform which you put on automatically. Avoid it by consciously planning your week's wardrobe. One of the most successful businesswomen I know always spends just five munutes each night organising her clothes for the next day. Others I know do it for the week on Sunday night.

Give your personality and clothes-confidence time to grow in any new job — and be conscious of the way your colleagues dress.

And finally . . .
If you find all advice such as the above demeaning, insulting and patronising, I am delighted! You are your own woman and you do not need the likes of me and that is exactly what this book is aiming to make you.

You can often afford to be bold with a blouse and it can have a considerable impact with a plain suit — like this stunning striped and draped high-collared one does.

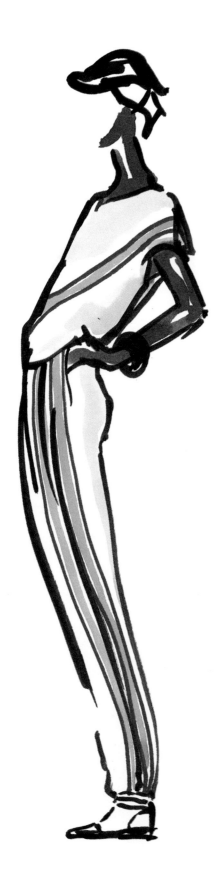

Leisure and sportswear have moved out of the gym and tennis court onto the streets — or, at least, about the house and garden. Shorts are perfectly acceptable for informal occasions and so are tracksuits and T-shirts. They provide the perfect solution for all those women who cannot be bothered with clothes.

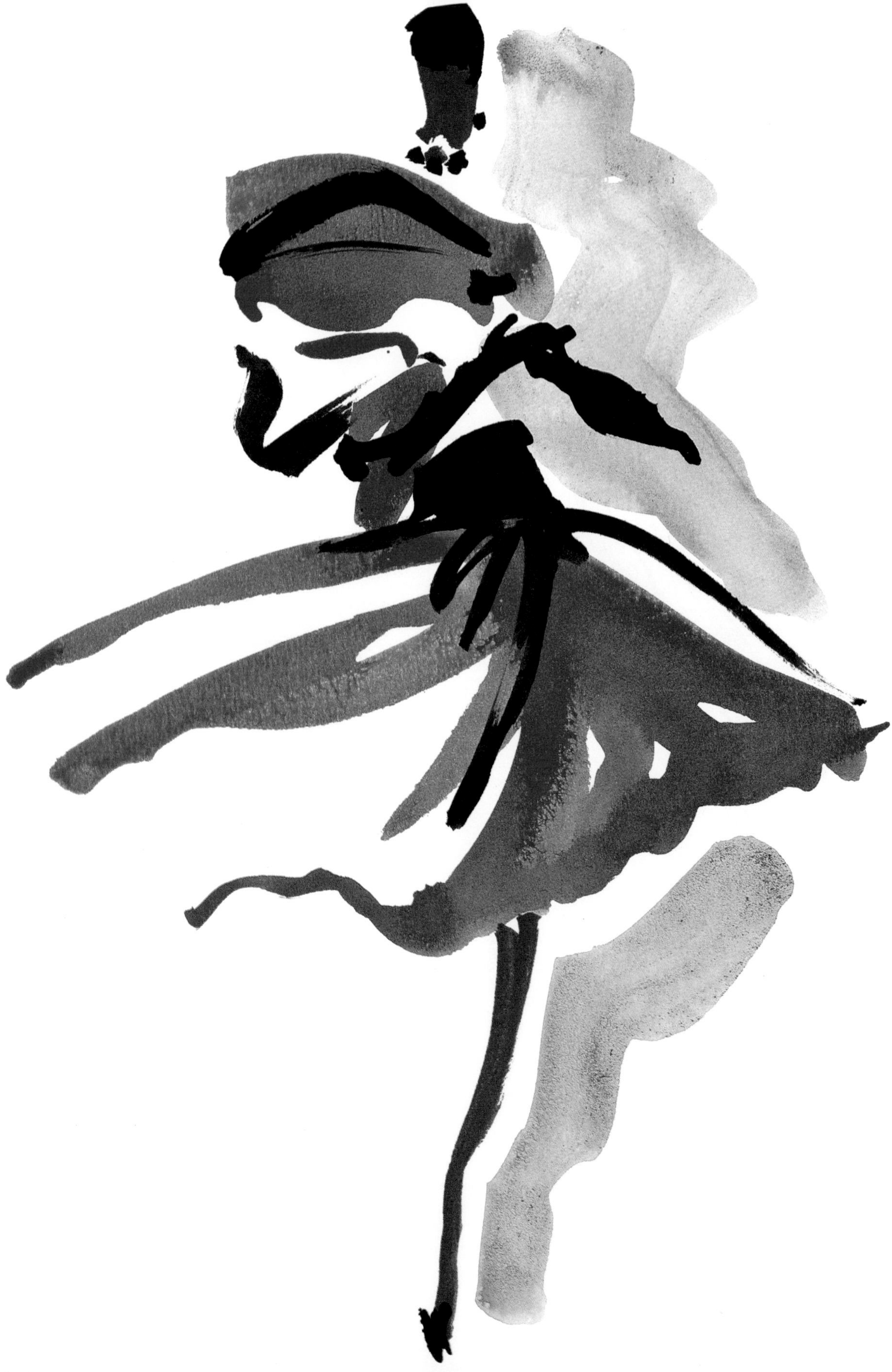

chapter 6

The finishing touch

You can spend a fortune on your back and still look nothing special. You can buy within a limited budget and always look great. It is largely to do with style, but it is also to do with what you wear with what. You and your frock are the picture, it is common sense to frame it in the best way possible.

Your frame consists of your hair, your make-up and your accessories. Get them right and you will highlight the rest. Get them wrong and they will dim even the twenty-two carat gold shimmer of the most exclusive designer dress. Although this book is not the place to discuss hairstyles and make-up in detail, a few basic points might help you to exploit your full potential.

Your crowning glory

I don't think any aspect of the average woman's appearance causes her so much trouble and grief as her hair. My theory is that this is because it has a will of its own and, unlike your face and figure, it is not static. Once you have done your make-up it stays more or less as you want it — but not your hair. Wind, rain and its own nature can undo all your handiwork in no time at all. Furthermore it is not called your crowning glory for nothing — it can make or mar your whole appearance.

Nothing but the best

Many women resent the money they pay at the hairdressers and try to get their hair done at the cheapest possible rate or, worse still, never let a hairdresser near them and trim and chop away whenever their hair gets too unmanageable. What a mistake! No matter how impatient and fed up you are with your

The newest coats are long, broad shouldered and very simple. They make their impact with their scale — which is fuller than at any time since Dior's new look, almost forty years ago. Obviously, if you are short and squat they must be approached with care.

hairstyle never be tempted to cut it yourself. To cut hair properly requires a trained eye and a skilled hand. Your amateur hacking can undo years of professional work and make it very hard for your hairdresser to get it back to a good style.

Remember, you wear your hairstyle every day of the week and my advice is to spend as much as you can on a really good cut and a first-class style, but make your time at the hairdresser a positive one.

Active haircuts
Instead of passively sitting there dozing off and gossiping with the stylist, become actively involved with what is being done. Ask questions, how and why, and learn the tricks of the hairdresser's trade. You won't be able to copy the trained hairdresser's skills but you will learn how to make more than an adequate shot at keeping your hair the way it was when you walked out of the salon.

Practice makes perfect
Put your new knowledge into action, don't go back to washing your hair and leaving it to dry after a quick dash through with a comb. Practice blow-drying it the way you saw the hairdresser do it. Talk to your hairdresser and find out which styling brush he recommends for your hair — using the right one could make all the difference. The first attempts may not look quite as chic as the original, but you will get there in the end.

Be loyal
Don't keep changing your hairdresser, ever searching for the perfect cut. Stick to one stylist and he will get to know exactly how your particular hair behaves and what you want from him. And don't be afraid to complain if you don't like the style. So many women say "He ruined my hair, I'll never go there again." You must go back the next week and show him why it is wrong for you. Only then can he hope to get it right next time. Most mistakes at the hairdresser occur because the client has failed to communicate exactly what she wants the end result to look like and only by going again and getting it right will you ever be satisfied.

Keep it clean
Clean hair is essential. If you have a greasy scalp then you must wash your hair every day, otherwise every two or three

days will be enough. Remember that if you live in a city your hair will get clogged with grime more quickly than if you are out in the country.

When you wash your hair at home remember that drying it is very much part of the process and not just an after-thought. Wrap a thick towel around your head like a turban and pat it dry. Do not be tempted to rub it roughly as this will damage it and lead to split ends.

Shampoos

Spend time experimenting with shampoos. Ask your hairdresser for advice and don't begrudge spending money on an expensive one if it is going to be right for your hair. There is no doubt about it, a good shampoo can have a much more beneficial effect upon your hair than merely cleaning it. As a general rule you do not need to use much shampoo to wash your hair and, the better the quality, the less you require.

Conditioners

If you wash your hair frequently that is not the end of the story. You must treat and condition your hair. There are masses of treatments on the market — buy the best you can afford. Hair care is a highly sophisticated field where clinical and beauty developments have been exploited to such a degree that the perfect product for every possible hair type is now available.

Blow-drying

If you are blow-drying your hair do so gently and do not use a comb — finger comb it through whilst the blow-dryer is working on it. Keep the blow-dryer a good distance from your head because, if you don't, the heat will leave your hair dry and lifeless. For a really sleek finish leave a touch of dampness in your hair — over-drying can make it fluffy and full of static, particularly in the winter when the weather is frosty.

Ring the changes

Remember that you can change your hairstyle to change your mood. Women in the public eye, like the Queen and Mrs Thatcher, have to be always recognisable and so they must stick with the same hairstyle day and night, day after day. You are luckier. Playing with your hair is the cheapest and easiest way of changing your mood — and it is fun as well. Pile it up on top of your head, slick back the sides, have it smooth and sleek one day, windswept and riotous the next.

Gels and mousses

One of the major break-throughs in recent years has been the development of gels. With them you can almost sculpt your hair. They fix you style in any way you want so that it can be sleeked like the fifties' Brylcream boys, wildly spiked or luxuriously curled. You put the gel on to towel-dry hair and scrunch it in to stiffen and thicken it. For a wet-look you can add more gel after you have dried and styled your hair. If you want to freshen up your hair but haven't the time to wash it, just add some more gel and style it. Once the gel has set you have no more worries.

Mousses condition the hair and give it much more body, and hair sprays can exert control and keep the hair in place.

How far can you go?

If you are the wife of the local vicar, you probably feel that to appear at the church social with your hair sprayed with colour or glitter would be an error. I do not necessarily agree, but don't forget that colour or glitter sprays and temporary dyes and colour mousses wash out very easily so the purple streak which wowed them at the Hallowe'en party need not embarrass you at the check-out the next morning.

Experiment a bit with bows, combs and glitter pins, but be careful. It is horribly easy to look like Enfield's Shirley Temple, which is not at all what you should be aiming at. The classic Chanel bow looks marvellous on women of any age — provided not a hair is out of place.

The perm

To perm — or not to perm, is not such a simple question. There is hardly a woman I know who has not, at one time or another, been disappointed with her perm and even now it is a tricky business.

The fluids, solutions and heat to which your hair is subjected cannot damage it if done by an expert, but the outcome can be unpredictable. All hair reacts in a slightly different way and it is wise to only have a perm from someone who knows your hair very well, and that is your regular hairdresser. And do not expect miracles. Although it will make your hair wavy or curly, this is not the only idea behind a perm. It also adds body and texture which is an advantage if you have fine and naturally oily hair, but if your hair tends to be dry a perm will worsen that aspect and it could end up looking very bushy and fluffy.

Big shapes and strong flashes of pure colour can make quite ordinary items of clothing interesting. Here (on the left) an over-size jacket and long loose skirt would look very elegant on a tall woman. The red scarf is visually important. It stops everything appearing to drain down towards the floor. The central figure demonstrates another well-known fashion fact: neutral shades need a ''punctuation mark'' or two if they are not to look dull. The strong colour of the belt and bandau gives this outfit a lift. A man's large white shirt (right) is one of the most relaxed and sexy items you can have in your wardrobe. Here it is worn with a plain skirt and is enlivened by a man's red cotton handkerchief casually knotted at the neck.

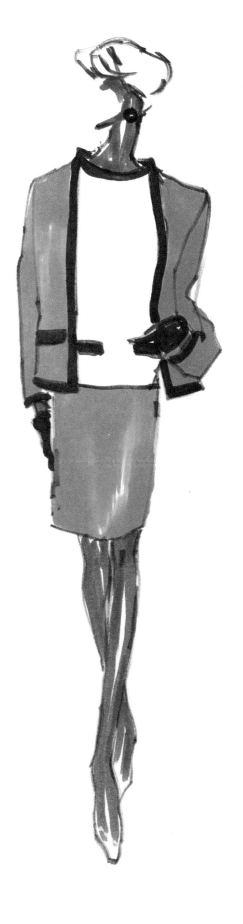

To accessorise or not to accessorise? Fantasy hats and big pieces of costume jewelry can give clothes an enormous impact — or they can steal their thunder. The draped wool dress on the left could well stand without its hat but the satin top and skirt (centre) are given great style by the addition of an over-scale hat and heavy costume jewelry. The Chanel-type suit stands perfectly assured without any additions — although Madam would have probably draped lots of gilt chains around the neck, without spoiling the suit's impact in any way.

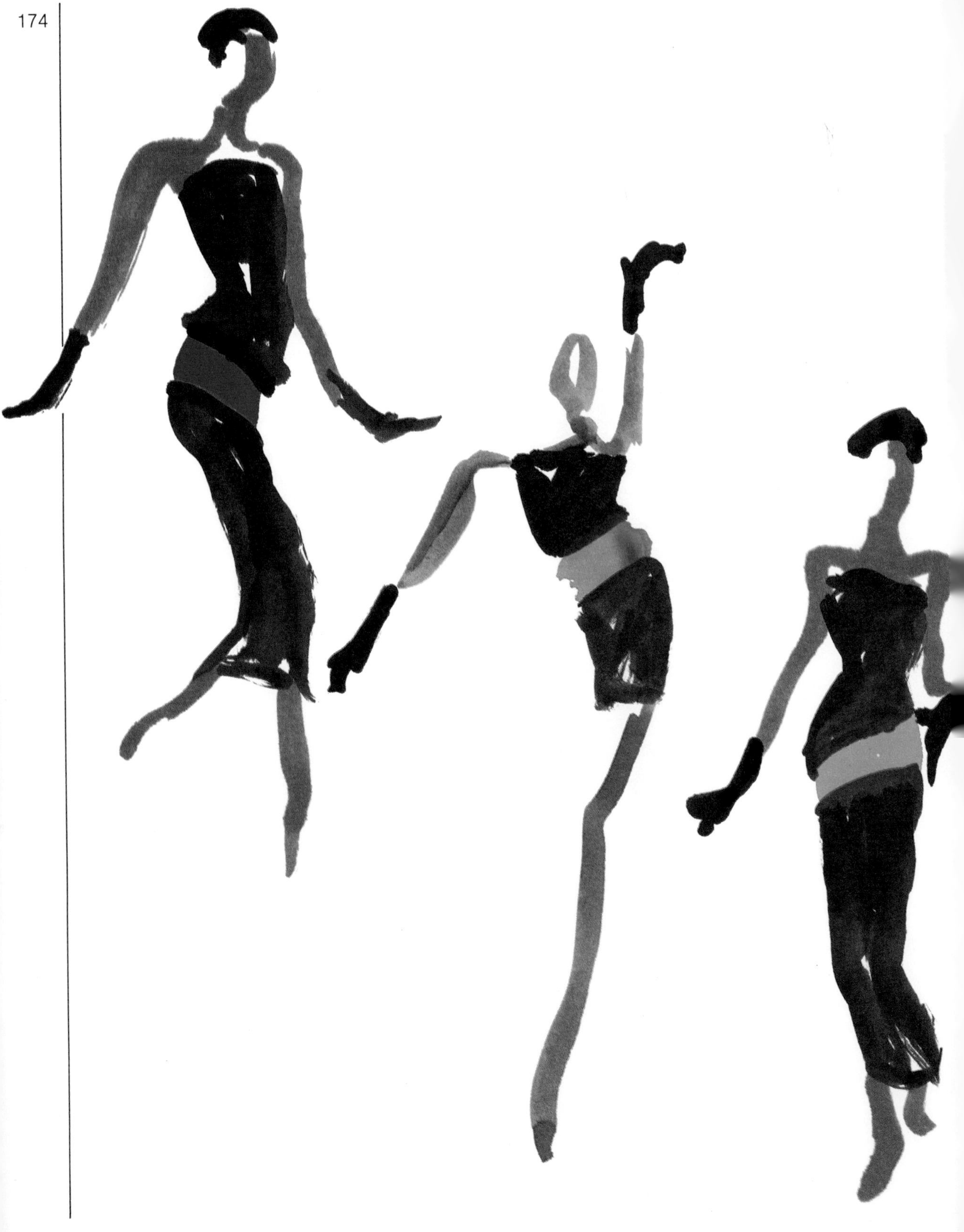

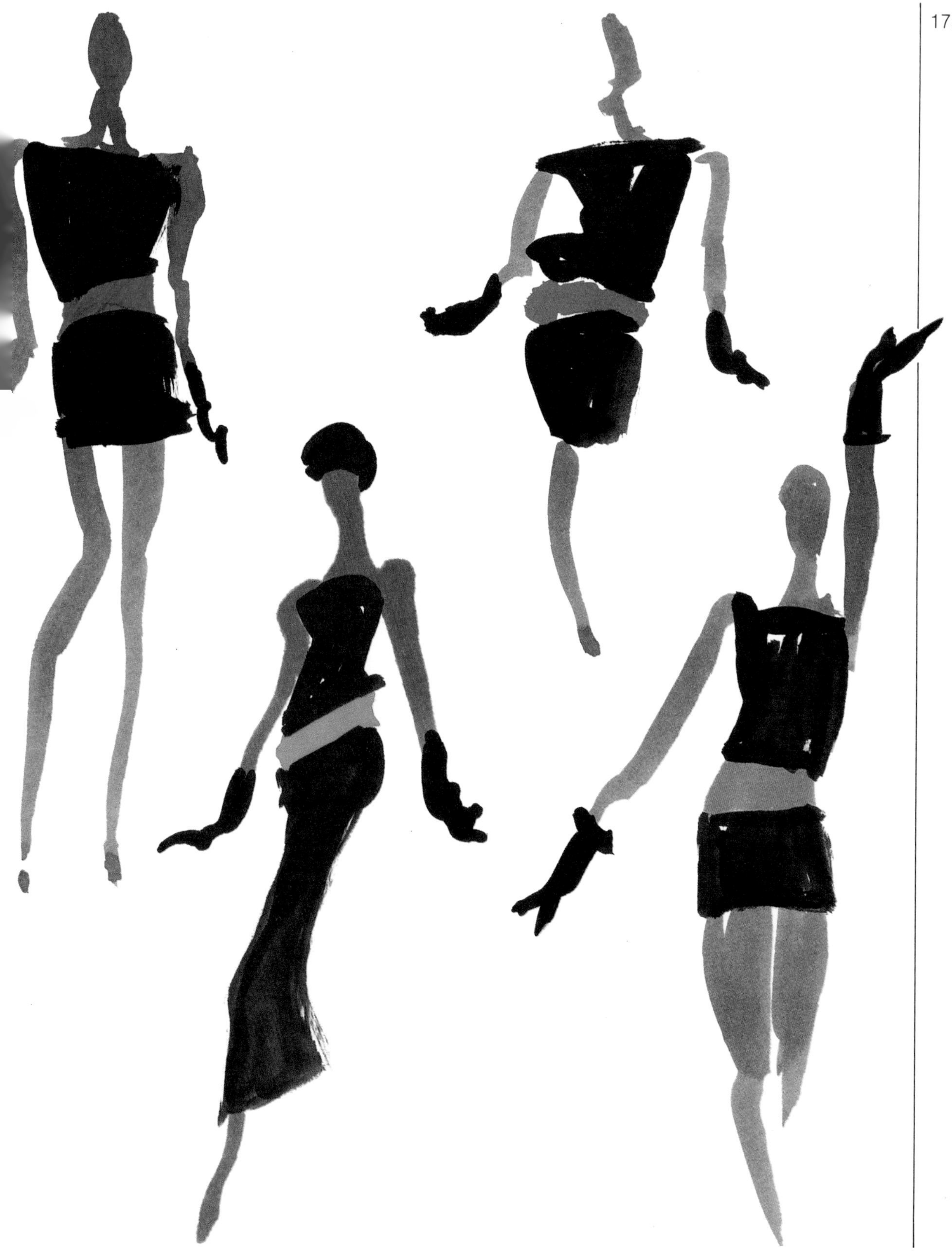

Draped and swirled semi-diaphanous evening looks always spell glamour — if you have a very firm figure and a lot of confidence.

Brushing your hair

The Victorian precept of brushing your hair vigorously at least fifty times is quite wrong. It stimulates the sebaceous glands and can make your hair greasy. Keep brushing to a minimum and make sure that you choose the right brush. Natural bristles are best and if they are widely-spaced they will be less likely to damage the hair. As a general rule the thicker your hair, the thicker the bristles should be.

Short hair

If your hair is short you can have great fun with those gels and mousses. You can plaster it down in a wet-look mood or you can pull it forward into feathered spikes. Hang your head upside down when you dry it for maximum volume. It is possible with slightly longer hair to use mousses to thicken and give body to it so that you can sculpt and shape it into any baroque arrangement that you want — and then just wash it out.

Unfortunately many women have their hair cut short believing it will be less trouble than long hair. In many cases the opposite is true. Short hair needs to be extra clean, more beautifully conditioned and carefully cut or you run the risk of looking drab and masculine. It also needs to be offset with careful make-up because so much more of the face is on view.

Hair colours

If you are streaking or highlighting your hair for the first time, try to afford a professional hairdresser to do it. It is possible to do it perfectly successfully at home, but you will get a much more professional look if you have carefully monitored every step taken by an expert. Every woman I know who has coloured or high-lighted her hair has found that it has given her an enormous psychological lift and really boosted her confidence. If you have never done so, it is well worth considering.

Do your homework

There are a number of magazines on the market now devoted to hairstyling. Flick through them for ideas. They are also a great help when it comes to explaining the style you want to your hairdresser because they illustrate exactly what the trade understands as a bob, a crop, or a square cut for example. Make a note of model's styles in fashion magazines and steal a few daring ideas from the pop world.

Remember that labels inside garments give vital information. Always read them before you make a purchase.

Details borrowed from the male wardrobe can look extremely feminine and sexy when worn with gentle jackets and soft skirts as here. The shirt and tie, along with the cap, look perfectly at ease.

A style to grow with you

Keep an open mind about your hairstyle. Women who have had long hair in their youth find this particularly hard, and there is nothing more aging for a woman in her forties than long, straight hair. Age reduces the amount of natural body in the hair and it ends up looking thin and lifeless. A sudden change in style at this age can bring back all the bounce and vigour to a woman's hair and knock years off her appearance.

Make-up

Women are the luckier sex. With make-up they can transform a face that looks like something the cat brought in into something radiant and appealing. Nothing gives more confidence than a well made-up face — not only to the owner but also the onlooker!

Find the time

In my experience, far too many women think that a careful, total make-up look is only for special occasions and that a quick slap-on will do for everyday. I disagree. We are back to the quality of the frame again. If your clothes are right and your hair is perfect, you must make-up to the image that they are projecting.

Busy women tell me that they cannot spare the time. I say that they must spare the time. A practised hand can make-up a face in a remarkably short time. Certainly it takes a little longer than cleaning your teeth, but with practice and a lot of concentration you can get it down to five minutes and anybody can afford that amount of time.

Avoid your time zone

Another danger of wearing make-up only for special occasions is that because you make-up so seldom your methods remain very outdated. You can tell at a glance with some women when they were having the time of their lives and making-up regularly. The scarlet lips and eyeliner of the fifties, the pale face and white lips of the sixties, the blue eyelid and glossy lips of the seventies. Change your methods of application more frequently than your colours and you will never look dated.

Understand your colouring

You cannot treat your face as you can your hair. You must learn what colour lipsticks and blushers suit you and then more or less stay within that colour range. Broadly speaking with lipsticks for example, reds range from orange-yellow at one end of the spectrum to purple-blue at the other. Somewhere along this line will be the point at which the lipstick colour and your colour chime together. On either side of that point will be tones that work for you but you must remember that if, for instance, your colour is towards the orange end, a purple red will never look right on you.

You have rather more freedom with eye shadows. Don't get stuck in the rut of blue eyeshadow for blue eyes and brown for brown. Our eyes are made up of many different colours, even the bluest have flecks of brown and green in them. Experiment with pinks and yellows, golds and blacks.

Night lights

You can have a lot of fun making-up for parties and evenings. Blue or black lipsticks, glossed with white, gold and silver glitter can look exciting for one-off occasions. Don't be afraid to go for strong effects after dark: heavier make-up, stronger tones, unusual effects — experiment and be confident.

Always apply your make-up in a light strength similar to the one you expect to spend the evening in. If you make up your evening face by the light coming through a summer window, your make-up will disappear when you get into the subdued lighting of a restaurant. Similarly, do not use strong artificial light to put on your day face or you run the risk of looking over made-up in the street.

Get the basics right

The right foundation is the essential base for your make-up and when choosing it you must look at your pigmentation. It is worth considering a consultation with the experts for this. Most make-up departments in large stores have experts who will be happy to discuss your colouring with you and to suggest the right tones for you to choose. Half an hour of discussion is time very well spent.

Spend time learning how to apply foundation correctly. You should use it to prepare the background for your make-up, which should be a flawless skin without blemishes or dark patches. Foundation should enhance the colour of your own skin. You cannot make yourself look more healthy by applying lashings of tan coloured foundation if the skin underneath is not tanned. You must use blusher, not foundation to alter the colour of your face. One exception to this rule is if you tend to

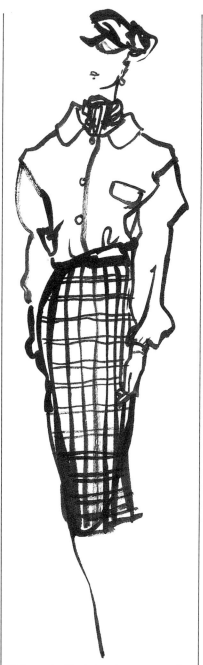

This sort of look has been around, with a few variations in scale, for fifty years as a country-based form of dressing and it still looks good. It was worn by Katherine Hepburn in countless thirties films (as was the masculine-feminine look opposite); Grace Kelly carried it through the fifties and it is going strong still. Why? Because it is soft, yet tailored, and would flatter virtually any figure type.

Understated dressing requires flat heels, sophisticated looks need high heels. If your ankles are not your best point, the higher the heel the better the ankle will look.

flush. A foundation with a green base (which does not show once it is on your skin) tones down any redness you may suffer from.

The older face

The older you are the more attention you should give to your foundation and blusher and the less to your eyes. Wear a little eyeshadow but avoid anything with a sheen or a glitter as this highlights the crepey texture on the lids.

Beautiful eyes

The point of balance for a successfully made-up face is the eyes. They link lips, cheeks and hair. They require some thought, and the right eyeshadow, skilfully applied can make even the flattest eye come to life. Again I think you should turn to the experts for advice. Study the beauty pages in your favourite magazines, they all print the make-up worn by their cover girls and often say how it has been applied. Treat the girls on the make-up counter as consultants, not just salesgirls, and don't be afraid to give new colours and products a try. Make-up may seem expensive, but how often have you actually used up a complete eyeshadow or lipstick? A little goes a very long way.

Mascara

This product is full of pitfalls for the unwary. Avoid intense tones. You will look very old-fashioned if your mascara is too heavy. It is all too easy to end up looking like Coco the Clown when what you are really aiming for is Coco Chanel. This is a particular problem as you grow older so, if you are of a certain age, go easy. Avoid waterproof mascaras if your face is no longer youthful. The extra scrubbing needed to remove every trace can damage the delicate skin around the eye.

   It always surprises me how few women ever consider having their eyelashes dyed. The process is not expensive, it lasts for quite a long time, it does not hurt and, if done by expert beauticians, looks completely natural. It is now also possible to buy preparations for dyeing your eyelashes at home.

Through a glass darkly

If you wear glasses remember that you can make-up your eyes more strongly and dramatically. When you are choosing frames, think not only of the shape and size of your face, but also of your colouring. Have you hair done before you go to the opticians — its shape and length will affect your face and influence your final choice of lens size and frame shape. Take plenty of time to make your choice and, if you can't decide on a clear winner, don't panic. Leave the choice and arrange to come back the next day — getting it right is more crucial than doing it quickly.

Nailing it

Far too many women don't bother to manicure their nails. It should be done once a week. Although time consuming, it is time well spent. If you use nail varnish, it will highlight any deficiencies in your nails, so work to get them right before you start to paint. Nothing looks worse than chipped or scratched nail varnish so the moment it is damaged, take it off.

Accessories

Do not neglect this important area. Well chosen accessories can give your clothes extra style, wit and class. Badly chosen, they can destroy the most carefully planned outfit. Good accessories look as if they are part of the the clothes, not merely desperate additions at the last moment. The accessories you wear depend on your way of life.

Jewelry

Some of the most elegant women I know never wear jewelry, others would never allow themselves to be seen without it. Few, however, would go so far as one friend who always wears her pearls in bed. As she says, ''You never know who is going to drop in . . . !''

If you are a jewelry person you can take various courses in building up your collection. You can buy only the real thing, buy mainly the real thing or buy largely junk jewelry. There is something to be said for each approach.

The real thing

If you buy the real thing you will build up your collection slowly but you will do it surely because good jewelry is well designed and made to last. Classic pieces give a touch of tone to any outfit. It is often said that gold is ageing. I do not think so but I do agree with the growing chorus against thin gold chains — they do nothing for anyone.

Ethnic-print linen skirts are a perennial fashion story. Their popularity lies in their graphic strength. Worn with a T-shirt they can see you through virtually any occasion. They can be casual day-wear or can carry themselves well on more formal evening occasions.

We should be thankful that in Britain at least there is always room for the way out or eccentric! These flock velvet pantaloons and cut-away coat were made by a design student and could be copied easily enough by the woman who wants to be original.

The mixture

If you buy certain key pieces of real jewelry and supplement them with cheaper, short life additions, you give yourself more flexibility. For example, a basic pearl necklace, gold bracelet and top quality antique cameo can be supplemented with fake diamond clips, coral or wooden bracelets and plastic rings or pins and still look good.

Junk jewelry

If you buy largely junk jewelry you can create any effect you want. You can strengthen complementary colours in your outfit with earrings and bangles, you can gamble on an up-to-the-minute clip or pin knowing you can throw it out the following season. You can go for the out and out joke accessories — wristwatches in exactly the same colour as your outfit for example. Browse around the junk shops for decorated hat pins and brooches from a past fashion era.

Imitation jewelry

Do not run away with the idea that you can get glitzy imitation rocks for a song. Some of the prices at Monty Don, Butler and Wilson and Kenneth Lane might surprise you and the magnificent costume jewelry from Saint Laurent or Lagerfeld is definitely expensive — but it looks fabulous.

Quick tip

It is all right to be a classic dresser but liven up your look with one strong feature (a powerful colour or dramatic piece of jewelry) otherwise there is the danger of being so classic that you fade away.

Handbags

Up until the sixties it was an unwritten piece of fashion folklore that a woman was known by the quality of her gloves, shoes and handbags — especially the latter. A lady's handbag had to show its direct line of descent from the world of top horsey tackle. The best and most supple leather, the most craftsmanly brass or silver clasps, the perfect stitching proclaimed the top-quality product.

How much should you spend?

The old school view was quite simple — buy the best. French women in particular believed that buying cheaply was false economy. So they bought classic items that cost a lot but were guaranteed to outlive several changes of wardrobe over the years.

Many of them still do. I know a very elegant Frenchwoman who lived in Rome. Her well-cared for winter handbag was frequently admired and commented on by her friends. She confessed to me that she had persuaded her first husband to buy it for her from Hermes in Paris shortly before she left him. She certainly understood investment dressing — the bag had cost a fortune but it still looked marvellous twenty-five years later! Conversely an English friend swears that an expensive white bag is a waste of money. No matter what it costs, she believes it will have a life of only one season.

Classic or current

Nowadays accessories are seen less as an anchor in a wardrobe and more as highlights so there is a strong case for an off-with-the-old, on-with-the-new approach to them each season. It depends on how faithfully you wish to follow the latest fashion fad. Certainly there are still very good reasons for buying classic, understated accessories as investments which will repay their initial cost by giving your wardrobe years of service and will look right over many seasons. There are still plenty of women who save to buy a classic leather handbag and perhaps buy only half a dozen in a lifetime.

Where to go

The top places to go for such classics are Aspreys (who provide the Queen with her handbags), Hermes or Louis Vuitton. However, most women pay considerably less than the prices charged at these establishments. If you want a top quality, modern design in leather at about a hundred pounds, the best buys, as I have already pointed out, are undoubtedly the Italian Enny bags. They are now very generally available. If you visit Italy you can pick up marvellous bargains at open-air markets — Florence has an especially fine one, selling bags of every possible design.

Belts and braces

Here again you can choose between top quality classics or amusing flavour of the month ideas. Certainly, you can have a lot of fun with belts and braces — they are cheap, expendable and versatile, unless you spend a fortune on the best leather

Keep silk squares for the country.

A dark hat and shoes enclose a small figure.

bearing one of the grandest designer names. It is a good idea to buy one or two investment belts which are traditional in design, well-made and in natural colours. You can wear them with jeans, skirts or even to belt a straight top coat.

Fashion belts
Do not forget that elaborate and even exaggerated fashion belts can do wonders. Take care over choosing belts with heavy embossed or moulded metal buckles. A wise choice can give you a dramatic focal point in your wardrobe for years, an unwise one can soon look flashy, vulgar and second rate. If you are in the habit of holidaying in Spain be especially vigilant. Although you can buy very beautiful top quality leather and silver belts, the cheap ones are as stiff as boards and the buckles discolour or lose their surface very quickly. A good leather belt should be soft and strong and should follow the shape of your figure.

Shoes
It seems ridiculous to begin with the old adage that, in shoes, comfort is all. Yet, every year thousands of women buy simply on appearance and find they have a pair of shoes that cripple them and they limp around inelegantly wincing with pain until their conscience lets them toss them out. Nothing is more calculated to make you look tired and old than this sort of torture so be really sure that shoes are wearable before buying.

It is said that women's feet get larger with age, particularly if they have had children. Some women have found that their feet go up one to one and half sizes in their middle years. Don't be foolish and cling stubbornly to the size of shoe you wore when you were a teenager — accept it as part of the maturing process and buy a size larger. No one else will notice a difference at all.

Fashion pundits tell us firmly that cheap shoes are always a waste of money but I do not entirely agree. For example, if you want to buy the latest fad style (and why shouldn't you?) which says "now" and will be dead next season, it seems ridiculous to pay the same price as you would for a traditional style high quality leather shoe that might last for the next five years.

High fashion, junk or classic
You can take your pick but wise girls have a mixture in their wardrobes. There are signs that the simple flat pump that has

been a standard for so long for fashion-conscious girls, including the Princess of Wales, is likely to be given a nudge by the return of the glamourous high-heeled shoe. There is no doubt that, putting comfort aside, a high heel definitely glamourises an outfit. It makes the foot look smaller because less area is in contact with the floor; it pulls the calf-muscle up making the ankle slimmer and the leg more shapely; and it makes it impossible to stride. You are forced to tuck you bottom underneath and take small delicate steps. But even if the high heel makes a dramatic comeback, flat shoes will surely remain staples in the majority of modern women's wardrobes.

Training shoes and plimsoles available in every pattern and colour imaginable, are a must for many women as are ankle boots in leather, plastic, suede or rubber.

Emergency measure

If your shoes pinch, fill them with hot water, leave them for a few seconds then pour out and quickly put the shoes on. The water will have softened them and they will stretch with your feet and your problems will be over.

Sinking feeling

Wearing satin or damask-covered shoes to garden parties, marquee balls or outdoor weddings is a problem if the grass is soft. Heels sink in, become stained and are ruined. Clear sellotape wrapped around the heels solves the problem and is easy to strip off afterwards.

Scentsations

Perfume, fragrance, scent — what you call it will probably depend on your age, but whatever the name, you should use it as a daily essential. It does wonders for your morale and feminine wellbeing and is far too good to be kept for special occasions.

Plenty of choice

The range of perfumes now available is staggering and new ones seem to come out almost monthly — although the high price of many means that they do not always push out old favourites. With scent, the adage that you get what you pay for is probably true. Cheap scents are dreadful — it costs money to get rid of the sweetness and cloying quality that they have.

The classic loose coat which avoids all extreme details is always worth paying a bit extra for — because it will repay its higher price by giving you much more service.

Many women have one scent and remain faithful to it forever. I think that this is a pity. With so much choice it seems sad not to experiment and find different ones for different moods, occasions, and stages in your life. And don't throw away the old scent bottles — take off the tops and fold them between the clothes in your drawers as an alternative to the lavender bag.

Keep it subtle
Remember, no matter how exclusive the scent, it can overpower you if you slap on too much — and it can annoy your neighbours. I have had many a meal ruined by the over-insistent perfume of my companion. French women never seem to make this mistake. Perhaps, as with everything else, they tend to go for the best and leave only an aura of beautiful scent when they pass. With expensive scents a little goes a very long way, so apply the minutest amount and reapply it only occasionally. In that way your aura will be subtle. If you are still aware of the scent yourself half-an-hour after applying it, you are probably wearing too much.

Topping it off

Headlines like ''Welcome back hats — all is forgiven'' suggest that women are turning back to millinery in their thousands. It is not the case and it is unlikely that it ever will be.

Changing hairstyles
The problem is not so much with the hat as with the hair. For years hair was dressed to go under a hat, styles were evolved with the interest concentrated at the back or sides of the head. The hat was always uppermost, in every sense.

The hair revolution of the sixties has meant that this situation has changed forever. The appeal that was previously concentrated on the hat by and with the hair became concentrated on the hair, which took on the role of the hat as well. The fact is that most modern hairstyles are spoilt by wearing a hat and, for most of us, life is normally sufficiently informal not to require a hat.

Special occasions
If you decide to buy a hat, especially if it is for a wedding, be very careful. Do not buy one if you cannot see yourself in a full length mirror. The way a hat works with your face is only half

the battle, the really crucial thing is the balance between it and your body. For weddings many women seem to be attracted to the glamour of the broad-brimmed hat, even though in practical terms such a hat is rarely worn a second time. If you buy one, avoid the little Welsh lady look. Check the depth of the crown and the width of the brim very carefully against your overall scale or you will look quaintly top-heavy.

Warming up

How do you keep warm without looking like a Michelin man? Layering has gone out of fashion — which is just as well as it made all but the slimmest woman look a bit like a yak. A doughty Yorkshirewoman said to me when layered dressing was a new thing, ''I don't know what the fuss is all about. With the winds we get up here we've been layering for years.''

Warm or sexy

The sad thing is that sophisticated, sexy underwear is not particularly warm, and warm underwear is not sophisticated or sexy. Few can afford silk French knickers and in any case, they're not exactly the thing to wear under jeans. Pure silk next to the skin is warmer than nylon, so a camisole vest or petticoat in silk is often the answer for keeping off the chills in evening dress. But the best answer for daywear is probably Damart. After all, that's how the Princess of Wales keeps warm — wearing underwear based on a discovery by her great, great, great, great grandfather.

Marks and Spencer are trying to break the tradition of granny underwear with their new thermal undies, lace trimmed in shell pink. However, most girls I know can't bear the bulk of woolly underwear and brave it with cotton briefs and tights — proving that the female is as tough as the male. Speaking personally, I wear underpants and no vest winter and summer — in fact, I do not possess a vest — and I don't feel the cold.

Warm legs, warm heart

The range of tights available now largely solves the problem. They can be as wooly and warm as you like in solid colours, patterned or textured.

Although layering is no longer chic, a woman can produce a very stylish and warm look by wearing shirt, waistcoat, jacket and top-coat all together provided it is all carefully coordinated

Bold stripes for a pair of silk pyjamas make a particularly sophisticated evening look but all it is about is taking the shape and silhouette of day wear and translating them into evening fabrics. This approach can work for you, as well.

and does not look cramped. After all, men have been keeping warm in this combination for many years.

If your feet suffer badly from cold during the winter, make sure that your shoes are not too tight. The old saying goes that nothing is more conducive to chilblains on the toes than tight shoes. A looser winter shoe allows an insulating layer of air to surround the foot, and with an ankle or full length boot, it leaves enough room for an extra layer of sock over your tights. If you really feel the cold it is worth investing in an insulating insole for really cold weather — you trim the insole to fit inside your shoe.

The body beautiful

You will all remember the old saying that a woman can never be too rich or too slim. Although both parts of this statement are debateable, it is a fact that it is very hard to look elegant if you are too overweight. Save your pennies if need be and then go to a health farm for three or four days. The treatments will not only give you a marvellous sense of wellbeing, but also you will be keener to work at getting fit by joining a health club afterwards.

Perhaps you feel that, as with the make-up routine, you just don't have enough time to fit in a regular exercise programme. This is just another excuse to put off the evil hour. Ten minutes a day is all that is necessary to push your metabolism up and make fat-shedding easy. You don't have to become a fitness freak, but you do have to be committed and really want to look better. Remember, when you feel good you look good.

Double or quits

It is a sad fact of life that, as we get older, lots of us develop a double chin. Exercise can help to eliminate its more obvious effects but, short of a face-lift, it is something one has to learn to live with. The obvious way to help it is by creating a soft, non-geometric neckline by using scarves or ties loosely knotted. Above all, avoid anything tight such as chokers or high-necked sweaters. A V-neck will always be the most flattering neckline for someone with a double chin.

Remember that if you wish to be sophisticated and elegant in the way you dress you must pare everything down to the minimum — you should take as your motto the famous adage "less means more".

The ideal necklace is a string of pearls. If you have more than one strand choose an odd number.

Looking after clothes

Lady's maids are very much a thing of the past, and so are the careful instructions about packing which girls' boarding schools used to insist upon. So, how do you keep your clothes looking right at home or when travelling.

The first point to remember is that much of the work done by a lady's maid was manufactured to keep her occupied and out of mischief. The vast majority of standard treatments meted out by a maid on Edwardian clothes were unnecessary and some were probably harmful. Modern working women want a vigorous routine that takes the minimum amount of time.

Dry cleaning

By American standards, the British are pretty filthy. I do not refer to our personal hygeine, but to the state of our clothes. We wash our underwear, blouses and tights as frequently as any do, but when it comes to sending our clothes to the dry cleaners, we definitely lag behind. Far too many clothes never go to the cleaners unless they get stained. The concept of regular cleaning to remove the grime which gets caught in the fibres has never really caught on here as it has in America. It is a pity because regular cleaning and professional pressing keeps garments looking fresh and helps to preserve their shape.

Brushing

Millions of women go through life hardly ever brushing their clothes — and they and their clothes survive. Nevertheless, clothes do benefit from a good brushing after a few wearings. It removes dust and dirt particles which, if they become embedded in the fibres, will cut and tear them. Obviously a good brushing makes clothes look fresher.

Any valet or lady's maid could have told you that the most efficient and least tiring way of brushing clothes was to lay them flat and brush with a semi-circular movement, avoiding scrubbing. Brush against the nap to clean the fabric and then *with* the grain to leave a smooth finish. As simple as that. Remember that velvet does not take kindly to being brushed against the grain.

For a quick way of removing fluff or specks from your clothes, wrap sellotape around your fingers, sticky side outermost, and dab them all over the garment.

Black hats work marvellously with black or blonde hair, but less well with other shades.

How to hang your clothes

No matter how tired, drunk or eager to get to bed you are, you should always hang up your clothes at night — if you want them to last and keep their shape. This will be helped by using the right type of coathanger. Wooden or moulded plastic ones are best as they are shaped and simulate the contours of the shoulders. Padded ones are acceptable for delicate dresses but wire ones should never be used.

Protect the shoulders with dust covers. Clothes that are not regularly worn, such as evening clothes, can gather quite a lot of dust even when they are hanging in a closed wardrobe.

Basic rules

Remember to empty all the pockets before you hang up your clothes. Make sure that shoulders are evenly placed on the hanger and that the garment is hanging straight. Use clamp hangers for pleated skirts — they ensure that the pleats hang straight. A lady's maid would always tack the pleats down before hanging up a skirt. Be careful to hang trousers with the creases correctly aligned or you will get a tram-line double crease effect. Don't cram too many clothes together. Your wardrobe should have enough space to allow air to circulate so that garments can breathe.

Never hang woollens, jersey-type materials, lightweight or delicate fabrics in a wardrobe — they will stretch and distort. Fold them and store in a drawer. Clothes cut on the bias should not be hung on hangers — they will sag and stretch unevenly, so fold them.

The art of packing

Nothing is such a downer as unpacking and finding that before you can get down to the piazza to sip a Campari you have to press your dress. This situation is easily avoided.

Tissue paper

Reams of the stuff were used by lady's maids and valets when packing the huge trunks with which all Edwardians travelled — and they knew what they were doing. The principle of packing is to interline everything with plain white tissue paper (coloured paper could get damp, run and ruin your clothes). Tissue paper helps to retain the vital ingredient for keeping clothes uncreased which is, simply enough, air. As you fold each garment, slip a layer of tissue paper between each fold. Bunch up a little paper to stuff into the shoulders so that they don't get flattened and, if possible, slide each item into a plastic bag. The air trapped in the bag will stop the garment from becoming too squashed — which is vital if you want your clothes to come out of the case looking as pristine as they went in.

Packing shoes

Shoes should be put in a shoe bag, plastic bag (supermarket ones will do) or wrapped in tissue paper. If you can't do this make sure that you wrap something around the high heels to stop them causing damage.

Packing pleats

Pleated skirts can cause trouble but if you take a little time you can ensure that they will also travel well. The secret lies in hair grips or paper clips which you slip over the hem of each pleat to keep it in place. Very fine accordian pleats, especially in silk or chiffon, need to be laid one on top of the other with great care so that the skirt forms a cylinder. You can then slide it inside an old stocking before placing it in the case.

Emergency measure

If all else fails and you haven't got a travelling iron, remember that the steam from a shower will get rid of light creases so hang your crumpled dress in the bathroom while you shower or bath and with luck it will look better when you come to put it on.

Think before you pack

There is probably not much point in saying this, but nine times out of ten we tote far too many clothes around the world "just in case". It is much better to take a few carefully selected garments, correctly packed, than to cram a case full of things which won't be worn and which are bedraggled and squashed on arrival.

Your suitcase

One last point — in my opinion the soft-sided grips that are becoming very popular are not nearly as good to travel with as a case. Reserve the grip for things that do not pack flat such as your shoes, camera, books, hairdryer etc.

The advantage of packing a case is that it is rigid and has a greater horizontal than vertical area. Clothes can be packed

Nothing is as unbecoming as briefs that cause a bulge. If you are wearing a thin, fine fabric that clings, wear French knickers or boxer pants underneath.

flat and will remain that way, which is vital if they are to be wearable at the other end. More and more airlines charge per number of bags now instead of by weight, so you may as well have one very large, stiff-sided case instead of a number of smaller fabric ones.

Shoe care

Feet are bad for shoes — they distort them. Shoe care must counteract the problems you cause by wearing shoes all day. Ring the changes. Nothing exhausts shoes quicker than being worn day after day with no time to rest.

Cleaning

Feed leather shoes by polishing them — use real polish and a brush. The sprays that shoe shops always try to sell are, in my opinion, a poor substitute for two minutes' brisk elbow work in the traditional way. Brush suede shoes very regularly as they are prone to absorb dust and dirt. Do not use a wire brush, it merely destroys the surface of your shoes. You need a rubber brush or a soft clothes' brush to keep suede shoes clean without tearing them to pieces.

Keep them smart

It is amazing how few women bother with shoe-trees. They are invaluable for retaining your shoes in good shape. Alternatively, stuff old socks into the foot once your shoes have had time to cool down.

Don't get down at heel — nothing looks shabbier than shoes that need to be heeled. Never force a shoe on — you will break its back. Use a shoehorn, the back of a teaspoon or even a hankerchief to ease your foot in.

Treat your shoes well and they will prove a good investment.

*Dear K
Many.

your support and
for an exciting
cooperation,
in 0at.*

WATER
AND
PEACE FOR THE PEOPLE

POSSIBLE SOLUTIONS TO WATER DISPUTES
IN THE MIDDLE EAST

Jon Martin Trondalen

COMPASS

United Nations
Educational, Scientific and
Cultural Organization

UNESCO Publishing

International
Hydrological
Programme

To the people in the region
who are longing for water and peace.

Published in 2008 by the United Nations Educational,
Scientific and Cultural Organization
7, place de Fontenoy, 75352 Paris 07 SP, France.

ISBN 978-92-3-104086-3

Photo credits:
Cover (from left to right): iStockphoto.com/Christine Balderas; iStockphoto.com/
Giovanni Rinaldi; iStockphoto.com/Khonji
Back cover: Hans Petter Foss
All other photos are taken by the author, except for the following for which permission
has kindly been granted:
- Photo 36: Ministry of Water and Irrigation of Iraq
- Photos 20, 21, 22: Joseph Guttman
- Photos 5, 12, 16: Lebanese photographer who prefers to remain anonymous
- Photo 37: Hans Petter Foss

Cover design: Maro Haas
Typeset by UNESCO Publishing/La Moncet
Printed by UNESCO

Also available in Arabic and Hebrew.

Printed in France

Acknowledgements

This publication is about the people, the water and the land of the Middle East, and it is thanks to the guidance from and co-operation with friends and colleagues over the years that I have formed my perception of these matters. I would like to express my personal appreciation to all of them, especially to the political leaders and experts from the various countries who have the courage to share their thoughts regarding solutions to these intricate disputes (in alphabetical order):

- **Iraq:** The many officials and the water experts have over the years given me a unique insight into their daily and long-term challenges. Their hospitality over the years will never be forgotten.
- **Israel:** Very few countries in the world have such a high expertise in water resources management. I have been enlightened by their knowledge, and received a greater understanding and respect of their concerns and hopes.
- **Jordan:** Due to its geographical location and political situation, Jordanian officials and professionals have given valuable perspectives I would otherwise not have received.
- **Lebanon:** The many officials and water professionals have over the years given me a deeper understanding of their way of handling the water issues.
- **Palestinian Authority:** I have had the pleasure to work with many leaders and experts, even before the Oslo Accord, and have learnt to better understand and respect their aspirations and how to handle the problems.
- **Syria:** Warm hospitality has always been shown by the many leaders and experts, and without their guidance through endless meetings and conversations, I would not been given such an appreciation and understanding of their country, of their people, and their waters.
- **Turkey:** Even since the first visits and meetings, officials and water experts have shown me great hospitality and insight, and gained my respect for what they have achieved and still want to pursue.

This book would never have been written if it had not been for my wife Bente. For years, she has walked beside me over the hills and through the valleys – and continued to encourage my work.

I am greatly indebted to my teacher of many years, the late professor Just Gjessing, who taught me to use science for the benefit of people. The foundation of this book is work conducted since the early 1990s, based on systematic notes and photos, which Just always prompted me to take despite the hassle of this mental exercise in the midst of the operational tasks and travelling.

I am profoundly grateful for a few people's encouragement throughout the years, and Kari and Hans Petter Foss are among the first ones to be mentioned.

This book is very much based on technical studies and numerous consultations with delegates from the various countries, and I am indebted to several people who put in a tremendous effort into studies of the Euphrates and Tigris Rivers. The first to be acknowledged is Bjørn Børstad. He has been my close aide and friend, and was responsible for leading the hydrological and water quality modelling of the two rivers as well as for compiling and editing the technical study of the Euphrates and Tigris. He received valuable assistance from his colleagues in COWI and other consultants. Special thanks to David Barton for his insight into water economics.

Many of my students from the University of Oslo became close associates and have over the years been most helpful in every area of water disputes.

Heidi Thorstensen managed the difficult tasks patiently with excellent results. I am also very grateful to Knut Aasberg for his capable work on combining the substance with the computers, especially maps and figures for this publication.

The book would not have been possible without decisive advice and guidance from people in the region. There are many to name, although only a few will be mentioned to represent insights from various countries (in order to avoid sensitivities, political leaders are not mentioned here, although some have had a profound impact on some of my work and proposals). In alphabetical order: Nazih Bandak, the late Ali Ihsan Bagis, Fadi Comair, Moshe Israeli, Badr Kasme, Fadel Kawash, Jacob Keidar, Antoine Nammour, Yigal Salingar, Adnan Shuman and Olcay Unver.

Also outside the region, I have benefited greatly from essential advice and support throughout the years, especially from Vigleik Eide, Les Woller, Tom Bøe, Sir Kieran Prendergast, Michael Möller, Chuck Lawson, Simon Mason, Arne Solli, Ola Vråmo, Henric Immink, Yngve Hanisch as well as from colleagues of COMPASS and, some years ago, former staff at the CESAR Foundation – Ulf Gürgens, Tor Wennesland, and Asgeir Føyen among many others.

A book this long has required meticulous translation, and two associates have undertaken this daunting task. Magdy Hefny made the Arabic translation and another dedicated collaborator the Hebrew one. They are of course not responsible for the content, but should be credited for any fruits that this publication may yield. The English text was initially improved by Gerd Mathisen. My good friends Kathryn and Christopher have, respectively, been responsible for the English editing and the initial design layout. Their skills are not only highly appreciated, but obviously displayed for all throughout the publication.

It has been a great privilege to work with the dedicated staff at UNESCO in Paris, and I am very grateful to András Szollosi-Nagy for his leadership and insight into international water resources management and current affairs. Léna Salamé has provided assistance and guidance, for which I am also greatly indebted. The highly dedicated staff of UNESCO Publishing has done an outstanding task.

Finally, but not least, I am deeply thankful to Christina and Andreas. They have remained remarkably patient and supportive despite an absent father throughout all these years. Their generation will be the one "to make a difference".

Above all, I am grateful to the various Departments and Agencies of the UN, and the Ministries of Foreign Affairs of Norway and Switzerland, for their support of various projects in the region.

All the people mentioned above are part of any success of this publication, but have no responsibility for any failures, unintended misrepresentation, or errors in this book.

Table of contents

This book presents a compelling case for water as a source of co-operation in an area that is otherwise loaded with conflicts.

Dr. Trondalen, a seasoned veteran of multilateral peace talks on water in the Middle East, offers comprehensive solutions in which water connects rather than divides. Just as in nature, one could argue. This is a major work that will hopefully be an eye-opener for all concerned: politicians, water experts and, most importantly, the people of the region. Peaceful solutions do exist and could serve everybody's interests, provided there is the will to find them.

This is the first publication in the International Hydrological Programme's new series on 'Water and Conflict Resolution'. It is an important contribution to UNESCO's paramount mandate, to nurture the idea of peace in human minds.

Andras Szollosi-Nagy
Secretary of the International Hydrological Programme
Director, Division of Water Sciences
UNESCO

List of abbreviations

AIC	Actual incremental costs
CESAR	Centre for Environmental Studies and Resource Management
CFR	Compensation for foregone resettlement
COWI	International consulting group
CSD	Commission on Sustainable Development
DOP	Declaration of Principles
DMZ	De-militarized zones
EAWAG	Swiss Federal Institute of Aquatic Science and Technology
EBSAP	Ecological Benefits Strategic Assessment Plan
ETI	Euphrates and Tigris Basins Initiative
ETI-TF	Euphrates and Tigris Basins Initiative Trust Fund
EU	European Union
FAO	United Nations Food and Agricultural Organization
GEF	Global Environment Facility
GS	Gaza Strip
GWMS	Golan Heights Water Resource Monitoring System
GAP	Southeastern Anatolia Development Project [Turkish: Güneydoğu Anadolu Projesi]
GWh	Gigawatt hour
ICARD	International Center for Agricultural Research in the Dry Areas
ISA	Incremental step approach
JSET	Joint Supervising and Enforcement Teams
JTC	Joint Technical Committee
JWC	Joint Water Commission
MCM	Million cubic metres
MIC	Maximum incremental costs
NAFTA	North American Free Trade Agreement
NBI	Nile Basin Initiative
NGO	Non-governmental organization
NSC	National Security Council
O&M	Operation and maintenance
OECD	Organisation for Economic Co-operation and Development
PA	Palestinian Authority
PLO	Palestine Liberation Organization
PWA	Palestinian Water Authority

RWMO	Regional Water Management Organization
SAP	Subsidiary Action Programme
SIWI	Stockholm International Water Institute
SVP	Shared Vision Programme
TBSAP	Tigris Basin Subsidiary Action Programme
TDS	Total dissolved solids (expression for the dissolved minerals in the water - TDS impact on water)
TF	Trust fund
TPCM	Third party compensation mechanism
UN	United Nations
UNDOF	United Nations Disengagement Observer Force
UNDP	United Nations Development Programme
UNEP	United Nations Environment Programme
UNIFIL	United Nations Interim Force in Lebanon
US	United States
WB	West Bank
WBGS	West Bank and Gaza Strip
UNCED	United Nations Conference on Environment and Development
UNFCCC	United Nations Framework Convention on Climate Change
UNCUIW	United Nations Convention on the Law of the Non-navigational Uses of International Watercourses (often called UN Water Convention)
UNTSO	United Nations Truce Supervision Organization
UNECE	United Nations Economic Commission for Europe
UNESCWA	United Nations Economic and Social Commission of Western Asia
WGWR	Working Group on Water Resources

Explanation of terms

- 'Dispute' is used synonymously with 'conflict'.
- 'Parties' refers to Turkey, Syria, Iraq, Lebanon, Israel and the Palestinian Authority – in some cases meaning only some of them.
- 'Palestinian Authority' (PA) refers to the formal Palestinian Authority (PA) as defined by the PLO (DOP, 1993).
- A 'river system' comprises both the main course and each of the tributaries that feed into it. The area drained by the river system is known as the 'catchment' or 'watercourse'.
- 'Basin' is used synonymously with 'watershed', 'catchment' or 'watercourse'.
- An 'aquifer' is considered to be any water-bearing or aquiferous stratum.
- 'International water resources/watercourses' is preferred over 'shared international water resources'.
- A 'water management regime' is a water arrangement that specifies the use of water flow according to certain timescales and water quality specifications.
- 'Return-flow' refers to the drainage water from irrigated land that could go to surface- and groundwater (compared to 'runoff' which is natural drainage).
- 'Bargaining' addresses the positions of the Parties, while 'interest-based negotiation' addresses the real interests or concerns of the Parties.
- 'Conflict management' comprises prevention, avoidance, settlement and resolution.
- 'Sustainable governance' in this context means sustainable solutions to management of international watercourses.
- The lake in the Upper Jordan River Basin is referred to as Lake Tiberias (also known as Lake Kinneret or the Sea of Galilee, a Biblical expression).
- The contemporary expression of the geographic area of the West Bank is used instead of the Jewish expression of Judea and Samaria, which includes a larger area.
- Some names have different spellings, such as Hasbani, Hasbanye or Hasbanya (termed *Snir* by Israel). As far as possible, the most common names in the English literature are applied.
- 'Virtual' or 'invisible' water refers to water that may be substituted, for example by importing food that would have required national water if produced locally.

Various 'water monitoring and verification systems' are proposed, using the following concepts:
- 'Monitoring': the systematic surveillance and measurement of defined parameters.
- 'Verification': confirmation, by examination and provision of objective evidence, that results have been achieved or that specific requirements have been fulfilled (or status of requirements).
- 'Auditing': a systematic, independent and documented process for obtaining evidence and evaluating it against agreed-upon, pre-set criteria.
- The 'rule curve': a function that defines the use of water – either for power production or for irrigation.

List of maps

List of tables

List of figures

List of photos

Preface

This publication not only presents information about, but proposes possible remedies to, the serious challenges faced by countries in managing their international water resources in the Middle East. International water conflicts are becoming more entrenched, and unless solutions are found the whole region will face even more serious water problems than today. In the foreseeable future, this may threaten the already fragile stability in the Middle East.

Demand for water in the region is constantly increasing. This is due to the combination of rapid population growth and a steady social and economic development that is incommensurable with existing natural water resources. It is therefore easy to overexploit and pollute the waters at the expense of coming generations. Water disputes in the region are hindering effective water use as well as fuelling political flames that have already been lit.

Some may say that the political questions should be settled first, with water disputes being addressed afterwards. However, water is such a valuable and basic human need that countries have an intergenerational duty to solve the problems relating to it. Such an obligation is also rooted in the three monotheistic religions – Judaism, Christianity and Islam.

Remedies to the water disputes in the Middle East are a long-term imperative. Conciliation between countries should not be destroyed by such disputes. Indeed, providing water and peace to the people, and especially for the poorest, is far more important than short-term political schisms, however entrenched.

Therefore, despite the limitations of the outlined proposals, this book offers at least some ways out in order to grant people access to water for drinking and food security.

Background

Hope for peace and prosperity has gradually vanished over recent years for most of the people in the region. They have learnt that governments are hard to trust and that dwindling natural resources are becoming scarce. History has also revealed that unless hope and some degree of trust are built up, no progress will be made.

In principle, each country could adopt a unilateral approach to managing sovereign natural resources such as water. Unfortunately, reality is less simple. Many of the contested waters cross borders that require some sort of jointly agreed-on arrangement. Since all Member States of the United Nations have signed several international environmental protocols and conventions, they have also accepted that issues such as transboundary water pollution must be tackled in co-operation.

The discussion and fight over water resources can provoke hostile relationships between countries. However, they also offer an opportunity for nations to co-operate and build cross-border confidence,

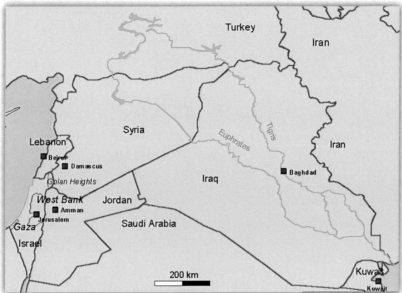

Map 1. Middle East region

in order to safeguard a basic need for their peoples and guide the usage of one of the most precious natural resources.

Conflicts over dwindling water resources in the Middle East are not new. Indeed, references to them date back as far as the Scriptures shared among Muslims, Jews and Christians. According to Genesis, Chapter 26, the two wells in the land of the Philistines were eventually called Strife and Hatred.

This publication deals with sensitive political, religious, cultural, social, economic and environmental matters. It may merely be considered as a good non-partisan effort, but some considerations should be taken into account:

▸ the results of the studies and many of the main elements in the proposals have evolved over several years, but were not made public previously as this was not considered conducive to finding common ground;

▸ the intent is to offer solutions from a non-partisan perspective that might otherwise have been perceived as one-sided if given by one of the Parties or by other concerned stakeholders; and

▸ the combining of epistemic work with actual engagement in processes, negotiations and even concrete projects has led to the conviction that the solutions to the disputes are to harmonize the interests of the Parties,[I] and that an explanation of the stated disputes cannot be found in a single discipline – in fact a single disciplinary approach is incorrect[II].

I.   As also expressed by the French diplomat, Francois de Calliéres (de Calliéres, 2002).

II. The author is well aware that an interdisciplinary approach runs the "risk of attracting the very sharp and even destructive analysis of elements of… [its] arguments by scientists with more specific disciplinary expertise in a particular episteme. In taking the scientifically hazardous interdisciplinary road one must be prepared for the ambushes of the scientifically well armed" (Allan, 2002: 21). However, this publication aims to offer realistic solutions that cannot be limited to a single discipline. See also Gjessing (2002).

There is a degree of uncertainty as regards the timing of the publication due to the unpredictability of events in the region. In any case, the need to manage the precious water resources and proposals are valid irrespective of the ebb and flow of politics.

Recent events

Since the manuscript of this book was completed at the beginning of 2006, dramatic events have taken place in the region. These include the increased hostilities between Israelis and Palestinians in Gaza; the Hamas overtaking of Gaza; and Hezbollah's subsequent targeting of Israeli soldiers at their common border with the ensuing skirmishes escalating into violent and warlike damage to humans and infrastructure. The latter event prompted a revised mandate of the UN Peacekeeping Mission, UNIFIL, in Southern Lebanon in the Upper Jordan Basin.

These events are important and dramatic. However, they do not change the basic diagnosis of the water conflicts, or the proposed solutions. On the contrary, they underline the importance of removing the causes of tension and conflict by proposing sustainable solutions.

Facilitating and building consensus among the parties

Crafting dialogue and understanding

Very little information is provided on how the crafting of dialogue, facilitation and understanding was carried out. This is first and foremost because such issues might draw public attention at the expense of the substance of the book. Secondly, the involvement of colleagues and partners is a sensitive issue, and the confidentiality of such processes should be respected. However, I discuss briefly below some of my involvement in dialogue and facilitation.

Lessons learned

The relationships between the countries of the Middle East are expressed in certain ways. One of these is the political drama, where rhetoric and various types of influence groups dominate. People outside the region often misinterpret such communication and assume that the status of relationships reflects the degree of tension in statements. One must therefore be aware that the political rhetoric sometime runs so high that it is hard to understand what is really going on.

There is, however, another layer of communication. This is often overlooked and consists of a constant flow of information between varying factions, constituencies and nations. Some of these channels, often named 'tracks', are public-diplomacy or 'behind-the-scene' initiatives. In some instances, leaders have one public channel of communication in addition to several secret or non-public ones. Quite often, the latter are characterized or supported by so-called 'track-two diplomatic approaches' where 'disinterested' diplomats, in collaboration with business leaders, scientists or other experts, craft channels of communication between the Parties.

I have worked primarily as a so-called 'impartial' or 'unbiased' expert, in the sense that I have not had any hidden personal, political or other agendas. In a politically-charged region such as the Middle East, it is obvious that what takes place behind the scenes should mostly remain there. Contrary to common belief, the main reason for this is not that clandestine activities or transactions are taking place. Rather, it is that certain issues are better dealt with in confined circles. Equally important, the individuals involved have a right to confidentiality. In some sensitive geographical, political and religious areas, such activities may even constitute a real danger not only to the process itself, but also to individuals' personal security.

Many facilitators, mediators and negotiators are therefore quite reluctant to outline how and with whom they work. I subscribe to such a discreet approach, and have in only two instances published experiences in setting up, facilitating and chairing talks in the Middle East. These include the process that led to the first trilateral water agreement in the Middle East – the so-called Declaration of Principles for Co-operation on Water-related Matters and New and Additional Water Resources of 1996 (see Trolldalen [Trondalen], 1997) – and a manual on dispute resolution (written for UNESCWA, Trondalen, 2004a).

Do personal experiences as a negotiator have a value for others?
Although it is quite common for envoys with a high public profile to publish their experience and lessons learnt, the value of these personal experiences for others is not always clear. This also applies to myself. However, as observers have challenged me to shed light on my experience working with the four disputes outlined in the book, a number of selected reflections are highlighted below.

Any experienced negotiator has found his/her way of working through dedication, loyalty, empathy, analytical skills, knowledge and the ability to handle stress. There are no panaceas for resolving international water disputes. However, some lessons that may be applicable are like common denominators in an equation, which you must strive to find in order to improve your own performance and that of your delegation.

One may wonder whether a successful negotiator always gets what she/he wants – irrespective of circumstances. Some observers may have a clear answer; I do not, simply because success is hard to define. Both success and common errors are briefly discussed below:

Some workable principles in setting up and developing a process
In many ways, the crafting of a process is an expression of both an explicit attitude (and values) and a modus operandi. In the two publications, the author focused on the following principles:
- understanding of and sensitivity to the political and cultural context of the dispute;
- problem identification and understanding of positions and interests, to be carried out prior to and during the negotiations (such as: What are the main questions? What data do we need to answer those questions, and how reliable and valid are these data?);

- development of a common understanding of collective concerns. This requires some basic understanding of the core issues, or at least a willingness to clarify them;
- providing information and data for an interest-based negotiation (versus bargaining process);
- establishing official contacts at a certain stage in the process, i.e. legitimizing efforts in a diplomatic context by 'track-two' bridging with other diplomatic approaches;
- mobilizing existing experience through government agencies, resource people and non-governmental organizations (NGOs); and
- involving the public. This can be quite difficult as the processes are not by nature 'open' and transparent. However, experience in the region has shown that lack of public ownership of agreements may severely hamper implementation.

Some lessons for delegates

Selected condensed and simplified lessons learnt for negotiations are listed below:

- Although not entirely obvious when delegates are in the middle of a tense negotiation, it is important to clarify interests, not positions. This does not mean that tactical points should be given away, but rather that the other Party should be guided towards solutions that are more important for your Party's interest.
- In practical terms, this means that a delegate must constantly develop her or his options and consider those of others. Any experienced negotiator will intuitively devise options for mutual benefit, simply because this is where the solutions are.
- An obvious lesson, but still hard to apply, is distinguishing between people and their constituencies. Many scholars argue hard for this point, but I am somewhat more pragmatic in my dealings. A skilled negotiator is able to convey his/her country's point of view in such a way that the other Party is constantly challenged by this distinction. Delegates may be able to act respectfully without jeopardizing their own country's interests.
- This leads to the next and obvious point – treat people with respect – irrespective of the circumstances.
- One of the best ways for a delegate to avoid the most obvious pitfalls is by improving his or her understanding of the other Party's cultural background and psychological frame of mind.
- In any case, a delegate must mentally process simultaneously a set of technical, political, diplomatic and emotional issues. This is demanding, and sometimes the pressure will make it even harder. (For a more in-depth discussion, see Trondalen, 2004a).

Common errors

Common errors are sometimes easier to identify than successes. Irrespective of political, cultural, political and technical complexity, at least four major findings are applicable to a negotiator and to a delegation as a whole:

- not listening to the other Party(ies), especially when the talks are getting tense. Equally detrimental is not showing that you are listening;
- focusing on positions; ignoring interests. This sounds easy, but is very hard in real negotiations. In everyday conversations, very few people make an explicit distinction between what is said and what is really behind the phrases. Any skilful negotiator will achieve this decisive ability;

▸ lack of knowledge of the particular subject or related issues is also, unfortunately, typical. The consequences of this are in most cases disastrous in terms of reaching an agreement. Most unskilled negotiators will block proposals and develop a defensive and reactive behavioural approach;

▸ limiting options (inventing vs. deciding) is often a consequence of the latter point. However, a delegate may have substantial knowledge about the matter, but not the right mindset. Inventing options is more about attitude than technical understanding. If the head of a delegation or anyone on the team has neither the power nor ability to invent/decide on options, they will probably not reach a solution unless the negotiations are taking place over an exceptionally long time (probably years rather than months).

What can change a gridlocked situation between watercourse countries?

There are hardly any panaceas for changing gridlocked situations, especially in the Middle East. The following techniques are often advocated in more academic literature, but I have also experienced their usefulness first-hand:

▸ new substantive information – or rather, new information provided to key decision-makers;
▸ new trade-offs between two or more of them;
▸ a changed general political climate or relationships; and
▸ new external power brokers (extra-regional Parties).

Quite often, the broader conditions are beyond the influence of negotiators and delegates. An interesting question becomes: What underestimated factors hamper progress?

Underestimated factors in international water negotiations

▸ The role of an individual negotiator: Experience has shown that 'able negotiatiors are able to negotiate'. Indeed, discussions on 'smart', 'hard or tough', or even 'soft' negotiators is of more academic than practical value. Negotiators that both understand the substance and have talents in dealing with complex issues as well as personal relationships are – without a doubt – the best envoys for the respective Parties.

▸ In many instances, the delegates should possess satisfactory bargaining power: A too-strict mandate often hinders new perspectives and development of options.

▸ In addition, the format and setting of the meeting: where it takes place, and under what kind of circumstances. Practical factors ensuring that the meeting will take place under secure and confidential conditions have been proven to be surprisingly important. They include in which country (a 'neutral' one) the meeting is held, at what time, whether there is accommodation close to the negotiating tables, etc. In this respect, the facilitator/mediator must be sensitive to the delegates' personal well-being (even on issues like family considerations and safety).

Reservations

Despite the attempt to crystallize some lessons learnt, my experience is that a general humbleness to the sheer complexity of the relevant water disputes, peoples and political concerns, limited realistic options and financial constraints is not only wise, but necessary for fostering sustainable solutions. Quick-fixing may provide short-lived rewards, but long-term agony for the people in the region could be the final outcome of such an approach.

The suggested solutions to the four water disputes should be viewed as an effort to incorporate the lessons and make a contribution that could foster sustainable water management while addressing the concerns of the people.

Water and peace for the people

In 1997 in Iraq, I met Abdullah, a farmer living in a village on the riverside at Al Hilla (in the ancient city of Babylon, 100 km south of Baghdad), close to the Euphrates River. He showed me the salt layer on the topsoil that was destroying his field – a plot his forefathers had cultivated for centuries. Together with his countrymen and women, he was tired of bearing the burden of the international sanctions against Iraq. He asked only for a small pump in order to get rid of the drainage water that could save the land of his village (in 1997, UN sanctions did not allow for the easy import of pumps).

■ Photo 1.
An irrigation channel on the plain east of the Euphrates River in Mesopotamia.

■ Photo 2.
A water pump in Gaza

In the Gaza Strip, Nasser painstakingly cares for his precious pump, which provides water for a small vegetable garden behind his house. Despite the salty taste, his family drinks the water from the aquifer situated under the Gaza Strip. Yet Nasser lives in constant fear, as he can only run the pump at night. This is because it is one of the thousands of so-called 'black wells' in Gaza, an unauthorized well beyond the control of the Palestinian Authority. "What kind of options do I have?", he asked me, "I was hard pressed! I have a family as well!".

In Israel, in the Upper Jordan River just before it reaches Lake Tiberias, the figures were convincing, the data was reliable and the conclusions were conclusive. Avi – the dedicated scholar – gave me the hard facts: Unless the sensitive hydro-ecological Lake Kinneret and the mountain aquifer are protected, Israel will face a water crisis beyond imaginable dimensions. The country will simply dry out. He goes on to describe how they are turning to manufacturing water and reducing water consumed by the agricultural sector. Desalinized water from the Mediterranean is one of the scant options in order to secure water for his growing nation.

■ Photo 3.
The Jordan River just before it reaches Lake Tiberias

In Turkey, close to what religious texts refer to as the birthplace of the Patriarch Abraham, near

the Euphrates River on the plains of Sanliurfa in the south-eastern part of Turkey, Suleiman was obviously very pleased that his village could finally make full use of the richness of the soil to double, and even triple, agricultural production. He considered that the central government was paying attention to the concerns of his village and family, after having been backlogged for decades. Now, huge hydropower installations not only benefited the people in the area, but also responded to the rest of the country's increased demand for energy and food. He was proud of his country's accomplishments, which I could readily understand.

■ Photo 4.
An ancient building in *Al Hilla* of the old Babylon

In Southern Lebanon, in the not-so-distant past, there were armed clashes in the area around the village of Amid. Today, however, his extended family, living in the picturesque landscape in the southern part of Lebanon, is benefiting from calm conditions as they wait for the new water pipe to be installed, so that drinking water and agricultural production may develop. He admits that they all are tired of political strife and simply want a little water in order to sustain their daily life and live peacefully – finally, after all these years.

■ Photo 5.
Water pipes at the Wazzani Springs in southern Lebanon

In Syria, higher up on the Euphrates River, Adnan, a young engineer at the new Thesreen dam project in Syria, showed me around the dam site under

construction. He knew he was part of a national effort to improve the efficiency with which the water of the Euphrates was used, for the benefit of people in the major cities and for agriculture. The area suffered from lowering of the groundwater and an increasing number of dry wells. The rapidly growing city of Aleppo, in the vicinity, was struggling to maintain a clean water supply. Adnan told me that there were plans to supply Damascus with drinking water from the river. He felt privileged to be a part of one of the major engineering works in his country.

■ Photo 6.
The fertile plains outside Aleppo in Syria

Executive summary

The book is divided into three sections. It pinpoints some of the current water conflicts, stressing their gravity and magnitude, but more importantly outlining principles and procedures for solving them.

- ▸ **Section I** is divided into two parts. The first deals with the dispute related to the Golan Heights and Upper Jordan River Basins involving Syria and Israel, while the second deals with the more recent Wazzani Spring dispute between Israel and Lebanon.
- ▸ **Section II** is quite different in nature, dealing with the water dispute between the Palestinians and the Israelis.
- ▸ **Section III** deals with the challenges faced by Turkey, Syria and Iraq in managing the Euphrates and Tigris Rivers.

Some may argue that each of the four disputes should be assessed together, in the sense that water could be transferred from one basin to another. I do not take this view, simply because the political setting – for the time being and in the near future – is not conducive to such proposals.

Introduction

Before turning to the four disputes, and in an attempt to explore overall and universal reference points applicable to the prevention and resolution of water disputes, some background, methods and policies are set out below.

Reference points in the discussion on water disputes in the Middle East

Over thousands of years, everyday problems in the Middle East have demanded urgent solutions – quite often with a dramatic outfall of historic proportions. For people living there and for outsiders, the waves of political events often reduce their perspectives and demand urgent actions.

Water has played its part in the historic web – for good and for bad. It remains at the centre stage of the daily life of people as well as in the relationship between nations, and gives a way to hope. However, there are some new traits in water management, some of which are alarming even within the perspective of one generation.

This publication aims to incorporate the constraints and opportunities in the proposed solutions to some of the most pressing water disputes in the region. It is important to understand that the causes of the conflicts are many and complex, and that any solutions should be presented with the utmost caution and reservations. The danger is that solutions will be outlined that are too associated with the point on the timeline and not in an intergenerational perspective, from which any water management should be viewed.[1]

> The key problem, however, appears to be how to enlarge the pie rather than try to enlarge one of the pieces at the expense of another Party.

The proposals to the disputes outlined aim to incorporate the hard facts on the ground. Half of the urban populations in the larger cities in the region do not have adequate drinking water facilities. Moreover, pollution of surface and underground water is rapidly developing, a problem for which the governments do not have proper remedies. Lack of agreement between the Parties hinders the effective and fair use of resources, leading to short-term and temporary solutions.

> ...creating a gap between the reality at the negotiation table and the reality on the ground has been a mistake in many past efforts...

Lessons learnt from deliberations with the Parties[2] have shown that creating a gap between the reality at the negotiation table among leaders and the reality on the ground – even among the enlightened public – has been a mistake in many past efforts.[3] Experience has shown that in the course of the political rhetoric, the public has sometimes not been given a picture of what might be realistic and what may even be factually incorrect information. This publication attempts to promote moderate positions in situations where every contester wants a larger piece of the pie than might be physically feasible. The key problem, however, appears to be how to enlarge the pie rather than try to enlarge one of the pieces at the expense of another Party.

Historic lines

Three basic historic lines appear to be of importance in proposing solutions to the water conflicts. A Biblical perspective cannot be isolated from contemporary history. However, in the search for solutions, current statehoods and borders as well as international agreements and water practices seem to be of more significance.

The first line is characterized by the recent centuries of water management of the major rivers and aquifers, which has occurred with few changes. During the Turkish Ottoman era (around 1570-1920), all of the current 'four disputed waters' were handled by the institutions under Turkish control and management. Except for a general shortage of water and more or less regular annual acute scarcity, the disputes were solved by the administration at the level of the Governor, or even among villages and cities.

The second line began *circa* 1923 with the establishment of the contemporary Arab nations as we more or less know them today and the founding of the State of Israel in 1948. Then, in 1967, as a result of the Arab-Israeli war with the subsequent annexations by Israel of the Gaza Strip from Egypt, the Golan Heights from Syria and the West Bank from Jordan, borders were created that form a central part of the disputes.

The third line encompasses the intervention in Iraq by an international coalition in January 1991 and, subsequently, the invasion of March 2003. The present Iraqi-US relationship is expected to influence not only internal Iraqi affairs, but also its relationship with other countries in the region. This situation has created a geopolitical situation of particular significance for any agreement to jointly manage the Euphrates and Tigris Rivers.

Neither of the conflicts can be understood and therefore resolved unless these historic lines and political realities are accepted. Most people take a normative point of view on some of these events. This publication does not belong to an unreal world that pretends that these events are not disputed. Rather, it argues that the solutions to the water disputes are to be found in mirroring the past with current political opportunities rather than constraints.

Today's situation

Unfortunately, water issues cannot be detached from current and protracted political events in the region (see Allan, 2002: 242 who also refers to Lowi, 1990: 375, Shapland, 1997 and Turton, 1997: 32). The situation today is grave, and will be even worse tomorrow unless political events take a rapid and positive turn. This is because scientists have demonstrated that the Middle East will be the first region in history to run out of water (Allan, 2002: 9; Rogers, 1994; and Allan, 1994). As one of the most renowned international water experts phrased it: "Meanwhile, the peoples and their leaders in the region refuse to recognise these resource and economic realities.

Their interpretations of Middle East hydrological and economic contexts are at best underinformed and at worst dangerous; their perception of global hydrological and economic contexts is unsafe" (Allan, 2002: 9).

The Middle East will be the first region in history to run out of water.

This publication argues that there are ways out of this situation. However, they require action to be taken by the Parties involved and the international community. Some commonly accepted international water management principles that will be applied in proposing solutions are therefore outlined below.

Transforming policy into concrete strategies[III]

Principles of water management are hard to agree upon, especially if they are concrete enough to have an operational meaning. Vague policy concepts may prove useful academically, but in the reality of the Middle East have hardly any value. Much effort has been put into policy development and the design of international principles, yet very little into the translation of those principles into concrete and lasting governance. There is indeed no shortage of well-developed policies and legislative frameworks. The problem is rather that countries apply these policies and principles according to what serves their tactical and strategic interests. Some of them are listed below:

1. International water laws, such as the UN's Convention on the Law of the Non-navigational Use of International Watercourses[4] and the Helsinki Rules. The first (which is still not ratified) is the most quoted by the international legal community.[5] Despite the weakness of these legal instruments, they are considered to contain the most important principles in managing international watercourses.

2. Other international water agreements in specific regions (such as for the UN ESCWA Region) are setting precedence for future ones (including customary law). International law, in general, and environmental laws specifically include emerging codes of conduct, declarations, protocols and conventions in global environmental matters. The UNCED meeting in Rio de Janeiro in 1992 (UN Conference on Environment and Development) and more recently the Johannesburg Summit with its UN Commission on Sustainable Development (CSD) affirmed relevant principles in order to achieve sustainable development at the local, national and international levels[6].

3. Regional agreements and legislation, as in the European Union, Organisation for Economic Co-operation and Development (OECD) and North American Free Trade Agreement (NAFTA), from which we may draw lessons transferable to the Middle East. These may include guidelines developed by international institutions such as the Operational Directives of the World Bank and other regional development banks, which set a code of conduct for international water management.

Many nations adhere to these principles. However, when the stakes are high enough, legal tools are often applied both ways. For example, the notion of 'equitable utilization' set out in the UN Framework Convention on the Law of the Non-navigational Uses of International Watercourses can 'conveniently' be applied to countries situated both upstream and downstream in a river basin.

III   See also Trondalen, 2004a.

Special water arrangements for the Middle East?

Contrary to some observers dealing with international water management, I argue that sustainable governance of most water resources is a matter of complex political sensitivities, especially in the Middle East. Ready-made regional co-operative models of water management are therefore not directly applicable to every geographical, political, economic and social setting.

Special arrangements should thus be developed. There are several reasons for this. Each country has its own history in using a particular international water resource; quite often, the internal political situation is such that water usage may change. In addition, strained and other inflexible relationships with neighbouring countries call for a constant search for applicable principles – so-called 'yardsticks' that can be used in developing common understanding. Finally, each existing water agreement in the region is tailored to the specific physical and political conditions.

Some would argue that a single approach to resolution should be applied in all of the four cases. However, in practice this has proven to be very difficult. There are, of course, some economic and legal yardsticks applicable to all four cases. However, the emphasis should be different due to the specificity of the conditions stated above.

What kind of yardsticks may be applied in sustainable governance of international watercourses in the Middle East?[IV]

In some cases, countries share and allocate international water resources in the spirit of 'good neighbourliness', 'equitable utilization', and even 'non-appreciable harm'. The academic literature records several success stories, especially in Europe and even in more complex areas such as the Mekong Basin in Indo-China and the Indus Basin (Kammerud, 1997). It therefore seems wise to look at some experiences from other parts of the world that may provide us with some clues as to how things may work out in the region.

Management of international watercourses offers unique opportunities for co-operation between the states concerned. Notably, 158 of the world's 263 international basins lack any type of co-operative management framework. Furthermore, of the 106 basins with water institutions (that are in charge in one way or another of a basin), approximately two thirds have three or more riparian states, yet less than 20 per cent of the accompanying agreements are multilateral. Despite the recent progress noted above, treaties with substantive references to water quality management, monitoring and evaluation, conflict resolution, public participation and flexible allocation methods remain in the minority. As a result, most existing international water agreements continue to lack the tools necessary to promote long-term, sustainable governance of water management (see also Wolf, Natharius and Danielson, 1999).

> Management of international watercourses offers unique opportunities for co-operation between the states concerned.

IV   Derived from Trondalen, 2004a.

Sustainable management of international watercourses can be discussed from various perspectives. Traditionally, water disputes are analyzed from either an upstream or a downstream perspective. In practice, however, an interest-based perspective is quite different from the conventional upstream-downstream doctrine. This more pragmatic – and possibly more contemporary – viewpoint overweighs the earlier approach, and is based on the concept of sustainable development (as utilized in Trondalen and Munasinghe, 1999). It relies on the balanced application of three of the most important principles in dealing with international resources: social equity; economic efficiency; and environmental protection (including public health).

These widely accepted principles also have implications for activities in other sectors that use natural resources, such as energy, trade, tourism and transport.[7] For most complex watercourses, any mechanism must be simple in application, but thoroughly developed in its economic, social and political contexts.

Before discussing these principles in more detail, the development that has led to international acceptance – including by countries in the Middle East – of these principles is outlined below.

Historical development of internationally accepted principles[v]

National and international environmental and resource management problems were first put on the international agenda at the United Nations' Stockholm Environmental Conference in 1972. Since that time, the international community, national authorities and local groups have frequently discussed environmental problems, often in view of sustainable development. The World Commission for Environment and Development or so-called 'Brundtland Commission' of 1987 is first and foremost highly regarded due to its achievement of worldwide acceptance of the notion of 'sustainable development'.

As a result of the universal acceptance of this concept, the United Nations organized the largest conference of its kind on environment and development: the United Nations Conference on Environment and Development (UNCED) that took place in Rio de Janeiro in 1992. All of the members of the United Nations accepted a document called AGENDA 21, which recommended, among others, four main principles in order to achieve sustainable development at the local, national and international levels.

These principles are:
1. the polluter pays principle;
2. the precautionary principle;
3. the principle of national responsibility for transboundary pollution (including subsequent compensation); and
4. the principle of institutionalized or mandatory environmental impact assessment.

---

v   Trondalen and Munasinge, 1999.

All four principles have been embedded in several recent major international environmental conventions, such as the Basel Convention (international transportation of hazardous materials), Montreal Protocol (protection of the ozone layer), Forestry Protocol and most importantly the UN Framework Convention on Climatic Change (UNFCCC)[VI].

These widely accepted international principles have implications for activities in other international sectors that use natural resources such as water, energy, trade, tourism and transportation.

In parallel to the deliberations for the protection of the ozone layer, Forestry Protocol and UNFCCC, the UN drafted the Convention on the Law of the Non-navigational Uses of International Watercourses. This latter includes the purpose of these widely accepted international principles, although three major upstream states – China, Turkey and Burundi – voted against the convention.

The principles

In terms of extracting relevant principles for water management from the widely accepted principles of the existing international environmental agreements, the Water Convention (UNCUIW) and UNFCCC are perhaps of most interest. The precautionary principle is interpreted here to mean that lack of knowledge is not a valid reason for inaction, especially if such inaction entails potentially disastrous consequences. The polluter pays principle is recognized by urging the watercourse countries to shoulder the burden of the response strategy.

At first, the complementary principle prohibiting pollution and assigning responsibility was limited to the protection of the territory and the resources of other nations. They were later extended to cover protection of the marine environment in general, including the 'high seas'. More recently, they have been extended to cover the protection of common areas, resources and the environment as a whole.

What is of interest in the field of international waterways is that the principles relating to liability for environmental damage caused seems to be developing significantly, and the damage does not need to be of a direct economic nature in order to attribute responsibility. A general requirement of the harmonization of liability insurance seems to be emerging so as to ensure adequate compensation for the victims. This has been applied particularly to the field of marine pollution and transportation of hazardous goods. Both the 1989 Convention on Civil Liability for Oil Pollution and the Convention on Civil Liability for Damage Caused during Carriage of Dangerous Goods by Road, Rail and Inland Navigation Vessels apply to such regimes.[8]

As of today, there are no water agreements in the Middle East relating to environmental or resources damage and liability between any of the Parties (except in the case of damage in relation to oil

---

VI   A so-called second generation environmental convention.

pipelines). It may be premature to include such clauses in current water agreements, but due to the general development of environmental liability, they will have to be integrated in future.

Political sensitivities in the region, even on straightforward matters such as water quality standards, are an argument in favour of the development of simple water agreements. However, unless they also include the increasingly generally accepted principles described above, they may backfire down the road. Nevertheless, any sustainable water management regime must be simple in application, thus reflecting political realism.

All the Parties[VII] dealt with in this publication are signatories to the UNCED-declaration and the UNFCCC, and are therefore in general agreement with the underlying principles described earlier. An incremental approach based on these principles may be used as an input to the proposed water agreements. The following three fundamental aspects mentioned above should therefore include:

Economic aspects
▸ Consider costs and benefits of water production and use (including shadow costs of externalities) for each individual Party.
▸ Allocate costs and benefits equitably: polluter pays; those gaining compensate losers to help build consensus.

Social equity
▸ Identify all stakeholders as well as the incidence of costs and benefits of water production and use among them (including externalities).
▸ Compromise between extremes for allocation of water benefits.
▸ Grandfathering, based on past usage patterns.
▸ Equal right to meet basic human needs (e.g on a per capita basis).
▸ Adjust the costs of supplying water to meet basic water needs and affordability.

Environmental aspects
▸ Treat water as a scarce environmental resource that is not generally substitutable.
▸ Minimize both depletion and pollution based on dynamic/long-term considerations.

Water quality in international water agreements
Water quality is a critical part of the environment. Unless water is of a certain quality, it cannot be used for drinking or irrigation. Unless it is treated, or if the purchase of bottled water is not possible, the consequences are potentially catastrophic for the daily life of common people.

This has been increasingly acknowledged. More and more countries are including protection of water quality into agreements with their neighbours. The question is: How much of a tradition

---

VII Except for Iraq, due to its status in the UN since 1991, but there are strong reasons to believe that they will sign in due course.

is this? This was looked into by Hamner and Wolf (2000), who reviewed 145 treaties from the Transboundary Freshwater Dispute Database and found that most treaties focus on hydropower (39 per cent), with 37 per cent covering water distribution for consumption. Seventy-eight of the 145 treaties studied (54 per cent) have provisions for water monitoring. (It should be noted that CESAR commissioned the Department of Oregon State University to develop this study without their prior knowledge of the Technical Study of the Euphrates and the Tigris Rivers outlined in *Part III*.)

Sixty-three of the 228 agreements reviewed (or 28 per cent) contain references to water quality. Seven were classified as Category One agreements (explicit standards), 40 as Category Two (general objectives), and 16 as Category Three (vague commitments – see more discussion in *Part III*).

The new generation of water agreements and standards, such as the UN Convention on the Law of the Non-Navigational Uses of International Watercourses and the EU Framework Directive on Water, contain protection of water quality. The latter includes very strict water quality standards and monitoring procedures. Today, the Directive goes far beyond any existing water standards set in the Middle East.

In combination with the notion of national sovereignty over water resources, the above principles form the basic approach of this publication. However, a question remains: How may sovereignty be applied when developing solutions?

Water rights and national sovereignty over water resources

Each country that shares an international water resource with another state could claim rights to the resource in one way or another. An obvious consequence of the state's sovereignty is its claiming of the right to own, access, control and use the resource. Since the concept of sovereignty and water rights is frequently used in the public and professional debate, as well as in the legal terminology[9], a translation of these terms into concepts that might be applied in operational negotiations [for a water agreement] seems relevant. Despite the vagueness of the terms, the principles outlined below are derived from the concepts of 'water rights' and 'sovereignty'.

Water rights are interpreted differently in various parts of the world.

A country with water rights has rights to the particular resource concerning the following attributes: ownership; access; control; and/or use. Internationally as well as in the Middle East, there are several examples of water rights attributed to all four 'rights', alone or in various combinations (CESAR, 1996; Solanes, 2000). However, water rights usually entail the right to use, while ownership normally means "a usufructury power, and not ownership of the corpus of water itself" (Solanes, 2000: 265).

In Northern and Central Europe and in the Americas, it is quite common for either a state or an individual owner to own the land, but not necessarily the right to use the water or other derivates from the land-water ownership/access/control/use nexus.[10]

The question is whether experience from other regions in interpreting these water rights are bringing the Parties in the Middle East closer to a solution. What this illustrates is that water rights are interpreted differently in various parts of the world. This fact is perhaps the best argument for tailoring the four concepts into a meaningful and mutually acceptable context of each of the water disputes in the region.

I would argue that the concept of sovereignty, which is closely linked to the concept of rights, might be an appropriate term to translate in a negotiation arrangement. According to international law, sovereignty over any natural resource comprises two important legal principles:
- sovereign rights, i.e. rights of water in respect of either of the attributes mentioned above; and
- sovereign obligations, i.e. obligations to use the water in a certain way, such as sustainable use, environmental protection and economic efficiency (cf. national and international obligations as discussed earlier).[11]

Rights
One may argue that any water solution between Parties should include an interpretation of the four attributes[12] of water rights, such as:
- ownership of which part of the water resource (including recycled water)[VIII];
- access to which part of the water resources (e.g. parts of aquifers). However, this concept is mostly applied in a geographically-defined area, like access to a territory, and is therefore not such a useful concept in this context;
- control of which part of the water resource (including recycled water)[IX]; and
- use of which parts of the aquifers and recycled water.[X]

Obligation
Another meaning of sovereignty is obligation: Each state or state-like entity with rights over specific water resources is obliged to manage them, not only according to national laws,[13] but also according to internationally recognized obligations[14] and even religious law (such as the Sharia[15]). Protecting a semi-renewable or renewable water resource from depletion both in terms of quantity

---

VIII In this context, this refers to a 'property right entitling the owner of the economic value to the water' (cf. "[H]ence a dispute over water ownership can be translated into a dispute over the right to monetary compensation for the water involved". (Fisher et al. 2002: 11-25).

IX In this context, this refers to a 'mandate to protect the aquifer systems' which would also include 'study, monitor, and survey' separately and/or jointly according to a set of water management rules.

X In this context, this refers to a 'mandate to utilize/extract/pump for consumption and/or storage separately and/or jointly'.

and quality is one of the most important obligations of any Party. In this context, these obligations apply specifically to protection against pollution and overpumping (of aquifers).

The political temptation of a one-sided emphasis on water rights is therefore a double-edged sword for any country, since the notion of obligations is equally strong.

■ Photo 7.
Inside a water quality monitoring station in Syria

This reality is acknowledged by most countries in the region. The questions should therefore be:

1. How can an agreement between the Parties include incremental steps that would incorporate transfer of water rights and obligations in a sustainable and agreeable manner?
2. How can implementation of these steps be enforced in a realistic and structured way?

Quite a few of the water disputes could have been handled differently if the countries had focused on preventive measures rather than on resolution of conflicts after they had escalated.

Anyone who claims that there are quick-fix answers to these questions has limited experience in the region. Therefore, several reservations, particularly political ones, must be made concerning the proposals for resolution of the four water disputes. However, they should not prevent non-partisan observers from offering a proposal. In any case, the Parties will carry the burden of both successes and failures.

'Prevention is better than a cure'

It seems obvious that the most effective way of developing a sustainable water management strategy is to establish appropriate preventive measures, and to make sure that these can be modified if they prove inadequate. Some of the most common measures are listed below.

Monitoring procedures

Experience from inside and outside the region clearly underlines the importance of setting up national water quantity and quality monitoring programmes.

Most countries in the Middle East have, unfortunately, not yet implemented such programmes. This shortfall has hindered water agreements due to the lack of long-term data.

As the various parts of this publication will reveal, it is urgent to establish such programmes, not least for their input to national water management.

Exchange of data, prior notification and fact-finding procedures[XI]
A commonly asked question is: "What are the first steps to take in order to develop a non-committal co-operation with the other Party(ies)?" The answer seems obvious:

One step might be to begin with exchange of technical data and notifications of upstream changes both in terms of water quantity and quality. A next step could be to set up factfinding procedures and missions and, if feasible, develop joint research programmes. These initiatives may provide stepping stones or opportunities for more active approaches (such as diplomatic ones).

...begin with exchange of technical data and notifications of upstream changes both in terms of water quantity and quality...

Some Parties in the region have developed cautious and isolationist ways of thinking by hiding water and water-related data. However, this information will eventually be revealed, and at a time that may not be optimal from a tactical point of view. Those who still favour not sharing such information are overlooking that contemporary remote sensing (for example, even commercial satellite photos) and sensor-technologies give in one way or another the neighbouring country access to a major part of this information.

Monitoring of water resources, exchange of data, prior notification of unilateral actions and factfinding procedures are perhaps the most important and practical diplomatic means for a Party in order to commence non-committal activities.

Legitimacy of proposing solutions to international water disputes in the Middle East

A relevant question would be to ask how a non-partisan participant may propose solutions to the complex water disputes in the region. What are legitimate solutions when politics are overriding most water management concerns?

The external community has a duty to offer solutions in line with the principles and yardsticks outlined above. However the people living in the various countries must take responsibility for what they are willing to accept.

The external community has a duty to offer solutions. The people living in the countries must take responsibility for what they are willing to accept.

There are of course no simple answers. However, they should at least be in line with the countries' accepted *rights* and *obligations* to:
- practice sound environmental management for the benefit of coming generations; and, of equal importance;

XI   Derived from Trondalen, 2004a.

> ▸ provide its citizens with fundamental human needs such as water for the socio-economic development of their nations.

If those rights and obligations are in one way or another met through a Third Party proposal – irrespective of the ongoing political dramas – this may offer an opportunity for a way out that balances the Parties' various concerns as stated above.

Therefore, the proposals may not fit the political circumstances at the point on the timeline when this book is made public, but rather attempt to offer a possible solution as to how countries' rights and obligations may be met now and in the future.

The proposals should therefore be judged according to this, and not in relation to the constant flux and reflux of politics.

Endnotes

1   In addition, recent dramatic events such as the war and invasion of Iraq in January 1991 and March 2003 are determining both the present political and geopolitical climate, from which none of the solutions should be isolated.

2   See the author's experience as outlined in Trondalen (2004a).

3   Cf. the US Middle East Chief Negotiator, Ambassador Dennis Ross, "We never did anything to prepare public opinion [for peace]. Holding negotiations come what may got us nowhere. If I could do it all over again, I'd do it differently" (Enderlin, 2003: 360).

4   See Permanent Court of Arbitration (PCA) (2003b) as the most authoritative assessment of the law. See also Boisson de Chazournes, 2004.

5   Such as the PCA publication mentioned above.

6   All three principles have been embedded in several major international environmental conventions, such as: (1) The Basel Convention (international transportation of hazardous materials), (2) The Montreal Protocol (protection of the ozone layer), (3) The Forestry Protocol, and more importantly (4) The UN Framework Convention on Climate Change (UNFCCC) - a second-generation convention.

7   See further discussion in Trondalen (2004b).

8   A similar system is being considered in the development of a liability regime under the Basel Convention; the areas under investigation include the establishment of a Special Fund and a system of supplementing intervention by the contracting state (ranked subsidiary to state liability). These elements are considered supplementary to civil liability regimes serving to provide maximum protection and compensation to the victims of environmental damage.

9   The notion of permanent sovereignty over natural resources found its first expression in a UN context already in the 1950s (GA resolution 626, /UN GAOR, Supp. No 20 at p. 18, UN Doc A/2361, 1952) and is quoted and discussed in Tignino (2003).

10 This view is also supported by du Bois (1995: 111-126).

11 There is a vast international literature on state sovereignty. An example of one such discussion is outlined in Tignino (2003) and her references to the literature, especially on 'new sovereignty'.

12 There might be different ways of classifying these attributes, for example in Islamic Sharia Law, where the following categories are referred to: the 'right to thirst', the 'right of irrigation', 'categories of water', and 'priority of uses' as described in Kristjánsdóttir (2003).

13 For Israel, the Water Laws (5719-1957) amended in 1991, and for the PA the Water Law enacted in March 2002.

14 See for example the European Union's Water Framework Directive, among the most comprehensive and strict legislation in terms of obligations of each member country regarding water protection and sound management (http://europa.eu.int/comm/environment/water/water-framework/index_en.html).

15 Liability for misuse is a strong concept in the Sharia law:
see discussion and further reference in Kristjánsdóttir (2003: 365).

SECTION I

Upper Jordan River and the Golan Heights Basins

Part 1. The water of the Golan Heights –
the final quest for a comprehensive peace between Syria and Israel

Part 2. Boiling point at the Upper Jordan River –
the Wazzani Springs conflict between Lebanon and Israel

Part 1

The water of the Golan Heights -

the final quest for a comprehensive peace between Syria and Israel

Abstract

One of the most fundamental conflicts in the region is between Syria and Israel over the Golan Heights. Some would argue that if this conflict is resolved, a more comprehensive Arab-Israeli reconciliation and peace might be achieved.

Part I of this section outlines the relevant historical background for understanding how water resources, especially groundwater, have played and still play a key role in the Syrian-Israeli relationship. Reconciliatory measures such as the Shepherdstown negotiations of January 2000 are described in order to understand the positions and underlying interests of the two Parties.

Based on years of developing an understanding of the Parties' real interests and discussions of possible solutions, a proposal is outlined that should take into account Syria's territorial sovereignty and Israel's need for an uninterrupted flow of water from the Golan. The suggested agreement would allow Syria to resettle the original number of people on the Heights (as of 1967 plus natural growth) and assume full sovereignty of the Golan, including use of natural resources. At the same time, Israel would be able to maintain the current use of water quality and quantity in order to secure the fragile hydrological balance of the Upper Jordan Basin (including Lake Tiberias).

Establishing an internationally supported third party compensation mechanism would provide Syria with the necessary financial and technological know-how to optimize water use in such a way that pollution would be abated and efficiency increased.

Finally, a comprehensive water resource verification and monitoring system is also proposed as a prerequisite for implementing and maintaining compliance of the agreement.

Chapter 1

Water: both a stumbling block and an opportunity for peace

As outlined in the introduction, increasing demographic pressure in the region combined with economic growth and social development is widening the gap between available water supply and demand. This gap is also a concern for Syria and Israel from a humanitarian, security, political and environmental perspective. Water may be substituted, for example as 'virtual water'[1], yet there is still a growing gap between people's expectations of water availability and actual supply.

On the Golan Heights, this gap is compounded by politics. The contested control of water resources between Israel and Syria is one of the most significant and unresolved conflicts in the Middle East. Some would argue that if this conflict is resolved, a more comprehensive Arab-Israeli reconciliation and peace might be achieved.

The Golan Heights were neither part of the United Nations' Partition Plan nor part of the establishment of the State of Israel in 1948. During the war in June 1967 between the two

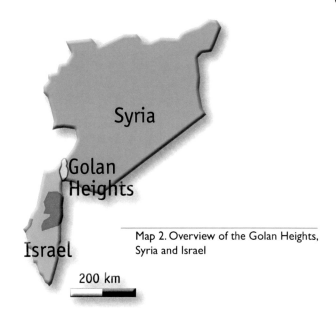

Map 2. Overview of the Golan Heights, Syria and Israel

states (in addition to Egypt and Jordan), it was occupied by Israel. Syria insists that any peace between the two countries would include a return of this territory.

The military significance of the Golan Heights for Israel has been much publicized. What seems increasingly relevant for any solution to the conflict is that a majority of Israeli military leaders argue that due to changes in military technology and strategy, its significance as a foreland has been reduced.[1] Nevertheless, publicly, the significance of the water resources seems to have increased.[2]

---

1   From an economic point of view, water may be substituted by so-called virtual or invisible water (non-evident water), which is soil water and water embedded in commodities that require water for their production. For example, production of a tonne of grain requires 1,000 tonnes (m³) of water. A community or economy can balance its water needs by accessing invisible water outside its boundaries (see Allan, 2002).

Both Parties have acknowledged throughout that the dispute over water resources on the Golan Heights, including the headwaters of the Upper Jordan River Basin, is the core of the matter. Unless this is resolved, peace seems improbable.

Before turning to a few relevant historic events and the present situation regarding the nexus of borders and waters, a brief description of the hydro-geographical environment on and around the Golan Heights is outlined.

Brief resource and geographical description of the Golan Heights

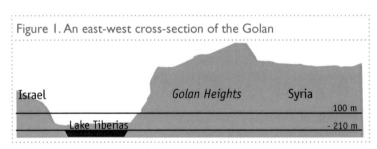

Figure 1. An east-west cross-section of the Golan

Israel

Golan Heights   Syria

Lake Tiberias

100 m

- 210 m

The Golan Heights are situated upland between Syria and Israel, and borders Lebanon in the north and Jordan in the south.[3] They take their name from the ancient city of Golan, having been known as Gaulanitis, as well as from Arabic, where 'Golan' is derived from the word 'Jaulan' meaning 'land filled with dust'. They consist of a rocky plateau overlooking in the east the plains towards Damascus, west over Lake Tiberias, and south-east to the Yarmuk River and the hills of Jordan.

The lake is known by various names, such as the Sea of Galilee or Lake Kinneret (the latter is commonly used by the Israelis). It will be referred to here as Lake Tiberias.

The Golan is made up of two geographically distinct areas: the Hermon Range (mostly limestone) in the north; and the Golan plateau in the south. The former is one of the highest mountain ranges in the entire region. The plateau slopes gently from north to south, descending from 1,200 metres above sea level on its northern edge to 300 metres above sea level at its southern rim. The area to the west of the Golan, however, encompassing the Hula Valley and Lake Tiberias, is 200 metres below sea level, and the dramatic disparity of the landscape creates a diversified scenery along the escarpment that marks the Golan's western border.

The Golan is situated in the Mediterranean climate zone, characterized by dry summers and wet winters. Snow falls for a few days every winter on its high northern end, where Mount Hermon is snow-covered from December to March, with snow patches remaining on the mountain throughout the year. Average annual rainfall ranges between 1,000 mm in the north (in the Hermon area), which is dependant on the winter rain, to about 450 mm of rain annually in the southern part of the Golan, with dry summers and large evaporation. The rainfall is the main determining factor for the surface and groundwater that is so crucial for the people on the Golan as well as for replenishment of the lake.

Surface water
Almost all of Golan lies within the Lake Tiberias catchment area. In addition to three of the Jordan River's main sources, the Hasbani River (originating from Lebanon) and Dan and Baniyas rivers that rise on the slopes of Mount Hermon,

Map 3. The Golan Heights and Upper Jordan River

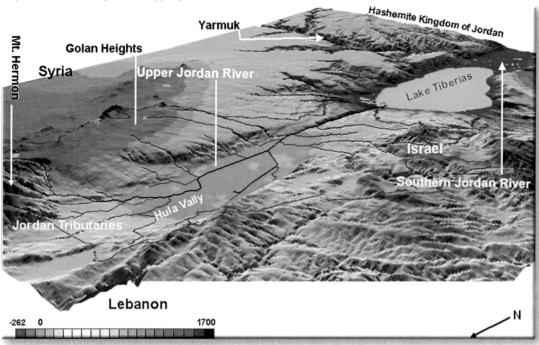

Note: The red line marks the catchment area of the Upper Jordan River.
Source: Data based on Hall, 1996.

Golan Heights – brief facts

Area	1,158 km²	Jewish population	16.500
Highest peak	2,224 m above sea level	Syrian population	17.000
Villages	36 (4 Syrian (druze) and 32 Jewish)	Main town	Katzin (the only town)
Nature reserve	246 km²	Cultivated area	80 km²
Grazing lands	460 km²		

several seasonal streams rise on the Heights and flow into the lake, either directly or *via* the Jordan River (Gvirtzman, 2002).

The drainage-divide-line of the Golan more or less coincides with the UN Armistice line (see *Map 3*). A significant part of the Lake Tiberias area drains from the Golan (350 km² drain into the Jordan River and 600 km² directly into Lake Tiberias). The remaining 200 km² drain into the Rokad and Yarmuk River basins. This means that almost all

of the water drains down ravines and canyons to waterfalls that hurl the melted snows of winter into a series of deep secluded pools towards the Lake Tiberias and Yarmuk River.

In addition, the Upper Jordan River Basin drains the water to Lake Tiberias and consists of three rivers:

▸ Hasbani ('Snir') River, with an average flow of 135 MCM per year. Most of its catchment area is located in Lebanon, including the recently-contested Wazzani Springs (see Omberg Hansen, 2004) (see also *Part 2*);

▶ Dan Springs, with an average of 250 MCM per year. Its aquifer is replenished mainly by snow from Mount Hermon; and

▶ Baniyas (Hermon) Springs, with around 120 MCM per year. Surface water and snow from Mount Hermon also replenish its aquifer. Originally assigned to the British Mandate by the 1920 Anglo-French Convention, the Springs were located 1 km inside Syria when the border was brought into legal force by 1923 (see Hoff, 2000 and Amery and Wolf, 2000: 151). The springs and a short stretch of the river came under Israeli control in June 1967.

Groundwater on the Golan Heights

The groundwater of Golan is a complex structure that primarily drains toward the lake. The Israelis have viewed the underground resources as vital to the hydrological balance of the lake, and have conducted in-depth analyses of the aquifers on the Golan in terms of both its natural and sustainable yields (pumping on a yearly basis) and its quality and pollution levels. It is beyond the scope of this publication to outline this science, except to point to the vast literature in this field.

The groundwater quality of the Golan Heights Aquifers is considered excellent, even though several cases of contamination (mainly by dairy farm manure) have been reported. The local (Basalt) aquifers in the Golan are sensitive to surface contamination, since it is mainly a phreatic aquifer.

There are about 100 springs of varying yields on the Golan, much of the water from which is used to service Israeli settlements (according to Shuval, 1994).

Although there seems to be a scientific consensus that the water quality is satisfactory, a more comprehensive automated water quality monitoring system is, from an Israeli perspective, desirable. This is regardless of the outcome of peace talks between the two countries.

Water reservoirs

After 1967, the Israelis developed the water reservoir system on the Golan to include 17 reservoirs. They are currently the basis of the irrigation water supply system. The total volume of the reservoirs is over 36M m^3.[4] In case no peace agreement has been reached, according to future Israeli plans there is an increase of 1.5M m^3 of water consumption for agriculture every year. Investments are planned mainly for wastewater treatment facilities, water reclamation systems for agriculture and improvement of water systems for domestic use. These measures and the construction of reservoirs are made primarily to catch the winter flood (for summer irrigation) and to avoid wastewater from reaching the lake or Yarmuk River.

Wastewater treatment on the Golan Heights

There is limited public information on treatment of water from the Israeli settlements, except that there is consensus among water professionals that wastewater is taken care of in a controllable manner.

The four Syrian/Druze Villages[II] – Masade, Bukata, Magdal Shams and Ein-Kunya – in North Golan Heights include approximately 17,000 Syrian/Druze inhabitants. Sewage in these villages is collected either into the main sewage system or into an absorption pit. However, the main sewage

---

II Syrians name them 'Syrian Villages', while the Israeli call them 'Druze Villages'.

Map 4. The basin of the Upper Jordan River and the Golan Heights

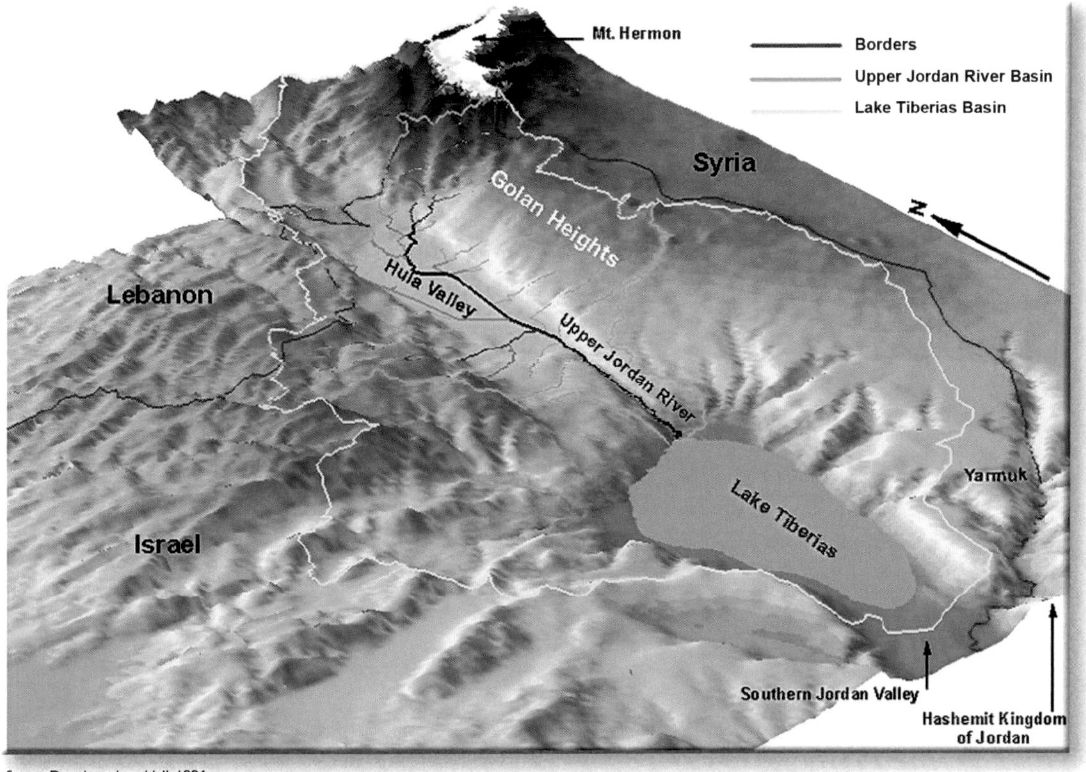

Mt. Hermon

Borders
Upper Jordan River Basin
Lake Tiberias Basin

Syria

Golan Heights

Lebanon

Hula Valley

Upper Jordan River

Israel

Lake Tiberias

Yarmuk

Southern Jordan Valley

Hashemit Kingdom of Jordan

Source: Data based on Hall, 1996.

Table 1. Comparison of share of discharge and allocation before 1967 and after, as well as Johnston Plan and early 1990, respectively

Discharge and allocation shares in the upper Jordan River Basin (including the Golan Heights) in MCM (per cent of total)[a]

Country	Share of discharge		Share of allocation[b]	
	Before 1967	After 1967	Johnston Plan	Early 1990s
Syria	560 (42%)	375 (27%)	130 (10%)	150 (13%)
U. Jordan R.	155	-	40	-
Yarmuk R.	375	375	90	150
Israel	335 (25%)	570 (42%)	400[c] (31%)	700 (61%)
U. Jordan R.	250	405	375	675
Yarmuk R.	-	-	25	25
Lebanon	95 (6%)	95 (6%)	35 (3%)	5 (0,5%)

a)   Soffer (1994) and Klein (1998)
b)   Allocation and use do not sum up total discharge as some water reaches the Dead Sea.
c)   Israel to receive excess water

Source: Revised after Feitelson, 2002.

system does not end in a proper wastewater treatment plant. Rather, it flows into the Sa'ar Stream and later to the Baniyas, one of the largest sources of the Jordan River. Wastewater from the east part of these villages seeps into groundwater and flows east into the Rokad River. An effluent treatment reclamation programme for the Syrian/Druze villages is planned. This will have an impact on environmental and groundwater protection from sewage pollution, and on the prevention of pollution of the Jordan River.[5]

Even today, there seems to be a need to further protect water resources from pollution.

Division of water resources among the countries

The combination of the complex hydrological structures of the Golan, including the Upper Jordan River, and the strained relationships between the countries has to date made a water agreement impossible. The only bilateral agreements are between Jordan and Syria through a Memorandum of Understanding on the Yarmuk River (which includes building a so-called 'Unity Dam') and between Jordan and Israel from 1994 encompassing, among other clauses, water allocation regarding flow from Lake Tiberias (see peace treaty between Israel and Jordan in Haddadin, 2001).

The relevant question is therefore: Could any yardsticks or points of reference be used in order to determine a water allocation scheme? The only proposed allocation formula was made by US Envoy Ambassador Johnston back in 1956[6]. The so-called Johnston Plan outlined a formula that reflected the 'facts on the ground' at that time, which were however somewhat different from today's situation (see further discussion in Chapter 3).

Some conclusions could be drawn from the overview, but only a few of these offer direct solutions to the present dispute. Although the Johnston Plan was never accepted by either Israel or the Arab States, it provides a point of reference for discussions on what water might eventually be allocated.

What Ambassador Johnston did not foresee was that the water quality would be contested as much as the quantity. The next chapter will assess how the water disputes were handled at the time and later, leading on to the following chapter that outlines solutions.

■ Photo 8.
The Yarmuk River in the background between the Golan Heights and Jordan

Chapter 2

Water resources on the Golan Heights: the conflict

The evolution of the Syrian-Israeli relationship

Historically, the two countries have been intertwined for centuries. They share many common traits such as religion, culture, people, customs and language. Trade and business over the years have mirrored the geographical features in major cites like Aleppo, Hama and Damascus, which have been linked to the east-west trade of the Silk Road as well as to the north-south movements along the Euphrates waterway. The proximity to the coast of what is now Israel have made it part of what the French call the Levant (today's Lebanon and Syria), an integral part of the cultural, economic and geographical landscape of the Middle East. Ancient and Biblical ties bind the people together in a remarkable way, and water resources have always played an important religious, cultural, agricultural and political role.

The fall of the Ottoman Empire at the beginning of the 1920s resulted in the establishment of the present states of Syria and Lebanon as well as the Zionist movement that increasingly evolved up to the 1940s. Syria and the then British-mandated Palestine did not have a tense relationship before the establishment of the State of Israel in 1948.[7] Several armed skirmishes took place, especially in the 1950s, related to the demilitarized zone, and leading to wars in 1967 and 1973.

Many view the Syrian-Israeli relationship as an indicator of the regional desire and ability to move into stability and, eventually, peace talks.

After 1973, little progress was achieved in improving relationships until the mid-1990s (see Ross, 2004: Chapter 5). Several initiatives were taken from May 1994 up until late 1999 that led to direct peace talks commencing in January 2000 under the auspices of the United States.

In May 1999, as the late Israeli Prime Minister Yitzchak Rabin had done, Prime Minister Ehud Barak set out a course to make a deal with the Syrians. Syria reciprocated Israel's call for talks by reiterating its longstanding position of a 'land-for-peace' formula. Together with Barak, the late Syrian President Hafez al-Assad made bold moves at the end of 1999, prompting the United States to undertake several secret consultations between Syria and Israel that culminated in the start of negotiations in the US on 3 January 2000. Prime Minister Barak and the Syrian Foreign Minister Farouk al-Shara headed each delegation.

According to the detailed accounts of the negotiations by US Chief Envoy to the Middle East, Ambassador Dennis Ross (Ross, 2004) and the book by former Secretary of State Madeleine Albright, *Madame Secretary* (Albright, 2004), a set of events made such a process feasible, including the increasingly unpopular occupation of South Lebanon and the loss of Israeli soldiers there. Barak promised the Israeli electorate to pull out the forces from South Lebanon within a year (after he resumed power). Likewise, he looked at himself differently from his predecessor, Benjamin Netanyahu, in the sense that he believed that he could make a peace deal with Syria. He was of the firm opinion that despite the hostile relationship between the two countries, the late President Hafez al-Assad would be able to stand by his commitments for a peaceful relationship, and subsequently get the Shiite Movement in Lebanon and those fighting for it under control.

Syria publicly reiterated their land-for-peace formula embedded in a statement that it would be 'without predetermined conditions'. However, it was obvious that President al-Assad would maintain the longstanding position: "No Syrian land to be handed over".[8]

There are strong reasons to believe that Syria was seriously preparing its population for a settlement with Israel, not only from detailed accounts from those involved in the talks, but also from how the public was being prepared for a peace. For example, posters and banners were being replaced in the major cities in Syria. One of the most striking signs was the replacement of the banner of the Commander-in-Chief President al-Assad with that of the peace-making Statesman President al-Assad (see photo on next page) outside the famous Souk El-Hammidya of Old Damascus (near the Umayyad Mosque).

Likewise, the Israeli public was, according to the polls, becoming increasingly optimistic about a possible peace with Syria. This was despite the fact that the opposing settlers on the Golan had joined forces with likeminded opposition in the West Bank and Gaza – and even in parts of the American-Jewish community in the United States (see *Rabinovich, 2004*).

US-led Shepherdstown negotiations

The US-led Shepherdstown negotiations[9] dealt with the two major challenges, "borders and water"[10], including three other more-or-less interconnected areas, together creating five 'groups':

- borders (demarcation/delineation of the exact border – although the 'border committee' never met);
- water (rights and control over water resources, particularly rights to Lake Tiberias, the Upper Jordan River and the Golan Heights, related particularly to use of and pollution from water resources on the Golan Heights);
- security and disarmament;
- normalization (such as diplomatic recognition, trade and tourism); and finally
- the 'Lebanese Track'.

The Parties had different views on whether these issues should be negotiated together, which was the Israeli position, or whether some of the matters, such as normalization and the 'Lebanese Track', could be postponed to a later stage. The Syrians argued in favour of this latter position.

Quite early, however, it became clear that the interconnection of water management and the exact location of the boundaries along the north-eastern part of Lake Tiberias and the Upper Jordan River would determine whether or not there would be peace.

■ Photo 9.
Souk El-Hammadya of Old Damascus in December 1999

The stakes were – and still are – high on both sides:

▸ Since 1967, Syria has been steadfastly concerned with its territorial sovereignty. The political significance domestically, as well as in the Arab world, of getting the Golan back should never be underestimated.[11]

▸ From a strategic, economic, water management and even humanitarian point of view, Israel was firm that the vital water resources had to be protected and the flow uninterrupted, as the lake makes up about 35 per cent of all its freshwater resources (see Gvirtzman, 2001).

The few publicly-available substantive reports from the Shepherdstown negotiations can be found in former US President Bill Clinton's memoir, former Secretary of State Albright's memoir, French Middle East Journalist Charles Enderlin's insightful publication and, not least, the detailed and narrative book by former US Chief Middle East Envoy Dennis Ross. The respective publications vividly describe how negotiations reached a point where the water/border nexus remained the main obstacle to further progress.

The water/border nexus

The conflicting interests of the two Parties regarding 'safeguarding the water' for the Israelis and the territorial sovereignty for the Syrians were linked to two matters perceived as irreconcilable:

▸ How could the surface and underground water resources from the Golan Heights and Upper Jordan River be secured in terms of quantity and quality when Syria demanded a boundary that might infringe on control of the water resources?

▸ In addition, how could the water be protected when Syria demanded resettlement on the Golan by a population amounting today to almost half a million?

With hindsight, an interesting question is whether a peace agreement would have been possible if the dispute over the 'water/border nexus' had been resolved in 2000.

The talks in Shepherdstown ended without a solution, although a 'working text' from the US – which *de facto* reflected more or less the Parties' positions at that time – was leaked to the press.[12]

The US continued to work behind the scenes in the coming months, with the efforts ending in a final meeting between President Clinton and President al-Assad in March 2000 in Geneva.[13] The meeting bore no fruit and created perhaps an even more unsettled climate than before. During it, Clinton presented a map to al-Assad on how Israel anticipated the borders at the strategic land strip around the lake. The proposal was perceived by al-Assad at that time to be unacceptable (Clinton, 2004: 903) because it did not reflect their interest regarding the border and territorial sovereignty (which included the demand for resettlement of Syrian 'refugees' on the Golan).[14]

Is water always going to be the stumbling block for peace between the two countries?

Several reasons may explain why the Geneva meeting did not yield an agreement.[15] However, there are strong reasons to argue that the solutions presented back in 2000 were not fully developed, and it is further known that these matters were discussed again after the Geneva meeting. However, time was running out. On 10 June of the same year, the Syrian President al-Assad died, President Clinton stepped down in January 2001, and subsequently the Israeli Prime Minister Barak lost the election to Ariel Sharon.

With hindsight, an interesting question is whether a peace agreement would have been possible if the dispute over the 'water/border nexus' had been resolved in 2000.

The short answer is, probably, yes. There were, however, several unresolved issues, such as the public mood in Israel, the issue of the succession of Al-Assad and the overall political situation in the Middle East. This was primarily the relationship between Israel and the Palestinians

as well as factors such as the relationship between Syria and the United States[16], between Syria and Lebanon, and the 'Iraqi situation' that together determined the outcome.

The nexus of water and borders along the Upper Jordan River and Lake Tiberias is complex in political terms. One assumption is that none of the countries, or the US as a Third Party, had developed timely solutions to the problems. This may be one of the reasons for which the water/border dispute derailed a peace agreement.[17] Due to the role of the US in the Syria-Israel talks, very few other actors contributed to the talks.

The author argues that the two principal and as yet unresolved water-related problems[III] are solvable.

Recognition of borders

Already in the aftermath of World War I, controls of vital water resources were high on the political agenda. When Britain and France entered into detailed negotiations to draw the frontiers, water was at the forefront of their concerns. According to renowned scholar David Fromkin, Palestine and Syria-Lebanon were still vague terms, and it was unclear where one ended and the other started:

> "For the French pictured the frontier as between France and Britain in the Levant, and took an uncompromising position ...
> At stake in the negotiations of Palestine's frontiers were the valuable headwaters of the Jordan and Yarmuk rivers – which the French successfully insisted on obtaining for Syria-Lebanon." (Fromkin, 2001: 441)

III   (a) Control and access to the water flow to Lake Tiberias, as well as (b) use and protection of the water resources under resettlement of Syrians to the Heights.

Map 5.   Present and historic borders between Israel, Syria and Lebanon (the black line represents the so-called 'blue line' set by the UN between Lebanon and Israel/Golan Heights)

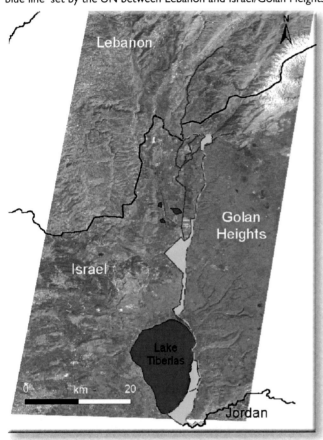

The **Turquoise** Line marks the old border between Syria and at that time called Palestine. In March 1923, the Anglo-French Boundary Commission completed the work on th Border Posts – thus this is know as the 1923 International Boundary.

The **Red Line** represents the July 20th 1949 Armistice Line between Syria and Israel. Following the War in 1948, UNTSO determined the boundary where it differed from the 1923 International Boundary, and Syria agreed to withdraw from the land west of the 1923 Boundary (i.e., on the Israeli side, becoming the Demilitarized Zones (DMZs).

The **Yellow Area** represents the DMZs. The Armistice Agreement did not decide on the sovereignty rights in the DMZs.

Sources: Data from Lebanon derived from Landsat ETM and ESRI from other areas. Data processed by MAPS Geosystems s.a.r.l., Beirut, Lebanon. The 'International border' is based on data from UN Map 'Levant 50J19 Houle' and the current Lebanese/Israeli border is based on the UN 'Blue Line'.

When Great Britain finally accepted the French Trusteeship of the Levant (presently Syria and Lebanon), voices advocated that the crucial water sources should be within – at that time the anticipated – Palestine. The so-called *Balfour Declaration* was embodied in the League of Nations[IV] entrusting Palestine to Britain, and the Zionist leader Chaim Weizmann wrote to British Prime Minister Winston Churchill in early 1921 that the agreement with France "cut Palestine off from access to the Litani, deprived her possession

of the Upper Jordan and Yarmuk and took her fertile plains east of Lake Tiberias which had hereto been regarded as one of the most promising outlets for Jewish settlement on a large scale" (Fromkin, 2001). Justice Brandeis, the leader of American Zionism, sent a similar cabled message to Balfour towards the end of 1921, deploring the loss of water at the Litani River (in what is now Lebanon) (Fromkin, 2001: 513).

Several border proposals were discussed between Britain and France in the early 1920s. Some of the various borders are outlined below, including the

---

IV   The forerunner of the United Nations.

Sykes-Picot borders, which were not only limited to the 'Palestine-Syria-Lebanon' borders.[V]

The basis for the current so-called pre-1967 border between Syria and Israel is the March 1923 border, known as the 'international border'. The difference between that border and the border of 4 June 1967 is that the latter contains two sets of boundaries. The first dates back to March 1923, while the second is the Armistice Line from 1949, including four demilitarized zones (from the northern Baniyas areas to the south at El Hamma at the Yarmuk River; see *Map 5*).[18]

The exact geographical locations of the borders are significant as regards management of water:

1. The border in the northern part of the border area makes Syria a riparian part of the Upper Jordan Basin, i.e. the perennial sources of Baniyas are located some 200 metres into undisputed Syrian territory.

2. The March 1923 border is on the riverbank of and not in the Jordan River all the way down to Lake Tiberias. This is interpreted by Israel in such a way that Syria has no riparian rights to the river itself. However, Syria has argued all along that that this is not so important,

since it is already a riparian (due to the Baniyas sources).

3. The March 1923 border along the lakeside until almost the middle of the lake is 10 metres from – at that time – the shoreline (i.e. lake/land intersection). According to international law, a country is not riparian if the border is 10 metres or more away. However, the Syrians had access to the lakeshore until June 1967 due to the Anglo-French Convention of 1923, which enacted a "good neighbourly relation" in 1926.

4. The border at the El Hamma (Hamat Gader) that forms the enclave at the Yarmuk River is disputed, since it is on the Israeli side according to the March 1923 border, but later came into the hands of Syria. If El Hamma belongs to Israel, it will become a riparian Party to the Yarmuk River.

In addition, the recent dispute between Lebanon and Israel over the Wazzani Springs of the Hasbani River has further complicated the matter. The border issue has therefore not been divulged and there is no mutual recognition of water rights.

In *Chapter 3*, the border/water/resettlement of Syrians to the Golan nexus is assessed in relation to the Parties' positions and concerns, with the aim of proposing a solution (see *Chapter 4*).

V   Mark Sykes and Francois Georges Picot were respectively the British and French negotiators on national borders beginning in 1915.

Chapter 3

What are the Parties' positions and real concerns?

Over the years, the Parties have made public statements that appear to be mutually irreconcilable regarding the as yet unresolved water/border nexus and water-related problems on the Golan Heights. However, up to the late 1990s, neither of them authoritatively set forth their respective position, much less their minimal requirements (see also Hoff, 2000 and Amery and Wolf, 2000). From 1999 onwards, the positions became more explicit. Below, they are described primarily based on an assessment of:

- public oral and written statements by the leaders of Syria and Israel;
- the 'official working text' as reflected by the US from the Shepherdstown negotiations[VI];
- the accounts of the negotiation at Shepherdstown as outlined by former US President Clinton, former US Secretary of State Albright and Chief Negotiator Ross in their respective memoirs;
- documentation from the French journalist Enderlin (2003) and the American writer Swisher (2004); and
- the author's familiarity with both Parties' positions and concerns.

The Parties' positions on the water disputes over the Golan Heights may be outlined in relation to:

- the exact location of the borders[VII];
- control over, access to, and protection of the water resources, and
- the return of Syrian citizens to the Golan Heights.

From an academic and historic perspective, discussion is merited on the meaning of the notion of territorial sovereignty as regards almost every metre along the borders of Golan (except on the eastern border, i.e. the area of the UN Disengagement Observer Force). The purpose of this publication is, however, to assess relevant information in relation to a proposed solution. The following outline therefore focuses on what has been achieved to date in order to bring the discussion forward towards a possible conciliation of the different positions.

The overarching principle in any conflict resolution[VIII] is that the solutions must address the important concerns of both Parties. In an academic sense, it should be possible to sharply

---

VI   Made publicly available on the Internet for some days after the Shepherdstown negotiations in Israel.

VII   Syria and Israel preferred the terms 'delineation' and 'demarcation', respectively.
VIII See Trondalen, 2004a

Map 6. The Golan Heights seen from a Syrian perspective (westward)

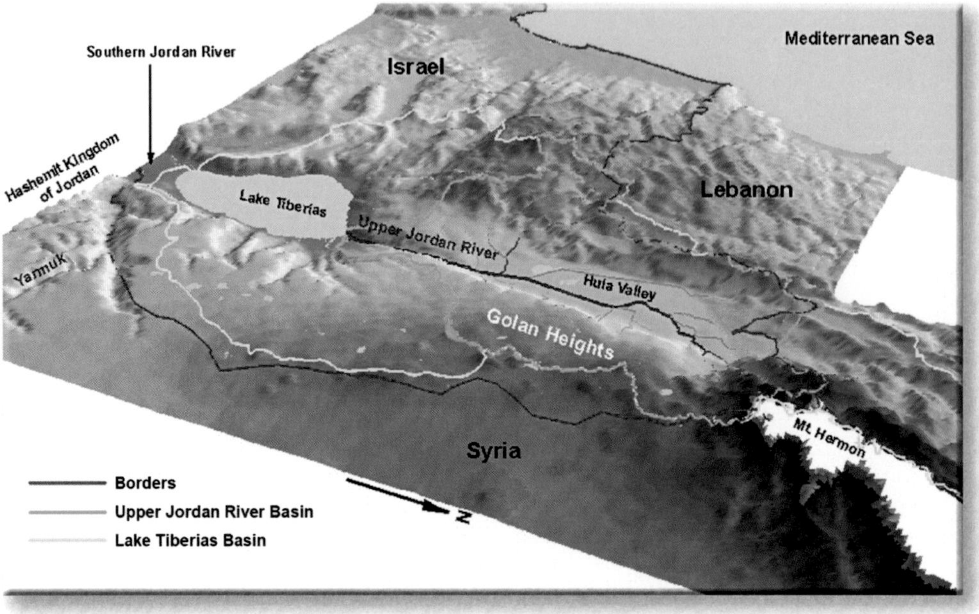

define their positions. In reality, however, neither of the positions is carved in stone. Sometimes the total sum of the factors is different from the sum of isolated factors. In political terms, this means that one of the countries may be willing to yield on one position assuming there are some concessions on other positions, or that the overall outcome justifies the compromises. The order in which subjects should be negotiated was also significant for Al-Assad and Barak, on different matters.

Syrian positions and concerns

Syrian perception of the borders

Syria claims the return of all occupied land in compliance with UN Security Council Resolution 242 according to the 4 June 1967 line. The belief that "all the land must be returned in exchange for peace" should not be underestimated in terms of pride, policy and being treated equally with Jordanians and Egyptians (in their peace deals with Israel).[19] This is clearly

understood as "full territorial sovereignty over its land up to the external borders" – including the borders to Israel and Lebanon. Syria has indicated a willingness to allow international control, monitoring and verification of provisions associated with its border with Israel. In practical terms, this means that the country would probably not only allow, but even welcome some sort of international presence – like the existing United Nations DOF – along the border. This issue was handled by the security/disarmament nexus of the Shepherdstown negotiations.

In this context, the border at the lakeside has become the crux of the matter. Syria has publicly stated that since Israel insisted that it had to secure the water rights and free flow of water resources draining down from the Jordan River and the Golan Heights, "in case the border should be drawn East of Jordan River and of the Eastern Shore of Lake Kinneret, it would be a gift and not an acquired right" (Clinton, 2004).

It is further understood from the Shepherdstown negotiations that Syria eventually agreed that "50 metres' 'access land' away from the shore line" should be given on the condition that Israel would accept the 4 June 1967 line (Clinton, 2004: 887). This position also coincided with the old Syrian position that the border would constitute the shoreline (i.e. the land-water intersection)

> Syrian President Bashar Al-Assad's made an explicit statement about water as an integral part of a comprehensive agreement.

at the time in 1967.[IX] Since then, the lake has shrunk by approximately 4.5 metres down to the present level of 213 metres below sea level. Consequently, the shoreline has geographically moved 120-300 metres west[20] of the 1923 line. Moreover, in the draft text leaked to the *Al-Hayat* newspaper on 9 January 2000, Syria recognizes that: "the line of June 4th is not a border and has not been marked out, and it therefore agrees to participate in the determination of this line" (Enderlin, 2003: 134).

In terms of principles, Syria's insistence on the 4 June 1967 line could contribute to paving the way towards reconcilable positions, i.e. that both countries be able to claim their historic rights. As in any negotiation, however, this position was given at a point in time when other factors were being taken into account. Afterwards, the late President Al-Assad made a statement that may be interpreted as a slight backing-down from this position.[21] However, Al-Assad's statement must be understood in the light of the timepoint

when he received the 'very disappointing offer' from Prime Minister Barak as communicated by President Clinton during the Geneva Meeting (on 27 March 2000).

Control, access and protection of the water resources
Syria's concern throughout has been territorial sovereignty, and their positions on the water resources were derived from that notion. The country therefore claims that a resolution of water issues should be: "based on relevant international principles and practices" and "mutually agreeable arrangements with respect to water quantities and quality from the surface and underground waters in the areas from which Israeli forces will withdraw."[22]

In what might be considered to be Syrian President Bashar Al-Assad's first interview after he succeeded his father in July 2001, he made an explicit statement about water as an integral part of a comprehensive agreement.[23] However, Syria has made it clear that they will not claim water rights for the lake or on the Heights *per se*, and explains this by claiming that it would have developed the resources before 1967 if it had had such ambitions.[24]

Syria's position on water on the Golan must be seen in the wider context
It seems obvious that Syria's concerns for water resources on the Golan must be seen in a wider context. Hydro-politically, the country is in an extraordinary position: it is both an upstream and a downstream country on the Euphrates and Tigris Rivers (see *Section III*), meaning that Syria ought to balance carefully the hydro-political doctrines that favour down and upstream countries.[25] All along, Syria has therefore been meticulous in not linking the Jordan River Basin with the Euphrates and Tigris Basins.[26] This is

---

IX   Both countries have developed certain interpretations of the rights to the various borders. However, for the purpose of this publication, this discussion is not taken further.

further underlined by the fact that Syria is upstream of Jordan on the Yarmuk River, and would like to avoid a comparison between their upstream behaviour and that of Turkey.

For various reasons, there is almost consensus among Syria, Turkey, Iraq, Jordan, Lebanon, the Palestinians and Israel not to link the hydro-politics of the basins. This is despite the fact that the proposed water-transportation-by-ships agreement signed in 2002 between Turkey and Israel was portrayed in Syrian media as linking them (i.e. "transferring water away from the Euphrates Basin to the port of Manavgat in Turkey", which in strict hydrological terms is however incorrect).

Recently, the cautious and carefully worded response from Syria on the water dispute over the Wazzani Springs at the sources of the Hasbani River between Lebanon and Israel illustrates Syria's sensitivity as regards linking water disputes whenever the Golan or the Euphrates are in question.[27]

Syrian demand for development of the Golan Heights, including returnees of Syrian citizens to the Golan Heights

Syria has for some time argued that *territorial sovereignty means the right to develop the area, including re-establishing a population on the Golan* equivalent to the Syrian population living there in 1967 plus natural population growth, calculated at 3.8 per cent per annum.[28] This may be equivalent to a population of around 450,000 people in the year 2004.[29]

Prior to 1967, Syria had ambitions to develop the water resources as in 1965-1966, following a decision by the Arab League. It began to implement a large-scale project for diversion of the Jordan headwaters directly into the Yarmuk

River (see Naff, 1994 and Feitelson, 2000). Such actions must be viewed in light of the Syrian perception of territorial sovereignty at that time.

Although re-establishment of the Syrian population was not an explicit mainstream theme in the Shepherdstown negotiations, it was an important matter throughout as it was a natural consequence of the country's longstanding interpretation of territorial sovereignty. One of the most forceful statements was made by Syrian Foreign Minister al-Shara in a written speech to President Clinton and the Israelis on 15 December in Washington DC:

> "...[the media] tried to arouse the sympathy of the international community on behalf of several thousand Golan settlers, arrogantly ignoring over half a million Syrians living in dozens of villages on the Golan, [which] today, have been totally destroyed, though these [are] villages where their ancestors had lived for thousands of years ..." (Enderlin, 2003: 131).

Israeli positions and concerns

Israeli perception of the borders

Israel's claims are legitimized by the March 1923 borders and interpreted in such a way that the borders should be drawn in order to secure primarily Lake Tiberias as well as the flow and quality of the Baniyas, Dan and Hasbani Rivers.

The borders in the north at the headwater of the Upper Jordan River Basin and along the lake are of utmost importance for Israel. *Map 5* (as well as *7* and *8* in *Part 2* of this section) outlines the March 1923 and so-called 4 June 1967 borders. The Parties formally dispute their rights to the demilitarized zones. However, the border delineation/demarcation seems indeed solvable.

It is the interpretation of what the borders mean in relation to control, use and ownership of the water that is contested.

Israel has always advocated for an absolute minimum distance of the border from the lake of 10 metres and stated that this was agreed on. This is due to a rule in international law that land adjacent to a river at a distance of 10 metres gives a nation the right to the water.[30]

Four sections of the boundary are of special significance (see *Map 5*):

5. the demilitarized zone at the northern border at the Baniyas River – the March 1923 border is desirable from an Israeli perspective;

6. along the Jordan River and south to the point where the river reaches Lake Tiberias. There are reasons to believe that Israel will accept that the border is at the riverbank as described in the March 1923 agreement. The DMZs will probably under no circumstances be handed over. Israel might, however, insist that no additional riparian rights be granted (except for the Baniyas area) as a consequence of that line;

7. the border at the lakeside up to the middle (at Kursi) where the old border is located 10 metres from the former shoreline will remain and preferably be expanded due to lower water levels of the lake. The same principle might be applied in relation to the Armistice line from 1949 and the disputed demilitarized zones. A trade-off between this area and El-Hamma might be feasible (see *Part II* of this section for further discussion on this);

8. finally, the El-Hamma Spring situated at the Yarmuk River (the latter being shared between Syria, Jordan and Israel). The sources of this river are mainly located in Syria. It forms the pre-1967 border between Syria and Jordan down to the tripartite border

at the El-Hamma, south-east of Lake Tiberias, then the Jordanian-Israeli border towards the point of confluence (Naharayim) with the Jordan River (see *Map 5*). There has never been a separate agreement on the Yarmuk River between Syria and Israel. Instead, Syria and Jordan signed a separate agreement in 1953 and 1987 on building a dam, the so-called 'Unity Dam' including use of the stored water in the dam. The Peace Treaty between Jordan and Israel contains specific provisions on water allocation between them (Alster, 1996). There are strong reasons to believe that Israel will not demand riparian rights to Yarmuk if no rights are granted to Syria on Lake Tiberias.[31]

> Israel's position is that a resolution shall ensure "the continuation of Israel's current use in quantity and quality of all the surface water and underground waters in the areas from which Israeli forces relocate."

Control, access to and protection of the water resources

Israel's principal position is that a resolution on water issues shall ensure "the continuation of Israel's current use in quantity and quality of all the surface water and underground waters in the areas from which Israeli forces relocate".[32] Israel claimed arrangements to include "all necessary measures to prevent contamination, pollution or depletion of the Kinneret/Tiberias and Upper Jordan River and their sources" (hereafter called the 'Israeli current use claim').

It is acknowledged that the Israeli position to date has been full riparian rights to Lake Tiberias and unrestricted natural flow of the Dan, Hasbani and Baniyas rivers as well as the springs that naturally drain to the lake (see Alster, 1996). The water draining to the lake should be of a quality

■ Photo 10.
The Baniyas River before it reaches the Jordan River

no less than the existing water quality, or should not be allowed to vary outside agreed limits.

Since the Shepherdstown negotiations, the Wazzani Springs Dispute between Lebanon and Israel has escalated and in some ways complicated matters. This is because it is impossible – in hydrological terms – to de-link the latter dispute from the question of water rights related to the Golan Heights. The two disputes are discussed separately from a technical and hydro-political point of view. However the dispute resolution processes ought to be seen in relation to each other (see *Part 2*).

It appears that Israel's positions as stated above are not the absolute bottom line, since the Israelis

are implicitly accepting Lebanon's demands of water from the Wazzani.[33] The country's stark objection to unilateral action from Lebanon is more related to how it is carried out rather than to whether they use a certain amount or not (see further discussion in *Part 2*).

The Israeli position on the Syrian demand for the return of citizens to the Golan Heights

The Syrian position on returning its citizens to the Golan Heights has been a realistic and disturbing concern for Israel.[34] However, some have argued that as long as Syria agrees to ensure continuation of Israel's current use in quantity and quality, it is not up to Israel to decide how this is carried out.

Nonetheless, the reality in the Middle East is not as simple. It is anticipated that the proposed military/security monitoring arrangements (that were more or less agreed on in Shepherdstown) might be expanded to include the water resources. Israel is extremely concerned with the practical implementation and enforcement of any water agreements, and the Israeli behaviour in Shepherdstown might be better understood when this is taken into account.

Just before the departure of the Israeli delegation from Israel to Shepherdstown, the Israeli Water Commissioner appeared before the Knesset's Committee for State Control and underscored this concern.[35]

> "If the Syrians settle the Golan with hundreds of thousands of inhabitants who do not handle sewage and pollution in proper fashion, this will spell certain doom for the Kinneret – without any doubt."

The Israeli Mekorot (the National Water Corporation) makes it clear in its report that unless Israel arrives at some "reasonable arrangements with Syria", it must "refrain from evacuating the Golan" – in terms of both securing a strategic water supply and controlling pollution.[36]

It seems obvious that both countries are concerned about the implementation of any agreements, especially on water. They will therefore probably favour a comprehensive water monitoring verification programme (for further discussion on this, see *Chapter 4*).

Up to now, neither the Parties nor external brokers such as the US have come up with any solution to this challenge – except to focus on the exact delineation/demarcation of the border. *Chapter 4* outlines a possible way out for both Parties, attempting to reconcile both positions and concerns.

Section I   part 1

Chapter 4

Proposed solutions to the water dispute over the Golan Heights

The need for a comprehensive solution to the water dispute

Any water proposal would be viewed as part of a larger agreed-upon package. Sometimes, this means that concessions in one area may yield benefits in another. The water-land conflict-nexus over the Golan Heights is of such significance, although strategically different for both Parties, that a comprehensive solution ought to be achieved. In this context, a solution to the water disputes means not only reaching an agreement on exact borders, disengagements, legal rights and handing-over of territories, but also taking into account the practical implementation and enforcement of any water agreement from a short-, medium- and long-term perspective.

Why make public the following proposed solution?

As with any proposals made public in the Middle East, this one must be viewed at a point in time (2006). For years there has been little, if any, progress in the negotiations. There are reasons to believe that if the political climate had been more conducive to talks, indirectly or directly the proposal might have been further communicated bilaterally before public disclosure. A few leaders from Syria and Israel did however receive the proposal shortly after the failed Geneva meeting. From a long-term perspective, it is therefore to be

hoped that the two countries may use this proposal as constructive input towards obtaining public support for the fact that these matters are complex and important for both countries, and that each Party has legitimate concerns.

Each Party will have to display not only utter flexibility in reaching an agreement, but equally importantly, a full commitment towards implementing it.

> A solution to the water disputes means not only reaching an agreement on exact borders, disengagements, legal rights and handing-over of territories, but also taking into account the practical implementation and enforcement of any water agreement from a short-, medium- and long-term perspective.

What does the proposal attempt to achieve?

This proposal attempts to make both Parties' positions compatible with each other in such a way as to allow both Syria and Israel's concerns (often described as underlying objectives[x]) to be met.

More specifically, this means that the Israeli positions on ensuring the continuation of Israel's current water use in quantity and quality are

---

x   In negotiation terms: the Parties' interests.

to be compatible with Syrian territorial claims, including their demand to develop and thereby re-establish a population of up to 450,000[XI] on the Golan Heights.

In addition, implementation of any agreement is expected to be ensured by a comprehensive water verification and monitoring programme.

This proposal is valid irrespective of the 'exact' location of the disputed section of the border, as long as the interpretation of territorial sovereignty includes the conditions below.

Only a part of the pre-4 June 1967 border is disputed

So far, the negotiations indicate that only the sections of borders discussed above are disputed. As long as the principles in this proposal are agreed on, the exact 'drawing down to the metre' might be carried out at a later stage and at a more technical level. One prerequisite of the proposal is that Syria will not claim riparian rights to Lake Tiberias (which has not been done to date).

...implementation of any agreement is expected to be ensured by a comprehensive water verification and monitoring programme.

As a minimum however, the ten-metre strip seems to be already agreed on. This is, in recent years and in geographic terms, around 120-300 metres away from the June 1967 water-line intersection. Syria gets 'all' its geographic territory back, and Israel will achieve 'full sovereignty of the lake' and the most wanted 'access-buffer strip' to the lakeside.

The concerns of both Parties will be addressed

Respecting Israel's 'current use claim' and Syria's 'territorial rights' (by meeting the water use needs of the above-mentioned population increase) would entail additional costs to Syria in the form of measures to mitigate water pollution and replace net water consumption.

Any agreements between the two states would require support from other Arab countries and the wider international community. Any deal would therefore entail a commitment from the international community assisting the Parties to establish and implement any agreements.

The basic principle is that Syria should be able to resettle a population beyond the 1967 figure, but also receive compensation from the international community that guarantees their ability to maintain current Israeli water quantity and quality downstream (given the agreed maximum population level)[37] – see illustration of the proposal in *Figure 2*.

More specifically, the proposal consists of the following principles:

1. The international community, and especially Third Party constituencies (hereafter called International Third Parties – such as the UN and World Bank as well as groups of nations such as the US, Russia, EU, Japan, Germany, Switzerland, France, Nordic countries and some Arab States) offer to cover the additional costs of providing and protecting the water resources from pollution up to an agreed-on maximum population level, i.e. the maximum population that Syria has a right to on the Golan Heights must first be determined/ negotiated. These additional costs (hereafter called the maximum incremental costs) are

---

XI   Implying an average population density of about 389 persons/km², assuming no geographical resettlement restrictions within the 1,158 km² of the Golan Heights. It is assumed that there were around 130,000 Syrians on the Golan prior to 1967 (Maar'l and Halabi, 1992).

part 1

Section I

Figure 2. Past, present and possible resettled population on the Golan Heights in relation to water resources usage with the third party compensation mechanism (TPCM) and water monitoring/verification system

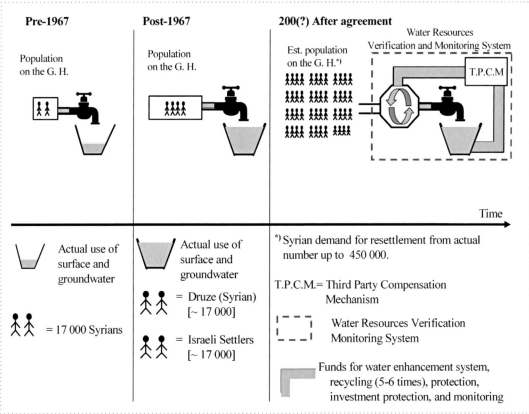

calculated as Syria's real costs[XII] of water resource management measures[XIII] that guarantee maintaining current Israeli water use downstream[XIV], given the agreed maximum population level. Exactly what incremental costs may be considered is discussed below.

2. The actual population resettled may be lower than the agreed maximum population. The International Third Parties will,

however, provide compensation for the actual incremental costs incurred, as well as compensation to Syria for resettling fewer people than the agreed maximum population. The latter will hereafter be called compensation for foregone resettlement.

3. Compensation for foregone resettlement may be used freely by Syria. It may be taken as compensation for the costs of alternative resettlement sites within Syria for that part of the maximum population that would have settled the Golan Heights.

4. Compensation for foregone resettlement (CFR) is defined as the maximum incremental costs

---

XII Real capital, operation, maintenance and certain opportunity costs.

XIII Water resource management measures encompass enhancement of water quantity and quality characteristics.

XIV Defined as the Upper Jordan River and Lake Tiberias.

Figure 3. Costs related to implementation of suggested measures

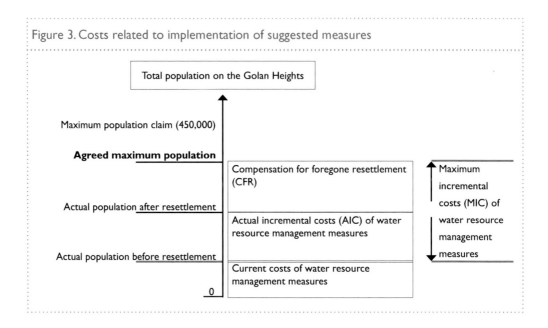

(MIC) minus the actual incremental costs (AIC) of water resource management measures. In other words, maximum incremental costs = actual incremental costs + compensation for foregone resettlement (see *Figure 3*).

5. The maximum Syrian claim of a population total of 450,000 on the Golan Heights may not be the maximum population finally agreed on by the Parties as the basis for calculating maximum incremental costs.

6. A separate publication by COMPASS defines the methodology for determining maximum incremental costs at different possible levels

of maximum population agreed on by the Parties.[38]

Alternative population levels considered in the publication are listed in *Table 2*.

Compensation principles and water resources constraints

Compensation principles
Compensation may include a set of various and, from an academic perspective, quite intriguing factors. However, as an attempt to narrow down

Table 2. Alternative scenarios for agreed maximum population on the Golan Heights

	Scenario 0 (baseline)	Scenario 1	Scenario 2	Scenario 3	Scenario 4
Maximum agreed population	17,000	100,000	200,000	300,000	450,000
Incremental population	0	83,000	183,000	283,000	433,000

Note: Assuming total relocation/withdrawal of all Israelis presently in the Golan Heights.

Source: COMPASS, 2005.

this discussion to the essential point, namely to come up with some figures that could give a realistic picture of such compensation, some assumptions are made in the calculation.

The compensation mechanism has been developed based on at least six assumptions:
1. Agreement on the maximum population that Syria has a right to resettle on the Golan Heights.[39]
2. Agreement on the principle that only incremental (additional) costs to the Parties due to the agreement will be admissible. This implies that compensation for investments in water resource management infrastructure, which is not a consequence of the Agreement, will not be given to either of the Parties.[40]
3. Agreement on the valuation principle that compensation for foregone resettlement will be measured in terms of avoided incremental costs of water resource management measures.
4. Agreement that actual incremental costs will be calculated using the most cost-effective water resource management options available relative to the agreed-upon standards that guarantee continued current Israeli water resource uses.[41]
5. Agreement on the interpretation of water quantity standards that guarantee continuation of current Israeli water resource uses.
6. Agreement on the interpretation of water quality standards that guarantee continuation of current Israeli water resource uses.[42]

Water resource use constraints
Certain suggested standards and constraints on human resettlement to the Golan Heights would follow from the draft peace agreement and common practices in water resource management.

Total mitigation costs will be a function of the levels of these water resource use constraints.

Water quantity constraints
Israel's claim to continued 'current use in quantity' of all surface and underground waters, and for 'measures to prevent depletion' of Lake Tiberias and Upper Jordan River and its sources will be interpreted as follows:
1. Upper Jordan River at mutually agreed-on monitoring stations:
   a. Current total annual flow is maintained[43].
   b. Current seasonal flow patterns must be maintained[44].
2. Underground water[45]:
3. Underground water level is established and new wells must not decline below current annual average groundwater level.
4. Maintaining current flow and variation should ensure protection of aquatic communities.
5. Respecting these quantity constraints means that any increase in net water consumption will have to be replaced by importing water from areas of Syria outside the Golan Heights. Increases in net water consumption can be expected with any population increase above current levels due to water consumption in the new domestic, service, agricultural and industrial sectors.
6. Total net water consumption of domestic, service and production sectors on the Golan Heights will depend on agreement of target levels for wastewater reclamation and reuse.

Water quality constraints
1. Israel's claim to continued 'current use in quality' of all surface and underground waters, and for 'measures to prevent contamination and pollution' of Lake Tiberias and the Upper Jordan River and its sources, will be

Table 3. Different scenarios of the cost of resettlement

Cost types	Capital costs (million US$)		Present value of recurrent costs (million US$)		Source in text
	Low estimate	High estimate	Low estimate	High estimate	Table
4.1 Costs of monitoring	1.4		1.5 (12%) 1.8 (6%)		1.1
4.2 Cost of water supply	Capital costs of distribution on GH not included		145 (12%)	499 (12%)	2.1
			248 (6%)	853 (6%)	
4.3 Costs of waste water collection and treatment	80	215	31 (12%) 52 (6%)	86 (12%) 145 (6%)	3.1
4.4 Costs due to solid waste disposal	All costs of waste transport are assumed recurrent		34 (12%) 63 (6%)		4.1
Total incremental costs (12% discount rate)	81+	216+	212	621	
Total incremental costs (6% discount rate)			356	1063	

Note: All costs in US$ for year 2000. (%) indicates discount rate used to calculate present values. The present value of total incremental costs is obtained by summing horizontally along the rows of Table 3.

* See COMPASS (2005).

interpreted as maintenance of the current level of predefined water quality parameters – hereafter called the current quality standard[46] (water quality parameters that may be considered in the current quality standard are discussed in COMPASS' publication).

2. Respecting these quality constraints means that any increase in wastewater generation will have to be completely mitigated by treatment processes.[47] Increases in wastewater generation can be expected with any population increase above current levels, due to net use of water in new domestic, service, agricultural and industrial sector processes.

Land use constraints

1. Respecting water quality constraints in terms of nutrient loading and turbidity requires certain restrictions to be placed on land uses, particularly in agriculture. The types of costs associated with these constraints are discussed further below.

2. Full Syrian territorial sovereignty implies that any previous delineation of areas, such as nature reserves, will be determined by Syria.

3. Approximately 21.2 per cent (246 km²) of the Golan Heights is currently managed as a nature reserve for conservation of endangered flora and fauna. Other conservation areas may be set aside for the protection of certain sensitive groundwater infiltration zones. In these areas all human settlement, agricultural and industrial activities would be excluded (exclusion of these land uses would entail opportunity costs – foregone net benefits – that are further discussed in COMPASS (2005)).

What are the estimated costs for such compensation?

Based on the assumptions outlined, the following cost types in *Figure 4* are taken into account. The proposal includes the first approximation order-of-magnitude cost estimates for cost types 1-4.

Based on the assumptions outlined, and as calculated in COMPASS (2005, *Third Party Control Mechanism of the Golan Heights*[48]), *Table 3* gives an illustration of the costs involved.

The total costs

The present value of total incremental costs would be in the order of US$293-837 million using a discount rate of 12 per cent, or US$446 million–1.279 billion using a discount rate of 6 per cent. Although these are in the order of magnitude estimates, they are considered 'low end' (see the technical assumptions detailed in the *Annex*).

In political and technical terms, a total amount of about US$1 billion is probably realistic. The exact amount would be set during implementation of the agreement.

Figure 4. Various cost estimates

Costs of monitoring (Type 1)
Costs of water supply and treatment (Type 2)
Costs of wastewater collection and treatment (Type 3)
Costs of solid waste disposal (Type 4)
Costs of measures to reduce diffuse discharges (Type 5)
Opportunity costs of water rationing (Type 6)
Opportunity cost of land use restrictions (Type 7)

Comprehensive water resources verification and monitoring systems

As outlined above, both Parties are concerned about compliance with any agreements. It seems obvious that both Parties not only want, but would even insist on, some sort of assurance of a mutually accepted Third Party's verification and monitoring of the other Party's implementation of the agreement. Due to the embedded scepticism

and suspicion of the other Party's intentions, comprehensive verification and monitoring systems that are specifically tailored to the water resources should be established as part of any peace agreement.

Documented compliance with such systems would eventually reinforce the Parties' conviction that they made the right decision.

Such a mechanism is a prerequisite for implementation. The other important element in this proposal is therefore establishment of a comprehensive 'water resources verification and monitoring system' involving both countries and a Third Party as a guarantor. Internationally, the importance of monitoring agreements is increasingly recognized.[49] Monitoring systems based on a standardized concept would provide continuous, reliable and standardized data with respect to climate and water quantity and quality for the water resources in question. Such systems would verify all phases of the water monitoring programme to ensure that it meets the intention of the agreement.

When an overall agreement on the Golan Heights has been reached, including an implementation plan, a 'Golan Heights Water Resources Monitoring System' (GWMS) should be established. This would take into account issues of pollution, water quality and quantitative aspects as well as procedural systems. The Parties should agree on rules for setting up and operating monitoring and verification programmes, including measurement systems and devices, analytical techniques, data processing and evaluation procedures.

The complex relationship between natural conditions and the manmade impact on water resources requires that the GWMS define status and trends, and identify possible early warning events. Such a GWMS will form the basis for a continuous verification process that may consist of four parts: planning; implementation; operation and maintenance (O&M); and reporting:

▸ During the planning phase, verification will focus on the proposed programme ensuring that the proposed procedures have been prepared. The main focus will be on the administrative procedures.

▸ During implementation, verification will focus on the monitoring sites, such as location, instrumentation and equipment, operation, data collection and processing, and reporting. Furthermore, the presence of relevant procedures for O&M, including analytical and monitoring methods to be used, data handling and reporting will be verified. The main focus will be on the technical procedures.

▸ During operation and maintenance, verification will include the monitoring stations, personnel, laboratories and other institutions participating in the programme. It will check that the procedures, manuals, O&M plans and contingency plans that have been prepared are used by programme participants, and that the monitoring programme is operated in conformity with these procedures as well as with written agreements and regulations.

▸ Verification of the reports will ensure that they are in accordance with the procedures made for the three types of reports: executive summary; data report; and O&M report. Verification statements will be prepared based on the verification documents/reports.[50]

▸ Non-conformities identified will be reported in draft reports, and corrective action must be undertaken by the national programme manager within a given deadline. Follow-up of the corrective action will be carried out and a final report prepared.

Systematic, independent and documented auditing processes will be established by a recognized Third Party arrangement.

Another effective confidence-building measure would be approved procedures for mutual visits and exchange of information between the Parties. This should ensure complete transparency, maximum efficiency and accountability. Reliable and auditable data collection principles and procedures are an integral part of that, and the Parties should have access to information about the GWMS according to agreed-upon rules. This access would contribute to creating mutual trust in the GWMS.[51]

Syria and Israel would, in mutual agreement, decide on the scope of the GWMS. Criteria for the selection of monitoring sites, monitoring programme and data assessment will then be established. A crucial question is how to deal with non-conformity data. Procedures for handling non-conformity should be worked out, and a proposal on how to deal with this developed very early in the process.

Initially, a Third Party would, as an independent auditor, verify and certify (if requested) the whole system arrangement and its establishment in conformity with agreements, regulations and procedures. It might also be that a third Party should have overall responsibility for the operation of the GWMS in such a way that both Parties are confident with the work and quality of the results obtained.

Transforming the proposal into reality

This proposal has been developed over the years in order to address the real concerns of Syria and Israel. It aims to reflect their genuine interests. However, as in every real-life situation, there are different ways of looking at such a proposal. Most likely, both countries will favour comprehensive arrangements related to the water conflict. Syria has done this recently in its bilateral agreement with Lebanon on Nahr el Kabir River signed in 2003 and in the Orontes River agreements, which involved a set of mechanics to be put into action.[52] It has also made clear that such monitoring and verification programmes are desirable in the Euphrates and Tigris context.[53]

Likewise, Israel's peace treaty with Jordan and the preliminary agreements with the Palestinian Authority are meticulous and contain detailed provisions for implementation.

What about the costs of implementation?

How would external stakeholders view these cost estimates compared to the possibility of no agreement? Over the past century, 'compensation' in various forms has been used both to secure settlements and to increase the chances of maintaining such arrangements.[54] Any extra-regional benefactors take a self-interested perspective and calculate the economic cost *vis-à-vis* the foreign and economic interests of their country in combination with its political course. Historically, for example, the US has had a different perspective on the Middle East to the French, but both would probably consider the economic cost to be low compared to the long-term political and economic benefits of peace and increased stability in the region.

The 'peace dividend' therefore seems to be high enough for international actors to commit funds to such a compensation mechanism.[55]

In addition, multilateral institutions such as the World Bank and United Nations (UNDP and UNEP) have for years set up funds for such purposes, such as the Global Environmental Facility (GEF)[XV] and Nile Basin Initiative. The role of the World Bank with its technical and financial expertise corresponds to its desire to focus on such activities.[56]

The two countries in question may, however, put different weights on various factors in this proposal.

A Syrian perspective on the proposal

The majority of the population in Syria will probably agree on a peace agreement with Israel as long their leadership is in favour of it, bearing in mind the following principles:

1. Any peace must be based on a formula that should not be underestimated from a Syrian perspective: "land for peace". To date, this has been interpreted as the territorial sovereignty of Golan.[57] The present proposal specifically addresses this matter. As discussed earlier, any other matter that follows such an agreement appears secondary to this formula.[XVI]

> For the Syrians, return of occupied land on the Golan is a national symbol and a matter of pride.

XV   Dealing with four areas: international water, forestry, protection of the ozone layer, and mitigating global climate change (see www.gefweb.org/)

XVI   Such as military disengagement zones and normalization, for example in trade and diplomatic representations.

■ Photo 11.
The watershed of the Baniyas River on the Golan Heights (northwards)

2. The principle of territorial sovereignty is interpreted in such a way that the 'right to return of the foregone population of Golan' must be accepted.

3. There is, to some degree, uncertainty about the extent to which progress on establishing a Palestinian State is necessary for a deal on Golan. Some have argued that this is desirable in the eyes of the Syrians – and of the Arab world as a whole.[58]

There are strong reasons to believe that Syria would favour peace with Israel.[59] Such a position cannot be isolated from events such as the US-led coalition invasion of Iraq in 2003 and subsequent US sanctions against Syria in 2004. However, one should not anticipate that Syria would sign a peace treaty if it feels it is being cornered. Any deal must be mutually perceived as honourable and fair. This is true not only from a political point of view, but equally importantly from an emotional, ideological and economic point of view. For the Syrians, return of

occupied land on the Golan is a national symbol and a matter of pride.

Specifically, as long as the two conditions (1 and 2) above are fulfilled, the peace dividend for Syria is potentially large. A normalization by the international community and specifically a lifting of US sanctions may pave the way for rapid economic and social development.

An Israeli perspective on the proposal
There are equally strong reasons to believe that Israel would favour peace with Syria. Quite a few scholars have argued that former Prime Minister Barak was ready to provide the Syrians with the border delineation/demarcation (through the so-called 'Rabin Deposit'[XVII]) (see Ross, 2004: Chapter 22; Enderlin, 2003: Chapter 3; Swisher, 2004: Chapter 8). This was some time ago,

---

XVII The late Prime Minister Rabin deposited a sort of 'bottom line' with President Clinton that should be applied in the end-game if a peace between Israel and Syria can be reached.

however former Prime Minister Peres and later Barak confirmed the 'deposit'.

One should not, however, underestimate the embedded psychological, intellectual and political scepticism as regards relying on the Arab countries' compliance with any agreements on strategic water resources.[60] The academic literature is quite interesting in discussing and reflecting various options and strategies, but it all boils down to the following question: Do the benefits outweigh the risk and costs (see for example Rabinovich, 2004)?

Most Israelis and their leaders may answer yes to that question[61], but at the same time add: What kind of insurance for compliance do they get, for what kind of cost and at what risk? In the end, such a decision would have to be made by the Israeli leadership together with the people. It will definitely be

> Most Israelis and their leaders may add: What kind of insurance for compliance do they get, for what kind of cost and at what risk?

made according to the overall political and psychological climate in the region.

In any case, the options exist for sustainable solutions.

Concluding remarks

Syria and Israel have much to lose and much to win by resolving the conflict over the Golan Heights. When the timing seems right for one of the Parties, it does not appear so for the other side. The failed Geneva meeting of March 2000 was in fact a missed historic opportunity, but may have occurred due to lack of a practical solution to the disputed waters. This proposal is not the only way of handling the water file, but rather one way of taking the Parties' key concerns into account.

Since the year 2000, little progress has been made. This may be because of the convoluted geo-political situation in the region. However, the 'irreconcilable positions' are the same – and proposals such as this may become even more relevant than before.

Section I   part 1

Chapter 5

A proposed water agreement between Israel and Syria

Preamble

The following text is a preliminary proposal for an input to a possible water agreement (as part of a peace treaty) between Israel and Syria – hereafter known as the 'Water Agreement'.

> **Reservations:** The author does not expect that a water agreement between the two countries will look exactly like that proposed. Any agreement is subject to political and technical negotiations. It does, however, attempt to illustrate what some key issues in such an agreement might look like (some formulations are derived from the 'Shepherdstown text').

Article I. Resolution of all water issues

The Parties recognize that the full resolution of all water issues between them constitutes a fundamental element in ensuring a stable and lasting peace based on international principles and good neighbourliness, the Parties have agreed to establish arrangements that ensure the continuation of Israel's current use in water quantity and quality of the surface and groundwater in a selected part of the Upper Jordan River/Lake Tiberias basin (north of ... degree of latitude and east of ... degree of longitude) pursuant to Article ... as detailed in Annex ... while at the same time enable Syria to utilize the water resources for its social and economic development on the Golan Heights.

Article II. Bilateral Water Management Committee

For the purposes of this agreement as outlined in Article 1 and Annex ..., the Parties will establish a Bilateral Water Management Committee which has a supervision and enforcement capacity as outlined in Annex ... The Quartet [UN, US, EU, and Russia] will be permanently represented (with each of its members) in the Committee and act as a guarantor for this agreement.

Article III. Third Party Compensation Mechanism

- (i) As a basis for the agreement outlined in Article I and II, the Parties have together with the Quartet agreed to establish a Third Party Compensation Mechanism which will serve the purpose of enabling Syria to develop the water resources while preventing pollution and depletion of the resources in accordance with Article I.

- (ii) The Mechanism will technically and financially be administrated by a secretariat managed by GEF's implementing agencies under instruction of the Bilateral Water Management Committee.

Article IV. Water monitoring systems

All agreed water monitoring systems in a selected part of the Upper Jordan River/Lake Tiberias basin – as detailed in Annex ... – are subject to verification by the Bilateral Water Management Committee. The committee shall approve verification procedures before they are put into force.

Article V. Notification of any planned measures

The Bilateral Water Management Committee shall be notified of any planned measure which may have an adverse effect on the selected basin environment for verification and approval. Such notification shall be accompanied by technical data and information including the results of any environmental impact assessment.

Article VI. Licensing of wastewater discharges

The Bilateral Water Management Committee shall license wastewater discharges. The water discharge licensing shall include all types of Return-flow and shall contain directives on how to handle unforeseen outlet situations.

Article VII. Protect the environment and prevent pollution

The two Parties shall, individually, and where appropriate jointly,

▸ (i) protect and preserve the ecosystems of ..., and

▸ (ii) prevent, reduce and control pollution that may be in contradiction to the agreement outlined in Article 1.

Endnotes

1 Several military leaders have made such statements, and recently the Israeli general Moshe Yaalon: "From the point of view of military requirements we could reach an agreement with Syria by giving up the Golan. The army could defend Israel's borders wherever they are": BBC, 13 August, 2004 (news.bbc.co.uk/go/pr/fr/-/2/hi/middle_east/3561334.stm).

2 This is also illustrated by the fact that former Military Chief of Intelligence General Uri Sagy who became the Chairman of the Israeli water company Mekorot also negotiated the water questions during the Shepherdstown talks. Or as stated by Israeli Minister of Agriculture Ya'acov Tsur who served both under Prime Minister Rabin and Peres when the evacuation of the Golan was seriously negotiated in the *Jerusalem Post*, 27 December 1995: "The water resources on the Golan [are] a critical, vital and even fateful matter in terms of the future of the State [of Israel]. I have to say that I am not aware of any replacement for this water" (see also: Proceedings of the Herzliya Forum Conference: 'Water Crisis in Israel', in: Starr (2001: 30). Or as stated by the authoritative Israeli journalist on strategic matters (Shiff, 1993): "If the Golan's military significance for Israel is primarily operational, specifically the defence of Galilee, the need to defend the water sources is absolutely strategic and indeed existential".
Or as stated in the Israeli newspaper *Ma'ariv,* 19 July 1995, quoting Prime Minister Rabin when he was addressing some Israeli ambassadors: "the greatest danger Israel has to face in the negotiations with Syria is the possibility of losing control over the Golan Heights' water resources".

3 The description of the resource geographical environment of the Golan Heights is based on the following open sources references:
- Hydrological Service, 1999.
- Arad and Bein, 1986.
- Bergelson, Nativ and Bein, 1998.
- Rimmer, Hurwitz and Gvirtzman, 1999.

4 Shuval (1994: 162) indicates between 40 and 50mm.

5 The planned project includes: a) restructuring and completing the internal wastewater system; b) construction of a new main line, 11 km long, that will connect the three big villages; and a wastewater treatment plant near Bukata. The treated effluent will be used to irrigate large areas of apple plantation in the region. Plans for the year 2010 predict an annual treated water production of 1.1 MCM (130 m^3/hour). The approved programme includes collection systems, oxidation basins, and a reservoir for effluent water on the Rokad River.

6 In 1955, the US President sent out an envoy, Ambassador Johnston, to develop a plan for allocation of the water in the larger Jordan Basin. See details in Murakami (1995).

7 Cf. Naff (1994) which gives a detailed description of the Syrian-Israeli relationship.

8 Confirmed also by US State Secretary Madeline Albright, 2004.

9 Which started on January 3 in the small American city of Shepherdstown in the State of West Virginia, not far from Washington DC, so the US President flew to and fro daily.

10 See Ross's (2004) detailed accounts (especially pp. 517 and 521 and Chapter 22), and as stated by the Israeli Negotiator Reserve General Uri Saguy, "We really defined the essential problems of our relationship with Syria"; and "The border; the question of the line June 4, 1967; water" as quoted in Enderlin (2003: 126).

11 This point was underscored in Syrian President Bashar Al-Assad's first comprehensive speech to the Arab League in September 2000, such as: "certainly it will use them [ed: i.e., the power elements and cards related to, among other things, Lebanon] for the service of the national cause, namely the issue of Golan. But before that, it will use them in the service of the pan-Arab cause…"

12 Presented in *Al-Hayat* (a daily Arabic-language and London-based newspaper) on 9 January 2000 and in the Israeli Newspaper *Haaretz* on 13 January.

13 At the Intercontinental Hotel in Geneva on 26 March.

14 Syria raised this matter with the author already in the December preceding the Shepherdstown talks in January 2000 as well as just after. The Israeli had a passive approach to this matter as the demand was not placed high on the agenda by the Syrians since the final border was demarked.

15 The most detailed assessment of this might be found in Ross (2004: 580-590), but it should also be viewed in relation to a slightly different perspective by Swisher (2004).

16 The adoption by the US Administration of the Syrian Accountability Act of May 2004 and the subsequent UN Security Council Resolution 1559 have not fostered that relationship.

17 See President Clinton's senior Director of Near Eastern Affairs at the National Security Council, Bruce Riedel, "In retrospect the US should have pressured harder to get a deal with Syria and put down own ideas about resolving the outstanding territorial issues on the front" as quoted in Swisher (2004: 122).

18 See further discussions about the demilitarized zones, their status and "authoritative interpretation" in Naff (1994), in Muslih, (1983) as well as in Feitelson (2000).

19 Cf. also the statement by President Clinton's advisor Gemal Helal regarding the US perception of the Syrian position (as quoted in Swisher (2004: 119). See also the newly published article in Science Po, Paris, by Marwan Doudy that deals extensively with this issue (Doudy, 2005b).

20 The horizontal distance from the present land/water intersection to the pre 4 June 1967 line varies between 40 and 200 metres due to different slope gradient of the terrain.

21 Ibid: President Clinton was citing President Hafez Al-Al-Assad of Syria in the last meeting on a peace for the Golan Heights between Syria and Israel as he realized that the peace talks between the two countries broke down – in Geneva on 27 March 2000: "[President Al-Assad] wanted to sit on the shore of the lake and put his feet in the water" (in Lake Tiberias)" (Enderlin, 2003).

22 According to the draft Syrian-Israeli agreement on water from Shepherdstown, January 2000.

23 For example: the Syrian President Bashar Al-Assad's statement in July 2001 to the leading Saudi pan-Arab daily *Asharq al-Awsat*: Q: "..are the Israeli positions still the same concerning the [eastern shore line of Lake Tiberias] and .. the water issue?" Al-Assad: "We refuse to discuss any issue unless agreement is reached on the essence, on the basic principle ...What is the point of agreeing on the water issue if we agree on the land, which is the main issue? Hence, Syria will not discuss any issue until it guarantees the return of all its territory up to the June 4 [1967] borders." (As translated from Arabic by the *Middle East Mirror*, 9 February 2002.)

24 Syrian Vice Foreign Minister Walid Moalem in interview with Swisher (2004).

25 This is also illustrated in the paper presented by then Syrian Head of the International Water Department at the Ministry of Irrigation, Eng. Abdul Aziz Al Masri (2003).

26 However, this does not coincide with President Clinton's statement that if the Israeli insisted on guarantees on the quantity and quality of water flowing from the Golan into the lake, "Syria agreed as long as it got the same guarantees on its water flow from Turkey", (Clinton, 2004: 886). The author's interpretation of this is that Syria believed they could obtain US assistance in pressuring Turkey. Today, after the US invasion of Iraq, the situation might be almost the opposite.

27 Some observers argue that Syria may want to demand water from Baniyas in order to give it to the Arab population downstream of the lake (cf. Hoff, 2000: 160). The author does not believe that Syria would link such an agreement with Jordan and the Palestinians as that would set a precedent by hydro-politically linking the basins.

28 According to the average population growth over the past 35 years. This figure should however, be open to being further determined/negotiated. See also the description of the Syrian demand on returning population in Gruen (2000) or as anticipated by Hoff (2000: 162).

29 As for example outlined in Foreign Minister's Farouk al-Shaara's speech on 16 December at the White House Rose Garden in Washington, DC. See also Swisher (2004: 72).

30 Alster (1996) represents one of the more authoritative Israeli points of view.

31 Riparian rights give in accordance with international law a set of rights and obligations (see for example the 'Helsinki rules' and the 'UN Framework Convention on the Law of Non-Navigational Uses of International Watercourses').

32 The 'Clinton Administration Proposal to Jerusalem and Damascus' in the Shepherdstown negotiations in January 2000.

33 See the Israeli letter to the UN Security Council of 21 November 2002.

34 See also Hoff (2000: 152), "Israel will likely seek Syrian assurances that this reservoir network will not be expanded and that steps will be taken to mitigate pollution runoff".

35 The Israeli Water Commissioner Meir Ben Meir, 3 January 2000, as translated by Martin Sherman, Proceedings of the Herzliya Forum Conference: Water Crisis in Israel, ed. J. Starr, April 2001.

36 Mekorot (1996: 19; IV in *Summary and Conclusions*); Sherman (2001).

37 This proposal is in line with the interpretation of sovereignty in terms of both 'rights' and 'obligations' (to among other things protect the resources) in relation to water resources (see the introductory part).

38 See COMPASS (2005). Determining what proportion of maximum incremental costs is actual incremental cost, and what proportion is compensation for foregoing resettlement, is not required at this point in time. In other words, deciding on "the size of the pie" must take place before deciding on "the sharing of the pie" between actual incremental costs and compensation for foregone resettlement.

39 Without agreement on the level of Syrian resettlement there is no basis for calculating maximum incremental costs.

40   It must be determined whether Israel will claim any form of compensation for existing infrastructure. An argument against such compensation would be that the infrastructure would continue to benefit mainly Israel, by reducing discharges of pollutants and reducing water consumption (e.g. drip irrigation systems).

41   Using the cost-effectiveness principle avoids inflating maximum incremental cost.

42   Subject to agreement on the activities that are to be considered as part of current Israeli water uses.

43   Baniyas River may get a separate arrangement, but for simplicity's sake is not included in this calculation.

44   Possibly defined as a minimum average flow during the dry season months (month 1–month 6), and a minimum average flow during wet season months (month 7–month 12).

45   Are any of the aquifers under the Golan Heights also tapped by Israeli wells (that are located outside the 4 June 1967 border)? If so, a total sustainable rate of withdrawal must be calculated and allocated between Israel and Syria.

46   An alternative interpretation of "continued current use in quality" is that current uses can still be continued at some lower water quality level – hereafter called a safe minimum standard of water quality. Wastewater treatment costs would then be lower under the safe minimum standard of quality than under the current quality standard.

47   There are other examples where one country has agreed to meet certain water quality standards and a water treatment plant has been installed at the border such as the Yuma area between USA and Mexico on the Colorado River. See Frank Leitz and Ewoldsen (1978).

48   See COMPASS (2005) www.compass-org.ch/Selected_literature/selected_literature1.htm

49   See for example the guidelines of OECD (1994) and the World Bank (1996).

50   Revised technical non-paper (2000) from Veritas to CESAR.

51   As in the case of the disarmament process in the Balkans as conveyed by the Chief Disarmament Negotiator General Vidleik Eide [former CHOD] (personal communication, February 2000).

52   Cf. the most comprehensive description and assessment of these agreements is in Comair (2003).

53   Expressed through personal communications with relevant ministers over the years.

54   As described historically in several cases from the Middle East by Fromkin (2001) and more recently in the case of the Egyptian-Israeli and the Jordanian-Israeli peace accords.

55   See also the long-standing US Envoy, Ambassador Ross' statement (Ross, 2004: 772) when summarizing lessons learnt, "We can offer guarantees on security; financial assistance to demonstrate the material benefits of hard decisions, all of which may be important in helping each side to cross historic threshold". Cf. also ODI, ARCADIS and Euroconsult, (2001).

56   See World Bank Technical Paper (Kirmani and Rangeley, 1994), "It focuses mainly on the Bank's role in international water affairs and recommends that the Bank should play a more proactive role in promoting dialogue, improving data base and analysis, and assisting riparians in establishing co-operative arrangements to plan and use their water resources efficiently. Further, it suggests that the Bank should strengthen its capacity to respond to riparian requests for assistance in an objective, competent and effective manner." WTP 239, Washington DC, Retrieved from www-wds.worldbank.org/servlet/WDS_IBank_Servlet?pc ont=details&eid=000009265_3970311122714

57   As emphatically stated by the Syrian President Bashar Al-Assad in July 2001 to the leading Saudi pan-Arab daily *Asharq al-Awsat* (as translated from the Arabic by the *Middle East Mirror*, 9 February 2002).

58   Cf. Syrian Foreign Minister's Al-Shara's speech (as he outlined the Syrian policy towards the negotiations with Israel) to the Arab Writers Union on 13 February 2000 (as quoted in Rabinovich, 2004).

59   See for example the Syrian President Bashar al-Assad's message on 24 November 2004 to (at that time) UN envoy to the Middle East Terje Rød Larsen, "… the Syrian leader has an outstretched hand to Israel and is willing to go to the negotiation table with Israel based on the relevant Security Council resolutions and the principles of land for peace, without conditions..." (cf. UN News service www.un.org/apps/news/printnews.asp?nid=12640), which was also repeated by BBC World Edition on 5 January 2005 on Turkey's Foreign Minister Abdullah Gul who spoke of "Syria's readiness for peace talks, during a landmark visit to Israel" (http://news.bbc.co.uk/2/hi/middle_east/4145587.stm).

60   Sherman (2001: 28) cites several Israeli scholars and politicians that have an "aversion to surrender control over water supplies to an alien power ..." as well as grave concerns regarding "non-compliance of the peace process".

61   Israeli Army Chief General Moshe Yaalon stated that Israel "could leave the Golan" and that "the move would not endanger Israel's security" (see BBC News 13 August 2004, http:// news.bbc.co.uk/go/pr/fr/-/2/hi/middle_east/3561334.stm).

Part 2

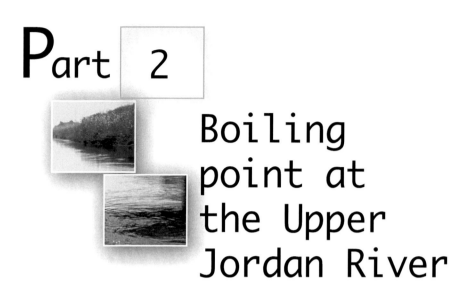

Boiling point at the Upper Jordan River

the Wazzani Springs conflict between Lebanon and Israel

Abstract

The evolution of the relationship between Israel and Lebanon is complex, and in many ways hard to understand for outsiders. Most of the international attention has been on the civil war in Lebanon (which ended in 1990), the role of Syria, and the high tension in southern Lebanon that erupted in armed confrontation as late as July 2006.

Quite a few key actors and observers argue that the Israeli–Lebanese relationship and, especially more recently, the role of Hezbollah as the dominant Party in the southern part, are predetermining the resolution to any dispute, whether this is over borders or water resources in that area.

This may be correct, but does not hide the fact that in case a solution is worked out, there should be some principles on which such an agreement may rest.

Part 2 describes the concerns of the Parties. It sets out the hydro-political complexity, especially in relation to the Golan Heights, and that any resolution here would be a precedent for resolution of the Golan dispute.

In short, the proposed solution contains provisions for a sharing/allocation regime of the Hasbani River, of which the Wazzani Springs are a part.

■ Photo 12.
Valley of the Hasbani on the Lebanese side of the border

Chapter 1

The water is boiling

Water in the southern part of Lebanon and northern part of Israel constitutes the Upper Jordan River Basin (in addition to the Golan Heights as dealt with in *Part 1*). It is located in a sensitive

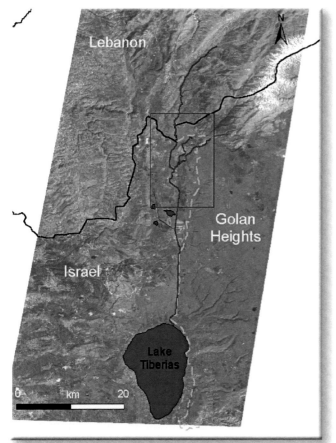

Map 7a-7b. Present and historic borders between Israel and Syria, and Lebanon (the black line represents the so-called 'blue line' set by the UN between Lebanon and Israel/the Golan Heights).

Note: Lebanon is disputing the area around the Sheeba Farms by claiming they possessed it before 1966.

Sources: Data from Lebanon derived from Landsat ETM and ESRI from other areas. Data processed by MAPS Geosystems s.a.r.l., Beirut, Lebanon. The 'International border' is based on data from UN Map 'Levant 50J19 Houle' and the current Lebanese/Israeli border is based on the UN 'Blue Line'.

Map 8.   Location of the Wazzani Springs with the Hasbani, Dan and Baniyas Rivers

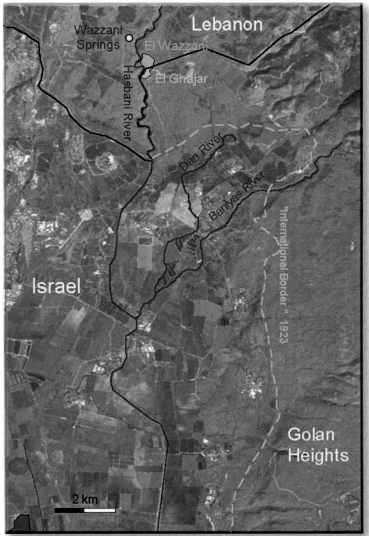

the Hasbani River[1] that flows into Israel only 2 km downstream. When an agreement on the Golan Heights (with the pre-1967 lines in this area) comes into force, Syria may also become a riparian, since the river forms the border for just over 2 km.[1] Recently, the spring has been 'boiling', not because of a conflict over a huge amount of water, but because of national priorities, politics and a fragile hydrological system.

As part of its reconstruction and development efforts in the south, Lebanon wanted to use the Wazzani Springs, while Israel reacted strongly to this because of the way in which the Lebanese started to use the water. Their reaction was due to the extreme hydro-ecological sensitivity of the Upper Jordan River Basin and its vital inflow to Lake Tiberias as a stable freshwater supply to Israel (if this flow is not sustained, a significant amount of all water supply in Israel may be disrupted).[2] Such a mixture does not usually create favourable conditions for sustainable solutions.

geopolitical area with a long history of quests for water resources since the establishment of the Jewish State in 1948. The only peace agreement signed to date has been with Lebanon in 1949 (i.e. a 'truce'). The particular dispute in question, the Spring at the Wazzani Village hereafter named 'Wazzani Springs', is located in Lebanon. It feeds

---

I   Or the Snir River as the Israelis call it. Hasbani River is more often used internationally, and is therefore used here.

This part of the publication does not attempt to duplicate descriptions of the hydrology of the area, nor the political analyses by eminent hydrologists[3] and political experts from the two countries and outside. Rather, it attempts to briefly describe the relevant historical and hydrological situation of the dispute. Based on some of the methodology and reasoning described in the introductory and preceding parts of the publication, it proposes a way to proceed in order to come to a mutually satisfying solution.

In simplistic terms, this conflict is discussed in terms of *the way it could be resolved* rather than *the exact allocation* of water. The reasons for this situation are complex, due particularly to popular public perception in both countries. Several scholars, such as Amery (2000), have studied the dispute, primarily from an epistemic perspective.[4]

As in the case of the two preceding water disputes discussed in this publication, any proposals should be careful in ascribing quick-fix solutions to such complex matters – especially due to the changing political climate in the region. The fact that this is a non-partisan proposal serves to increase its credibility for Israel, Lebanon and any other stakeholders, while also potentially removing obstacles towards a peace agreement.

Section I   **part 2**

Chapter 2

The border landscape in southern Lebanon and northern Israel

Thousand-year-old cedar trees are scattered throughout the rugged landscape of the high mountains in Lebanon. Even today, the beauty and mystery of the trees demand respect from anyone walking among them. According to the Scriptures, the Jews built their Temple in Jerusalem of the finest timber; the Romans burned them to make arms; and until recently they were unprotected and used for buildings and firewood. As the cedars have been precious throughout history, the water running down from the mountains has formed civilizations on the plains of Lebanon and in the fertile Hula Valley in Israel, contributing to the determination of the religious and political societies of the ancient and modern world. Their ability to use the water in the valleys and on the costal plains for agricultural and drinking purposes enabled, among others, the Phoenicians to develop a remarkable intellectual and technological supremacy 3,500 years ago. The fruits of civilization stretched out in all directions of the old world. Even today, the contemporary Western alphabet is derived from their work.

The southern part of Lebanon and northern part of Israel is a beautiful landscape with mountain and river scenery that is stunning to any visitor. The warm morning sun creates a magical light that makes picturesque spots on the slopes and waterfalls, and in the numerous villages in the foothills. The beauty of the landscape is hard to associate with its rugged contemporary history. Indeed, the area has been an arena for military clashes and political drama ever since the 1970s. The Israeli desire to secure the valuable water sources of the Upper Jordan River Basin is not new.

The water in the Upper Jordan River has played a significant part in history, even more so after May 2000, when Israel withdrew their troops in Lebanon from the so-called 'Security Zone' (see *Map 10*). Today, the disputed springs are located within the UN Peacekeeping zone, UNIFIL.

The *border landscape* in a Lebanese context

Lebanon is historically a part of the *Levant*. It was therefore a province under the Ottoman Syria region, becoming a sovereign nation as a result of the Anglo-French Convention in the 1920s. The present geographical location is quite similar to ancient Phoenicia. The borders cut across ethnical groups, confessional domains and natural resources. The Ottoman era reflected this mosaic in such a way that the cities of Aleppo (in today's Syria) and Tripoli governed

Map 9.   Location of the Hasbani River (H.R.) seen in relation to the Upper Jordan River Basin

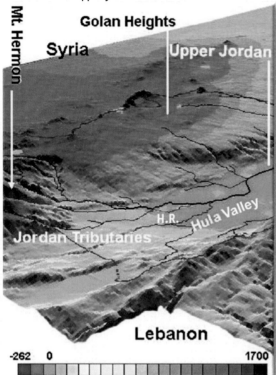

Evidently, the correlation between confessional and political 'areas of influence' is quite high. This means that the political landscape in the south is dominated by the predominately Shiite communities, such as Hezbollah and Amal, which are both a combination of political parties and Shiite movements, despite the fact that there are some Christian villages in the area.

The interrelationship between Hezbollah, Syria and Iran is complex. It is beyond the scope of this publication to describe it, except for one important aspect: most observers agree that there is a relationship between Syria and Hezbollah. Various factors determine this connection, but in this context the Syrian interest in the 'triangle of headwaters of the Jordan Basin' is significant (see further discussion in *Chapter 4*).

In the late 1960s, Lebanon was drawn into the ongoing conflict between Israel and the Palestinians for various reasons, including cross-border attacks on Israel by Palestinian militia. Internally in Lebanon, and due to the complex political landscape, several factors eventually led to a complex and destructive civil war over 18 years that ended in 1990. In the south, the Phalanges militia fought the Palestinians and Israel supported the so-called South Lebanese Army. In 1978, a UN Peacekeeping Force (UNIFIL) was established upon a request from the Lebanese Government, and still exists today. In June 1982, Israel invaded South Lebanon in an attempt to stop the Palestinian militias' attacks on its northern border.

After May 2000, when Israel withdrew from Lebanon, there was unanimous national support for integration through reconstruction and development of the south.

the north, Damascus the centre, and Sidon the south. Coastal Lebanon and the Bekaa Valley were directly governed from Istanbul, while Mount Lebanon had a semi-autonomous status.

A simplified description of the various religious affinities may explain this. Arab tribesmen settled the southern part after the spread of Islam in 700 AD and the Christian Maronites settled in the mountainous north. In 1100 AD, the Druze faith (a derivate of Shiite Islam) spread, while other groups of Shiite Muslims settled at the northern and southern fringes of the slopes and in the Bekaa valley. The coastal areas became mainly Sunni. To a large extent, the confessional geography is more or less unchanged.

Still a sensitive *border landscape*

South Lebanon is a remarkable area with long historic ties. In 1999, the Government's High Relief Committee and the United Nations Development Programme (UNDP) described it in the following terms:

> "South Lebanon has been heavily affected by 30 years of conflict. The area possesses important potentials for development; the availability of water; sites of touristic value, resourceful and dynamic inhabitants, and a geographic location that could offer the region a promising future once the conflict is over. What matters today is to preserve this potential and to operate a transition between the politics of emergency assistance and those of development. This would permit, as soon as the conflict ends, an invitation of ambitious projects, including the return of the displaced, as an answer to the reconstruction challenges and in order to consolidate the post-conflict situation with socio-economic progress." (Government's High Relief Committee and UNDP 1999)

This description illustrates the desire of the Lebanese and the international community to develop the area. In the south, around 350,000 people live in precarious economic conditions, with a quarter of households having a monthly income of less than US$300 for an average family of almost five. In addition, social problems exist that are directly related to the

post-conflict situation (High Relief Committee and UNDP, 1999).

The border landscape displays marks of conflicts such as minefields, burnt areas and deserted terrain. The region is less developed than the rest of the country, although the Lebanese Government has undertaken efforts to repair

■ Photo 13.
Water supply near the border between Israel and Lebanon

and maintain public networks, and launched new projects for Tyre and Nabatiyeh, primarily focusing on water and sanitation.

From the central government's point of view, it has been important to promote national integration of South Lebanon and ensure an adequate level of services equivalent to that of other regions. According to the government, unless adequate development of the area takes place it may experience multiple negative defects such as:

▶ "the uncontrolled return of thousands of displaced people to the South, leading to a multiplication of problems related to distribution of water and energy.

Map 10. UN peacekeeping forces in southern Lebanon (Wazzani Springs in red)

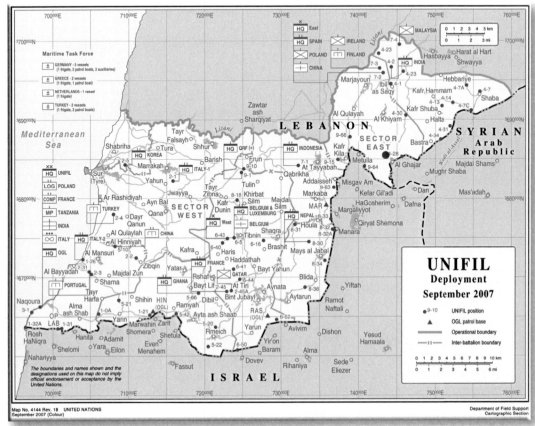

Section I   part 2

▸ the phenomenon of retaliation and conflict between families and villages can take place and even persist, and

▸ the water streams might witness irreversible degradation due to uncontrolled movement of reconstruction." (High Relief Committee and UNDP, 1999: 10)

Within such a context, the government emphasized the need to develop the water resources for the people in the Hasbani and the Marjeyoun regions (*cazas*), amounting to about 150,000 people. Such efforts were stepped up after the Israeli withdrawal from the area in 2000.

The *border landscape* in an Israeli context

As described earlier, the strategic water resources are the main concern. However, in this context, the security situation in its northern part is important. The area has been fully developed despite an unstable security situation, and much effort has been put into monitoring and managing the headwaters.

Brief description of the water resource situation

It is quite common in the academic community to compare water availability to a country's population, as an expression of what might be a guiding principle in water allocation between states. The author takes another perspective, in the sense that a comparison of water availability may be relevant for today's situation and that of the future, pending development of various sectors (especially agriculture), but may not offer principles for solving international water disputes. As in the preceding case of the Golan Heights, as well as with the Euphrates and Tigris Rivers, the relative availability between the states does not determine the respective share, but rather underlines the importance of finding sustainable solutions that could provide a stable and foreseeable water supply for each country.

With this in mind, it is worth noting that Lebanon, on a national level, enjoys a relative surplus of water compared to countries in its proximity. 'Surplus' is, however, a relative concept. This is particularly true as Lebanon, like any other country, aims for socio-economic development that empirically raises demand. The country's own interpretation is that there is a deficit of water resources[5], not least in terms of management of water quality (El-Fadel, Maroun, Semerjian and Harajli, 2003). The only Lebanese international water resource associated with the Upper Jordan River Basin is the Hasbani River, with an average flow of 135-140 MCM per year[6] to which the groundwater is connected.

Lebanon's climate is subtropical, with rainfall between October and April that averages between 600 mm and 1,000 mm yearly at the coast, but may be as much as 1,300 mm in the high altitudes. The Bekaa Valley – from which the Orontes, El-Khabir, and Litani rivers originate – is in the rain-shadow and averages between 350 and 650 mm. The combination of rainfall and snow melting in the spring gives fairly steady flows. Irrigation in the area is necessary, since there are about three to four months with complete aridity. The mountainous

geological composition in South Lebanon has little permeability, and because of this water is forced to the surface as springs and small rivers. On the top of the mountains the topsoil is poor, but the lower slopes are intensively irrigated with terraced hills. The coastal area has relative high clay content retaining moisture that produces favourable conditions for agriculture.

The total amount of water is roughly estimated at about 4.5 billion m³/year. However, due to loss by infiltration and evapotranspiration, the available amount is set at 2.5 billion m³/year. Of this, surface water constitutes around 2 billion m³/year, whereas extractable groundwater for the rest represents about 0.5 billion m³/year (High Relief Committee and UNDP, 1999). The major river, Litani, flows south in the Bekaa valley and then turns westward before reaching the ocean not far from Sidon. In the mid-1960s, an irrigation and hydropower dam at Qir'awn in the Bekaa Valley reduced the flow in lower Litani to 300-400 m³/year (see Kolars, 1992).[7] In the South, the Water Authority of Jabal Amel (including Bint-Jbeil, Marjeyoun, and Hasbaya *cazas*) manages the water from the following sources: Litani River; Aquifer of Marj El-Khawkh; Sources of Sheeba; Aquifer of Wadi-Jilou; and other sources including Ain-Qenia and Khalawat that feed the same villages of the same names in the *caza* of Hasbaya.[8]

The upper part of the Hasbani Springs is located only 2 km from the Litani River that runs from the Bekaa Valley. The latter is about four times larger than the Hasbani River and used solely within the country.

Development of the water resources in the south has received widespread national support. With the exception of the Hasbani Springs, none of

Section I part 2

them are controversial from an international perspective.[9]

The Lebanese Government's justification of the need for about 7 MCM/year (planned to increase to 9 MCM/year) from the springs was primarily related to a "response to a request from the inhabitants to resume the pumping of water to the villages that had been customary before the Israeli occupation. In its time, the latter had deliberately destroyed the Lebanese pipeline and pumps and had deprived the population of the use of the water for drinking, household use or irrigation".[10]

Use of the water for irrigation became a priority as a part of the development efforts in the south (as described above). In 1999, the government estimated the existing irrigated land (in the Hasbaya *caza*) at 300 ha out of almost 6,000 ha (High Relief Committee and UNDP, 1999: 37). In the *Lebanese 2002 Position Paper* to the United Nations, the government estimated that it needed far more than that. It may be necessary to almost double the existing figure depending on the influx of people as well agricultural ambitions. The land capability suitable for irrigation is, however, set at between 5,000[11] and 8,000 ha (High Relief Committee and UNDP, 1999).

Irrespective of the difference, the point here is that the Lebanese Government has a politically-driven development ambition in the south in which development of the water resources will play a central role, particularly due to the impact on poverty reduction and the environment (High Relief Committee and UNDP, 1999: 104).

Lebanon is therefore claiming that it has a need for use of the Hasbani Springs. However, as in the case of any international river, that is not necessarily reconcilable with the downstream country's need for the steady flow of the Hasbani into the vital Upper Jordan River, which in turn feeds into Lake Tiberias.

Israel argues that the Lebanese demand can be met by using water from the Litani River, of which a portion runs into the sea in any case. It is further stated that some of the villages in question used water from the Litani (and through the *Conveyor 800*) prior to 2003.

Both the central and local government in Lebanon are well aware of this sensitivity, not only historically, following the Anglo-French Convention in the 1920s, but also during the Israeli occupation of the south and subsequent events.

The hydro-sensitivity of the *border landscape*

The relative abundance of water in Lebanon compared to Israel, and the Hasbani Springs' proximity to the Israeli border, have fuelled various theories of diversion of the Litani River to Israel. These aspects have been extensively dealt with by several scholars (such as Amery and Wolf, 2000), but despite their rhetorical value, such a diversion seems, in the views of enlightened leaders and experts, unrealistic.

During the Israeli military operations in 1978 and subsequent invasion in 1982, the South Lebanese Army leader Major Sa'ad Haddad became a protégé of Israeli interests. In addition, Major Haddad's militia was reported to have protected the Jordan River's headwaters of the Hasbani by closing some wells and preventing digging of others.[12] Some contest these reports, primarily because, according to Haddad, there were "two taboos – our land and water" (Wolf, 1995: 58). Plans were made by the Israelis to divert 5-10 m^3/year from the Wazzani Springs for irrigation in Shiite southern Lebanon and Israel (Wolf, 2000: 92). This too was detested by Haddad, but incidents like these illustrate two

to the wish to secure the headwaters of the basin.[13] In this context, however, this discussion may not yield much benefit, as the two aspects (mentioned above) appear to remain valid. Rather, the question is how to find a solution that is satisfactory for both countries.

Even with this sketchy hydrological and historical glimpse, it seems obvious that the two countries have apparently contradictory interests concerning the management of the Hasbani River.

■ Photo 14.
The Hasbani River in the northern part of Israel

aspects: (i) the headwaters are not only hydro-strategically significant, but indeed vital for Israel's main freshwater source, Lake Tiberias, and (ii) the springs are geographically located in a sensitive area from an internal Lebanese perspective.

Academic literature has extensively examined the invasion of Israel in 1982 from a hydro-strategic perspective, i.e. on the assumption that the Israeli invasion was primarily due

■ Photo 15.
One of the small waterfalls of the tributaries to the Hasbani River in northern Israel

Section I   part 2

Chapter 3

What has been done to solve the dispute?

As in most places in the Middle East, this contested water resource cannot be isolated from other stakeholders and political agendas. One example of such a linkage is that the relationship between Lebanon and Israel cannot be understood without considering the role of Syria (see also Allan, 2002: 254). The interrelationships are complex. However, it seems correct to argue that a peace treaty with Syria is not a necessity for a Lebanese-Israeli water agreement, or at least some sort of 'water understanding'. The Lebanese Government would nonetheless carefully balance its relationship with Syria, the interests of internal political constituencies such as the significant influence in the south of Hezbollah and Amal, and national development efforts.

In contrast to some observers, who set 20 February 2001 as the starting date of the dispute, it seems apparent that a more accurate perspective situates the unsettled management status of the Hasbani River as dating back to 1948. On that date, the local Lebanese authorities began laying a four-inch wide water pipe from the Wazzani Springs to the Wazzani and Maysat villages.

As outlined in the Golan Heights case above, due to the extreme sensitivity in maintaining a predictable and steady flow from the headwaters of the Jordan Upper Basin, Israel immediately reacted through its Minister of Infrastructure, Avigor Liberman. He stated that "nobody heard me say wars break out over water..., but factually that is correct, I regret" (Morris and Smyth, 2001).[14] Similar statements were given by key decision makers during the spring of 2001.[15]

Lebanon responded with letters to the UN General Assembly and Security Council defending and justifying their decision. Israel also submitted a letter to the same consignee on 21 November 2002.

The intensity of the rhetoric ebbed and flowed up until March 2003, when the US-led-coalition attacked Iraq. Prior to this, the EU, US and UN made attempts to solve the conflict. In the fall of 2002, the US dispatched several envoys to the two countries. The EU also sent its EU Rapid Reaction Mechanism with the aim of providing the following outputs:

> "(i) a hydrological impact assessment of the Wazzani pumping station; (ii) an assessment of water needs for the area served by the Wazzani pumping station and a preliminary assessment of the technical options for meeting these needs, and (iii) identification of the parameters affecting the use of water resources in the wider Hasbani

■ Photo 16.
Water pipes at the Wazzani Springs in southern Lebanon

France and Russia, strongly urged the Parties to solve the dispute peacefully and through talks.[17] Some argued that good winter rains in 2002/2003 "took the edge off the dispute for the time being" (EU Rapid Reaction Mechanism, 2004: 4).

Procedural obstacles in resolving the dispute

The aim of this publication is to propose solutions, an in-depth answer as to why the dispute has not yet been resolved. It seems relevant, however, to clarify that the dispute is both an 'isolated' water dispute over the Wazzani Springs, and at the same time a prelude to how the

basin, including their possible impact on downstream water users." (EU Rapid Reaction Mechanism, 2004)

The UN reacted in several ways in 2001 and 2002. It made several offers to the Parties to provide its *Good Office* to the dispute, but was not prepared to mediate between intermediaries (i.e such as through the US or EU).[16] After that, the UN followed the dispute closely, but did not make any diplomatic attempts to mediate.

The dispute was not resolved. Nonetheless, the EU, US and UN, with input from nations such as

■ Photo 17.
One of the small streams that runs into the Hasbani River (Mount Hermon in the background)

Golan Heights dispute might be solved. The way in which the Wazzani conflict is dealt with may be considered by the Parties to set a precedent for how the Golan dispute will be resolved. Thus, Israel would prefer to have the US as an interlocutor and guarantor in any agreement with Lebanon, while Lebanon (like Syria on the Golan) would want not only the US, but also the UN and possibly the EU.

Therefore, with the danger of simplifying complex Lebanese and Israeli political issues as well as procedural matters, it seems correct to conclude that Lebanon was insisting on using the UN as the interlocutor and guarantor, while Israel wanted the US to play a similar role.

None of the Parties has excluded important actors like the EU, the French or the Russians. However, the procedural stalemate prevailed up to 2005.

However, this creates an opportunity to offer a third party solution that might accommodate both procedural and water management concerns. This part of the publication must be viewed as a desire to use such an opportunity.

The procedural problems should not blur the complexity of how to manage the headwaters of the Upper Jordan Basin. The next chapter attempts to clarify the Parties' positions and real concerns in order to understand how the headwaters may be managed in the future.

Section I   part 2

Chapter 4

What are the parties' positions and real concerns?

Contentious water resources were not, until Israel withdrew its armed forces from Lebanon, explicitly at the forefront of political rhetoric in either of the countries. In May 2000, after all of the territory in the south of Lebanon came under the sole control of the Government of Lebanon, as the Israeli forces withdrew, according to the UN[II], in compliance with UN Security Council Resolution 425[18], major efforts were made to reconstruct and develop the area.

Since then, the Parties have made public statements that appear to be mutually irreconcilable on the as yet unresolved problems of the headwaters of the Upper Jordan River. The positions and interests of the two countries are outlined below, based on an assessment of:

▸ public oral and written statements by leaders of Lebanon and Israel as well as other international actors such as the UN, the EU, and the US;

▸ official dossiers from the Parties to the UN General Assembly and the Security Council;

▸ a Position Paper elaborated by Lebanon (9 October 2002)[III];

▸ a Conflict Assessment report from the EU;[19]

▸ international literature on hydrological conditions and chronological escalation of the conflict[20]; and

▸ the author's familiarity with both Parties' positions and concerns through discussions.

The Parties' positions on the water disputes over the Wazzani Springs are related to:

1. the right to use water with or without an agreement;
2. the amount of water to be used by Lebanon;
3. the need for a bilateral agreement regarding the Hasbani River; and
4. procedural matters.

As illustrated in the preceding disputes, from an academic and historical perspective it is quite interesting to discuss how the disputes evolved and the complicated history of the Parties' relationships. The purpose of this part of the publication is, however, to assess relevant information in relation to a proposed solution. Therefore, the following recapitulation is confined to the relevant history of the Parties' positions and concerns thus far, in order to

As in every dispute, the Parties publicly express their positions. However, it is important to recall that the rarely-stated underlying concerns of the Parties are more relevant for finding solutions.

II   According to the 'Blue Line', which was demarked by the UN. Lebanon is still requesting the Sheeba Farms as claimed by Syria in the 1960s.

III   Not publicly released.

bring the discussion forward towards mutual conciliations of the different positions.

As in any proposed solution to water disputes in the region, the underlying concerns of the Parties must be addressed (see for example Trondalen, 2004a). It is also recognized that the total sum of the factors is different from the sum of isolated factors. In this context, this means that the two countries may be able to work out an agreement, but it appears that this cannot be isolated from Syria.

As in every dispute, the Parties publicly express their positions. However, it is important to recall that the rarely-stated underlying concerns of the Parties are more relevant for finding solutions (Trondalen, 2004a).

Despite the complexity and gridlocked nature of this dispute, it seems to be solvable to the satisfaction of both Parties. However, the *way* in which this solution is worked out, as described above, is significant. For example, a mediating effort or even a proposal from the US may be viewed differently in Lebanon and Israel to a proposal received from the UN.

> Both Parties have stated that they wish to maintain peace and seek a speedy resolution to the dispute through dialogue and negotiation.

This proposal therefore has no political attachments to either of the Parties, nor to any other external stakeholders. Indeed, it is an independent proposal based on *principles of peaceful settlement of disputes* and *sustainable management of water* for the people in the area.[IV]

Both Parties have stated to the UN General Assembly and the Security Council that they wish to *maintain peace*[V] and seek a *speedy resolution to the dispute through dialogue and negotiation*.[VI] Such a mutual political desire further justifies the attempt to develop solutions that could be mutually satisfactory.

Before proposing a possible solution, some of the most relevant positions and real concerns of the Parties must be understood.

The Lebanese and Israeli positions must be seen from a wider hydro-political perspective

International law in itself does not offer a solution to water conflicts, but provides legal elements to guide part of a possible resolution (see Boisson de Chazournes, 2003: 91). The UN framework Convention on the Law of the Non-navigational Uses of International Watercourses of 1997, other similar laws such as the so-called 'Helsinki Rules' (UNECE, 1992) and the associated Protocol on Water and Health (UNECE, 1999) as well as customary laws do not directly offer a solution to the dispute, nor guarantee co-operation.

However, there appear to be a few cases where co-operation has been established and sustained without a legal framework anchored in international law. The legal framework must therefore be carefully weighed by each Party in relation to several factors, such as the following:

▸ In addition to Lebanon, Israel shares waters with Syria, Jordan and the Palestinian Authority (PA). In some instances, Israel is situated upstream and downstream of the water resource (such as the Gaza Aquifer

---

IV   Along the line of arguments similar to the author's philosophy and approach as described in UN ESCWA (2004).

V   Lebanese letter to the UN Security Council of 12 September 2002.
VI   Israeli letter to the UN Security Council of 21 November 2002.

100

and Golan Heights, respectively). The Israeli would therefore probably not subscribe to a rigid upstream or downstream doctrine, but rather advocate balanced principles that serve their interests in a wider regional context. This approach paves the way for reaching a possible 'balanced' solution with Lebanon.

▸ Lebanon is upstream with Syria and Israel regarding all of the three international watercourses (Nahel el Kabir, Orontes and the Hasbani, respectively). However, as in any international agreements, Lebanon's position on the Hasbani disputes cannot be isolated from the agreements already reached on the Nahel El-Kabir and Orontes Rivers. Neither agreement reflects a rigid doctrinal watersharing position. Rather, they take both Lebanon's and Syria's legitimate concerns into account.

What may at first glance seem to complicate matters is the long and special relationship between Lebanon and Syria. The latter, as a Party to the unresolved water disputes over the Golan Heights and the Euphrates and Tigris Rivers, should therefore be taken into consideration. Although the water basins *are not hydrologically connected*, legal and water management principles advocated by Syria in one of the international water disputes (for example with Turkey and Iraq) will obviously have implications for any other water disputes in which it is involved (such as with Israel on the Golan). Syria may therefore consider the Lebanese/Israeli Wazzani dispute as some sort of a 'prelude' not only of the procedures, but also of water management principles in a possible agreement on Golan.

One may argue that such a connection complicates rather than simplifies opportunities for reaching an agreement on the Wazzani Spring. Another way of considering this is that the dual upstream/

downstream concerns of both Israel and Syria open up the possibility for a 'balanced doctrinal' approach.

Some of the *common* concerns expressed by Israel and Syria are outlined below. These arguments (or rather principles) were aired by Israel when dealing with Jordan and the Palestinian Authority (see *Section II* of this publication) as well as by Syria in dealing with Turkey and Iraq regarding the Euphrates and Tigris Rivers (see *Section III*). They include:

▸ prior consensus with – and notification by – the upstream user, i.e. before the upstream country uses the river;

▸ non-appreciable harm, meaning in this context that the upstream country cannot use the water without mitigating the pollution and regulating the river without harm to the downstream country (UNECE, 1999);

▸ in line with the UN Water Framework Convention, both Parties also argue that the riparian states should establish joint mechanisms and commissions in which riparians participate in the regular exchange of information and data, as well as give notification of planned measures;[21]

▸ similarly, due to their dual up and downstream positions, principles such as equitable usage, reasonable use and no appreciable harm have been aired.

Relevant factors in understanding the Lebanese concerns

One should not infer from this that the Syrian positions will have a direct impact on the Lebanese position in relation to the Wazzani Springs dispute. Nevertheless, due to the geo-political situation in this part of the Middle East, Lebanon's positions cannot be totally isolated from Syria's positions. At least two important aspects are considered below.

Section I   part 2

First, it is in Lebanon's and Syria's best interests that co-operation over scarce water resources take place – irrespective of their relationship with Israel. The implications of the lack of such an agreement on the Euphrates and the Tigris Rivers are evident for Syria, which over the past 30 years has pressed for a trilateral agreement.

Second, to date Lebanon has not taken a typical upstream position[VII] (cf. the agreements on the *Nahel el Kabir* and *Orontes* rivers). Because of this, it is setting a sound precedent for international water agreements in the region.[22] In fact, Lebanon has underlined the significance of the following aspects (see UN Convention on the Law of the Non-Navigational Use of International Watercourses, 1997):[23]

▶ "[f]actors relevant to the equitable and reasonable use of water (Art. 5 and 6);

▶ "[o]bligation not to cause significant harm" (Art. 7);

▶ "[o]bligations to co-operate and regularly exchange data and information" (Art. 8 and 9);

▶ "[p]rotection and preservation of ecosystems and the prevention, reduction and control of pollution" (Art. 20, 21 and 23);

▶ "[m]anagement, regulations and installation" (Art. 24, 25 and 26); and

▶ "[s]ettlement of disputes" (Art. 33).

Lebanon has therefore, both in reality (by signing the two water agreements with Syria) and in terms of principles (by making agreements with explicit reference to sound and well accepted principles), shown that they are willing to agree on an agreement anchored to the UN Convention.[24]

VII Often called the 'Harmon Doctrine' or the 'Absolute Territorial Sovereignty Doctrine' – a position taken by a country that simply argues that the amount of water originating in their own territory is theirs.

Relevant factors in understanding the Israeli concerns

Likewise, Israel has signed water agreements with Jordan as part of the Peace Treaty of 1994 as well as with the Palestinians in the Israeli-Palestinian *Interim Agreement* of 1995 (cf. *Section II*). In the latter case, however, a 'final' water agreement has not yet been reached.

Despite its polarized political rhetoric on the Wazzani dispute (especially in the period September 2002 to March 2003)[25], Israel has conveyed to the UN that it supports international law as a yardstick and guide on international waters:

▶ "Customary international law provides that states sharing an international river have a legal right to use its waters".

▶ "....equitable and reasonable, and that the states are required to take appropriate measures to prevent causing significant harm to other states along the river. In this context, great importance is attached under customary law to existing and historic uses of the river."

▶ "Equally, a basic obligation of states, according to international law and practice, is to co-operate with all states along the river ...".[26]

Israel has not only developed its arguments along commonly accepted international principles, but also conveys that it wants a "speedy resolution to the dispute through dialogue and negotiation".[27]

So, are all these arguments bringing the dispute closer to a resolution? The answer may be that if the Parties' main concerns are reconciled, a solution could be at hand. Currently, the concerns listed below must be addressed – in one way or another – in any agreement:

Lebanon

1. is retaining territorial sovereignty, in this context meaning ownership, control and use of water within its own border;
2. asserting the rights to use the water for the socio-economic development of the area – to date the country has claimed up to 9 MCM yearly;[28]
3. requesting the UN to be an interlocutor and guarantor in one way or another in resolving the dispute; and
4. demanding that the dispute be resolved within an international legally accepted framework.

Israel

1. is objecting to unilateral actions by Lebanon without prior notification and agreement;
2. demanding an agreement that includes water quantity, but equally importantly some kind of assurance that the water quality[29] is kept within certain levels (probably through a monitoring programme);
3. requiring an assurance that unilateral actions will not be taken in the future; and
4. making sure that the UN is not the sole interlocutor and guarantor, but also that the US is involved in one way or another in both capacities.

Syria

To date, the country has not made a direct public statement on its rights to the Hasbani River. As noted in the introduction, however, Syria considers that it will be a riparian when the dispute over the Golan Heights is resolved, and the author assumes that the Hasbani River might be part of the arrangement between Syria and Israel as proposed in *Part 1* of this section.[30] Syria is therefore not included below in the proposed solution to the dispute between Lebanon and Israel, as it would be dealt with under that arrangement.

Although many observers underline the sole importance of maintaining a steady flow of the headwaters of the Upper Jordan River to Lake Tiberias, the exact amount of water is not the crux of the matter for Israel. Rather, how the sharing of water is arranged and guaranteed is crucial. In this context, however, Lebanon is more concerned about obtaining acceptance of its *territorial integrity* and thereby the right to use its 'own' water for socio-economic purposes.[31] From an outsider's perspective, the Parties are two sovereign states that have legitimate and real concerns that must be addressed to mutual satisfaction. Any uneven or unfavourable solution will be unsustainable. This situation is the crux of the matter.

The Parties' concerns in this dispute bear a striking resemblance to those in the water dispute over the Golan Heights. This situation is open to many different kinds of solutions. Although it is not exactly the same as the situation on the Golan Heights, some of the same principles can be applied. The next chapter presents one possible means, among many, of solving the conflict.

Section I part 2

Chapter 5

Proposed solutions to the water dispute

As outlined in the introductory part of this publication, the author argues that it is not up to the external community to accept any solution on behalf of Lebanon and Israel. Rather, it should attempt to offer answers to a legitimate question: What kind of yardsticks for a successful agreement can stand the test of historic judgment from people of both countries?

This proposal consists of two elements:
▸ an allocation/sharing formula; and
▸ an incremental way of developing the approach.

Development of an allocation/ sharing formula

There appear to be no simple answers such as a specific allocation figure (e.g. a water flow of X m³/year). However, as mentioned above, both Parties have accepted that they have *rights* and *obligations* to:
▸ practise sound environmental management for the benefit of coming generations; and equally importantly to:
▸ provide their citizens with fundamental and universal basic human needs such as water for the socio-economic development of their nations.[32]

If those *rights* and *obligations* are in one way or another met through a third party proposal, this might offer an opportunity for a solution that balances the Parties' concerns. This proposal may therefore not play into the flux and reflux of today's politics, but rather attempt to offer a sustainable solution as to how Lebanon and Israel's *rights* and *obligations* could be met.

As also thoroughly discussed in *Section II*, it is argued that the concept of *sovereignty*, which is closely linked to that of 'rights', might be an appropriate term to translate in a negotiation arrangement. According to international law, the notion of *sovereignty* over any natural resource comprises two important legal principles:
▸ sovereign *rights*, i.e. 'rights' to water in terms of one of the attributes mentioned above; and
▸ sovereign *obligations*, i.e. 'obligations' to use the water in a certain way, such as sustainable use, environmental protection and economic efficiency (see national and international obligations as discussed in the introductory part of this book).[33]

Rights: One may argue that any water solution between the Parties should include an interpretation of the three attributes of 'water rights', such as:

▸ ownership of a *de facto* portion of the river; i.e. proprietary rights of the economic value[VIII];

▸ control of the river, especially related to protection of the water quality[IX]; and

▸ use of a portion of the river.[X]

Obligation: Another interpretation of *sovereignty* is obligation. Every state with *rights* over specific water resources is *obliged* to manage them according to national laws[34], but also according to internationally recognized obligations.[35] Protecting an international river from depletion both in terms of quantity and quality is one of the most important obligations of any riparian Party.

The politically tempting concept of water 'rights' is therefore a double-edged sword for any upstream user, since the notion of obligations is equally strong. This reality is acknowledged by both Parties, and the questions would rather be:

1. How can an agreement between them grant Lebanon its legitimate ownership of a portion of the river and provide Israel with an essential portion to Lake Tiberias in an agreeable manner?

2. How can Lebanon control depletion, especially in terms of protecting the river and the groundwater?

3. How can the Parties agree on a *formula* that regulates usage?

VIII In this context, means a "...property right entitling the owner of the economic value to the water" (cf. Fisher *et al.,* 2002.) The dispute over water ownership is therefore translated into a dispute over the right to monetary compensation for the water involved.

IX In this context, means a "mandate to protect the river system", which would also include "study, monitor, and survey" separately and/or jointly according to a set of water management rules.

X In this context, means a "mandate to utilize/extract/pump for consumption and/or storage".

Proposed application of the Parties' water rights and obligations

In any approach, experience from any other international water agreements must be based on certain agreed criteria or so-called parameters.[36] In this case, a step-by-step approach could be based on a *formula* that specifies each Party's *rights* and *obligations* according to specific parameters, some of which are outlined below.

A *step-by-step approach* is proposed based on an agreed *formula*. Any agreement is probably also

---

The following parameters could be included in developing mutually satisfactory formulas:

Proprietary rights of economic value (right to monetary compensation for the water involved)

Control ('protect the river systems' also includes 'monitor' and 'survey') separately and/or jointly (in this context, means a mandate to protect the river according to a set of water management rules).

Allocation/share for use (utilize/extract/pump for consumption and/or storage) (expressed in MCM) from the river might be determined in relation to:

a) the need for development and reconstruction locally in Lebanon, and expressed need;

b) the amount of water to be leased to Israel, or in a form which is mutually agreed, to be based on principles for leasing permits, which could also include some sort of compensation mechanism;

c) water balance management: use of the shared/allocated water according to an agreed formula in relation to a sustainable yield (based on a set of hydro-geological/climatic parameters from the past 6-12 months).

Figure 5. An *allocation/sharing formula* for the Hasbani River based on three categories

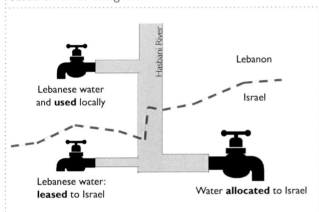

Hasbani River

Lebanon

Israel

Lebanese water and **used** locally

Lebanese water: **leased** to Israel

Water **allocated** to Israel

as different investment in infrastructure and degree of water consumption to economic development).

In this particular context, three important parameters in the formula are:

▸ proprietary rights of the economic value;
▸ control; and
▸ allocation/share of the Hasbani River.

This distinction is made because the Lebanese and Israeli *proprietary rights* to and *control* over the water may be different from the *usage* of the water. The Parties should have equal rights to control the water (as defined), although the usage will be different.

Another important feature in the formula is the difference between the allocated/shared amount of water and actual usage. Due to the need to achieve a rightful and equitable deal between

dependent on the provision in the *approach*. As an illustration of how such a formula may look, see *Figure 5*.

The outlined formula may appear quite complex. This is due to the complexity of the hydrology, with two quite different countries being involved and an intricate water management history (such

Section I   part 2

An example of an allocation/sharing formula of the Hasbani River

Proprietary rights (of the economic value)
Total: 135 M m³ (MCM) (100%)

	Lebanon	Israel
• Hasbani river	10%	90%

Allocation/share for use ("Utilize/extract/pump for consumption and/or storage")
Total: 135 MCM (100%)

	Lebanon	Israel
• Hasbani river	10% (13.5 MCM)	90% (121.5 MCM)

Time period:	Immediately	25-y. lease	Immediately	25-y. lease
• Water usage	5% (7 MCM)	7% (9.5 MCM)	95% (128 MCM)	93% (125.5 MCM)
• Leased water to Israel	5% (7 MCM)	3% (4 MCM)		

Control: "Reciprpoal responsibility to protect the river systems" (also include "monitor, and survey").

Note: Syria's rights, allocation/share, and control of the river are tentatively being dealt with under the Golan Heights Arrangement.

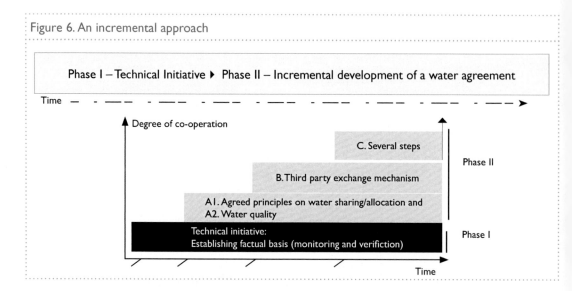

Figure 6. An incremental approach

Phase I – Technical Initiative ▶ Phase II – Incremental development of a water agreement

Time

Degree of co-operation

C. Several steps — Phase II

B. Third party exchange mechanism

A1. Agreed principles on water sharing/allocation and
A2. Water quality

Technical initiative:
Establishing factual basis (monitoring and verification) — Phase I

Time

them, Lebanon may be granted, for example, 10 per cent of annual discharge as its *proprietary right*. If Lebanon uses this amount now, there would be severe and immediate negative implications for the flow of the Upper Jordan River to Lake Tiberias. Since that constitutes the backbone of Israeli freshwater supply, Israel may lease a certain amount of water (of that 10 per cent) from Lebanon rather than making new and additional supplies (for example through expensive desalination). In the figure below, it is suggested that Israel *lease* 5 per cent of annual discharge, but reduce that amount to 3 per cent over the lease period. Such leases could be negotiated on a regular basis, such as every 25 years.

An incremental step-by-step approach

Recognizing that politics and the history of the Parties' relationship cannot be isolated from any proposal, a step-by-step approach should be designed around a more technical water agreement in order to create a framework that gives both Parties a sense of trust and accountability.

Such an approach may consist of following two incremental steps (see also *Figure 6*):

Phase I – Technical initiative

A Third Party[XI] should directly or indirectly conduct a technical fact-finding mission that aims to provide factual matters that are undisputed by both Parties. Answers should be given to the following questions regarding the Hasbani River as it crosses the border:

▸ What are the annual and seasonal variations of water [quantity] volumes?
▸ What is the average and what are the variations of the current water quality parameters?[XII]
▸ Are there any differences in recorded historic data from Lebanon and Israel?
▸ What changes of the groundwater influence the Wazzani Springs?[XIII]

XI Probably neither the US nor the UN unilaterally, at this stage, but either with both or by another Party that would be (tacitly) accepted by both.

XII Such water monitoring has unilaterally been conducted by Israel (see for example Salingar, Geifman and Aronwick, 1993).

XIII These questions are especially relevant due to the global climate changes.

In order to answer these questions, a monitoring and verification system could be established where the Hasbani River crosses the border; for example in the form of a water quantity and quality monitoring station on each side of the (Lebanese–Israeli) border, in addition to stations for the groundwater. These *technical and bilateral initiatives* should at one stage be *translated into some sort of institutional mechanism* that would function as a 'bridge' to the next phase. The management of these stations could offer such an opportunity.

■ Photo 18.
A water quality monitoring station in the Middle East

At this stage, the monitoring stations may be managed by the respective national experts together with an independent support and supervision committee consisting of, for example, delegates from the quartet (e.g. the UN and the US) executed by a small technical secretariat provided by one or two 'concerned' nation or nations (for example from countries involved in water issues in the Middle East such as Switzerland, Norway, France, Japan or Germany).

Phase II – Incremental development towards a water agreement

Either as *Phase I* evolves, or at the same time, the Parties could enter into direct or indirect deliberations with an aim of establishing a bilateral water agreement that may contain the following steps:

▶ A1) *Agreed principles for a sustainable, reasonable, and equitable use of the Hasbani River, including:*
  • extraction volumes (in Lebanon according to agreed parameters such as last year's rainfall); which may also be determined in relation to
  • principles for "leasing water quota [volumes]"[XIV]
▶ A2) Agreed water quality standards at the border point.
▶ B) Establishment of a third party exchange mechanism that would handle the leased water, maintain a certain water quality and improve water efficiency according to the set standards (see an example of such a mechanism in the textbox).[37]
▶ C) *Several steps* are expected to be included in the agreement:
  • identified institutional and political entity(ies) accountable for the agreement from each Party;
  • agreed duration of the agreement in terms of years, such as the duration before re-negotiating the terms of the [so-called] leasing period, for example 25 years;

XIV As in any international river context, one may expect that the demand of those upstream, i.e. the Lebanese, is higher than what those downstream, i.e. Israel, expect to obtain. One option is to grant the Lebanese their proprietary rights, but for Israel to lease a certain amount of water (possibly connected to an exchange mechanism – see textbox). Such 'water wheeling' would give Lebanon the opportunity to lease parts of the water amount and use the funds for socio-economic development.

Section I   part 2

Third party exchange mechanism (TPEM)

As a basis for a water agreement, the parties have, together with the quartet, agreed to establish a TPEM that will enable Lebanon and Israel to use the Hasbani River while preventing pollution and depletion in accordance with further agreed-upon specifications. A certain amount of water will be leased to Israel.

The funds from the lease are earmarked for projects in Lebanon that aim to increase the water efficiency and treatment according to the set standards; such as:
- financing water-efficient technology and infrastructure;
- financing use of environmentally sound technology; and
- financing water substitution technology.

Independent Support and Supervision Committee
The TPEM could technically and financially be administrated by [a joint (GEF) Secretariat under the auspices of the] 'Extended Quartet' (e.g. France, US, UN, Russia and the EU).

- agreed procedures and milestones and a 'performance review process' involving the Independent Support and Supervision Committee;
- agreed measures in case of breach of agreements between the Parties and a dispute settlement mechanism; and
- the exact mandate and the duration of the Independent Support and Supervision Committee as a guarantor of implementation according to specific criteria (including the financial commitments).[xv]

...both would probably consider the economic cost to be low when compared to the long-term political and economic benefits of peace and higher stability in the region.

How would Lebanon and Israel perceive such a proposal?

First of all, this proposal aims to address the main concerns of the Parties in accordance with their rights and obligations. There may be other factors outside the hydro-political framework that could determine quite a different outcome, or even a continued gridlocked situation.

As in every real-life situation, there are different ways of looking at such a proposal. Most likely, both countries will favour a simple but fair arrangement related to the water conflict. Indeed, Lebanon has done this recently in bilateral agreements with Syria on Nahel el Kabir and the Orontes River and even proposed a step similar to that outlined in Phase I.[38] In the same way, Israel's dossier to the UN goes along the line proposed, and past agreements with Jordan and preliminary ones with the Palestinian Authority follow the principles of need for a factually-based water agreement.[39]

What about the costs of implementation?

This question was asked in all of the preceding water disputes. Again, there are strong reasons to believe that external stakeholders would view these cost estimates as 'recoverable' as compared to the costs of potentially continued instability. As in the preceding cases, any extra-regional benefactors take a self-interest perspective and calculate the economic cost in relation to the foreign and economic interests of their

---

XV   Including questions relating to the role of a larger international constituency in financing implementation of the agreement.

country. For example, historically, the French have a different perspective on the Levant than that of the US or Russia. However, both would probably consider the *economic cost* to be low when compared to the long-term *political and economic benefits* of peace and higher stability in the region.

Such a 'settlement dividend' therefore seems to be high enough for international actors to commit funds to such a mechanism. Moreover, it appears quite evident that multilateral institutions such as the joint United Nations/World Bank Global Environmental Facility (GEF)[XVI] would also be relevant for such a function. An important question would be whether the international community as a whole can afford to see this conflict go unresolved; there is an international moral obligation that transcends politics.

Constituencies inside – and indeed outside – each country may well put different weights on the benefits of an agreement. However, the bigger question is, as always: do the Parties want an agreement and, if so, what kind of price are they willing to pay?

The Wazzani dispute does not determine the political climate; rather, the political climate generates the dispute. In any case, legitimate solutions are there to be agreed upon.

Concluding remarks

As in the case of the preceding and interconnected dispute, the Golan Heights, Lebanon and Israel have *much to lose and much to win* by resolving the conflict over the Hasbani River. There is, however, one complicating factor, namely the interests of Syria in both cases. However it is also an opportunity in the sense that when there

is general willingness to negotiate solutions, Syria would be in both nexuses.

This book attempts to present one way of handling both water files based on the same principles, and by taking the Parties' concerns into account while at the same time ensuring that water is sustainably managed.

Despite the ebb and flow of local and geo-politics, managing these precious water resources will continue in one way or another. As time goes by, the urgency for some sort of water agreement increases, making sustainable and realistic solutions even more relevant.

■ Photo 19.
Small stream in a pristine environment in the Upper Jordan Basin

Section I   part 2

Endnotes

1   It is obvious that Syria considers that it is a riparian to the Hasbani river. Cf. the former Advisor to the Syrian Minister of Irrigation, Eng. Majed Dawood's statement, "Hasbani... runs for 3 km as an international boundary between Syria and Lebanon", "the river ... can only be fairly and sufficiently shared by Syria and Lebanon under international laws after release of South Lebanon and the Syrian Golan under Security Council Resolutions 242, 338, and 425", in Dawood (1995). However, if the boundary is drawn so that the 'Sheeba Farms' become Lebanese, Syria will not border the Hasbani River.

2   There are a variety of sources for these statements. See for example Gvirtzman (2002).

3   See, for example, the study of a twenty-year time series of the water quality in the Upper Jordan Watershed Basin by Salingar et al. (1993).

4   For one of the most comprehensive overviews of the sensitivities of the water of Lebanon both from a Lebanese and Israeli point of view by Amery (2000).

5   Deficit may be interpreted as not sufficient to reach the objectives of the government. In this case, Lebanon's five-year water master plan has clearly identified a water demand short of existing and available water resources. Cf. General Directorate of Energy and Water (2001).

6   Almost all publications quote this figure (such as Salingar et al., 1993). However, recently Israeli officials are stating (personal communication) that the annual average flow has been reduced to 105-110 m³/s. See also Amery (2000).

7   At a national level in Lebanon, there are uncertainties about the water quality, particularly since there is no database. UNICEF estimates that about 60-70 per cent of the resources are contaminated in one way or another. The major pollutants of surface water are untreated municipal wastewater discharge, industrial effluents, improper solid waste disposal and runoff from irrigation. The drinking water networks are quite old and are in urgent need of rehabilitation since almost 50 per cent of the water is unaccounted for. See also METAP (2001) (http:/www.metap.org.files/water%20reports/country/%20Rreport/ LebanonWaterQualityReport%20Report.pdf).

8   Data based on government figures as presented in High Relief Committee and UNDP (1999: 32-36).

9   According to senior Lebanese officials.

10 Cf. the Lebanese Letter to the UN General Assembly and the Security Council on 23 March 2001 and on 12 September 2002, and respectively stating:
    • "on 20 February 2001 the competent Lebanese authorities began to lay a pipe from the Wazzani spring in order to supply water to the villages of Wazzani and Maysat in response to a request from the inhabitants to resume the pumping of water to the villages that had been customary before the Israeli occupation. In its time, the latter had deliberately destroyed the Lebanese pipeline and pumps and had deprived the population of the use of the water for drinking, household use or irrigation", and in
    • 12 September 2002: "The quantity of water of which Lebanon has been availing itself since liberation is estimated at approximately 7 million cubic metres yearly. ...At present the Lebanese authorities are laying pipes to ensure the supply of water to the villages in the basin of the Hasbani and Wazzani rivers. The maximum quantity to be pumped will be 9 million cubic metres yearly, which is far below Lebanon's legitimate entitlement." Available at: http://domino.un.org/unispal.nsf/9a798adbf322aff38525617b006d88d7/3ceb1a678c9f1 7b285256c39004f03b7!OpenDocument&Highlight=2,A%2F57%2F404

11 General estimates by Lebanese professionals.

12 Naff and Matson (1984: 49).

13 With reference to several Arabic, Jewish and external scholars, Amery and Wolf (2000) discuss various perspectives.

14 Morris and Smyth in Financial Times, 16 March 2001. See also Anders Omberg Hansen's extensive analysis over the chronological evolution of the dispute, especially from 2001 to 2005 (Omberg Hansen, 2004).

15 Such as PM's Advisor Ra'anan Gissin (Financial Times, 16 March 2002) and General (Ret.) Uri Saguy (BBC News 15 March 2001). PM Sharon was reported by BBC News on 10 September 2002 to have said on Israeli Army Radio that: "...he had notified the United States that Israel could mount military operations should Lebanon begin pumping water out of Hasbani or its tributary, the Wazzani River".

16 Several actors from the UN were involved such as the UN HQ's Department of Political Affairs, the UN Special Envoy to the Middle East, and the UN SG's Special Representative to Southern Lebanon as well as the UN Economic and Social Commission of Western Asia (ESCWA) based in Beirut, whereas the latter submitted a report stating more or less explicitly that Lebanon had full rights to utilize the water.

17 Cf. According to Jordan Times, 15 September 2002, the Russian Foreign Minister called on both Parties to "solve the problems peacefully, through talks".

18 UN Security Council Resolution 425: Mideast situation/Lebanon – establishment of UNIFIL – Security Council Resolution 19 March 1978 (http://domino.un.org/unipal.nsf).

19 Cf. EU Rapid Reaction Mechanism – End of Programme Report – Lebanon/Israel Wazzani springs dispute, January 2004 (http://europa.eu.int/comm/external_relations/cpcm/rrm/wazzani.pdf).

20 In the latter case, see, for example Omberg Hansen (2005).

21 "In determining the manner of such co-operation, watercourse states may consider the establishment of joint mechanisms or commissions, as deemed necessary by them, to facilitate co-operation on relevant measures and procedures in the light of experience gained through co-operation in existing joint mechanisms and commissions in various regions".

22 Cf. Director General Fadi Comair's comprehensive paper on the experience gained from the water agreement with Syria on the Orontes River and the Nahr el Kabir River, "Hydro Diplomacy of Middle Eastern Countries along with the UN Convention on Non-Navigational Uses of International Water Courses: Case Study Orontes & Nahr el Kabir", in: UNESCWA (2004).

23 *Ibid.* (p.13).

24 *Ibid.* Quotes from the agreements such as:
   • "Place of a storage dam abides to several conditions": "socially, technically, economically";
   • "Allocation based on technical and economic studies" (p.7);
   • Flexible formula: "Allocation volume to Lebanon (64 MCM) but only 40 in dry years" (also specified) (p.7);
   • "Rightful and rational distribution / benefiting of international riparian rivers" (p.11).
   • Formula of using their upstream portion: "IF either Syria or Lebanon wish to use certain amounts of water from the upstream portion of the river within the limits of their parts (60 per cent and 40 per cent respectively), all with respect to the ecological considerations mentioned in Article 5, this amount shall be deducted from their share of stored water. Any country that does not use its entire share of stored water by the end of the hydrological year, according to the schedule of water intake shown in Annex 2 of this Agreement, is not allowed to use this share during the coming year" (p.11).
   • Join efforts by building a dam on Nahir El Kabir (p.12).

25 Cf. Anders Omberg Hansen's chronological analysis of the conflict level, 2005.

26 See the Israeli letter to the UN Security Council of 21 November 2002 (p.3).

27 *Ibid.* (p.6).

28 Some high officials in Lebanon argue that their "share" should not be restricted to this figure, that figure was only as a first step in further water development.

29 Due to the extreme hydro-ecological sensitivity of the influx of water to Lake Tiberias (cf. *Part I* on the Golan Heights).

30 As stated earlier, if the boundary is drawn so that the 'Sheeba Farms' become Lebanese, Syria will not border the Hasbani River.

31 This does not mean that Lebanon is not concerned regarding water quality. See for example two of the publications from the Lebanese Ministry of Environment (1996) and "Decision 8/1 related to standards for wastewater discharges", 2001.

32 Cf. the introductory part of this book with reference to Israel's and Lebanon's signatories to relevant international conventions ("Some reference points in discussion of water disputes in the Middle East").

33 There is a vast international literature on state sovereignty, and an example of one such discussion is outlined in Tignino (2003) and her references to the literature, especially on "new sovereignty" (list of references in footnote 81, p. 390).

34 For Israel, the Water Laws (5719-1957), amended in 1991, and for the Palestinian Authority, the Water Law enacted 3/2002.

35 See, for example, the European Union's *Water Framework Directive* as one of the most comprehensive and strict pieces of legislation in terms of obligations put on each member country concerning water protection and sound management (cf. http://europa.eu.int/comm/environment/water/water-framework/index_en.html).

36 *The International Water Dispute Data Base* at Department of Geography, University of Oregon.

37 The need for such measures are also described in World Bank (2001a).

38 Lebanon has in fact advocated this. The Lebanese President for example invited the EU "... to provide technical assistance to establish objective baseline information on the water resources of the disputed area" in the EU Rapid Reaction Mechanism's Report (2004: 2). See also official statements such as those of the Lebanese Director General (Directorate for Energy and Water) in UNESCWA (2004: 16):

- "adaptable management structure incorporating a certain level of flexibility allowing for public input, changing basin priorities and new information and monitoring technologies";
- "clear and flexible criteria for water allocation and quality: allocations, which are at the heart of most water disputes, are a function of water quantity and quality as well as political fiat";
- "effective institutions must at least identify clear mechanisms for water allocation and water quality standards that simultaneously provide for extreme hydrological events, new understanding of basis dynamics and changing societal values";
- and statements related to "distribution of benefits", "protection of the environment ecosystem of the basin as a whole".

39 Israeli letter to the UN Security Council, 21 November 2002.

SECTION II

Contested water between the Israelis and the Palestinians

Abstract

As in the case of the water disputes discussed previously, this part of the book does not prescribe a quick-fix solution to a complex dispute. Indeed, the Israeli–Palestinian relationship is intertwined with local and international politics and the contentions over *water* are embedded in the ongoing political drama. The intention, however, is to make a contribution to the ongoing debate and negotiations between the Parties and other stakeholders in order to remove one of the obstacles for a sustainable peace.

This publication does not attempt to quote the many Palestinian–Israeli water experts, but rather distil some of their ideas in such a way that certain elements are filtered out as a basis for a possible solution to the disputed water.

There is therefore no presentation of 'new' information nor of a 'one-text proposal', but rather a reflection of various ways of thinking by suggesting specific steps to be taken.

Some of the key questions relate to how to co-operate, and along which timeline. The proposal outlines an incremental step approach whereby each gatepost implies fulfilment of mutual rights and obligations in combination with the establishment of a comprehensive performance review process. In short, water rights are interpreted in various ways based on a formula detailing an allocation/sharing regime.

The two main concerns – managing the water resources in a sound manner while taking the interest of the Parties into account – are incorporated in such a way that the precious water may create an opportunity for peace.

Chapter 1

Water as a contender for peace

As we have seen above, water disputes are complex and hard to solve. The *Palestinians* and the *Israelis* are also caught in an entrenched water conflict in the Middle East. This one is quite different from the three others due to the complex intertwining of the two people geographically, historically, politically, religiously and, not least, emotionally.

The dispute in the same land can be traced back to Biblical times, during the era of the Patriarchs in Palestine, as described in Genesis (21:25, 30-32). According to this religious text, Abraham went to King Abimelech for a permit to use a well, which he obtained. A generation later, like his father, Isaac went to King Abimelech, and despite political differences, made proper arrangements and was granted continued use of the water (Genesis 26:18-23, 26-32).

Today, the conflict over water is similar to those described above. Yet while it is an obstacle to peace, it may possibly provide the conditions for making peace.

Connecting the past and the present
Obviously, knowledge of the past is important to understanding the current situation. In this setting, however, only a few points on the

Map 11. Israel and the West Bank and Gaza

timeline will be highlighted. The present water dispute cannot be viewed without considering the evolution of the Arab–Israeli relationship. This includes historic ties between the Palestinians, Jordanians and Israelis, including the pre-1948 period, the establishment of the State of Israel in 1948, and its socio-economic evolution. It further includes the challenges of the Palestinian communities since 1949 and 1967, including the Palestinian refugees, and subsequently the establishment of the Palestinian Authority in 1993. The latter event led to the setting up of Palestinian public institutions, including the Palestinian Water Authority (PWA), which was formally announced in April 1994.

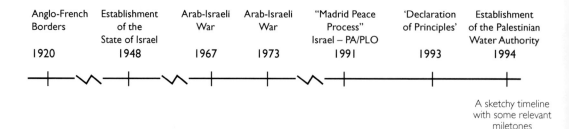

Anglo-French Borders	Establishment of the State of Israel	Arab-Israeli War	Arab-Israeli War	"Madrid Peace Process" Israel – PA/PLO	'Declaration of Principles'	Establishment of the Palestinian Water Authority
1920	1948	1967	1973	1991	1993	1994

A sketchy timeline with some relevant miletones

Emphasis is placed on a brief overview of the nature of the dispute and the Parties' concerns. Some of the international and bilateral responses to these problems are also briefly described. Finally, a proposal on how to consider moving foward is outlined in *Chapter 4*.

As in the case of the preceding water disputes, one should be cautious in prescribing quick-fix solutions for such complex matters – especially when they involve the ongoing political drama of the Israeli-Palestinian conflict. The proposed approach should therefore be interpreted as *one of several ways out of the problem*. The intention, however, is to make a contribution to the ongoing debate and negotiations between the Parties and other stakeholders in order to remove one of the obstacles for peace.

Israeli and Palestinian water experts are not only internationally renowned for their general competence on water issues, but even more so for their specific knowledge of the nature of the water problems and remedies in their region. This publication does not attempt to recite all of them, but rather distils what some of their leading experts have propounded. It will not be a repetition, but will rather filter through possible approaches that may encapsulate some of the Parties' real concerns through a non-partisan perspective.

What also makes this dispute different to the others is that since the 1993/1994 period,

the Parties have worked more closely together and more or less *clarified the factual basis* for deliberations on water issues.

This section of the book is therefore different from the others, since there is no presentation of 'new' information nor of a 'one-text proposal'. Rather, it reflects various ways of thinking by suggesting specific steps to be taken.

Such an endeavour could easily become an academic exercise. Instead, however, it attempts to propose solutions as a result of scholarly perspectives combined with discussions with relevant actors from each of the Parties, thus without their official approval.

Nonetheless, one should not hide the fact that constituencies exist within each Party that strongly argue for *unilateral* approaches and believe that any co-operation with the other would endanger its own course. The author understands the arguments and acknowledges the risks involved. However, the 'Siamese twin' relationship between them, due to the sharing of vital aquifers, requires at least some form of basic co-operation. The key questions are how to co-operate, and along which timeline. The latter point is highly uncertain due to the unpredictability of political events in the region, but some steps may exist that can already be taken at this stage, or at least seriously considered by the Parties, before their common water resources dwindle to an extent that may threaten the humanitarian situation and stability of both societies.

Human suffering due to inadequate water facilities, especially among Palestinian communities, has already reached a level that by all international standards is unacceptable.

This in itself justifies the proposal outlined in the following pages.

Before turning to a discussion of various models of co-operation and a proposed approach, a brief geographical description of the water resources are outlined in the next chapter.

Map 12. Illustration of the West Bank with the Mountain Aquifer divide

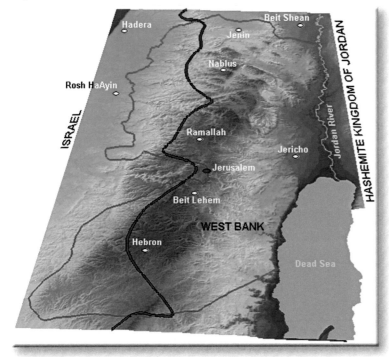

Blue line: *the divide between the Western and Eastern Aquifers. Ground water flow directions are west and east, respectively.*

Green line: *the Green Line (1967 borders).*

Note: The extension of the Western and Eastern Aquifers as well as the replenishment areas are not shown here. The boundaries of the Western Aquifer are complex – in some areas they are west of the coastal line and in some cases east. There are also sections below the Coastal Aquifer. In the Eastern Aquifer, the Jordan River delineates its eastern boundary (Gvirtzman, 2002).

Chapter 2

The water resource situation and what has been done to solve the problems

Water is a scarce resource in Israel as well as on the West Bank and Gaza Strip, hereafter also named 'areas under the Palestinian Authority (PA)'. The area[I] is situated in an arid zone with low and high variability of rainfall. The water resources are beyond any doubt insufficient to supply the needs of the people today. In fact, both peoples are facing a looming water shortage of critical proportions.

Historically, water management in the area remained more or less unchanged for centuries, until the building of the Israeli State in the 1950s. The aspirations of the Israeli founders were quite clear. In the aftermath of the First World War, controls of vital water resources were high on the political agenda. When the two European allies, Britain and France, entered into detailed negotiations to draw the borders, water was at the forefront (Fromkin, 2001). As described in *Section I*, the Upper Jordan River was of vital importance due to the securing of the headwaters for Lake Tiberias[1], and the so-called Mountain Aquifer amounted to approximately 30 per cent of freshwater supply to the Israeli and

70 per cent to the Palestinian population on the West Bank (see an illustration of the horizontal east-west water divide of the Mountain Aquifer in *Figure 7*).

Some reservations in describing disputed water resources

Both Parties have different ways of describing the status and physical locations of the resources, as this could potentially strengthen or weaken their respective arguments. It appears evident that the Palestinians would focus on the following parameters:

▸ historic use of the water resources – such as the wells and springs on the West Bank and Gaza Strip, as well as the Jordan River;

▸ which resources are recharging from which areas and who has the control of which parts of the hydrological systems, including recycled water;

▸ which Party uses how much per capita and from which resource or recycled water – especially a comparison of per capita consumption of water by the Israelis versus the Palestinians;

▸ who has *de facto* control of which resources and recycled water;

▸ the use of water in Israeli settlements on the West Bank compared to other Palestinian towns and villages;

I   In this context, the 'area' means the territories of the internationally recognized State of Israel, the West Bank (irrespective of the exact location of the Green line (pre-June 1967 line) and Gaza Strip. The exact borders and territories are not defined more precisely at this stage.

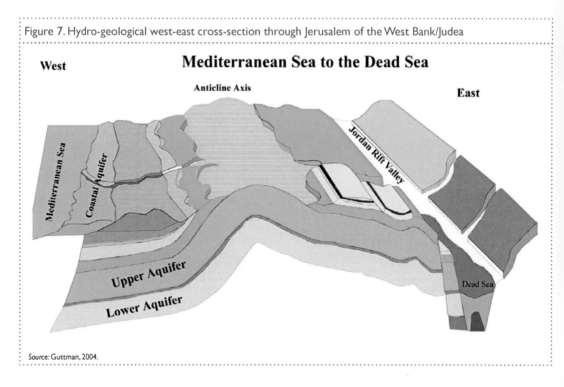

Figure 7. Hydro-geological west-east cross-section through Jerusalem of the West Bank/Judea

Source: Guttman, 2004.

- the possible implications of the Israeli National Water Carrier on the local climate; and finally
- the 'strategic' location of the Israeli wells on the Green Line of the West Bank (see for example Kawash, 2004; PWA, 2004a).

On the other side, Israel would highlight:
- the net benefit to Palestinians of the meticulous management of the scarce resources, especially management of recycled water and protection against pollution and overpumping since 1967;
- provision of water supply and building up of water infrastructure during the time when the West Bank and Gaza Strip were under complete Israeli military administration – especially with regard to the water carrier system;
- supply of water to the Palestinian communities despite the recent hostilities;

- the benefits of long-time monitoring and study of the various hydrological systems as a basis for management control; and
- explanation of the difference in water consumption between the two peoples due to a higher socio-economic level in Israel than among the Palestinians.[2]

The different way of describing the water resources certainly makes even hydrological presentation quite a politically sensitive matter. Despite the danger of being viewed as biased, some relevant parameters have been selected below as a background for proposing a possible approach to solving the dispute.

Some general trends in the water resources for the area

Both Parties agree that water resources are deteriorating – some of them slowly and others more rapidly. This is primarily due to the following driving factors:

▸ population growth plus an increase in the standard of living and thus demand for more water;

▸ global climate change;

▸ deterioration of the water quality (pollution); and

▸ decrease in natural recharge to groundwater aquifers as a result of increased urbanization.

Map 13. Intertwined Palestinian and Israeli water infrastructure on the West Bank

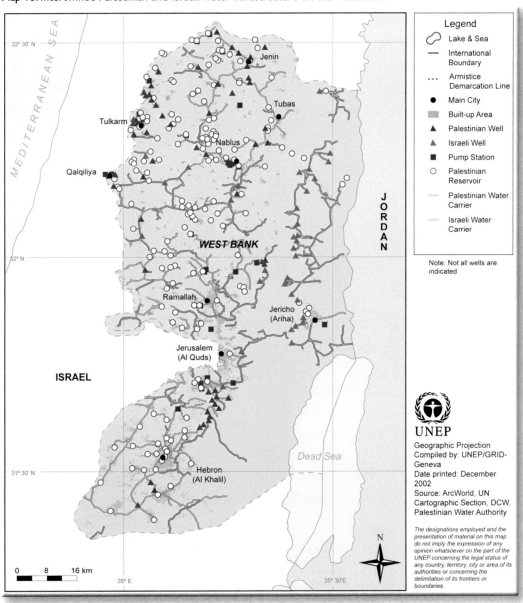

Geographic Projection
Compiled by: UNEP/GRID-Geneva
Date printed: December 2002
Source: ArcWorld, UN Cartographic Section, DCW, Palestinian Water Authority

The designations employed and the presentation of material on this map do not imply the expression of any opinion whatsoever on the part of the UNEP concerning the legal status of any country, territory, city or area of its authorities or concerning the delimitation of its frontiers or boundaries.

Section II

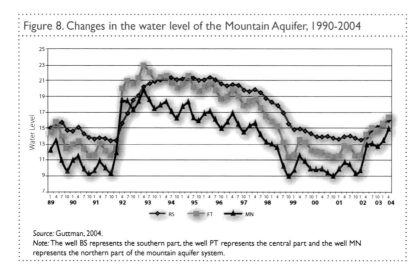

Figure 8. Changes in the water level of the Mountain Aquifer, 1990-2004

Source: Guttman, 2004.
Note: The well BS represents the southern part, the well PT represents the central part and the well MN represents the northern part of the mountain aquifer system.

At present, and in contrast to the disputes related to the Euphrates and the Tigris Rivers, there is little controversy over the water data.

Furthermore, the conclusions are irrevocable: the aquifers must be managed very carefully. If they are not, the sustainable yields and storage capacity may be reduced to the detriment of further generations of Israelis and Palestinians alike. The Mountain Aquifer system is often classified into the following aquifers: the Western, the North-Eastern and the Eastern. However, recent research shows that the demarcations between them are not so clear (see Gvirtzman, 2002; Shuval, 1992).[5]

The hydro-geology is such that the aquifers drain west and eastward along a watershed as indicated in *Figure 7*. It is obvious that since the drainage patterns of all the aquifers involve areas from both Parties, some form of co-operation or at least co-ordination is necessary. The recharge of the complex hydro-geological systems is less than what is extracted.

The water level has significantly decreased over the past 15 years (1990-2004), as expressed in *Figure 8*. There are several reasons why the levels have varied, such as recharge, pumping and management of outside water resources.[6]

Since both Israelis and Palestinians are pumping from the same water resources, it is obvious that – at least up to now – most of the water

In the near future, none of the abovementioned trends are likely to change. On the contrary, the two Parties will face:

▸ probable successive drought years;
▸ continued exploitation of natural resources, causing their depletion;
▸ delays in the introduction of desalination; and
▸ delays in adjustment of demand and water prices to the desalination age.[3]

In addition, it is also understood that fulfilment of the obligation to supply water, as required by international agreements, from Israel to the PWA and to Jordan, will further reduce the current existing amount of water.[4]

Description of the Mountain Aquifer system

There is a vast amount of Israeli, Palestinian and international literature regarding the nature of water resources in the area. What is relevant in this context, however, is a brief description of the disputed water resources, including their geographical location.

infrastructure has been intertwined, as illustrated by *Map 13*. The resources are 'shared' between the two Parties. They will have to co-ordinate and co-operate even more in the future, since the stress on the resources for the West Bank and Gaza will increase.

Another contested resource is the Jordan River running from Lake Tiberias and down to the Dead Sea. The Palestinians are demanding that the river be included in the upcoming negotiations.[7] This will be quite a complex matter due to the sensitivity of Lake Tiberias as the main water supply for Israel, further complicated by the fact that many of the salty sources naturally draining towards the lake are diverted into the Jordan River after the outlet from the lake.

The salt content of the river is therefore very high even before it reaches the Dead Sea. In addition, Jordan has also *de facto* excluded the Palestinians as a riparian, through signing the bilateral Peace Treaty between Israel and Jordan in 1994.

Since this has been tabled by the Palestinians, however, it would have to be addressed in the upcoming bilateral talks.

Brief description of water resources in the Gaza Strip

The water situation on the Gaza Strip is undoubtedly in a very grave situation. Due to overexploitation and despite both international efforts to identify the problems and mitigating efforts (such as recharging and water treatment measures), the aquifer systems are extremely exposed to irreversible damage.

There is general consensus among national and international water-professionals (Vengosh *et al.*,

2005) that the PWA's official statements are not an exaggeration, as illustrated below:

"1. The demand greatly exceeds water supply.
2. More than 70% of the aquifer is brackish or saline water, which leaves no more that 25% of the aquifers suitable for drinking purposes.
3. Gaza water resources need to be protected from pollution since they are subject to severe contamination caused by wastewater and agricultural activities.
4. New water resources need to be added to the aquifer system in order to minimize the water deficit and to improve the groundwater in terms of quantity and quality."[8]

Total groundwater abstraction is estimated at 140-145 MCM/year divided into:

▸ agricultural, 85 MCM/year – from 3,800 wells,
▸ municipal, 54 MCM/year – from about 100 wells,
▸ Israeli settlement-related, 5-7 MCM/year – from about 40 wells.

The PWA further states that the extent to which the aquifer may be impacted by other pollutants such as organic chemicals, metals and pesticides has not yet been fully defined. Pollutants can reach the shallow water table quickly. Sixty per cent of reported diseases in the Gaza Strip are water-related.

The current gap between supply[II] and demand[III] of water on the Gaza Strip is calculated at 55 MCM/year (in 2003, see PWA, 2004b).[9] This figure is confirmed by a comprehensive study under the auspices of the German Technical Co-operation

---

II   Rainfall and 'sustainable' groundwater yield.
III Actual consumption.

Map 14. The Gaza Strip (with the Wadi Gaza) under the Palestinian Authority

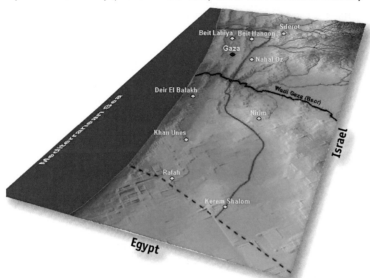

Comparison of supply and demand of water for Israel

It has long been acknowledged that the gap between supply and demand, even if theoretically no water is shared with and allocated to the Palestinians, is rapidly increasing, and that new and additional water resources must be provided now if human suffering for the impoverished part of the population is to be avoided. The Israelis are aware of this situation, as various public awareness campaigns have been carried out for decades.

Today, investment in the water sector as well as its economic significance

(GTZ, 1998). The GTZ study estimates that there will be an investment need for high priority projects[IV] in Gaza alone amounting to at least US$734 million (GTZ, 1998: Table 2.2 (Evaluation Report)). These figures are staggering.

Comparison of demand and supply of water for the Palestinians on the West Bank and Gaza Strip

For obvious reasons, the existing water resources are simply not sufficient to satisfy the demands of both people. As of today, the situation is as expressed in *Figure 9* for Palestinians on the West Bank and Gaza.

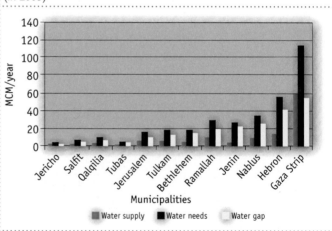

Figure 9. Current Palestinian municipal water supply needs and gap (in 2003)

is illustrated by the fact that the Israeli water company Mekorot is one of Israel's 15 largest companies, with an annual turnover of approximately US$500 million.

Water consumption in Israel in 2003 was estimated as outlined in *Table 4*, with 1,862 million cubic

IV   Such as conventional water resources, demand management, treated wastewater reuse, brackish water desalination, freshwater supplies and treated wastewater supplies.

Table 4. Water consumption in Israel in 2003 (in MCM)

Use	Rigid consumption	Potable water consumption	Entire water consumption
Residential	689	689	689
Neighbours	96	96	96
Industry	90	90	122
Agriculture	-	497	955
Total	875	1,372	1,862
1991	527	1,453	1,762

Source: Mekorot, 2004.

metres (MCM) being consumed per year. The renewable water resources are considered to be 1,750-1,800 MCM.

Additionally, lack of water for the agricultural sector would have negative socio-economic implications. Many countries have adopted a high degree of self-sufficiency in food production, especially if there is a risk of embargoes during tense geo-political situations. Israel is no exception; in fact, agricultural production is used as a domestic incentive in settling the population of the whole of Israel, including in the Negev desert. Despite the fact that water for the agricultural sector is decreasing and efficiency (output per unit of water) increasing, there seems to be no doubt among Israeli water experts and international observers that in the future the agricultural sector will not receive the amount of water it receives today.

Israel participated in the international GTZ Study (under the Multilateral Peace Process), not to obtain a better overview of its own state of 'water affairs', but rather to obtain increased international legitimacy regarding a major shortfall of water. Years ago, Israeli experts predicted today's situation. GTZ estimates that demand will rise from past use (in 1994) of 1,904 MCM/year to 2,135 MCM/year in 2010 (see *Table 5*).

Such projected demands are quite staggering if these scenarios actually eventuate. There is no doubt that the gap will increase, but Israel has the knowhow and skills to handle this (Oren, 2004). Shortage of financial means, however, will probably be one of the main obstacles. The cost of transferring economic sectors from high water demand to non-consumptive sectors will place a burden on the consumer that will not make such transitions without complications.

Section II

Table 5. Current water use and future demand

Core party areas	Current use (MCM/a)	Low demand scenario (MCM/a)			Base demand scenario (MCM/a)			High demand scenario (MCM/a)			Sustainable demand scenario (MCM/a)		
Year	1994	2000	2010	2040	2000	2010	2040	2000	2010	2040	2000	2010	2040
Israel	1904	2005	2052	2428	2039	2135	3766	2057	2387	4066	1787	1881	2300

Source: GTZ, 1998.

■ Photo 20.
Desalination of brackish water is one part of the solution for both Parties

What can be done to fill the gap between supply and demand of water for the Israelis and the Palestinians?

In brief, there seem to be three ways of filling this gap:

▸ use existing water resources more efficiently with a variety of measures, such as a higher degree of recycling, improved technology and demand management such as application of policy instruments (e.g. incentives for saving such as pricing);

▸ new and additional water resources, such as desalination of brackish water as well as sea water, import of water by land[V], and import of water using sea transport[VI]; and

> Both Parties have acknowledged that unless co-ordinated efforts are taken to protect the most exposed water resources, they will simply be destroyed.

▸ substitution of the water by restructuring the agricultural sector for both the Israelis and the Palestinians, meaning that water use for domestic food production is substituted with importation of food (i.e. the notion of 'virtual waters') (Allan, 2002).

From a professional point of view, various means of filling this gap must be initiated, and some of them have already been put in place, such as a 50 MCM/year desalination plant in Israel. For both Parties, rising to the challenge of filling this gap is imperative for further development of both communities – and at the least will be granting people a basic need. Nevertheless, the Parties must handle the question of 'division' of the water resources on the West Bank and the Gaza strip, irrespective of how the gap is filled. The question of whether or not they should co-operate on filling the gap may be handled regardless of the attempt to solve the water dispute.

The author therefore assumes that the Parties will co-operate on one or more of the ways of filling the gap. However, the extent of such co-operation will probably not influence how the existing water resources (including recycled water) are 'divided'. This leads to a more specific discussion on the sensitive nature of the areas and resources in question, particularly in relation to protection of and sovereignty over existing resources.

Sensitive water resource areas on the West Bank and Gaza

Both Parties have acknowledged that unless co-ordinated efforts are taken to protect the most exposed water resources, they will simply be destroyed. The grave situation is further substantiated by the United Nations' comprehensive study on the environmental situation of the West Bank and Gaza Strip (UNEP, 2003a). The PA, through its water authority and relevant ministries, must develop plans to handle the urgent water challenges (MOPIC, 1998).

V   Although politically not feasible, according to GTZ, 1998; from other river basins in the areas including Turkey.

VI Such as surplus water from Turkey (Manavgat River on the Mediterranean coast).

Section II

Israel has decades of experience in meticulous surveying and monitoring of the water resources, including on the West Bank and Gaza Strip. Through institutional, legislative, financial and scientific means, the management aspects are handled carefully – probably one of the most well-developed practices worldwide.[10]

Unilateral management of water resources by the Parties is complex in itself. Co-operation represents an additional complication, since several technical and political problems must be handled together, both prior to and during co-operation. There seems to be no doubt that neither of the Parties have any illusions that the water can be divided and managed in complete isolation.[11]

This drives the water management situation into what is, at times, an involuntary co-operation. The challenges are enormous, but not insurmountable as long as there is a willingness from the Parties to co-operate and from the international community to assist their endeavours. Some of the challenges are outlined below.

Water as a territorial and sovereignty challenge

Water resources are considered by both Parties to be an integral part of territorial sovereignty (see further discussion of the concept in *Chapter 3* of this section). It is argued here that sovereignty and water are issues that must be tackled in conjunction with other factors, and not just from a strict 'what-is-on-this-side-of-the-border issue'. Sovereignty is a legal term, but also a highly political and emotive one, which can be deconstructed into 'domestic' or 'internal sovereignty', whereas the relationships between States or State-like entities are characterized as 'external sovereignty' (cf. Green Cross International, 2004: 44).

As a separate and internationally-recognized state, Israel's interpretation of sovereignty means full ownership and unrestricted access and control of the natural resources. However, even seen in isolation to its neighbouring states, any unilateral approach to management of international watercourses infringes on each Party's strict interpretation of territorial sovereignty. There is therefore a question as to whether the vague notion of sovereignty is the one that brings forward various models of co-operative action.

The question of sovereignty and borders[VII]

Many scholars and politicians argue along at least two lines: First, the inseparability of national sovereign rights of territory and resources, often named 'territorial integrity'. The proponents argue, more or less, that any water resources within their borders are theirs. The second, more pragmatic, view is that insistence on the inseparability of the sovereignty/border nexus is not bringing negotiations on disputed resources any further. As the coming chapters reveal, there are other ways of looking at sovereignty over one's 'own' water resources. Prior to this, however, a brief outline is provided of what has been carried out to date to solve these problems.

What has been done to date?

Academically, the history of the development of the relationship between the two Parties is quite interesting. An in-depth analysis of this might offer more insight into the past, but not necessarily into the future. There are, however, a few events that are important to bear in mind.

VII Already in the aftermath of the First World War, controls of vital water resources were high on the political agenda. When the two European allies, Britain and France, entered into detailed negotiations to draw the frontiers, water was at the forefront (see Fromkin, 2001).

First, from 1948 to 1967, the Palestinians managed their water under Jordanian auspices and through a quasi-institutional and legislative setup (CESAR, 1996). It was after 1967 and the Israeli annexation of the West Bank and Gaza that water management in the areas changed.

According to Israeli law, the West Bank and Gaza Strip were under Israeli Military Administration, meaning that the Israeli Government was obliged to provide the Palestinian citizens and society with adequate water. From 1967 onwards, Israeli settlements (up to 175,000 Israelis) were established on the West Bank and Gaza Strip.[VIII] The Israeli water carrier system (cf. Shoam and Sarig, 1995), to which Palestinian towns and villages connected, was increasingly built upon.

Management of water resources on the West Bank and Gaza Strip formally changed its nature in September 1993. A 'Declaration of Principles' became the first bilateral agreement between the Palestinians (formally the PLO) and Israelis. It was agreed that water issues should be discussed in a forum called the Permanent Palestinian Israeli Committee for Economic Co-operation.

The Gaza–Jericho First Agreement, signed on 4 May 1994, was a temporary arrangement that *de facto* established the PA. According to this agreement, a limited authority on water uses was transferred to the PA, which then received control over the water resources and related infrastructure in the West Bank (WB) and the Gaza Strip (the two areas) as well as over operation and management of the water systems.[12]

In 1995, the Interim Agreement (known as the 'Oslo II agreement') between the two Parties outlined temporary means of co-operation (article 40). These included measures to protect existing resources and produce new and additional ones, as well as sharing/allocation of water resources according to the following formula (see Annex II):

▸ Both Parties agreed that there was a future need of 70-80 MCM/year on the West Bank, and 28.6 MCM/year was made available by Israel to the PA as an immediate and interim measure – including 5 MCM/year to the Gaza Strip.

▸ The additional amount (41.4-51.4 MCM/year) should be developed by the PA from the

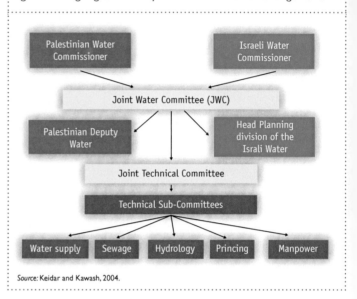

Figure 10. Organigram of the joint Palestinian-Israeli arrangements

Palestinian Water Commissioner

Israeli Water Commissioner

Joint Water Committee (JWC)

Palestinian Deputy Water

Head Planning division of the Israli Water

Joint Technical Committee

Technical Sub-Committees

Water supply | Sewage | Hydrology | Princing | Manpower

Source: Keidar and Kawash, 2004.

VIII The Israeli settlements on the Gaza Strip were abandoned under the Prime Minister Sharon government during the summer of 2005.

Eastern Aquifer and other agreed sources in the West Bank.

Since the signing of the Interim Agreement of 1995, they have worked together through a Joint Water Commission (JWC) and Joint Supervision and Enforcement Teams (JSET) as illustrated in *Figure 10*. Both have realized that co-operation has been essential for what has been achieved. Even during the turbulence of the Palestinian *Al-Asqua Intifadia*, the JWC met on a regular basis and agreed that the water infrastructure was of such importance that it should remain 'untouched' during hostilities.

The expectations of the results of the JWC might differ, and the Palestinians have conveyed a desire that the mandate cover additional areas (such as including *Areas C*).[13]

In addition, and since 1995, quite a few bilateral initiatives with the PA, especially from Germany, Japan, Canada and Norway have taken place. They have also been supported by a more structured multilateral engagement.

Multilateral initiatives

In 1991, the Madrid Process was established as an attempt primarily by the United States and Russia to solve the gridlocked crisis in the Middle East. The focus on the talks included five of the core Parties: Syria; Lebanon; Israel; and the Palestinian and Jordanian representatives, which formed one delegation until September 1993 and then became two separate ones.

Five working groups were formed. They included: Regional Economic Development; Arms Control and Regional Security; Refugees; the Environment; and the Working Group on Water Resources (WGWR). This latter is chaired by the US, with Japan and the European Union

serving as co-organizers. It has been divided into several initiatives, with the active participation of extra-regional parties like France, Canada, Germany, Oman, Tunisia, Luxembourg, Norway and, more recently, Switzerland.

Since the first regional conferences (in Madrid, Washington DC, and Moscow) between 1991 and 1993, only three of the five core Parties participated, namely Jordan, the PA and Israel. They addressed four areas to cope with some of the critical water issues[14]:

- enhancement of water data availability[15];
- water management practices, including conservation;
- enhancement of water supply; and
- concepts of regional water management and co-operation.

Since its inception, the WGWR has implemented several initiatives whereby each project enjoys the support, both technical and financial, of one or more of the WGWR's extra-regional donor delegations.

Quite a few observers argue that the multilateral framework has been a successful mechanism for addressing regional problems, not least in an Israeli-Palestinian context. The WGWR, in particular, is still successfully developing a cadre of high-level water decision-makers that work effectively together on regional water issues.

Others might argue that despite the fact that the WGWR projects continue to provide important benefits to participating regional parties, water allocation and water rights between the Palestinians and the Israelis have not been addressed. Such an argument might bear merit if the Parties had expectations of using the multilateral forums for such decisions. The fact is, however, that the three core Parties have jointly decided to co-operate on initiatives that are complementary to bilateral negotiations, such as in the case of the Jordanian–Israeli peace treaty of 1994, and the Interim Agreement between Israel and the PA in 1995.[16]

One of the fruits of the WGWR was the signing of the first trilateral water agreement between the Parties in 1996, the so-called Declaration of Principles on New and Additional Water Resources (Trolldalen [Trondalen], 1997). As an explicit reflection of the Parties' desires, no reference to allocation or interpretation of water rights was included. It did, however, provide some very important concepts for regional co-operation that might be highly applicable in the near future – if the Parties continue their co-operation. More importantly, and with relevance for the outlined proposal (in *Chapter 4*), is the fact that it reflected the level of mutual confidence at that time.

Regional initiatives on desalination of brackish water and seawater as a means of augmenting the nation's water supply have already been undertaken by the Gulf States for many years, as well as recently by Israel on a larger scale (by building and planning plants with a production capacity of about 435 MCM/year in the coming years). Under the WGWR umbrella in 1996, the three core Parties, together with several other countries[17], established a Middle East Desalination Research Centre in Muscat, Oman, paving the way for direct co-operation.

Another regional initiative of relevance to the Israeli–Palestinian relationship is the development of plans for *transferring water from the Red Sea via a hydro-power station down to the Dead Sea* (400 metres below sea-level) as a joint project between Jordan, Israel and the Palestinian Authority; the so-called Red-Dead Canal Project.[18] This project has been stalled for years. Recently, however, the Palestinians have become a partner to the project, which will provide around 870 MCM of freshwater a year to the three partners, as well as around 550 megawatts of electricity a year.[19]

Another alternative considered that would probably involve all three Parties is the Med–Dead Canal Project (by transferring water from the Mediterranean Sea to the Dead Sea either *via* the *Qatif* or the *Amakim* alignments, whereas the latter starts near Haifa or Hadera).

Transportation of water by ships would be yet another alternative, such as for example the agreement signed (in 2004) between Turkey and Israel on transporting water by ship from the Manavgat facility in Turkey to Israel, or other joint or/and national projects.

In any case, the three core Parties agree that regional co-operation is necessary and complements bi- and unilateral approaches.[20] Bilateral disputes and co-operative projects are also expected in the future to be dealt with directly and outside the 'multilaterals'. As *Chapter 3* shows, however, there are international stakeholders that cannot be neglected, either during the negotiations or while securing compliance with future water agreements.

Chapter 3

The Parties' positions and real concerns

As in most contentious situations, the Parties and their allies have, over the years, made public statements that seem to be mutually incompatible on water management. The solutions to the water disputes between them will probably not be found in past rhetoric and entrenched positions. However, they have real concerns that must not be overlooked in any proposed solutions. Unless the Parties – whether the leadership or the public, or preferably both – feel that their concerns and needs have been met in one way or another, past experience shows that the solution will not last long (Trondalen, 2004a).

As in any conflict situation, the perceived gap between the professionals, the political leadership and the public is posing, in this case, a particular challenge. Unfortunately, there is a gap between the political rhetoric and what can feasibly be achieved in a solution to the water disputes. Both Parties must be prepared to compromise and, equally importantly, prepare the public for the fact that not all national aspirations can be maximized. There are reasons why this has not been done, and it appears that it is not only due to political decisions, but also to the fact that neither Party wants to be perceived as 'giving in' in the preparatory negotiations.

The challenge of enlightening the public and preparing for a realistic solution may look trivial, but recent events such as the Golan Heights negotiations between Israel and Syria may serve as an example (see *Section I, Part 1*). In this case, public preparation was not carried out to an extent that gave the leaders the necessary 'mandate'. However, as some have argued[21], leaders must sometimes take steps that go beyond the popular public perception. The gap, however, must not be too large.

> ...leaders must sometimes take steps that go beyond the popular public perception. The gap, however, must not be too large.

With this in mind, the Parties' positions and interests will be described while bearing in mind that any sustainable solutions can only be found by reconciling their concerns rather than their positions.

As outlined in the following text, the Parties are approaching the water dispute from two quite different perspectives. Despite the striking moot points, it is recognized that the water crisis is severe and that both Parties have humanitarian obligations to provide water to the people that go beyond the present rhetoric and points of view. 'Water rights' are, in fact, essential to achieve the "right to a standard of living adequate for the health and well-being of himself and of his family".[IX]

This is the *raison d'être* that makes solutions possible. Before turning to those in *Chapter 4*, the Parties' positions and concerns are outlined.

Palestinian positions and concerns

The Palestinians' positions on the water disputes are related to:

- ▸ water rights, including water sharing;
- ▸ an agreed-upon formula for water allocation (between the two Parties);
- ▸ an exact location of the borders on the West Bank that will also determine control of the water;
- ▸ the West Bank Barrier/Separation Wall[X]; and
- ▸ control, access and protection of the water resources.

In an academic sense, it should be possible to clearly define the Palestinian positions. In real life, however, these positions are not carved in stone. The Palestinian leadership is well aware that the total sum of the factors is different from the sum of isolated factors. The Final Status negotiations either along the Quartet's Road Map (see further discussion in *Chapter 4*) or with a different formula may well create situations where either Party could be willing to yield

...there are reasons to believe that the Palestinians will demand water allocation on the basis of geographical and hydrological principles...

on one position if there are some concessions on other issues, or if the overall outcome justifies the compromises.

The main positions related to water rights, including water sharing

As discussed above, positions are not the same as interests or concerns, but are rather strategic and tactical. As of today, the PA takes the following positions (not necessarily in this order of priority):

- ▸ "to secure an Israeli commitment to respect international resolution on sovereignty;
- ▸ to exercise its right to permanent legal sovereignty and actual control over water regarding sources that lie within its territory – as in the case of Israel;
- ▸ to take whatever measures are needed to use water resources within the boundaries of its territory, including its share of joint aquifers, with commitment to respecting the rights of the other Party and refraining from causing it any damage;
- ▸ to have a share of the eastern wadis of the Gaza Strip. Methods for sustainable management of such wadis must be discussed; and
- ▸ to have a share of the Jordan River Basin. A comprehensive joint co-operation agreement that includes all other Arab countries riparian in such basis must be made."[22]

An agreed-on formulation of water allocation (between the two Parties)

Although this has not been claimed officially, there are reasons to believe that the Palestinians will demand water allocation on the basis of geographical and hydrological principles (i.e. the degree of contribution to the watershed such as geographical extension and/or rainfall within such parameters) as well as social and economic needs (including industrial and agricultural demands).[23]

IX   See the United Nations' Universal Declaration of Human Rights, Article 25.

X   A Palestinian term. The Israelis call it a Security Fence.

In addition, the PA states that:

► "any physical, administrative, or legal measures taken by the Israeli authorities relative to Palestinian water resources must not affect Palestinian water rights (to be negotiated);

► the Israeli side must give restitution to the Palestinian side for the losses of the Palestinian people as a result of Israeli measures in the field of water;

► co-operation on the use of shared ground or surface water aquifers cannot be discussed before reaching a clear agreement, according to which the Israeli side acknowledges the Palestinian water rights;

► the temporary agreements set forth in the Oslo agreements do not affect Palestinian water rights, given that those agreements are temporary and interim. The Palestinian people's rights to their water resources are permanent and unquestionable;

► water rights cannot be measured by the average individual's need or by dunums of land. Complete sovereignty over water resources within the boundaries of 'Palestine';

► the Palestinian State must be able to exercise its rights to use the water of the Jordan River Basin and to participate fully in the management of this basin;

► the Parties must review the mechanism for transferring the title of water infrastructure that belongs to the Israeli side and is located within the border of the West Bank and Gaza Strip to the Palestinian side; and

► the Parties must discuss the Palestinian share for the Jordan River Basin and how to benefit from such a share. A comprehensive joint co-operation agreement that includes all other Arab countries riparian in such basis must be made." (UNESCWA, 2004)

■ Photo 21.
A small stream draining to the Dead Sea

The PA has made a strategic decision to attempt to increase the legitimacy of its arguments by basing its positions on UN resolutions rather than on international law related to international watercourses (PWA, 2004a). A key issue is not whether that is wise or not, but rather that a set of explicit positions have been brought forward to the Israeli.

Location of the Green Line on the West Bank in relation to control of water[XI]

The Israeli decision to build a security fence has raised sharp criticisms from the Palestinian and Arab sides, who call it a 'separation wall'.

This highly contentious issue is further disputed since the route of the barrier is considered to have relevance for control of the water resources by creating 'facts on the ground'. According to the PA, the barrier has the following implications in relation to management of the water resources:

XI The Green Line is the ceasefire line on the West Bank as until 1967. It was normally marked as a green line on Israeli maps.

▸ "The wall will prevent the Palestinians from utilizing their own water resources in the Western Aquifer Basin."

▸ "Only a small portion of the Upper Aquifer utilization area in the Basin lies within the fenced-in Palestinian areas."

▸ Israel will "control 40 Palestinian water wells (...with a pumpage of about 5,23 MCM/year) located in the fertile agricultural land that lies between the Green Line and the wall".

▸ Furthermore, the PA is particularly concerned that "moving the political border [Green Line] a few hundred met[res] east would mean that G[round] W[ater] utilization areas would be under the control of Israel in the final settlement." (UNESCWA, 2004)

The PA uses the Latrun case (an area along the Green Line located near the highway from Jerusalem to Tel Aviv) as an example of where it is losing 'strategic' land that might be used as a bargaining tool in relation to allocation of the Western Aquifer.

For obvious reasons, their arguments are quite clear and founded on one way of thinking and reasoning. In this context, an interesting question is whether the route of the wall/barrier will have an impact of the permanent status agreement. There is, however, no clear answer to this political question. What seems obvious is that drawing borders in this area has never been insignificant (e.g. the Camp David negotiations in late 2000).[24] The proposed solutions (in *Chapter 4*) would have to take this factor into account, but any border and associated water allocation and sharing are all parts of a larger puzzle. One can hardly argue that a 'temporary'[25] fence would determine intergenerational water rights.

Israeli positions and concerns

Israel is approaching the water dispute with the PA in quite a different way to the Palestinians. Sovereignty over water resources has been at the forefront of the Zionist movement for over 100 years.[26] Systematic water studies and subsequent projects were conducted as early as the 1930s in preparation for the establishment of a Jewish state.

> Sovereignty over water resources has been at the forefront of the Zionist movement for over 100 years.

One of the first major efforts by the new state was the development of national water plans and projects, including draining of the Hula Valley (north of Lake Tiberias) and building of the National Water Carrier System, which included transferring water south to the Northern Negev desert.

A turning point took place after the war in 1967, where the Israelis took control of almost all springs and branches of the Jordan River as well as groundwater in the West Bank and Gaza Strip (WBGS). Since that time, major water infrastructure has been developed – primarily in Israel as well as in the WBGS.

Some major overriding Israeli concerns have and still prevail in all water-related matters, as discussed below.

Hydro-strategic concerns

Despite changing governments in Israel, a univocal affirmation of the strategic importance of proper management of water for the very existence of the state has been repeated. At present, the web of economic and social growth is very much determined by use of water. In the Israeli mind, sound management, or more correctly speaking proper stewardship, of the precious water has led to a situation whereby the country's water management policy and practice is a model for most nations. Conservation methods measured both in terms of efficiency and effectiveness are considered to be some of the best in the world. Therefore, protection and conservation of already-existing resources are essential concerns for all Israeli water professionals and managers.

Interestingly enough, the influential National Security Council (NSC) has made several statements on this matter. In 1999[27], the NSC warned of the danger of overpumping the Mountain Aquifer and of developing a joint management arrangement with the Palestinians due to what was considered to be their inability to enforce any agreement that may be reached. It further cautioned that extensive 'wildcat' drilling and over-exploitation would lead to diminution of the quantity and quality of the water in the aquifer.[28]

The professional establishment in Israel, such as the Water Commissioner, is somewhat more nuanced with regards to contentious issues like granting water rights to the Palestinians. The author is not aware of any updated *official* position paper on water regarding the upcoming negotiations. There are, however, quite clear official and expert statements in line with the Interim Agreement from 1995 that warn of the danger of not managing the water resources in a proper manner. There are a few overriding concerns.

A major issue is how to extract the water from the Mountain Aquifer System in a sustainable manner and in terms of sharing with and/or allocation to the Palestinians. Measures to prevent and mitigate pollution are considered to be critical

(see Schwartz and Zohar, 1991). The objectives would be to:

▸ prevent unregulated increase of the extraction of the groundwater at the expense of Israel's water supply; and
▸ prevent pollution of the aquifer as a result of uncontrolled activities such as untreated flows of sewage and other forms of waste.

It is further argued that principles of prior and present use on the definition of the source according to the location of the springs would be the guide in any negotiations rather than the outcrops of the aquifer. In addition, water should be allocated where there are the highest economic benefits (lowest production costs).

There is a water crisis and a severe water deficit

The political and professional establishment in Israel acknowledges that:

▸ water resources are scarce, and insufficient to meet present and certainly future needs (Schwartz and Zohar, 1991). This is further underlined by the fact that the water crisis has accumulated a deficit in Israel's renewable water resources amounting to 2 billion m³ – an amount equal to the annual consumption of the State[29]; and
▸ drastic adjustment in various sectors (including agriculture) must be taken in order to manage the crisis.

Co-operation on new and additional water resources

Israel is therefore requesting acknowledgement by the Palestinians that the water situation is alarming – including the Mountain Aquifer System and Coastal Aquifer – as well as that the Gaza Aquifer faces a risk of severe pollution. These problems are of paramount importance compared

Section II

to the amount of water to be shared.

On *Map 14*, the locations of planned desalination plants are, according to the Israelis, 'ready-made' for linking up to the Palestinian water system so that together they may provide new and additional water.

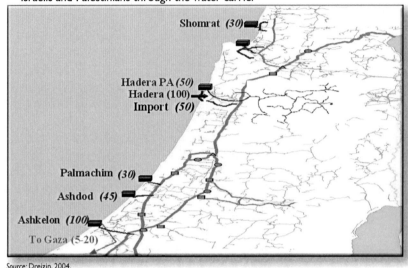

Map 15. Development of seawater desalination plants that could serve both Israelis and Palestinians through the water carrier

Source: Dreizin, 2004.

Israel further argues that a deficit cannot be shared and that co-operation will be possible on new and additional water resources in order to cope with the existing and future deficit.

The issue of water rights

Israel has already recognized that the Palestinians have water rights on the West Bank (see *the Interim Agreement of 1995, para.1*), and has expressed willingness to discuss the Palestinians' water needs. It is a general international impression that their position has been interpreted as 'rights to use water'. As will be discussed in the following text, translation of the vague political notion of 'water rights' into a concrete water management regime is a major challenge, especially since there is a definite limit of available resources.

Israel is well aware that water rights are a major issue for the PA, and that external observers will probably not know the exact Israeli position before real negotiations commence.

Arguments used by Israel in developing joint management arrangements

There are different views on the extent to which joint management mechanisms should be developed. Some argue that unilateral approaches serve best the interests of the state, based on the following argument: "...the profound difference, not only with regard to the substance of the hydrological interests of Israel and the Palestinians, but also over the very definition of the principles defining the right of ownership of the water adopted by each side, make it difficult to be optimistic as to the prospect of joint management" (Sherman, 2001: Appendix VIII).

This view may contradict the principles established in the Interim Agreement of 1995, which emphasizes joint arrangements not only by the establishment of the Palestinian-Israeli Joint Water Council, but also of the Joint Supervision and Enforcement Teams. Although there are different views in Israel about these matters, irrespective of ideology there are reasons to believe that the water resources must be managed through national and joint institutional mechanisms.

The fact that two separate political entities exist – one situated upstream and the other downstream – always increases the chances of friction and hence the failure of any joint management endeavour. Such tension may arise not as a result of intentional malevolence, but out of divergent views involving *bona fide* differences of perspective on given objective circumstances (see also Sherman, 2001).

> Tension may arise not as a result of intentional malevolence, but out of divergent views involving *bona fide* differences of perspective on given objective circumstances.

What are the individual Parties' perceptions of the other Parties' positions with regards to the water negotiations?

In any assessment of water conflicts, an understanding of the Parties' respective perception of the other Party's positions and concerns is relevant in order to develop any possible solutions (see Trondalen, 2004a).

The Israeli perception of the Palestinian concerns

There are no easily accessible public Israeli statements on the Palestinian positions. However, based on discussions in the area, there are good reasons to argue that the Israelis are very well aware of the PA's positions, such as that:

▸ the PA is demanding sovereignty over the water resources within the West Bank (and Gaza) without any guarantees of protecting the aquifer against pollution and overpumping[30];

▸ Palestinians demand that water rights be granted according to international law and codes of conduct, but so far without further specifications, especially in relation to obligations in line with international law[XII], as to when and how such rights would be acquired and which obligations would be accepted; and

▸ the PA acknowledges that sewage and pollution are a major challenge, but has, as of today, very few feasible plans, institutional or financial means or enforcement mechanisms of any policy that might be developed.

The Israelis are also aware (and from their perspective consider to be totally unrealistic) that the return of the Palestinian 1948 refugees will increase the number of people. This in turn will increase the Palestinian demand for the allocated/shared amount of water. This issue, however, is very much intertwined with the final status of the returnees, and under which conditions they return.

Palestinian perceptions of the Israeli concerns

Interestingly enough, the Palestinian Authority (such as the PWA) has made public its interpretation of the Israeli positions. This does not mean that their interpretation of the Israeli positions is 100 per cent correct, but it displays how the Palestinians perceive them, or at least wish them to be publicly portrayed.

XII Such as sustainable utilization, 'polluter pay's principles, and precautionary principles (cf. various environmental UN conventions).

As in any dispute, the fear of any Party is the intention of the other. The PA therefore fears that Israel is "trying to distract from its violation of Palestinian water rights by claiming that all available water resources are not sufficient to meet current requirements", and furthermore, that "what's behind this claim is a desire to rule out negotiations over water resources used now by the Israelis. According to Israel, there are no water resources to negotiate over, and both Parties should talk – but not negotiate – about co-operating to search for new water resources to be shared on an equitable basis" (PWA, 2004a: *the Political Framework*).

More specifically, *the PA has stated that Israel is arguing* that:

■ Photo 22.
The Feshka Springs of the Eastern Aquifer have eroded through the ground eastward to the Dead Sea

▸ "It is not possible to share a deficiency, but it is possible to co-operate in looking for new and additional water resources and work together to fill the deficiency. This is the only practical solution, and there is no other.

▸ The Israeli side is willing to discuss the issue of Palestinian water needs apart from politics, i.e. to deal with water rights as utilization rights only; the Palestinians will receive their water needs if available.

▸ The Israelis have no extra water, so they have decided to set up desalination units with a productivity capacity of 312 MCM.

▸ The Israelis hope to agree with the Palestinians on a co-operation and co-ordination mechanism for the protection of the aquifers through joint management.

▸ Israel does not want co-operation talks on water to be separate from co-operation talks on sewage.

▸ The Israeli side wants to separate water from other issues relevant to the permanent status negotiations.

▸ Israel's position is based on the 'first utilization' principle, and that the Israelis will not discuss their established rights in existing utilization. Their basis for their claim that they use the water by right is that Israel was utilizing prior to 1967 the same amount of water as now. (PWA, 2004a)

As for water resources in Gaza, the Palestinians understand the Israelis' positions as:

► The total quantity pumped from the ground aquifers in Gaza is 5 MCM, of which 2.5 MCM is supplied to the Palestinians.

► A further quantity of 2.5 MCM will be supplied to the Palestinians in the Gaza Strip from Israeli resources.

► The Gaza Strip will not obtain water from the West Bank aquifers, since those aquifers are shared between Israel and the West Bank.

The PA also believes that the Israelis want "the Palestinians to abandon their water rights and co-operate on looking for new water resources (e.g. seawater desalination, sewage water recycling, and importing water from Turkey)" (PWA, 2004a).

Furthermore, the Palestinian Authority summarizes the difference of opinions by stating that the "gap between the Israeli and Palestinian positions is very large".

As an external observer, a legitimate question would be whether the Parties' concerns are irreconcilable. The next chapter attempts to answer that question.

Section II

Chapter 4

A proposed approach to the water dispute

Various models for separate and co-operative water management

The intertwining of the ideological, economic, strategic, territorial and humanitarian aspects of the water dispute means that no solutions can be ascribed to a given water allocation formula in accordance with specific water quality standards. Any solutions must therefore address the Parties' real concerns in an incremental approach in which agreements are cumulative, in the sense that if the Parties agree on step A, they move to B and later to C, and so on.

> Any solutions must address the Parties' real concerns in an incremental approach in which agreements are cumulative.

As with the preceding Golan Heights dispute, no proposal can be viewed in isolation from a larger agreed package. Sometimes this means that concessions in one area may yield benefits to another. The water dispute between the Israel and the PA, however, means that use of the water resources must be solved in one way or another, irrespective of any agreements in other sectors. The proposed solution should probably be viewed as an integral part of a comprehensive *peace* between the two Parties, but may also be applied in isolation in the case of the unfortunate situation in which a comprehensive Permanent Status Agreement is postponed.

Before turning to the concrete proposal, one may ask, also in this case: Why make the proposal public? There is an increasing need for water professionals to communicate to a larger public audience about *realistic* options, since there seems to be a gap between, on the one hand, the political rhetoric and aspirations, and, on the other, realistic technical solutions. In addition, a proposal from an external observer might be viewed differently from a proposal from either of the Parties. Finally, as in the case of the Golan Heights, the following proposal should be viewed in light of the fact that very little progress in the talks between the two Parties has taken place in recent years.

Unless responsible leaders and the enlightened public realize that each Party must have great flexibility in reaching an agreement, and equally important, full commitment in implementing it, human suffering will occur, as will continuous fighting over the water resources.

What does the proposal attempt to achieve?

This proposal outlines a way of making both Parties' positions *compatible* with each other in such a way that PA's and Israel's underlying objectives[XIII] are *fulfilled*.

More specifically, this means that the Israeli concern regarding management and control of the water resources on the West Bank[31] such that Israel's water use is secured in terms of quantity *and quality* regarding the aquifers shared with the Palestinian Authority must be fulfilled. At the same time, this must be compatible with the Palestinian territorial claims as well as their demand for sovereignty to develop and use the water resources on the West Bank and Gaza Strip.

As in the case of the Golan Heights, implementation of any agreement must be ensured by comprehensive water verification, monitoring and enforcement programmes.

This proposal is valid irrespective of the exact location of the disputed borders on the West Bank, as long as the interpretation of sovereignty over the disputed water resources is agreed on. If consensus is found on the principles in this proposal, the exact drawing down to the metre on the West Bank might be done at a later stage and at a more technical level (including the implications of the barrier/fence on the West Bank).

Both Parties will have their concerns addressed

Respecting Israel's sound water protection claim and Palestinians' water rights by meeting

the water use needs of any population increase would incur additional costs to both Parties in the form of measures to mitigate water pollution and replace net water consumption.

Any agreements between them would involve the international community as a whole. Therefore, as in the Golan Heights case, any deal would entail a commitment from the international community to assist the Parties to establish and implement the agreements.

What kind of negotiable concepts may be applied?

As dealt with in the introductory section of this publication, the vague concepts of 'water rights' and 'sovereignty' should be clarified and translated into an operational context. A starting point might be that *sovereignty* encompasses both the notions of 'rights' and 'obligations', whereas the latter requires that every state or state-like entity is obliged to manage them according to national laws but also according to internationally recognized obligations (or even to religious law such as the *Sharia* for the Palestinians (see for example Haddad, 2000)). In this context, protection against pollution and over-pumping (of the aquifers) is one of the most important obligations of the two Parties.

Since water rights are interpreted differently in various parts of the world, this is perhaps the best argument for tailoring the three concepts of water rights (*ownership, control and use*) and the notion of 'obligations' into a meaningful and mutually-acceptable context of the West Bank and Gaza Strip. An official recognition of water rights was already granted to the Palestinians by Israel in 1992.[32] However, this raises another question: How to translate those obligations and rights into a mutually-accepted agreement?

XIII In negotiation terms: the Parties' concerns or interests.

Since experience on internationally-shared management of aquifers is meagre, it is not obvious that a proposed solution should specify all three concepts of water rights.

One could, for example, argue that an agreement on joint management would make such distinctions redundant.

There seem, however, to be two reasons why these three attributes should be translated into a *timelined agreement* or so-called *incremental step approach*. First, there is profound professional opposition in Israel to a dependency of the Palestinians in joint management of the Mountain Aquifer.[33] Second, since an incremental set of solutions is proposed, agreement on some of the attributes may be implemented at different stages in the implementation, as it is important for the PA to obtain an agreement so that long-term strategies might be developed.

The perceived politically-tempting concept of water rights is therefore a double-edged sword, especially for the Palestinians, as the notion of 'obligations' is equally strong. Israel has realized this even from a unilateral perspective. Over several years, and especially since 1999, its Water Commissioner has warned about unsustainable use of both surface and groundwater.[34] At present, Palestinian professionals[35] and the PA have officially recognized the significance of these obligations, but the Palestinian Authority does not have sufficient institutional, financial or enforcement abilities[XIV] to fully take on such obligations.

This reality is acknowledged by both Parties, and the questions would rather be:

▸ How can an agreement between them include incremental steps that would include transfer of water rights and water obligations in a sustainable and agreeable manner?
▸ How can implementation of these steps be enforced in a realistic and structured way?
▸ How can disputes between them be resolved during this process?

Anyone who claims that there are quick-fix answers to these questions is either naive or has limited real-life experience in the region. Therefore, the following alternative proposals have several reservations, particularly of a political nature.

Proposed solutions to the Parties' water rights and obligations

At present, no single formula or approach seems mutually acceptable. One formula that might seem appropriate at a certain point on the timeline may quickly be outdated due to a constantly-evolving political climate combined with dwindling water resources. However, the international community would have to act as guarantor for the implementation of whatever is agreed on. It may seem odd that the international community is counted in as a decisive factor in reaching any agreement, but unless stakeholders such as the US, EU, Russia and the UN (the *Quartet*) back any agreement on water, the chances are high that not only the proposed incremental step approach, but also any other approaches, may fail.

One may argue that a unilateral and isolationistic approach is favourable, as the risks are too high to rely on international stakeholders. The arguments probably bear some merits for the Israelis, but the alternatives also involve high

---
XIV The PWA has been granted this mandate in its water law generally (which was enacted in 2002), but it is assumed by most observers that it needs more time to take on such obligations – therefore, an agreed timeline is needed.

Section II

risks, especially related to depletion of the Mountain Aquifer System, unless an agreement has been reached with the Palestinians. Additionally, lack of a water agreement with the PA would be perceived by the Palestinians as politically and psychologically impossible[36], and could also deprive the Palestinians of basic human needs and rights that could (even from a national perspective) backfire on stability.

Questions to address in an incremental step approach (ISA)

Certain questions must therefore be addressed:

A) General questions.
   - Who is the institutional and political entity accountable to for the agreement from each Party?
   - What is the duration of the agreement – and what are the incremental steps?
   - What are the *milestones* and how would the *review of the process* be conducted?
   - What are the agreed procedures for reviewing performance?

B) Legal and practical interpretation of the four attributes of water rights separately and/ or jointly and in geographic terms (both horizontally and vertically of the aquifers)[37]
   - Who has ownership of which part of the aquifers and recycled water?
   - Who has control of which part of the aquifers and recycled water?
   - Who may use how much and at what time of which parts of the aquifers and recycled water?

C) Legal and practical interpretation of water obligations to use the water
   - How is sustainable use conducted?
   - How is environmental protection carried out and enforced – separately and/or jointly?
   - How will breach of agreements be handled (punitive measures)?

- How to use the water resource in an economically efficient way?

D) Monitoring and verification procedures
   - What kind of monitoring and verification procedures will be applied?
   - What is the role of the *Quartet* as a guarantor?
   - Who will finance the implementation of the agreement, and over what time period?

Some unresolved questions remain. For example, in case the Parties agree on 'compensation' to the PA in one form or another for foregone use of water on the West Bank (from a certain date), which parameters could be included and in which form? Another linked issue is compensation to the PA from the international community for guaranteeing maintainance of Israeli water uses downstream beyond an agreed level in terms of quantity and quality. These and other questions could therefore be discussed within the proposed incremental step approach.

The basic principle is that both Parties must have a sense not only that their main concerns have been taken care of in an agreement, but also that the chances of successful implementation of what is agreed on are higher than the risk of no agreement.

The need for incremental steps

It goes beyond doubt that the Parties must have some sort of minimum mutual confidence, which is necessary for the implementation of an agreement. Without such a gradual development of trust built into an agreement, proper implementation of even the most refined agreement will not take place. In *realpolitik*, however, no Party would enter into an agreement that would render it dependant on the other as

Outline of the incremental step approach

1. Agreement step ➡ 2. Solidification step ➡ 3. Implementation step ➡ 4. Review step ➡

regards vital strategic matters. Politicians from both Parties are proponents of water agreements that tie the Parties together, while others argue along unilateral lines. Likewise, the professional water community reflects this division (as argued in Feitelson, 2002: 10), including those that favour joint water management regimes such as the joint Israeli-Palestinian academic process (through Professors Feitelson and Haddad) (see Feitelson and Haddad, 2000)[38] or the 'opposing views' as expressed by Sherman[39] from the Israeli side.

As there are probably several ways to achieve such gradual implementation and development of a water agreement; one should be wary of

The following parameters could be included in developing mutually satisfactory formulas for water and recycled water for the West Bank and Gaza Strip. In addition, each parameter should be determined in relation to a timeline, such as 'at what time' and 'over what time period':

Separate and/or joint ownership of separate parts of the Mountain Aquifer System according to an agreed formula, such as X per cent by the Palestinian Authority, and Y per cent by Israel (and expressed in MCM): the Western Aquifer, the Eastern Aquifer and Gaza Aquifer – including recycled water.

Control of which parts of the sub-aquifers separately and/or jointly (meaning in this context a "mandate to protect the aquifer systems" according to a set of water management rules) according to an agreed formula, such as Z per cent by the PA, and V per cent by Israel (and expressed in MCM): the Western Aquifer, the Eastern Aquifer and the Gaza Aquifer – including recycled water.

The amount of water shared/allocation (expressed in MCM) from the sub-aquifers might be determined in relation to:
  a) what is already agreed in the Interim Agreement, 1995, Article 40, plus:
  b) the number of people living in the West Bank and Gaza Strip, estimated separately multiplied by a certain amount of water per capita. It is anticipated that a certain number of Palestinian people will return to the West Bank and Gaza Strip under a final status agreement;
  c) the amount of water to be leased to Israel in a transition period, or in a form that is mutually agreed on;
  d) principles for tradable permits/quotas/water wheeling, which also includes trade and compensation mechanisms;
  e) other related factors like joint arrangements for producing new and additional water resources; and
  f) water balance management: use of the shared/allocated water according to a joint formula in relation to a sustainable yield (based on a set of hydrogeological/climatic parameters from the past 6-12 months).

proposing the 'one and only' approach.[40] Some of the inside proponents mentioned above have worked over several years on designing possible approaches. The proposed *incremental step approach* is therefore derived from the following sources:

▸ the Israeli and Palestinian experience of implementation of the Interim Agreement of 1995 (so-called Oslo II agreement, Article 40 – see Annex II), and especially with the experience gained by the Joint Water Committee and Joint Enforcement and Supervision Teams[41];

▸ as an example of different perspectives, with the common desire to manage the resourcesin a proper manner, the two Israeli and Palestinian scholarly proponents mentioned above, although not limited to the two;

▸ discussions over the years with officials and water professionals from the two Parties; and

▸ relevant lessons learnt (by the author) from other parts in the region.

Without agreement on an incremental approach, the chances of any agreement becoming viable appear slim. The following proposal therefore aims to answer some of the questions described above, implemented as a carefully structured and gradual approach. It may be divided into four incremental steps (see outline above, as well as *Figure 11*):

Any approach, whether it is incremental or not, must be based on certain agreed-upon

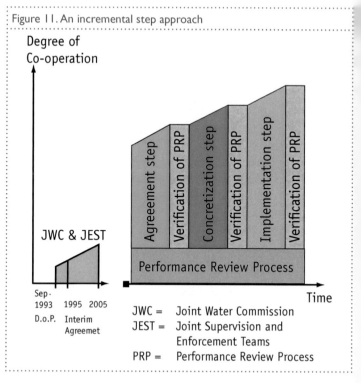

Figure 11. An incremental step approach

JWC = Joint Water Commission
JEST = Joint Supervision and Enforcement Teams
PRP = Performance Review Process

criteria or so-called parameters. In this case, the Incremental Approach could be based on a Sovereignty Formula that specifies each Party's rights and obligations according to some specific parameters. In the textbox on the preceding page, some of these parameters have been outlined. A possible integration of the formula with the incremental approach is developed in the following pages.

Proposed approach: an incremental step approach

1st agreement step: Following decisions must be made:

5. Identify institutional and political entity(ies) accountable for the agreement from each Party.

6. Duration of the agreement in terms of years – and time period for each incremental step.

7. Milestones and the review process, and procedures for reviewing performance.
8. Determination of separate and/or joint ownership with regard to parts of the aquifers; horizontal, vertical and recycled water (see *Figure 12*).
9. Control of which parts of the aquifers and recycled water (see *Figure 12*).
10. The amount of water shared/allocated from the aquifers and recycled water (on a yearly basis; see *Figure 12*).
11. Principles for sustainable use – including extraction volumes according to agreed-upon parameters (such as last year's rainfall or annual yields at a certain reference point, etc.).
12. Separate and joint environmental protection measures.[42]
13. Punitive measures in case of breach of agreement between the Parties and within each Party.
14. The role of the Quartet[XV] as guarantor of implementation according to specific criteria (cf. especially, 3 above).

2nd solidification step: Following decisions should be made:

1. Harmonization of the Parties' water legislation.
2. Procedures for monitoring and verification.
3. Principles for using the water resource in an economically-efficient manner.
4. Development of a Strategic Master Plan for the West Bank and Gaza Strip that includes the elements described above.
5. Development of a Crisis Management Mechanism: conflict resolution and enforcement arrangement that should deal with all sorts of crisis management (see Feitelson and Haddad, 2000: 464).

6. Implementation of some selected protective measures[XVI] in tandem with the allocation above.[43]
7. Development of joint plans for manufacturing water,[XVII] including the establishment of an Escrow Fund.[XVIII]
8. The role of a larger international constituency in financing the implementation of the agreement.

3rd implementation step: Following actions should be taken:

1. Adjustment of the respective water legislation.
2. Implementation of agreed allocation of water between the Parties according to the formula agreed on in the 1st step, especially in relation to: 5) - 8) (ownership, access, control, allocation/share).
3. Continuation of implementation of protective measures in tandem with the allocation above.
4. Development of tradable permits/water wheeling mechanisms, including an Escrow Fund.
5. Implementation of joint plans for manufacturing water.
6. The Guarantor should review performance according to agreed standards.
7. Continuation to the 4th step, or implementation of punitive or other agreed measures in case of breach of agreement between the Parties and within each Party.

XVI Anti-pollution; treatment; reuse etc.
XVII Such as desalination of brackish water and seawater or water transportation by ships.
XVIII It is implicitly recognized that some sort of joint initiatives will be undertaken – based on the fact that as long as a joint infrastructure has been developed in situations where the mutual gains are high, withdrawal from the project will also hurt the withdrawing Party.

XV Russia, USA, the EU, and the UN.

An application of a sovereignty formula of water and recycled water in an incremental step approach for the West Bank

Ownership ("Property right entitling the owner of the economic value to the water")

MCM:	Separate		Joint
	Israel	PA	Israel/PA
The Western Aquifer	V	I	X
The Eastern Aquifer	J	G	H
The Gaza Aquifer	X	K	L

Control ("Protect the aquifer systems" also include "monitor, and survey")

MCM:	Separate		Joint
	Israel	PA	Israel/PA
The Western Aquifer	A	L	B
The Eastern Aquifer	G	D	E
The Gaza Aquifer	O	K	P

Transition phase
Allocation/share for use ("Utilize/extract/pump for consumption and/or storage")

MCM:	Separate		Joint
	Israel	PA	Israel/PA
The Western Aquifer	Æ	K	Å
The Eastern Aquifer	H	L	IX
The Gaza Aquifer	S	Ø	T
New and additional	A	P	Q

Final
Allocation/share for use ("Utilize/extract/pump for consumption and/or storage")

MCM:	Separate		Joint
	Israel	PA	Israel/PA
The Western Aquifer	I	II	III
The Eastern Aquifer	IV	V	VI
The Gaza Aquifer	VII	VIII	IX
Leased Water	X	XI	XII
New and additional water	XIII	XIV	XV

Note: The Mountain Aquifer is for hydrological and allocation/sharing purposes only divided into Western and Eastern Aquifers. The shaded numerals refer to *Figure 12*.

The 4th review step: Following actions should be taken:

1. Continuation of allocation of water between the Parties according to the *formulas* agreed on in the 1st step – especially in relation to: 5)-8) *(ownership, access, control, allocation/share)*.

2. Implementation of *protective measures* in tandem with the above allocation.

3. Implementation of 'tradable permits'/'water wheeling' mechanisms.[XIX]

XIX In this context, this means short-term licenses to use each Party's water – no sale of sovereignty as a whole would be involved. One such example could be sale of recycled water from the Gaza Strip to Israel for agricultural purposes in the Negev Desert, which will have a double positive effect – not polluting the Gaza Strip aquifer and providing saleable water to the southern part of Israel (see also Fisher *et al.*, 2002: 25-14).

Section II

4. Continuation of implementation of joint plans for *manufacturing water*.
5. The Parties and Guarantors should review performance according to agreed standards.
6. Continuation along the established lines, or implementation of punitive or other agreed measures in case of breach of agreement between the Parties and within each Party.

Unfortunately, the political rhetoric has so far focused on figures and the possible negative impacts of an agreement rather than on the suggested principles. This is why a performance review process must be an integral part of the water agreement.

Application of a sovereignty formula together with an incremental step approach

The ISA should be based on an agreed formula, and some may argue that such an approach is worthless unless some hard facts and figures are agreed upon. The arguments bear some merit, but any agreement on the figures is probably also dependent on the provisions in the incremental approach. A possible matrix of how a formula may look is outlined in the textbox above.

The outlined formula may look quite complex, but this is attributed to the complex hydrology. Two quite different communities

are involved, and there is an intricate water management history (such as different investment in infrastructure and degree of water consumption related to economic development).

One of the important points in the formula is the relationship between ownership and allocation/share of water. This distinction is made since the Palestinian proprietary rights (ownership) of the Mountain Aquifer System may be higher than the amount to be used (allocation/share) by the PA. It may be an optimal solution for *both Parties* for the Israelis to use a larger share from one of the aquifers than its proprietary rights. This is due to the fact that an expensive water infrastructure is already in place. From an economic perspective, Israel could, for example, lease water from this particular aquifer (e.g. from the Western Aquifer), but provide water to another (e.g. to the Eastern Aquifer, where the PA has a higher need) – as illustrated in *Figure 12*.

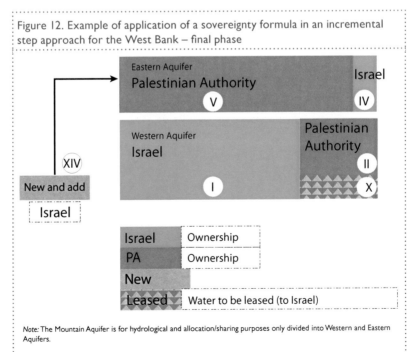

Figure 12. Example of application of a sovereignty formula in an incremental step approach for the West Bank — final phase

Eastern Aquifer
Palestinian Authority
Israel
V
IV

Western Aquifer
Israel
Palestinian Authority
II
I
X

XIV
New and add
Israel

Israel	Ownership
PA	Ownership
New	
Leased	Water to be leased (to Israel)

Note: The Mountain Aquifer is for hydrological and allocation/sharing purposes only divided into Western and Eastern Aquifers.

The need for a comprehensive performance review process by the guarantors

As outlined above, both Parties are concerned about the others' compliance with any agreements they may enter into. Both Parties not only want, but rather insist upon, the assurance of a mutually-accepted guarantor's review, verification and monitoring of the other Party's compliance, as well as the international community's implementation of the agreement. Such a mechanism is a prerequisite for implementation.

Internationally, the importance of verifying agreements is increasingly recognized, and the role of a guarantor should not be too controversial. The process would include reviewing and verifying all steps in the agreement to ensure that the Parties have made decisions and taken action in accordance with the agreement. The Parties shall harmonize rules for setting up and operating monitoring and verification programmes, including measurement systems and devices, analytical techniques, data processing and evaluation procedures.

As in the case of the proposed solution for the Golan Heights (*Section I, Part 1*), the guarantor should review performance according to clearly agreed-on standards and procedures.

What about the costs of implementation?

As in the case of the Golan Heights, how would external stakeholders view the cost of financing implementation of an agreement between Israel and the PA? There is of course no exact answer to this. However, they would probably view the cost according to what serves their foreign political and economic interests in relation to part of a settlement of the Israeli–Palestinian conflict and thereby the region as a whole.

It is hard to estimate the exact cost of implementation. Nonetheless, some scholars have estimated that this water conflict "...is unlikely to exceed \$100 M yr^{-1} and our results...show ... in fact less than that" (Fisher *et al.*, 2002). They go on to argue that "[s]uch amounts ought not to be a bar to agreement between nations". This line of argument implies that this water dispute is merely a dispute over money, not over life and death. An alternative cost estimate would involve asking "What are the costs of no agreement?" If human suffering is not treated as an externality today, the costs are obviously very high and will be even greater!

Such an economic perspective should not blur the political, cultural, social and strategic value of water for both Parties. For obvious reasons, the long-term political and economic benefits of peace, and thereby enhanced stability in the area, are obvious. The humanitarian impetus also appears obvious: unless the Parties, and especially the Palestinians, who already carry the weight of significant humanitarian suffering due to lack of proper water supply, obtain political and financial assistance for managing existing water resources as well as new and additional water, they will not be able to provide satisfactory water to their people. Dramatic changes need to take place in their production systems. Such changes normally take years, and in the short and medium-term the humanitarian cost will be far higher than today.

The humanitarian prerogative and 'peace dividend' therefore seem to be high enough for international stakeholders to commit substantial long-term funding to implementing the agreement.

How would the two Parties perceive such a proposal?

This proposal has evolved over several years in order to address the real interests of the Palestinians and the Israelis. It aims to reflect their genuine concerns, but as in every real-life situation there are different ways of looking at such a proposal. Most likely, both countries will favour a comprehensive and verifiable arrangement that is closely reviewed by a guarantor.

Although the 1995 Interim Agreement between Israel and the PA is of a temporary nature, the part on water (Article 40) contains detailed provisions for implementation that could be developed along the proposed lines.

Some constituencies within each Party may argue that this proposal falls short of a specific timeline and precise numbers of allocation/sharing as well as operationalizing the parameters of ownership, allocation/share and control of the various water resources. Such an argument bears some merit; it is not a final agreement, but the specifics of any agreement is an outcome of several independent factors such as the level of trust between the Parties, external stakeholders' involvement, the degree of compensation, extraction volumes at a certain period, the financing and speed of implementation of the various elements of an agreement, and the overall political settlement between the two Parties. In addition, global and local climate change may also affect the allocation/sharing, as well as the timeline in which the agreement is implemented. There are no complete, objective, fair and reasonable yardsticks between the Parties and in relation to the international community.

If the proposal is too specific at this point in time, it may therefore hamper development of constructive solutions rather than proposing principles for a water roadmap. One of the first concrete steps to be taken is to develop procedures for reviewing and verifying the Parties' implementation of an agreement (see 1st step, 3). Such draft procedures and principles may in fact be developed before the direct water negotiations begin.

Concluding remarks

Most Palestinians and Israelis would probably agree to the principles in the proposal, but some may ask: "Do we get more water than before?" Both Parties face grave water shortages in the near future – with or without an agreement between them. The agreement opens up opportunities – at least for the Palestinians – to obtain more water, although not to a level that satisfies the aspirations of some constituencies. There will be some who will always argue that enough is never enough, and that the notion of 'virtual water' will never be accepted.

The Israelis may argue: "What is in it for us, if we have to hand over water under our control to the Palestinians?" Some argue for the "restructuring of the entire water system so as to make the Israelis independent of all water sources under Arab control" (Sherman, 2001: 31). In case joint mechanisms are developed, what kind of insurance for compliance do we obtain and at what humanitarian, political and economic cost?

The longer an agreement is postponed, the more suffering will be inflicted on ordinary people, and the harder it will be to hammer out compromises and find a decisive solution. At the

> The longer an agreement is postponed, the more suffering will be inflicted on ordinary people, and the harder it will be to hammer out compromises and find a decisive solution.

Section II

end of the day, any agreement made, or even lack thereof, lies with the Palestinian and Israeli leadership and people. It will most certainly be made in light of the overall political and psychological climate between them. Irrespective of this climate, solutions will exist – and the international community must stand ready to assist.

1   See for example a detailed and narrative overview of water issues in Palestine (pre-1948) and of different Israeli initiatives seen from an Arab perspective: Muhammed Ali Habash (1995).

2   Primarily through statements by Israeli officials.

3   See also Dreizin's (Israeli Water Commissioner Office) presentation at Stockholm Water Week, SIWI, 2004.

4   *Ibid.*

5   Cf. Gvirtzman (2002). See also Shuval (1992), which is much quoted as to how the sub-aquifers are connected.

6   The fluctuations illustrate the complexity of the management of the Mountain Aquifer:
    *   The winter of 1991/1992 was rainy in the Middle East. The recharge into the aquifers that year was around three times above average.
    *   1992/1993 was also rainy, although less than the preceding year. After this year, the water reached its highest level. Then the pumping exceeded the recharge and the water level declined.
    *   1999/2001 was characterized by three years of drought and the water level dropped to the 'Red Line'.
    *   When the water level in well MN got closer to the Red Line, Israel reduced the pumping in this region and pumped more from the central and southern part.
    *   The rainfall in 2002/2003 enabled Israel to pump more from Lake Tiberias, thereby relieving the pressure on the Mountain Aquifier.

7   Cf. PWA (2004a) and as outlined by Isaac and Owewi (2000).

8   Kawash (2003) states that 25 per cent of the aquifers have a high salinity (more than 2500 mg/l of chloride), 30 per cent have medium salinity (a range of 500-1000 mg/l), and 20 per cent have a relatively low salinity (a range of 250-500 mg/l). See also PWA, 2004b – presentation at the ESCWA Conference: UNESCWA, 2004.

9   In 2003, cf. PWA (2004b).

10 Cf. public information such as the Annual Reports from the Water Commissioner. Several of the policy instruments applied are illustrated in the publication from the Israeli Water Commissioner (2002).

11 See for example:
    *   Former Israeli Water Commissioner Menahem Kantor, Kantor (2000);
    *   PWA (2004a).

12 Also in conjunction with the so-called A, B and C areas. Cf. PWA (1999).

13 In addition, the PWA has further stated that: "...co-operation should include water resources, supply, and infrastructure", "....lengthy procedures should be avoided", "....data should be exchanged on all needed elements, especially abstractions" (PWA, 2004a).

14 Not much information has been presented from these initiatives, but the following web reference is one of the few descriptions of its contents: http://www.mfa.gov.il/mfa/peace%20 process/regional%20projects/

15 See, for example, http://www.exact-me.org

16 Repeatedly and over the years stated by each of the three Heads of Delegation to the author.

17 The US, Japan, South Korea, the EU.

18 See the Israeli MFA's web-site for more information:
    http://www.mfa.gov.il/MFA/Peace+Process/Regional+Projects/The%20Red%20Sea%20 and%20the%20Mediterranean%20Dead%20Sea%20canals. The level of the Dead Sea has dropped by a third since the 1960s and continues to fall by about a metre a year.
    See also UNESCWA (2004).

19 Cf. AFP, Amman on 10 May, 2005. In the first years of discussions, the Palestinians were left outside the project (as outlined in UN ESCWA, 2004).

20 See one of the most explicit and public expressions of regional co-operation in a presentation made by a leading Palestinian and Israeli official at the Stockholm Water Week, August 2004 entitled "Regional Co-operation on Water Issues", SIWI, Stockholm.

21 Like the US President Clinton (Clinton, 2004) to Prime Minister Barak, urging him to take bold steps at a 'historic time'.

22 For the first time, the Palestinian Authority has officially systematized its positions and made them public *via* the Palestinian Water Authority's (PWA) official statements in Kawash (2003) and in UNESCWA (2004). The description in the text is derived from the written material.

23 See also *Tahal Report* (1990) as outlined by Schwarz and Zohar (1991).

24 Cf. for example the description of former Israeli Foreign Minister Shlomo Ben Ami's diary as presented in *Ha'aretz Magazine*, 14 September 2001.

25 Cf. the official Israeli term of 'Security Fence' in their web address of February 2005.

Section II

26 Such as the Herzl Declaration at the first Zionist Congress in Basel, in Switzerland and in the early 1920s (cf. the role of the Zionist leader Chaim Weizmann and Justice Brandeis, the leader of American Zionism).

27 As reported in the Israeli newspaper *Ha'aretz*, 7 November, 1999.

28 As referred by Starr (2001: 26-27).

29 See for example the Israel Water Sector, August 2002, Ministry of National infrastructure and the Water Commission.

30 Even confirmed in PA's official documents: MOPIC, 1998: Chapter 5, and especially Chapter 7 (pp. 51, 53.)

31 The water resources in the Gaza Strip are somewhat more complicated since the Israelis as of 25 October 2004, as affirmed on 20 February 2005, decided on a schedule for pulling out settlements and military installations from the Strip – and the control of the water resources will be changed.

32 First officially documented by a letter from Avraham Katz-Oz (the former Minister of Agriculture and) at that time Head of the Israeli Delegation to the Water Working Group of the Multilateral Peace Process (at the Geneva meeting in 1993) to Head of the Palestinian delegation Riyad El-Khoudary, and later in the Interim Agreement of 1995, Article 40, Para. 1.

33 See two important letters: A memo from 1989 from former Agricultural Minister Avraham Katz Oz to at that time Prime Minister Yitzak Shamir regarding "Water security in the State of Israel now and in the future": "urging the Israeli Government to retain control of water resources in Judea and Samaria in any political agreements with the Palestinians", and another from the Israeli Water Commissioner to Prime Minister Yitzak Shamir of "Danger of loss of control over water resources in Judea and Samaria", in: Sherman (2001: Appendix VI and VII, respectively).

34 See for example the widely distributed publication from the Ministry of National Infrastructure and the Water Commissioner entitled *Reduce Consumption*, August 2002.

35 See for example Zarour and Isaac (1993: 50) or the Palestinian Hydrology Group (1999).

36 Several analysts with different vantage points have argued that water has to be transferred to the Palestinians in one way or another, see for example Mier (1994) and Shuval (1992: 133-143).

37 See Annex 1 regarding an example of one way of classifying 'water rights' of the various resources: Figure A1.

38 See also the newly published book from Fadia Daibes-Murad that deals extensively with this issue.

39 As outlined in some of his publications, such as Sherman (2001).

40 See for example a Palestinian perspective (before the establishment of PWA) in Zarour and Isaac (1993) or an Israeli perspective as expressed by Shuval (1992) (even before the DOP between Israel and the PLO).

41 See for example the joint Israeli/Palestinian presentation about regional initiatives in Keidar and Kawash (2004), as well as PWA's written documentation from PWA (2004a) (*the Political Framework*), which may be summarized as follows:
   - "Goodwill and a genuine spirit of equality should prevail in implementation. Neither side should veto the water projects of the other side without just cause.
   - Co-operation between the two Parties was realized to be essential and enabled the management of some good services in the water sector.
   - Implementation should be timely enough to meet the basic water needs of the Palestinians.
   - Unilateral implementation of projects should be avoided.
   - Implementation needs to cover all areas, including area C, where there is the greatest need for water. Co-operation should include water resources, supply, and infrastructure.
   - Lengthy procedures should be avoided.
   - Data should be exchanged on all needed elements, especially abstractions.
   - An example of the need for improved co-operation is the Jenin Project."

42 See also Sherman (2001: 30-33) who argues for joint, but also specifically separate measures both in terms of water supply and protection.

43 Cf. also Feitelson and Haddad's approach (2000: 465-466): i) qualitative and quantitative monitoring, ii) addressing the main threats to the aquifers, iii) comprehensive long-term issues, and iv) joint planning and funding.

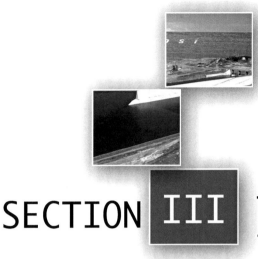

SECTION III The Euphrates and the Tigris Rivers – solutions for Turkey, Iraq and Syria in managing water resources

Abstract

This section describes the challenges faced by Turkey, Syria and Iraq in managing the Euphrates and Tigris Rivers. The welfare of millions depends on the supply from the rivers, which are mainly fed by rainfall in the northern parts. The three countries are bound together by their destiny to use and protect the rivers. If this is not soon done properly, they could easily become *rivers of fire* with far-reaching national and international impact. As yet, there has been no agreement on how to manage the rivers.

Internationally, little is known about the status of the waters. For the first time, therefore, information from Turkey, Syria and Iraq is made public. The countries have handed over authorized national data that has been applied in a comprehensive analysis of the river management. Although the study does not cover all aspects of their management, the technical findings are serious. They show that unless the three countries find ways to co-operate, the water quality may shortly be in a grave condition; particularly for the Euphrates in Iraq and subsequently in the southern part of Syria.

In order to adequately address this situation by maintaining a water quality level based on agreed standards, a desalination plant, in the first stage at the Syria-Iraq border, funded by a third party compensation mechanism, is proposed.

However, the challenges go far beyond the scope of a compensation mechanism. It is obvious that a *new overarching international initiative* must be taken: a Euphrates and Tigris Basins Initiative should be established with a partnership initiated and led by the riparian states. The initiative should benefit from full international support through an international organization such as the Arab development banks and institutions, together with, for example, the World Bank in co-operation with the UN.

The two main concerns – sound management of the water resources and respect of the Parties' interests – are incorporated so that the precious water may create an opportunity for co-operation.

Map 16. Location of the Euphrates and the Tigris Rivers

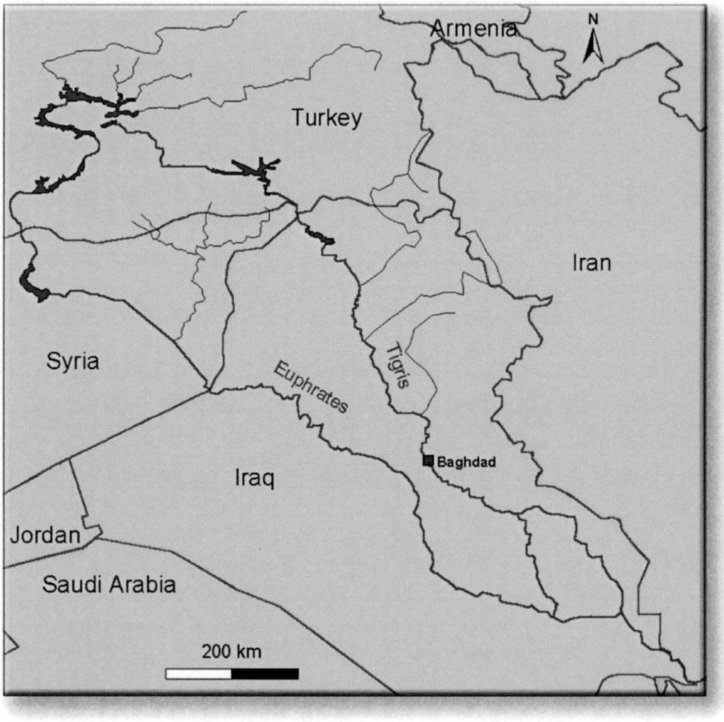

Chapter 1

Past, present and possible future use of the rivers

This section describes the immediate and enormous challenges faced by Turkey, Syria and Iraq in managing the Euphrates and Tigris Rivers. The welfare of millions of people depends on the supply from the rivers, which are mainly fed by rainfall in the northern parts.

The water belongs to the three countries. As of today, they have not agreed on how to manage the rivers. Since the water is of utmost importance for all three of them, the dispute has been lifted to the highest political level in the region.

Iran also feeds the Tigris river basin with 42 rivers that cross the 1,200 km-long and mostly hilly Iraqi/Iranian border. The author has limited the scope to the three riparians, since a bilateral co-operation agreement on the Tigris would most probably best be negotiated directly between Iran and Iraq.

Internationally, very little is known about the status of the two rivers. For the first time, therefore, information from Turkey, Syria and Iraq is being made public. These countries have handed over authorized national data applied in a comprehensive analysis of the water management of the two rivers, hereafter referred to as the 'technical study' (CESAR, 2005) or simply the study.[1] *However, this publication takes a perspective that goes beyond the technical results of the initial study.*

> For the first time... information from Turkey, Syria and Iraq is being made public.

The study does not cover all aspects of management of the two rivers. Nevertheless, the technical findings are so serious that unless the three countries find ways of co-operating, the water quality of the rivers may shortly be in a grave condition, particularly for the Euphrates River in Iraq and subsequently in the southern part of Syria. Equally importantly, the water resources will not be used effectively and the shortfall between need and availability will grow even larger. Human suffering would escalate to such a degree that the international community could not be indifferent towards it, and would eventually become involved in the situation.

---

[1] Although the three countries initially provided water resource data for the technical study, none of them is responsible for the classification, analysis and modelling of the information. They have not been requested to authorize any of the proposals made in this publication. In 2000, Turkey informed the author that it had withdrawn its authorized data for the technical study. All the authorized information was replaced with data from 'open international sources' (i.e. public Turkish information). However, that had no impact on the numbers and no changes were made to the conclusions of the study in the modelling or to the final outcome and technical recommendations.

Since the Middle East tends to have a surplus of problems and a deficit of constructive and sustainable solutions, this publication aims to rectify the latter. To that end, it describes, for the first time, the results of several rounds of consultations with the three states, as well as technical studies initiated in 1996/1997, resulting in thousands of pages of analyses and reports.

Credible and authorized data from the three countries were shared, and this information has been applied in the various studies and models. It is, however, impossible to transform the scientific findings directly to a water agreement. This is due particularly to the fact that the technical study chose to analyse the two rivers separately according to the so-called *separate-basin model*. However, it is subsequently acknowledged by the author that they could also be viewed as one basin, a so-called *twin-basin model*. By taking the Parties' concerns into consideration and deriving some of the technical results, elements for trilateral water agreements for the two rivers are proposed in *Chapter 5*.

Despite the uncertainties of transforming the technical findings directly into any agreements, this publication is probably among the very few, if not the first, to suggest a way out of the entrenched positions and problems.

The proposal is valid irrespective of the ebb and flow of the politics in the region

The three countries are bound together by the rivers – by a destiny to use and protect them. Yet if this is not soon done properly, they could easily become *rivers of fire* that would eventually have far-reaching international impacts. Countries inside and outside the region would then become involved, with unpredictable consequences.

Two rivers in the middle of a geopolitical minefield

Few, if any, rivers exhibit such historic affinities and associations as the Euphrates and Tigris. Over the millennia, it is not only the rise and fall of the ancient cultures of Mesopotamia, the Biblical dramas, the evolution of Islam and the growing Muslim dominance that have played out along and between the rivers, but also the rivers' role as a military and cultural crossover between civilizations from the East and West.

Some describe the ancient area between the rivers as the *cradle of civilization* from which intellectual and institutional advances were made, such as letters and scriptures, laws, accounting and monetary systems, and from which empires were built and fell over thousands of years.

Water disputes in the Euphrates and Tigris basins go back 6,000 years and are described in many myths, legends and historic accounts that have survived from earlier times (Altinbilek, 2004).

Contemporary history vividly illustrates the merging of the area's past and present significance, not only after vast oil resources were discovered in the 1920s, but also with the political dramas that have unfolded over the past two decades. The Iraqi–Iranian war of 1980-1988, and US-led coalition attacks in 1991 and 2003 on Iraq, took place on the plains of Mesopotamia, and underscore the strategic importance of the area. Until May 2003, the isolation of Iraq through UN-imposed sanctions created a distorted image of the state. Little, if any, international news about the dwindling rivers came out. Due to this geopolitical situation, little international focus has been placed on the water conflicts between the three states in managing the two rivers.

Preparation for the study – through numerous consultations with the three countries – began as early as 1997 and most of the basic scientific findings were completed in 2001. Some significant political events took place after this, with either short or long-term implications for use of the two rivers as well as their own resources:

Three events are particularly relevant: *first*, the coalition forces' attack on Iraq in March 2003 and the subsequent violent and unstable security situation, which, in addition to its major international implications, may result in transformation of a stable government and institutions; *second*, the increased tension between Iran and the US is also impacting on water co-operation; *third*, the Turkish accession process to the EU will potentially have implications for the management of both its own as well as international water, since the EU Water Framework Directive would be applicable to Turkey.

From more contemporary historic times and until the end of the Ottoman Empire in the early 1920s, the use of the rivers, primarily in the southern parts, has remained almost unchanged. After that, the three present states, Turkey, Syria and Iraq, obtained almost the same borders as today. The disputes between them stem back to the last 50 years (Altinbilek, 2004).

The relative abundance of water in more or less semi-arid and arid conditions in both Syria and Iraq has not stressed the water situation in terms of quantity or quality. The only constant and serious challenge to irrigation is the concentration of salt in the topsoil. Highly intensive irrigation as a basis for food production and the area's social-economic growth has characterized all advanced hydraulic civilizations in Mesopotamia. In many cases, salinization of the topsoil caused by intensive and improper irrigation practice led to collapse of food production and the sensitive water/soil-balance. The downfall of the advanced Sumerian Civilization in Mesopotamia more than 3,500 years ago is such an example.

Today, this salinization process is continuing to take place not only in Iraq, but also in Syria and even in Turkey. It will continue to do so unless mitigating measures are taken. The severe impacts would not be limited to Iraq alone, but to the river basins as a whole.

> Today, the 'silent' majority of people who suffer from lack of water for drinking and agriculture are growing in number and in terms of severity.

The 'matter-of-fact' description of the water situation above may seem quite abstract as long as the immediate impact on the daily life of the people is not considered by international media to be catastrophic. Let it be quite clear: today, the 'silent' majority of people who suffer from lack of water for drinking and agriculture are growing in number and in terms of severity: ordinary people's access to clean water is rapidly becoming worse. On top of this, the two rivers are increasingly deteriorating. The situation is grave both for ordinary people and for the states.

Problems and conflicts in management of the rivers

In recent years, the academic literature[1] has reflected concerns about the hydrological status of the rivers and unilateral approaches taken by the riparian states. The exact nature of the problems have not, however, been internationally recognized due to lack of reliable data and the above-mentioned overall political situation in the region.

Section III

In 1996, Turkey and subsequently Syria proposed to the author that a trilateral study specify the *factual basis* of the water management challenges of the basins. Syria and Iraq expressed serious concerns about the nature and magnitude of the problems, with emphasis on different aspects. Altogether, this led to the start-up of a comprehensive process of consultation with the three countries and technical analyses in which interim reports were periodically conveyed to the Parties, with a final report in 2001. The findings outlined some serious water management challenges that need to be handled by all three of them. It is the author's impression that they understood the magnitude of the challenges and became concerned.

As in any major river basin, there are challenges in co-ordinating activities even at a national level, especially regarding optimal management of the flow of the river in relation to hydropower production and irrigation.

Turkey's impressive development of the water resources of the two rivers in the south-eastern part of the country, the so-called GAP project in south-eastern Anatolia, is unprecedented not only in the region but also compared to areas with a long tradition in river basin development. Turkey has mobilized national and international funding and expertise in this effort, and has probably to a large extent fulfilled the GAP's objectives. There are national and international challenges, however, such as optimizing hydropower production versus irrigation, and treatment of the return-flow from

> A slowly growing and uncontrolled rise of the salt concentration of the Euphrates River in Iraq is taking place, assumed to be primarily due to return-flow from irrigation.

the vast irrigation areas that drain across the Syrian border.

As a mid-positioned state (downstream of Turkey and upstream of Iraq), Syria also uses the water, especially from the Euphrates, for irrigation, while maintaining a certain discharge to Iraq. The Syrian master plans, however, assume a significant increase of water use, including water from the Tigris River. Up to now, much of the irrigated lands between the two rivers had come from natural rainfall and extraction of groundwater. More recent studies have revealed significant lowering of the groundwater table in these lands, especially in the north (close to the Turkish border). Due to the overall water situation in Syria, there are also plans to extract water from the Euphrates for drinking purposes in the large cities of Aleppo and Damascus.

For the outside community, the water resource situation of Iraq has been largely unknown since 1990. More recently however, a bleak picture was drawn for the international community:

- "...the country's supply of clean water is being seriously threatened, because of shrinking funds.... and an outdated water treatment and sewage system.
- ...country's 229 operating water treatment plants are old and badly in need of repairs.
- ...sewage from cities and towns that lack processing networks - more than 90% of the municipalities around the country - seeps into the Euphrates and Tigris Rivers
- ..the Ministry provides services to 17 million Iraqis, or 70% of the total population. Of those 17 million, more than 30% have no access to drinkable water".[2]

Since 1991, much focus has been put on the marsh areas in the south and the anticipated 'politically driven drainage' (such as Clark and Magee, 2001) of the area. This led even the United Nations in 2003 to make headlines like *"Garden of Eden in Southern Iraq Likely to Disappear Completely in Five Years Unless Urgent Action Taken"* (UNEP, 2003b). The situation in the south was, and still is, a challenge, far removed from the simple manner in which it is portrayed in the media.

soon, within a few years rather than decades, first in Iraq and then in the southern part of Syria.

Figure 13 shows results from a calculated salinity concentration in south Iraq after irrigation extraction has theoretically been stopped upstream (year 0 – see technical discussion of this simulation in *Chapter 3*). The salinity concentration would then gradually decrease to the natural state situation[II] (where return-flow from irrigation is not included).

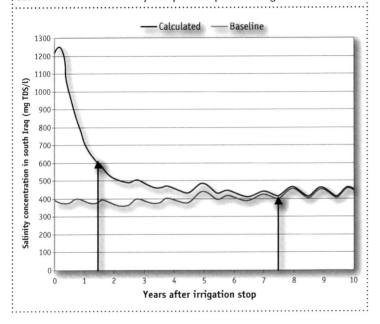

Figure 13. Long-term effect of high salinity concentration in the river basin reservoirs followed by complete stop of discharge

It is, however, totally unrealistic to imagine that irrigation (and thereby return-flow from irrigation areas) will stop for 7.5 years under the current water management practices in the three countries. The reality of the situation today is that at the Syrian–Iraqi border the salt content is already very high (with high-average around 1,000 mg TDS/l).

In fact, the technical study revealed a far more significant trend. A slowly growing and uncontrolled rise of the salt concentration of the Euphrates River in Iraq is taking place, assumed to be primarily due to return-flow from irrigation.

The most immediate problem is the accumulation of the salt content, especially in the Euphrates River, to such an extent that it may be irreversible and unusable for drinking and even agricultural purposes for decades to come unless return-flow from irrigation is controlled.[3] This may happen

In plain language, this means that water from the Euphrates River for irrigation in Iraq is threatened. According to Iraqi government sources from the Ministry of Water Resources, during parts of the year the water is unsuitable for drinking and irrigation in the southern part, especially in the Governorates of Basra, Dhi Qar, Qadisiya, Wasit and Babil. Considering the unbearable summer heat, it is hard to imagine the impact of this on people's daily life.[4]

II   Probably a realistic and recommended level taking the natural water quality into account.

Section III

■ Photo 23.
The downstream side of the Ataturk Dam on the Euphrates River in Turkey

There is no agreed allocation of water quantity to each country

Although time is ticking away, the existing problem is solvable, but requires co-operative action between the three countries. A number of agreements have been reached since the 1920s, the most important era of the negotiations on the rivers being between 1980 and 1986 (Altinbilek, 2004), leading to the establishment of trilateral joint economic and technical commissions (see an overview in *Annex II*). After that time, and up to 2003, little – if any – progress in the deliberations was achieved.

Today, each country uses whatever amount of water suits them, within certain parameters. On the Euphrates River there are two bilateral arrangements, one temporary, and a unilateral dossier by Turkey on the Euphrates flow into Syria issued when Turkey's famous Ataturk Dam

was filled up in the 1990s, obliging Turkey to provide an average annual minimum flow of 500 m^3/s at the Syrian border. Another, not yet officially announced (but commonly known), agreement is between Syria and Iraq, whereby the first has promised to provide Iraq with 52 per cent of what Syria receives from Turkey (while keeping 48 per cent for its own use).

Until now, no agreement on the Tigris River has been reached between the three countries. Today, Turkey and Iraq use the water, but Syria claims its rights from the 60 km river border it shares with Turkey.

Since there are no other agreements between the Parties, the following chapters attempt to provide a factual basis for the following hypothesis: optimal use of the Rivers in terms of hydropower production, irrigation and water for drinking purposes can only be reached if the countries co-operate.

There is no overview or agreement on safeguarding water quality

To date, the countries have not given high priority to monitoring the water quality of the rivers. Therefore, an overall understanding of the water quality in either of the rivers has never been achieved. Iraq made some calculations in the early 1990s, with however a high degree of uncertainty due to unverifiable water data from Turkey and Syria.[5]

As a response to that situation, three automatic monitoring stations were initially installed at three sites in Syria and one site in Iraq.[6] None of the data from these stations was used in the modelling, but the information has later confirmed the findings.[7]

■ Photo 24.
A manmade drainage channel for the Euphrates and the Tigris Rivers starting from west of Baghdad to the south designed with a projected average flow of 270 m³/s

The more up-to-date measurements thus further confirm the overall conclusion that unless a river basin agreement is reached in the foreseeable future, in a relatively short time the water quality will reach a level in which water from the Euphrates is no longer suitable for drinking or agricultural purposes, at least with existing technology and practices, particularly in Iraq and subsequently in the southern part of Syria. It is beyond any doubt that the human, political and financial costs of rectifying this situation will be staggering.

The value of water

The discussion of the value of water is therefore becoming increasingly interesting. The findings from the initial study, briefly outlined, are new to the international community, and are being made public in order to increase international attention and efforts in assisting the three states in promoting sound water management practices for the two rivers. Some would perhaps argue that compared to other parts of the Middle East there is a relative abundance of water, for example

compared to per capita consumption. This is true if figures are compared and not realities, but the facts on the ground are different:

1. All three countries have univocally given national priority to agricultural development, demanding a huge amount of water.

2. All three nations have claimed control and the right to use the water resources from the two rivers as an integral part of their territorial sovereignty.

3. Water has a tremendous cultural and spiritual value in the region, not only for the public, but also for the national leaders.

The author's approaches to the three issues are as follows:

1. Agricultural production may be viewed by economists as an essential economic commodity, whereby production should take place where the highest economic rate of return is, whether this is within or outside the country. The concept of 'virtual' or 'invisible water'[8] means that a country can balance its water needs by importing 'invisible' water from outside its national boundaries through import of agricultural products. It seems quite clear that from a strictly economic point of view, import of food ought to increase significantly in the years to come, simply because there is not enough water

> Unless a river basin agreement is reached in a relatively short time, the water quality will reach a level in which water from the Euphrates is no longer suitable for drinking or agricultural purposes.

to meet the rapidly-growing demand for food. In addition, and at a national level, if the negative implications of irrigation and especially pollution from return-flow are counted as an externality, the cost of food production will be even higher. Therefore agricultural production under existing conditions is, from an economic perspective, expensive and ineffective. However, and quite clearly, despite this situation none of the countries can change their respective agricultural practices in just a few years – decades of change are more realistic. In the

■ Photo 25.
Damside of the Tabqa Dam on the Euphrates River in Syria

foreseeable future, the economic perspective of irrigation at a national level is therefore more relevant from a theoretical and policy-setting point of view than in practical terms.

2. 'Territorial sovereignty' is a vital concept for any state in ascertaining control over natural resources. Worldwide, so-called *fluid* or *flow resources* like oil and water are geographically defined, and thereby subject to division according to a certain legal formula (see Gjessing, 2002). Sovereignty over an international/transboundary renewable water resource means that states not only have *rights*, but equally importantly *obligations*, according to any international law that deals with international natural resources (as will be further discussed). Any country's claim of sole control is therefore more complex than is sometimes portrayed in national political rhetoric.

3. Water as a symbol of both physical and spiritual life is rooted in the people of the three countries. This fact is perhaps the overriding determinant for usage of water. Adoption of alien concepts like 'virtual water' that might lead to changes in the water management policy[9], and subsequently to another agricultural practice, cannot be carried out in one generation. Any outsider – irrespective of his/her scientific credentials – that overlooks this fact does not have a firm understanding of the realities in the region. Any policies that change the people's perception of this value are deemed to fail, unless they are implemented gradually and with sensitivity to people's beliefs and identity.

Before turning to what might be done by the Parties as well as by the international community, the three countries' positions and concerns are outlined in the next chapter. *Chapter 3* outlines the technical findings followed by a more detailed examination of those relevant for the two alternative models of co-operation proposed (in *Chapters 4–7*).

Chapter 2

Positions and concerns of Turkey, Syria and Iraq

The three Parties' perceptions on how the Euphrates and Tigris Rivers should be used in the future cannot be viewed in isolation from the history of the civilizations that have risen and fallen.

It seems relevant to draw a comparison with the use of the Nile River, which is shared by nine countries today. Egypt's use of the Nile is a historic fact, its entire civilization having been created out of the Nile River. Today, both Sudan and Ethiopia, among other countries, have ambitions to use the water of the White and Blue Nile respectively as part of their legitimate development efforts. One may ask to what extent management of other river basins in the region, like the Nile, form a precedent or at least have relevance for the Euphrates and Tigris Basins. There are no simple answers to this, but there is at least one important observation: the up-and downstream positions taken by the Nile Basin states will be influenced by what might happen in the Euphrates and Tigris basins, and *vice versa*. The situation of Turkey, Syria and Iraq has not been described in comparison with the situation of the Nile basin, but rather to illustrate covariance of the positions taken by Turkey and Sudan/Ethiopia versus Iraq and Egypt.

Since any interpretation of the positions and concerns of Turkey, Syria and Iraq is a reflection of the perspective of an *external observer*, a brief description of the consultative process with them is outlined.

Creating a consultative process with the three countries

Due to the author's long-term engagement in promoting peaceful solutions to water disputes in the region, contacts with the respective governments were initially made through professionals. Over the years, the author conducted several consultations with the states, first and foremost in order to understand their concerns. At the same time, the Parties were able to assess the author's credibility as an unbiased facilitator and professional capacity to develop solid scientific models and results. This part of the process took over two and a half years, and at a certain point in time the consultations became official in the sense that only official delegates, primarily from the respective Ministries of Foreign Affairs and Water/Irrigation, were involved. By 1998, all three states were willing to provide not-yet published or authorized water-related information to be used in a series of technical studies, based on a commonly accepted scope for the work.

From the outset, it became obvious that it was not possible to develop a thorough understanding of the hydrological systems and water management of the two rivers unless all three countries participated. Earlier on, Turkey had clearly recognized this fact and proposed in 1982 to the two other downstream Parties that a comprehensive study be undertaken jointly (the so called 'Three-Stages Plan') (Turkish Ministry of Foreign Affairs, 1996; SAM, 1996; Allan, 2002). The three Parties met over a number of years and exchanged data and plans (see *Annex 3*). As the Turkish proposal was further discussed, Syria and Iraq withdrew their participation.

Since that time, several countries outside the region as well as the UN (specifically FAO and UNEP) and the World Bank have indicated their willingness to assist the Parties. Quite a few international studies have also been conducted, using data of unknown reliability.[10]

The basic idea for any kind of co-operative river basin management is that a common and comprehensive technical understanding must exist. This was the reason for over two years of preparatory consultations with the Parties, to reach an agreement on the scope of the work, leading to the launching in 1998 of the technical studies. Through co-operation with the three countries, the aim was to develop an integrated water resource management analysis of the Euphrates River and the Tigris River in Turkey, Syria and Iraq, the analysis being based on water resource data from the respective countries (national authorized and publicly

> The basic idea for any kind of co-operative river basin management is that a common and comprehensive technical understanding must exist.

available data), as well as reflecting data derived from international studies.[11]

The development of the analysis was based on indirect co-operation between the countries where the author acted as a facilitator with whom data and information was deposited.[12] It was expected that the results and a proposed trilateral framework agreement would lead to a situation whereby documentation could be applied as a basis for further deliberations between the three countries on the principles of integrated water resource management in the region.[13]

The positions and concerns of Turkey, Syria and Iraq

A well-established diplomatic tradition is that "no country will carve its negotiation positions in stone" (see for example Trondalen, 2004a). In public, they have however taken fairly categorical positions, with little room for manoeuvering. The stakes are obviously high, since water is so fundamental, whether economically, socially, culturally or environmentally. Nonetheless, the positions may not be as irreconcilable as they appear at first sight. A key is to go beyond the political rhetoric and obtain an understanding of their real concerns. Any sustainable solutions ought to address these concerns.

The position and concerns of the Parties, as described below, are derived from publicly-available government web sites, public statements by officials, various official publications, and discussions with water experts and other government officials. The countries' positions have been slightly adjusted over time, but some constant traits can be identified.

The positions and concerns of Turkey

Turkey's principal argument is that no one country has a fixed claim to the waters of the rivers, in the sense that historic usage of the downstream countries does not mean they have a "fixed claim on most of the waters, and only a very small residue above this to be shared".[14]

Their perception of a fair deal is the recognition that all three states have rights, and that the rivers are to be used in an equitable manner.

■ Photo 26.
The dimensions of the Turkish Ataturk Dam on the Euphrates River are enormous, with the sixth largest dam storage volume worldwide

Furthermore, Turkey is promoting a bi-/ trilateral arrangement without interference of a strong international actor like the United Nations, since international law is relatively weak in defining states' rights and obligations.

Turkey is also taking a conceptual position regarding the terminology of the Euphrates and Tigris Rivers that they are 'transboundary waters', i.e 'rivers that are crossing state borders' versus rivers 'running along a border' (i.e. 'international waters'). The implication of this is that if the river is international the division will be different than if they are transboundary.[15]

Furthermore, Turkey argues that the Euphrates and Tigris Rivers must be considered as forming one single transboundary watercourse system, as they are linked by both their natural merging in the *Shatt al-Arab* as well as by the manmade *Thartar Canal* in Iraq.[16] As a consequence of the Euphrates and Tigris Rivers forming one single transboundary watercourse system, Turkey argues that the existing and future water uses need not be derived from one river alone, particularly the Euphrates River.[17]

Turkish authorities claim that 'equitable and reasonable utilization' is the most acceptable principle in international law in the allocation of a transboundary river. In order to reach equitable usage of the waters of the two rivers, various socio-economic, legal, hydrological and

> Turkish authorities claim that 'equitable and reasonable utilization' is the most acceptable principle in in the allocation of a transboundary river. In order to reach equitable usage of the waters of the two rivers, various socio-economic, legal, hydrological and geopolitical factors in the riparian states should be taken into consideration.

Table 6. Area of the Euphrates–Tigris drainage basin in riparian countries (km²)

Country	Euphrates		Tigris	
	km²	%	km²	%
Turkey	121,787	21.1	53 052	14.3
Syria	95,405	16.5	948	0.2
Iran	–	–	175,386	47.2
Iraq	282,532	49.0	142 175	38.3
Saudi Arabia	77,090	13.4	–	–
Total	576,814	100.0	371 561	100.0

Source: UNEP, 2001.

geopolitical factors in the riparian states should be taken into consideration.

Another argument is that the waters should be used in Turkey where the land capabilities and thereby economic efficiency is highest.[18]

This argument is further underlined by the overview of the area of the drainage basin in relation to each country as brought forward by one renowned Turkish expert (see *Table 7*) (Turkish Ministry of Foreign Affairs, 1996: 18). Since 98 per cent of the runoff of the Euphrates River and 53 per cent of the Tigris River is produced in the highlands of Turkey, an equivalent and equitable proprietary right is therefore acquired (Turkish Department of Information, 1992; Altinbilek, 2004).

In addition, Turkey argues that the damming of the two rivers in Turkey has benefited Syria and Iraq, since there is a significant reduction of flooding and loss of much-needed water for irrigation and power generation downstream during the summer season.

Turkey further states that "many lessons can be drawn from comparison between the Euphrates River and the Orontes River" (where Turkey is the end-user), as well as the fact that Lebanon and Syria are upstream and use the lion's share

without any agreement with Turkey (Turkish Ministry of Foreign Affairs, 1996: 9).

In order to use the transboundary waters of the Euphrates and Tigris Rivers in an equitable, rational and optimal manner, Turkey has proposed a joint technical effort in which the three countries develop a factual water technical basis, the Three-Stages Plan, as an input into a water allocation scheme that "will determine the true water needs of each riparian country".[19] Turkey has clearly stated that optimal water usage based on the three countries' needs is unrealistic since the other two are overstating their demand (SAM, 1996: 6-7).

The above positions reflect a genuine national desire to develop the water resources as an important element in building a modern Turkish state. The symbols are strong, illustrated by the fact that Turkey perceives the GAP project as a legacy of the famous Turkish, post-Ottoman era leader Mustapha Kemal Ataturk: the dam-side of the Ataturk Dam is inscribed with the words "Proud is the one who can call himself a Turk" (see *Photo 26*). From a political view, this made sense, as Turkey used a significant part of its own wealth to develop the GAP project, with external actors like the USA, World Bank and United Nations initially supporting the endeavour. The achievements in terms of dam and water infrastructure are impressive. Recently, the Turkish authorities seem to be increasingly recognizing the international rights and obligations that pertain to such international water courses. This recognition and the possible adherence to the European Union and thereby compliance with the EU's strict Water Framework Directive (van Baal, 2003) provide an opportunity for a trilateral agreement that could satisfy Turkish concerns as well as those of the two others. In addition, and equally important, Turkey has repeatedly stated that a "fair deal is possible for everybody" – an attitude which should pave the way for constructive solutions (SAM, 1996: 24).

■ Photo 27.
From a harvested cotton field in Syria

The positions and concerns of Syria

First and foremost, Syria states that it has acquired thousands of years of water usage, and that these 'acquired rights' were upheld even during the Ottoman era.

Up to now, Syria has used the principle of *grandfathering* as the most important argument in tandem with Iraq. The as-yet unpublicized agreement of the Syrian–Iraqi 48 per cent – 52 per cent division of the Euphrates water must be viewed from that perspective. Along this line, Syria has also repeatedly stated that it will not sign a bilateral agreement with Turkey without Iraq.[20]

> Syria states that it has acquired thousands of years of water usage, and that these 'acquired rights' were upheld even during the Ottoman era.

In contrast to Turkey, Syria claims that the waters of the Euphrates and Tigris Rivers are international watercourses, i.e. "parts of which are situated in different States".[21] The difference is, from the Syrian point of view, only semantic and has no legal implications.

As in any modern state in the Middle East, Syria is increasingly relying on water resources in its social and economic development. Agricultural development, both rainfed and irrigation, has been a priority for decades (Daoudy, 1999). As an illustration of this, one of the few international agricultural research centres, the International Center for Agricultural Research in the Dry Areas (ICARDA), is situated close to Aleppo and in the vicinity of the Euphrates.

The national long-term water plans[22] therefore rely on the Euphrates Rivers as a source of drinking water for major cites like Aleppo and even Damascus, as well as for its ambiguous development of irrigation in the so-called Euphrates Valley. Due to rapid population growth, irrigation dependant on the Euphrates

Section III

River is increasing as the groundwater table is shrinking.[23]

Syria considers both the Euphrates and the Tigris to be international rivers (i.e. that the rivers should be treated as a shared natural resource), meaning that the waters should be allocated to each riparian state according to a negotiated agreement (primarily based on needs of each).

The Syrian position is that the two rivers must be viewed as two separate entities, based on the following arguments:

1. There is no surplus on the Tigris River allowing for any transfer to the Euphrates River.
2. The merging of the Euphrates and Tigris Rivers is downstream of Syria, and will not affect the use of water in other states (i.e. is not applicable to Syria).

Since Syria argues that the rivers are international watercourses, they must therefore be shared between the riparian states according to a quota that could be based on the following formula:

1. Each riparian shall claim its water demand on each river separately.
2. The capacity of both rivers (in each riparian state) must be calculated and agreed on.
3. If the total water demand does not exceed the total water supply, the water shall be allocated according to the stated figures on water demand for each riparian state.
4. In case total water demand exceeds the water potential of a given river, the exceeding amount should be deducted proportionally from the water demand of each riparian state.[24]

Syria is in a delicate position, as it must balance its interests as a downstream and upstream country. Its negotiation positions and concerns must be flexible and balanced, especially when it comes to the contentious question of water quality. Syria has on many occasions – and even recently – expressed concern about pollution from Turkey, not only in relation to the Euphrates itself but also regarding the *return-flow* from the large irrigation schemes just north of its long border with Turkey (between the two rivers).

The country's dual role as an upstream and downstream riparian also relates to its being situated downstream on the Orontes River[25] and Nahar El Kabir River from Lebanon, as well as upstream on the Golan Heights and Upper Jordan River Basin.

Syria has much to gain from a trilateral agreement, which would give it a predictable allocated amount of water with a certain level of quality. When this is achieved, the Syrian authorities could make long-term plans and obtain international assistance for sound development of their own water resources as well as for mitigation of pollution downstream to Iraq (see further discussion in *Chapter 6*). Syrian government officials are stating that they would eventually grant Iraq some of the same rights (for example, some sort of agreed-upon water quality standards) and obligations (such as a flexible allocation regime, which is dependent on preceding rainfall) if a trilateral agreement is established.

> ...Iraq maintains that it possesses *acquired rights* relating to its *ancestral irrigation* of the Euphrates and Tigris Rivers.

The positions and concerns of Iraq

Acquired historic rights of water are obviously the key argument of Iraq, illustrated by the following opening statement of its official dossier

■ Photo 28.
From the bank of the Tigris River that runs slowly through Baghdad city (as it looked in 1998)

Like Syria, Iraq states that the Euphrates and Tigris Rivers must be seen as two separate entities, based on the following reasoning:

1. There is no surplus on the Tigris River allowing for any transfer to the Euphrates.
2. The *Thartar Canal* connection between the two rivers (north of Baghdad) is manmade and only functions as a flood channel.
3. The fact that parts of the drainage basin of the Tigris river are also on Iranian territory makes the merging and negotiations relating to an allocation based on the notion of a 'one Euphrates–Tigris River Basin' unacceptable.

regarding the two rivers: "The life in Iraq since eternity depends on the waters of its two great rivers..." (Iraqi Ministry of Foreign Affairs, 1999). The Iraqis further stress that "Iraq has preceded the States of the basins in the use of the largest quantity of the Euphrates waters. Prior to 1917, Iraq was irrigating over half a million hectares and then after that date, the irrigation projects and land reclamation have developed. With regard to the Tigris, it is known that Iraq was the sole state...which utili[z]ed the waters of this river since ancient times" (Iraqi Ministry of Foreign Affairs and Ministry of Irrigation, 1999: 25).

Iraq also argues that the waters of the rivers are international watercourses, i.e. parts of which are situated in different states.[26] As the Iraqis consider the rivers to be international, they should be treated as shared natural resources, i.e. the waters of the rivers can be allocated to each riparian state according to a negotiated agreement (as argued by Syria; primarily based on its needs).

Not least, Iraq maintains that it possesses *acquired rights* relating to its *ancestral irrigation* of the Euphrates and Tigris Rivers. It also emphasizes two dimensions of the acquired rights, stating that for several thousand years the two rivers have given life to the people of the Mesopotamian Plain, constituting an acquired right to use these rivers. In addition, due to its long history of

■ Photo 29.
A part of the city of Baghdad bathing in the afternoon sun

use of the Euphrates and Tigris Rivers, Iraq has an extensive system of both modern and ancient irrigation and water infrastructure. The country has almost 3 million hectares of agricultural land, which is by far the largest in the river basins.

In the past, Iraq has declared that the waters of the Euphrates and Tigris Rivers must be shared among the riparian countries according to the following formula:

■ Photo 30.
A culvert for an irrigation field from the Euphrates River south of Baghdad

▸ Each riparian will present information about its present and planned water demand based on hydrological data on the Euphrates and Tigris Rivers that will be exchanged between the riparian states.
▸ In addition, as Iraq is experiencing deteriorating water quality, any agreement must contain rules, procedures and mitigating measures necessary to safeguard the water quality.[27]

The realism of their demands is such that Iraq will most likely advocate that any trilateral agreement should also take the upstream countries' interests into consideration. This recognition is, first and foremost, a reflection of the *realpolitik* in the region. Iraq is situated at the end of the rivers and dependent on a co-operative relationship with Syria and Turkey in managing the vital rivers. In addition, and increasingly so, the jeopardizing problem of water quality for Iraq[28] offers an opportunity for a sound trilateral agreement that Iraq will endorse and benefit from.

The concerns seem to be reconcilable

Despite diverging points of view of the three Parties on how to manage and allocate the two rivers, each of them acknowledges the need for co-operation.

One of the most prominent Turkish water experts, Dogan Altinbilek, has encapsulated the challenges by stating:

"Uncoordinated and independent actions of basin countries may result in some difficult problems for which remedies cannot easily be found. With proper and coordinated planning and implementation, however, many or some of the problems may be pre-empted, eliminated or greatly minimized". (Altinbilek, 2004: 28)

The challenge then, is to translate this desire into accepted management principles that are feasible to implement.

Chapter 3

Findings of the technical study

Approach of the technical study

The three countries accepted the basic idea that for any co-operative river basin management, a common and comprehensive technical understanding must exist. From the outset, however, it became obvious that it was not possible to develop a thorough understanding of the hydrological systems and water management of the two rivers *unless all three countries participated*.

Therefore, the development of a comprehensive study of the two rivers had to be based on *indirect* co-operation between the watercourse countries. There was, however, no direct co-operation between the states, since all communication went *via* the author.

Before describing the design of the analyses and the findings, some information about the specific objectives and structure is outlined. Additionally, a few reflections on the realism of the cross-section between science and politics are also given.

One may argue that even reliable technical findings may not determine a trilateral water agreement between the three countries. Any technical results, irrespective of the scientific accuracy of the findings, will never fully determine a negotiated agreement between any countries, especially in the Middle East. The reality is far too complex for that and, as history has shown, any agreement is a reflection of the combined political, economic and hydrological circumstances at that particular point in time.

It is, however, incorrect to draw the conclusion that a technical study, irrespective of its accuracy and reliability, will have no impact on a negotiated agreement. As this chapter outlines, the findings are expected to provide input into possible negotiated trilateral agreements, not determine an agreement. The transferability of the (more) technical results to a (more) politically designed agreement is dealt with more extensively in *Chapter 4*.

The three countries have never been asked to authorize the technical findings *per se*, but rather to give input to the applied data, methods and analytical models. In *realpolitik*, no country would approve technical results that would limit their negotiation options, especially before they had started. However, the objectives of the study, approach and methods, and the technical

> ...any agreement is a reflection of the combined political, economic and hydrological circumstances at that particular point in time.

results were extensively discussed with the three countries.[III]

General objectives of the technical study

Initially, the technical study aimed, through co-operation with the three watercourse countries, to develop an:

> "[i]ntegrated water resources management analysis of the Euphrates River and the Tigris River in Turkey, Syria and Iraq. The analysis will be based on water resources data from the respective Countries (national authori[z]ed and publicly available data), but will also reflect data derived from international studies."[29]

Collecting, documenting and analyzing data on the water resource situation of the rivers formed the basis of the analysis.

The overall objective of the technical study was to outline a possible water allocation and water resources management strategy that would provide conditions for a sustainable river basin environment.

At the same time, and based on input from the countries, it aimed to maintain the highest possible irrigation targets in each of them. The decision was made to analyze the rivers separately, i.e. using the so-called single-basin model. To fulfil this objective, it was expected that the initiative would lead to the following short and long-term results:

▸ "documentation that may be applied as a basis for further deliberations between the watercourse countries on the principles of

integrated water resources management in the region;

▸ processes that will encourage integrated water resources management through the application of Geographical Information Systems and modelling tools; and

▸ an optimal river management with respect to sustainable development."[30]

Analytical approach

The approach was based on a step-by-step integrated analysis with a focus on the most important elements to be included in a possible river basin management arrangement. In *Annex 3*, the water resource planning structure applied throughout the process as well as the role of the different working papers in this structure is outlined. The final technical report summarized and integrated the major findings previously presented in the working paper documents that were completed over the course of this analysis.[31]

Any comprehensive water resource analysis requires reliable and valid data in order to assess the status and compute the consequences of different river management regimes.[IV] The need for such data was accepted by all three states, and incidentally was the *raison d'être* behind the Turkish Three Stages Plan (see further outline of data and methods in *Annex 3*).

What are the implications of viewing the Euphrates and the Tigris Rivers as one single basin versus two separate river basins?

Turkey has all along argued that the two rivers should be 'treated', meaning that they should

---

III Turkey has not officially provided any feedback on the technical results.

IV A 'water management regime' simply means a water arrangement that specifies the use of water flow for different purposes on a certain timescale, and specifications of water quality standards.

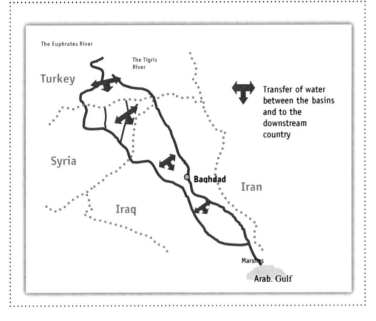

Figure 14a. Water transfer: twin-basin model (treating the Euphrates and the Tigris as one basin)

▸ each country could be given a certain amount of water to optimize within each territory;

▸ Syria and Iraq could receive a combined or a separate amount of water from the two rivers; and

▸ the states must agree on certain water quality standards of both rivers as they cross the borders into Syria and into Iraq.

From a practical and scientific point of view, this is feasible and may even have some merit. The initial study, however, is based on the separate-basin approach (see *Figure 14b*) because the preliminary

be viewed, as a single basin, a twin-basin model, as illustrated in *Figure 14a*. By doing so, water could be transferred between the rivers within each country in order to optimize national water usage. A crucial and legitimate question arises from this statement:

How should a study be developed if the two rivers are considered as one?

To date, Turkey has not provided a clear answer to this question, and no basin study has been conducted. However, if a single-basin study is developed, it should encompass at least the following considerations:

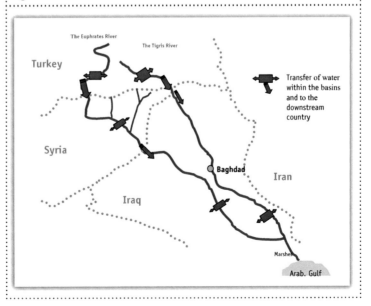

Figure 14b. Water transfer: separate-basin model of the Euphrates and Tigris Rivers

investigations anticipated that each country would receive a smaller allocated amount if the *twin-basin model* was chosen. Eventually, the findings from the study to a large extent confirmed this assumption, although not unambiguously as a comprehensive modelling of rule-curves with transfer of water between the rivers was never conducted. It must be recognized that this is a significant limitation of the technical study.

If, eventually, the countries decide to pursue a *twin-basin* approach, some sort of new estimation for optimized and co-ordinated use of the rivers must be designed, since water between them should certainly not be transferred randomly into the other river basin at any given time. The technical study has revealed that this is a highly complex matter. Therefore, despite the previously stated political positions on this matter, it would be wise for all three countries to establish a factual basis before a final judgement is made on the separate-basin model.

River basin description

General

Although it may seem obvious, the main characteristic of rivers in general is their continuous one-way flow in response to gravity, and this fact has a special significance for the two rivers due to the vast geographical area. In addition, due to changes in physical conditions such as slope, uncompacted material and bedrock geology, rivers are dynamic and may change several times during their course. When assessing the characteristics and water quality of the two rivers, it is important to bear in mind that they comprise not only the main courses, but also a vast number of tributaries (even from Iran into Iraq as regards the Tigris).

The rivers are greatly influenced by the characteristics of the catchment area, such as the climatic conditions influencing the water flow as well as geology in general (including alluvial deposits), riverbed characteristics and soil type. The latter also affects the mineral content of the water in the rivers.

In addition, exogenous factors such as activities within the basins affect the river systems in numerous ways, such as through forestation or deforestation, urbanization, agricultural development, land drainage, polluted discharge and flow regulations.

It seems evident that in order to obtain an overview of how the flow of the rivers varies over time, how the water quality changes as well as how the exogenous factors contribute to determining the surface and groundwater, a long-term perspective must be taken. Applications of long-term data series, but also inter-generational perspectives, were made in the study.

In the following text, a brief introductory description of the two rivers is given followed by specifications on use in Turkey, Syria and Iraq.

The Euphrates River

The Euphrates River is formed in the mountains of eastern Turkey by the confluence of the Murat and Karasu rivers at the Keban reservoir (north of the Ataturk dam in *Figure 15*). The main source of runoff in the catchment of these rivers is snow.

The Euphrates River flows southward, crossing the border with Syria at Jarabulus. Downstream of the border, the river is first joined by the Sajur River from the west, and further downstream by the Balikh River and Khabour River from the north.

These two rivers receive most of their water volume from springs immediately south of the border between Turkey and Syria, and have most of their catchments in Turkey (Kolars and Mitchell, 1991). After the entry of the Khabour River, no further water is added to the Euphrates River from permanent sources. Since 1995, little or no runoff has been recorded in the Khabour River and Balikh River.

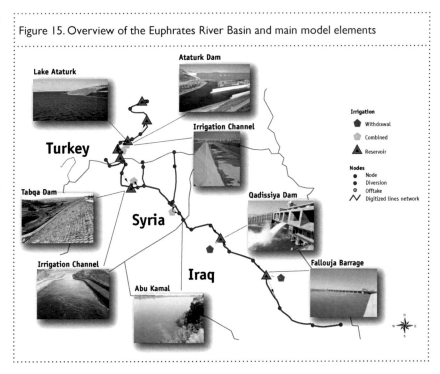

Figure 15. Overview of the Euphrates River Basin and main model elements

The Euphrates River enters Iraq at El Qaim south of Abu Khamal. Further downstream at Hit, it enters its alluvial plain, which is covered with fertile alluvial soils and formed by silt deposits from the Euphrates River. After confluence with the Tigris, the two rivers form the Shat al-Arab (Kliot, 1994).

The Tigris River

The Tigris River originates in the mountains of eastern Turkey. The first source is known as the Tigris River branch and the other as the Batmansu branch. These two branches are joined together near Ceffan to form the Tigris River which flows southward through Turkey. This then forms the boundary between Turkey and Syria before entering Iraq. Here, the Tigris River enters its alluvial plain between Fatha and Samarra. Unlike the Euphrates, the Tigris River receives water from several tributaries originating in the east. The first of these tributaries is the Greater Zab, which rises in the mountainous area around Lake Van in Turkey and enters the Tigris River between Mosul and Fatha in Iraq. The second tributary is the Lesser Zab, which originates in the Zagros Mountains in Iran and enters Tigris upstream of Fatha. The third tributary, the Adhaim River, enters Tigris between Samarra and Baghdad. The Adhaim, which flows entirely within Iraq, is a very small contributor to the Tigris River. The fourth tributary is the Diyala River, which originates in the Zagros Mountains in Iran and enters Tigris a few kilometres downstream from Baghdad. The last major tributary is the Kharun River, which originates in Iran and enters the Shatt al-Arab downstream of Basra.

In contrast to the Euphrates, the discharge of the Tigris River increases with distance downstream, as most of its water is added through the tributaries in Iraq. As the sources for the Tigris discharge are located further downstream, its lower parts are more prone to flooding than the lower parts of the Euphrates River.

Use of the Euphrates and Tigris Rivers in Turkey

The two river systems constitute about 50 per cent of Turkey's total surface water supply (see EIE web site).[32] The country also has a good supply of groundwater. Turkey embarked on its efforts to develop the Euphrates and Tigris in the 1970s. Due to the emphasis on industrialization in Turkey, the development of hydroelectric energy has received priority over other aspects of water usage, while irrigation has mostly been secondary. The increasing need for energy has led to a drive to expand hydropower as a source of energy totally owned by Turkey.

Through the south-eastern Anatolia Project (GAP), Turkey plans to foster regional and national socio-economic development by using the waters of the Euphrates and Tigris Rivers to increase electricity production and irrigation. The GAP consists of 22 dams, 19 hydroelectric power plants and 25 irrigation systems. If it is fully implemented, approximately 1 million ha of land will be irrigated with water from the Euphrates River; while another 600,000 ha will be irrigated with water from the Tigris River. On completion, the GAP with generate altogether 27 GWh/year (on Euphrates and Tigris with 20 GWh and 7 GWh, respectively)(GAP, 1996) and will double Turkey's hydroelectric production and increase the irrigated land by approximately 50 per cent (Broch and Lysne, 1992).

As described, the GAP is a central part of the Turkish government's ambition to raise income levels in south-east Anatolia, which borders both Syria and Iraq. About 70 per cent of the working population in the region are employed in agriculture (EIE web site). Farming today, however, is characterized by low productivity due to inadequately watered soil. With its new irrigation schemes, GAP aims to introduce intensive and profitable farming to the region. The expected increase in agricultural production may create new employment opportunities, trigger industrial growth and raise income levels in the region. Although hydroelectric development provided the initial incentive for the GAP, other aspects of the project are also of importance to Turkey.

Until now, Turkey's developmental efforts have focused on the Euphrates River, on which the largest dam of the GAP, the Ataturk Dam, is located (see *Photo 26*). When fully developed, it will contribute 7,500 MW/year, which is one third of GAP's total energy production, and irrigate some 500,000 ha of land (EIE web site, Altinbilek, 2004). With the GAP, Turkey's use of the Euphrates and Tigris Rivers can be expected to increase substantially in the future. The use of irrigation water, which has mostly been of a local character, is expected to expand rapidly in the future, especially around the Ataturk Dam.

Use of the Euphrates and Tigris River in Syria

Prior to 1950, Syria used little of the Euphrates waters. Use of Euphrates started during the 1960s and 1970s. Today, the river is very important to Syria, as it constitutes some 80-90 per cent of its surface water supply. In addition, Syria has a supply of groundwater, much of which has been overpumped and degraded by sewage and agricultural drainage.

Section III

Agriculture is very important to the Syrian economy. Consequently, Syria plans to increase its irrigated area (World Bank, 2001b). Dams for this purpose have been constructed on the Euphrates and Khabour Rivers. The future discharge of the Khabour River (and the Balikh River, which is mostly used in Turkey) is difficult to assess due to uncertainty on Return-flow from the Urfa Harran Plains, as well as Turkish pumping of aquifers supplying the springs in Syria. In addition, Syria plans to start pumping the Tigris River water for irrigation. Despite previous efforts to increase its irrigated area, there seems to have been a net loss of irrigated land since the early 1960s (see EIE web site). Land scheduled for irrigation in the Euphrates Basin has had to be abandoned as a result of various factors, such as soil characteristics, waterlogging, salinization and land reforms. Consequently, it is difficult to establish the amount of planned irrigated land that will actually be implemented in Syria.

In addition to supplying water for irrigation, the Tabqa Dam on the Euphrates is important for electricity production. At its peak, this dam provided 60 per cent of Syria's electricity (in 1979, cf. EIE). However, low water levels have often left the turbines idle, thus making hydroelectricity an unreliable source of energy in Syria. Lake Assad must be kept full if its hydroelectric potential is to be realized. This conflicts with increased water demands for irrigation projects and domestic consumption. Aleppo and the surroundings, for instance, are increasingly dependent upon Lake Assad for domestic, industrial and irrigation water supplies (EIE web site). The combination of the rapid growth of urban populations and a lack of reliable potable water supplies have already resulted in water shortages in Syria's urban sector. Thus, providing reliable water supplies to growing urban populations is an important future concern for Syria.

Use of the Euphrates and Tigris Rivers in Iraq

Use of the rivers began in Iraq in ancient times. Due to the high seasonal and annual fluctuations in the discharge of the rivers, water storage capacity is an important aspect in managing the water resources in the basins. In Iraq, water control structures have been in use since ancient times to prevent flooding and to irrigate land in central and lower Iraq. When the earliest Mesopotamian civilizations were at their peak, they supported large populations based on well-maintained irrigation and flood control structures, such as the Habbaniya and Abu Dibbis Lakes. Also in modern times, Iraq was the first country to start using the Euphrates and the Tigris waters. Modern engineering work in Iraq began with the construction of the Hindiya Barrage on the Euphrates during the years 1911-1914. It has continued since then, mainly to supply water for irrigation in the basin. Dams have been constructed on both rivers and their tributaries.

Approximately 98 per cent of the total surface water in Iraq is related to the Euphrates and the Tigris and their tributaries (Broch and Lysne, 1992). Iraq also has a small supply of groundwater. About 90 per cent of the water consumed in Iraq is used for agriculture.

Due to shortages in the urban water supply to cities like Baghdad and Mosul, Iraq must expand its domestic water supply. As a result of large oil reserves and the physical characteristics of the rivers, Iraq has no urgent plans for hydropower. Still, there has been a trend towards enlarging the hydropower capacity, and all new dams in Iraq have substantive hydroelectric capacities.

It is not easy to present a picture of Iraq's social and agricultural activities related to water use after the Gulf War in 1991, especially in the aftermath of those events. Some water infrastructures in Iraq have been degraded or damaged during and after the recent years of war in the country.[33] The Gulf War, subsequent UN sanctions (which among other things initially put a ban on dual-use items such as pumps) and the 2003 war also resulted in the disruption of electrical generation in Iraq, consequently halting water pumping for domestic and agricultural purposes including drainage. Major water and sewage treatment projects as well as modern drainage systems to alleviate soil salinity problems were initiated before the three wars.[34]

■ Photo 31.
On the riverbanks of the Euphrates in the southern part of Iraq

There is little available information on the present state of these projects, except for repeated statements by the Coalition Forces in 2004 that water and energy were priority areas for international funding.[35] These statements have been affirmed by the new Iraqi Government.[36]

Since Iraq is located furthest downstream on the Euphrates and the Tigris, all river developments undertaken in Turkey and Syria may have an impact on the water flowing into Iraq. Because Iraq has the largest population within the basins of the two rivers, it is obviously vulnerable to any changes in the quantity and quality of the water received from its upstream neighbours.

Economic efficiency of water – the Euphrates River in GAP

While keeping in mind that the study is based on a separate-basin model (as outlined earlier),

the relationship between energy production and irrigation on the Euphrates in the GAP area would determine how much water may be used in Turkey versus the two other downstream riparians. It is therefore important to understand how energy production and irrigation could be optimized from an economic perspective, as well as how that would influence potential negative environmental impacts.

The reason for focusing on Turkey is because use of the water in the GAP obviously has a major impact on the downstream countries both in terms of quantity and quality.

In the GAP project, two major activities generate economic outputs: hydropower production and agricultural production. These two activities 'compete' for use of water. Power production favours retaining the water in the watercourse, while increased agricultural output demands extraction of water from the watercourse. From an economic point of view, it is interesting to define the balance between power production and irrigation in order to identify the use that provides the highest potential national net benefits.[37] The following aspects were therefore dealt with: power production; the value of power production; crop increases due to irrigation; and crop value analysis.

A set of conditions are outlined in the study, but what is of relevance in this context is the overall result. Although the analysis is not based on verified national Turkish data, and the assumptions made deviate somewhat from national figures, the study concludes that:

▶ a new analysis could be performed based on revised national Turkish data in order to increase the degree of verification;

▶ from an economic perspective, Turkey should use less than the estimated 10 billion m³ per year if no mitigating efforts are put in place (such as treating the return-flow from irrigation and pollution). If the downstream countries' effects are accounted for – which they must be in one way or another – the amount used for irrigation will be significantly smaller.[38] A new analysis could be performed based on revised national Turkish data in order to increase the degree of verification.

Available and planned extraction of water from the rivers[39]

The Euphrates River
When the natural river flow was only disturbed by limited extraction of water for municipal, industrial and irrigation purposes, average annual runoff was calculated at 31.6 billion m³ at Biercik (close to the Turkish–Syrian border, 1938-1972). Together with the runoff of

2.7 billion m³ in Syria, the total amount becomes 34.3 billion m³. At Hit (north of Iraq, 1925-1969) it amounts to 29.4 billion m³ (see *Figure 16*).[40]

The study further presents the applied long-term average total river flow (catchment runoff) and planned use (so-called net irrigation extraction) in Turkey, Syria and Iraq (see *Figure 17*).[41]

The Tigris River
Water quantity data
Annual runoff at the Cizre gauging station (close to the Turkish–Syrian border) for the period between 1948 and 1994 is presented in *Figure 18* (Bilen, 1997). This set of data consists of measured values and includes changes in flow conditions caused by the establishment of reservoirs over recent years.

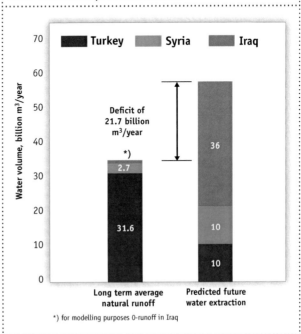

Figure 16. The Euphrates River: comparison of available water volume and predicted demand

*) for modelling purposes 0-runoff in Iraq

Figure 17. The Euphrates River: estimated long-term average total catchment runoff (left) and net irrigation extraction target as defined by the respective countries (right) in Turkey, Syria and Iraq (billion m³/year) (assumed net inflow of 2.7 billion m³/year in Syria, and assumed no net inflow in Iraq)

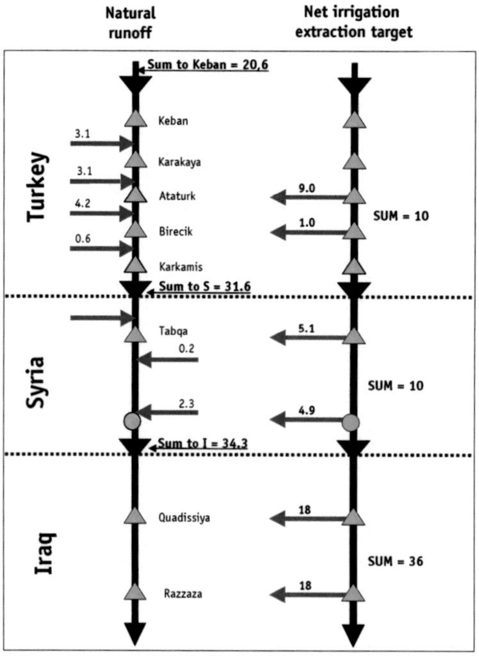

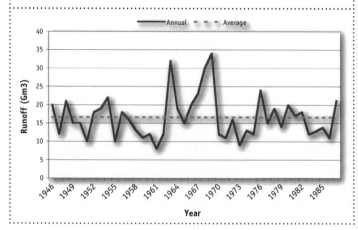

that must be considered when analyzing model output. Despite these limitations, the models can provide comparisons between water management alternatives. They are built to evaluate such long-term alternatives and the actual numbers derived are simply good indicators of trends.

A large number of results have been generated with a complex set of scenarios. Different models relating to both water quantity and quality have been applied to both rivers, except for water quality modelling of the Tigris due to lack of available data from the river. In the latter case, however, there are no reasons to underestimate the water quality challenges in Iraq.

In order to assess the recorded water quality in the Euphrates River, internationally accepted water quality standards were applied as standards of reference with a focus on drinking water and irrigation purposes, to:

▸ develop new models or modify existing modelling tools in order to perform sensitivity analyses of major parameters affecting the water quality;

Modelling of power production, discharge and water quality

In order to obtain a more comprehensive understanding of the flow, regulation and impact on the flow and quality of the rivers, two renowned but different modelling tools were applied.[42]

The technical study underlines that such models are merely best estimates of possible future events, and because the latter are unknown, models have limitations

Figure 18. The Tigris River: annual runoff at Cizre gauging station, 1946–1987

Section III

- describe and simulate possible future changes in salinity along the Euphrates River due to different irrigation strategies;
- evaluate effects of conveying water from the Tigris into the Euphrates in Iraq;
- assess the long-term effect of a deteriorating water quality;
- identify the full net irrigation extraction target; and
- reduce the net irrigation extraction target to 6 billion m³ per year in Turkey and Syria.[43]

Quite a few conclusions may be drawn from the matrix in *Table 7*. In this context, however, just a few relevant points (for the proposals in *Chapter 5*) will be highlighted.

The river flow at the Turkish–Syrian border as well as at the Syrian–Iraqi border is as illustrated in *Figure 19* (based on the figures marked in yellow in *Table 7*). The estimated average flow of 781 m³/s of the Euphrates River at the Turkish–Syrian border is higher than the existing

Table 7. Simulation statistics on selected main scenarios for the Euphrates River

All results are yearly average values, salinity concentration is flow-proportional. Flow restrictions in model: minimum flow at borders: T-S border = 450 m³/s; S-I border = 58 per cent of T-S border. Minimum flow in south Iraq = 150 m³/s. T= Turkey, S=Syria and I=Iraq.

Parameter	Natural runoff/baseline	Scenario			
		Full irrigation target		60% irrigation target	
		A1	A2	B1	B2
Assumptions/input data					
Minimum flow at T-S border (m³/s)	-	450	450	450	450
Return-flow concentration (mg TDS/l)	-	700	3500	700	3500
Return-flow ratio (%)	-	20	20	20	20
Return salinity concentration in reservoirs (mg/l) (T/S/I)	-	300/400/500			
Net irrigation target (billion m³/year)					
Turkey	-	10	10	6	6
Syria	-	10	10	6	6
Iraq	-	36	36	21.6	21.6
Net irrigation obtained (billion m³/year)					
Turkey	-	9.2	9.2	6	6
Syria	-	9.4	9.4	6	6
Iraq	-	9.7	9.7	15.1	15.1
Flow at border (m³/s)					
T-S border					
Average	1006	681	681	781	781
Min	493	450	450	463	463
S-I border					
Average	1091	467	467	671	671
Min	535	264	264	331	331
Calculated salinity concentrations at borders (mg TDS/l)					
T-S border					
Average	268	317	517	303	434
Min	330	369	623	352	533
S-I border					
Average	400	746	1395	573	906
Min	493	967	1841	753	1295

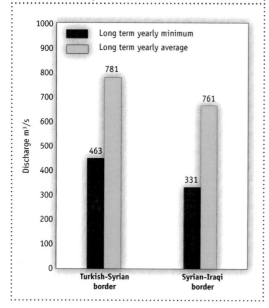

Figure 19. The Euphrates River: computed annual average discharge at the Turkish–Syrian border and Syrian–Iraqi border with reduced irrigation target values in the respective countries

user as a consequence of full irrigation, especially in Turkey.

What has been presented is at best a summary of the study and may run the danger of oversimplification. A more comprehensive presentation of the results, including the full irrigation target, is however given in the relevant sections in the study. There is, nevertheless, another matter that must be discussed, which is related to the possible irreversible or permanent pollution of the reservoirs of the Euphrates unless drastic steps are taken. Perhaps one of the most alarming findings is the long-term effect of polluted reservoirs.

Since the results show that water quality is becoming a major challenge for the Euphrates Basin, the water quality analysis is outlined in more detail. As a consequence of large reservoir volumes in the Euphrates River basin, the average detention period[44] in the river has increased dramatically compared to the natural runoff.

agreement between Syria and Turkey, which is in "not less than of 500 m³/s", although the absolute estimated minimum flow is lower (463 m³/s). *Therefore, the 'agreed river flow' (of 500 m³/s) and estimations (of 463 and 781 m³/s) are not directly comparable.*

A critical question is to what extent the amount of irrigation (i.e. the concentration of the Return-flow from such areas) determines the salinity of the Euphrates River at the two relevant borders. In the following tables, two scenarios are presented: one with a majority fulfilment of the planned irrigation target (*Figure 20*): 9.2-9.4 billion m³ *per year* and the other with 6 billion m³ *per year* (60 per cent of the planned irrigation target in *Figure 21*).

The tables clearly show that the water quality has severely deteriorated for the downstream

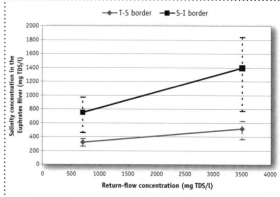

Figure 20. Average salinity concentration of the Euphrates River at the Turkish–Syrian (T-S) border and at the Syrian–Iraqi (S-I) border versus return-flow concentration based on a 40-year simulation period with: net average annual irrigation extraction = 9.4 billion m³ per year in Turkey and Syria. Return-flow ratio = 20% (ref. Scenario A1 and A2 in *Table 7*).

Figure 21. Average salinity concentration of the Euphrates River at the Turkish–Syrian (T-S) border and at the Syrian–Iraqi (S-I) border versus return-flow concentration based on a 40-year simulation period with: net annual irrigation extraction = 6 billion m³ per year in both Turkey and Syria. Return-flow ratio = 20%. (Ref. Scenario B1 and B2 in *Table 7*)

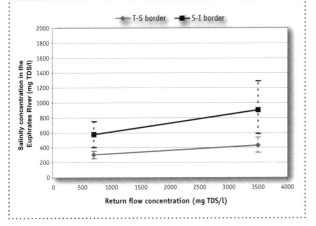

Figure 22 shows results from calculated salinity concentration in southern Iraq after irrigation extraction has been stopped (year 0). The salinity concentration should then gradually decrease to the natural-stage situation (where Return-flow from irrigation is not included).

Results show a reduction in salinity concentration in the Euphrates in southern Iraq after high irrigation/return-flow (until year 0) followed by no irrigation/return-flow. An assumed baseline salinity concentration in south Iraq is shown to illustrate how calculated salinity concentration will gradually be reduced to baseline concentration.

Perhaps one of the most alarming findings is the long-term effect of polluted reservoirs.

Based on the simulation results, if no irrigation takes place (i.e. no Return-flow), the following conclusions could be drawn:

▸ It will take about 1.5 years before the salinity concentration is reduced from approximately 1,250 mg TDS/l down to 600 mg TDS/l (halving).
▸ It will take about 7-8 years before the effect of highly-concentrated reservoir water is insignificant (close to the baseline situation).

Assessment of conveying Tigris water to the Euphrates River in Iraq

A *twin-basin model* involves the transfer of water from the Tigris to the Euphrates. One of the possible justifications of this model would be if the Euphrates River in the south of Iraq becomes polluted and inadequate for municipal usage and irrigation. In this case, the water from Tigris could be conveyed into the Euphrates to improve the water quality.

Since water quality data from the Tigris River was not made available for the study, only a rough and simplified assessment was carried out.[45]

Figure 22. Long-term effect of high salinity concentration in the Euphrates River Basin reservoir followed by complete stop in discharge

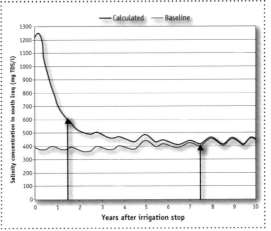

The 'mixing' of waters from the Tigris with the Euphrates in Iraq in order to improve poor water quality downstream *might* have insignificant benefits. This does not, however, exclude the possibility of Syria and Turkey transfering water between the rivers if this is carried out as part of an agreement based on far more comprehensive modelling.[46]

■ Photo 32.
The manmade drainage channel located between the Euphrates and Tigris Rivers in Iraq (1998)

Section III

Chapter 4

The findings and their relevance in developing solutions for sound river basin management

In this chapter, the separate-basin modelling of water quantity and water quality is summarized according to what is relevant in relation to a river basin management agreement. Only the most vital conclusions are outlined.

...special attention must be paid to the water quality aspects and particularly the impact of return-flow from irrigation.

Unexpectedly, the analyses have demonstrated that special attention must be paid to the water quality aspects in any water management strategy for each of the countries and particularly the impact of Return-flow from irrigation. In this respect, minimum and maximum river flow requirements at the borders between the three countries should be specified. Important key parameters, such as the contents of bacteria, metals, nutrients (phosphorus and nitrogen) and biota characteristics, were not made available. These parameters are, however, essential in performing an appropriate river basin assessment. There are reasons to assume that the situation might be even worse in terms of water quality.

Findings of the power production and water quantity simulations

With the separate-basin approach, the major findings indicated by the power and water quantity model simulations are summarized as follows:

The Euphrates River

▸ Increasing the minimum flow requirements at the border between Turkey and Syria from 300 m³/s to 500 m³/s will reduce energy generation in Turkey by approximately 1 per cent.

▸ Reducing the irrigation volume in Turkey from 10 billion m³/year to 5.5 billion m³/year will increase energy generation in Turkey by approximately 9 per cent (which could create a win-win situation for all three countries, except that Turkey may not fully use its irrigation potential).

▸ Full implementation of the irrigation schemes of the GAP project will reduce the longtime average discharge of the Euphrates River into Syria to approximately 650 m³/s, equivalent to approximately 20 billion m³/year as a long-term average value.

▸ It will be possible to maintain a minimum discharge of close to 500 m³/s at the border between Turkey and Syria after full implementation of the GAP project.

▸ Full implementation of the planned irrigation schemes in Turkey and Syria will reduce the long-term average discharge of the Euphrates River into Iraq to approximately 470 m³/s, equivalent to approximately 15 billion m³/year.

▸ The GAP region design irrigation volume of approximately 10 billion m³ per year may not be the economically optimal irrigation volume. The calculations show a possible optimal irrigation volume of 6-9 billion m³/year, even when environmental costs and interests downstream of the Turkish–Syrian border are excluded from the analysis.

The Tigris River

▸ Initial simulations carried out on the Tigris River indicate that it is possible to maintain a minimum discharge of 200 m³/s at the border between Turkey and Syria–Iraq, after full development of the GAP project. As the calculations are not solely based on national data, they must be verified by the watercourse countries.

Findings of the water quality assessment: present situation

From the limited available data, the following water quality assessment of the *Euphrates River* has been made.

Irrigation

At present, the river is already saline, but the question is: *What is an acceptable level?* The findings present a situation which all countries must address:

▸ Salinity measured in Syria appears acceptable for irrigation use. However, long-term annual average data from north Iraq (Hussaiba) showed that in about 50 per cent of the measuring period (1976-1998), salinity was so high that the water quality should be classified with slight to moderate restrictions regarding irrigation use.

▸ Sulphate concentrations were relatively high compared to internationally recommended levels (50mg SO₄/l). The average recorded sulphate concentration during the measuring campaign was 80 mg/l.

▸ Relatively low oxygen saturation measured along the Euphrates River in Syria, with a decrease from north to south (from approximately 77 per cent in the north decreasing to 68 per cent) indicates significant biological activity. This may eventually restrict water use for irrigation purposes, especially if the origin is domestic emissions.

Drinking water

One may argue that it is unprecedented for an international river of this magnitude to attain drinking water standards. Some use the Rhine River in Europe, which is shared by eight countries, and is treated several times before it reaches the Atlantic Ocean, as a comparison. The Euphrates is, however, compared to similar international rivers, of relative high quality:

▸ All parameters are typically above guideline values (especially sulphate concentration) but below the maximum permissible values, except for magnesium, where the maximum recorded values exceed the maximum recommended values.[47]

Water quality simulations

As described, water quality modelling has only been executed on the Euphrates River. The following findings are thought to be important regarding development of any river basin management strategy:

▸ Based on the assessment of the present water quality and the simulation results, it is recommended that a cautious strategy be chosen for implementing the planned irrigation schemes in the watercourse countries.

- The simulation modelling showed that with full irrigation targets (as stated by the upstream countries) the water quality will most likely not conform to user requirements. It is therefore recommended that an irrigation strategy implying less than 60 per cent of the full irrigation target be put into practice.
- If net target irrigation volumes are put into practice, a strict rule curve[48] operation must be applied; that is to say, as the volumes of water in the reservoirs are reduced, the permissible extraction of water for irrigation purposes must be reduced accordingly.
- Without a rule-curve regime, high peak salinity concentration will occur in dry years, resulting in a water quality not suitable for irrigation purposes. In practice, it is also an advantage to operate along a rule-curve regime in order to ensure that reservoirs are not emptied during dry seasons.
- Even with the rule-curve regime applied in the technical study, a critical worsening of the water quality occurred when the full irrigation extraction target was simulated, especially during dry years. Analyses of accumulated high salinity in the Euphrates and its reservoirs showed that restoring the water quality back to an acceptable level is a slowly reversible process, even if all discharges are stopped (which in itself is a highly theoretical assumption, and in reality probably not possible).
- A conceptual assessment of conveying Tigris water into the Euphrates River in Iraq to improve on poor water quality showed that under the assumed prevailing conditions this measure has a limited effect downstream. Further studies are necessary to determine this result.

Since irrigation must be reduced in relation to the Parties' ambitions, should the twin-basin model be adopted rather than the separate-basin model?

In order to compensate for the reduced irrigation and need to manage water quality, a possible transfer of Tigris water into the Euphrates Basin should be evaluated for Turkey. An analogous measure should be assessed for Syria, although in both cases as part of an agreement. On this basis, one may argue that the two rivers should be viewed as a twin basin (as Turkey argues).

One should not, however, hide the fact that from a negotiating point of view a twin-basin model seems complex to negotiate. This is because operation of the rule-curves of the rivers would be quite complex: if transfer of water within Syria and Turkey takes place between the two rivers, it must be co-ordinated by all three countries and included in an agreement.

Another relevant question is: to what extent are these findings valid, and how applicable are the results for future trilateral water agreements?

In order to verify and review the results of the study, an independent review was conducted by an international scientific institution and a leading international water scientist.

Third Party review of the technical study

It is obvious that with any technical water management study, and especially when simulations and models are included, the results are not carved in stone. The data, methods and assessments may be put into question. This technical study is by no means an exception; especially because it deals only with the separate-basin model and not the twin-basin one.

Section III

■ Photo 33.
Water-level measurement sticks
in the Euphrates River

It therefore seems evident that the technical findings cannot be exactly applied in a trilateral agreement – there are simply too many prerequisites set out in the study. Even more importantly, any agreement would have to be developed within a political context rather than in a confined scientific one.

The results nevertheless give a technical basis for any future deliberations. It therefore became evident that an external review of the study would either decease or increase the legitimacy of the results. Two independent reviews were thus conducted: a limited one by the British scientist J. A. Allan of the University of London's School of Oriental Studies, and a more comprehensive one by the renowned Swiss Federal Institute for Environmental Science and Technology (EAWAG).

Allan acknowledges that "[t]he study provides by far the most comprehensive account of the hydrology of the Tigris–Euphrates river systems so far assembled". He summarized the whole report by stating:

"The [technical study] is an important potential contribution to advancing agreement over the allocation of the Euphrates-Tigris riparians and their future quality. It could have an immediate impact as an input to technical discussions on water allocation and the management of water quality. Such discussions are essential."[49]

Subsequently, in early 2003, the EAWAG in Zurich[50] conducted a more detailed review of the study. The institute put together a team of water experts who answered a set of critical questions on it.[51] The specific questions and relevant answers are outlined in the technical study. EAWAG's overall conclusions were:

"In general, EAWAG is very positive about the analyses in the CESAR report with a view that it should serve as a 'start up document' to facilitate negotiations

■ Photo 34.
Monitoring of water quantity and quality as part of the compensation mechanism should go beyond today's situation

Section III

[my emphasis]. It is certainly recogni[z]ed that the study is unique, since no similar studies have been carried out. It should indeed be of the interest to the Parties to use the study as a *basis for negotiations to obtain a long-term sustainable solution*" [my emphasis].

It seems obvious from EAWAG's review that exact figures from the study should not be directly applied in any trilateral agreements. Their univocal recommendation is to use the *findings* as a critical input to further studies, in preparing realistic positions of the Parties, and for the political negotiations. This is exactly the author's purpose with this publication.

One of the strongest recommendations from EAWAG is that the three Parties should work together in developing further river basin studies in order to understand the exact nature of how the rivers may be optimally used, both in terms of quantity and quality.

Water quality aspects in existing treaties

As outlined in the introductory part of this book, the University of Oregon was commissioned to conduct a study on the extent to which water quality aspects were included in international water agreements.[52]

The new generation of water agreements and standards, such as the UN Convention of Non-Navigational Use of International Watercourses and the EU Framework Directive on Water, contain references to protection of water quality. The EU Framework includes very strict water quality standards and monitoring procedures. Today, the Directive goes far beyond any existing water standards set in the Middle East. In any case, the inclusion of water quality and monitoring in any agreements on the Euphrates and the Tigris Rivers is legitimized by a strong international trend (see also Iza, 2004).

■ Photo 35.
A railroad bridge with a water-measurement device over the Balih River on the Syrian side of the border with Turkey

Chapter 5

Two alternative models for a trilateral water agreement on the Euphrates and the Tigris Rivers

All three countries have officially and unofficially expressed a need for a trilateral water agreement. None of them will, however, enter into any agreement if the benefits do not outweigh the costs, either in terms of political and financial capital, or from a more technical water management point of view. When the *realpolitik* conditions will be optimal for an agreement is hard to predict, if not impossible. Each country, as well as other stakeholders, has its own perception of the right timing, and it is in the midst of this uncertainty that the following principles for a possible water agreement are made public.

Whether the conditions are optimal or not when this book is made public is not for the author to judge. Rather, the aim is to offer a proposal that might be considered an input *when* the three countries are ripe to enter into negotiations for an agreement. This proposal is a reaction to an imperative and urgent need for a trilateral water agreement, irrespective of the ebb and flow of politics.

This proposal is a reaction to an imperative and urgent need for a trilateral water agreement, irrespective of the ebb and flow of politics.

To reach such an agreement requires, first and foremost, political will from each of the countries. It is fruitless to blame any of the countries for not promoting the necessary co-operative willingness. Instead, before outlining a preliminary water agreement, it seems relevant to illustrate the advantages of co-operation as set out by Turkish water expert Altinbilek (2004).

Advantages of co-operative actions
- "The optimum plan for the basin as a whole can be formulated and implemented.
- Seemingly conflicting demands can be harmonized within a broad master plan that may incorporate many water-supply-augmenting and efficiency-improving measures.
- The waters for the Euphrates and Tigris can be utilized equitably and effectively, taking into account seasonal and yearly variations in flow due to floods and droughts.
- Joint regional research institutions, training centres and pilot farms ...
- Water-augmenting techniques ...
- Co-operative action may facilitate the achievement of environmental sustainability.
- Financing of joint and national projects from various international sources may be easier and more attractive".

Source: Altinbilek, 2004.

Altinbilek is proposing the transfer of water between the two rivers and between the reservoirs of the same river or two rivers.[53] At the same time, he adds the danger of politicizing the water issues to such an extent that they "may be heavily obstructed by inclusion of other issues and controversies".

As discussed in the preceding chapter, a key question is the extent to which the technical findings form the basis for a negotiated political trilateral water agreement. Before answering that question directly, some factual issues must univocally be considered when such an agreement is developed:

▸ It is urgent that a trilateral water agreement be reached as soon as possible, irrespective of whether a separate-basin or twin-basin model is chosen. If not, and if no remedial action is taken, irreversible damage, especially to the Euphrates watercourse in the lower part of Syria and in Iraq, may occur as irrigation volumes are increasing.

▸ In order to prevent the Euphrates River from being polluted – especially in dry periods – the application of rule-curves for extraction of water for irrigation is recommended. Discharge values at the Turkish–Syrian and Syrian–Iraqi borders might therefore vary, and even more so if climatic changes increase.

▸ The consequences of doing nothing on the above-mentioned points would be severe human suffering.

▸ An allocation of water quantity to each country must be determined by the need to maintain a minimum water quality for the users of both watercourses. The exact minimum discharge, which is technically suggested to be of 150 m³/s (for the Euphrates River at the point of convergence with the Tigris River in southern Iraq), may be discussed. However, the independent review by EAWAG[54]

underlines the importance of minimum flow and concludes that an amount of 150 m³/ might be sustainable. An agreement on this amount is not insignificant for determining the effects upstream.

▸ A precautionary principle should be applied for the planned irrigation schemes in the watercourse countries in order to maintain sustainable development of the river basins.

▸ A water quantity and quality monitoring programme should be implemented at the borders. A set of limiting value ranges for these parameters should be established.

▸ Transfer of sound environmental wastewater technology and joint research on development of low water demand crops and effective irrigation practices should also be intensified.

The three countries should also adhere to some general principles that would increase the sustainability of any solution:

▸ From a sustainable water management perspective, it is not conclusive whether there are two associated agreements for the rivers or one unified one, as long as an agreement is reached on how to manage the rivers for the optimal benefit of all three countries. From a negotiation process point of view, however, it seems appropriate to develop a single agreement, or at least two linked river agreements.

▸ Turkey has argued that the river basins should be treated as a single basin: the so-called twin-basin model. However, it is unclear whether this means that there should be a single agreement. The technical study has shown that in case the rivers are treated as one basin, transfer of water between them (at least in Turkey and Syria) without coordination with the downstream countries should be carefully assessed. Such a twin-basin approach is feasible, but seems more complex to negotiate and even more complex to operate at an international level (through rule-curves).

▸ All three countries have, as a principle, acknowledged the responsibility to protect and use the watercourses in an equitable and reasonable manner.

▸ All irrigation projects in the watercourses should be made subject to an extensive environmental impact assessment with respect to Return-flow, soil and groundwater effects.

Based on these principles, the two above-mentioned models are presented: a twin-basin model; and a separate-basin model as a basis for possible trilateral water agreements. Irrespective of the models, the common elements outlined earlier are included in the text as outlined in *Annexes 4* and *5*.

The allocation of water and water quality standards at the borders with either a *twin-basin* or a *separate-basin* model

A decision of the three countries to pursue either a twin-basin model or the separate-basin model will determine how the rivers are to be managed, i.e. the rule-curves (how to co-ordinate the various usages as such as hydropower, irrigation, storage and extraction of water).

As of today, relevant information is only available for the separate-basin model, which means operating the rivers separately (cf. the technical study). However, based on the experience gained from the study, it would be intellectually arrogant and politically unwise not to also consider a twin-basin model, since the findings of such a study are as yet unknown. Several studies must be conducted in order to find a complex but feasible formula that aims primarily to meet the following objectives:

▸ optimize water usage in Turkey;

▸ provide predictable and co-ordinated minimum flows of both rivers to Syria;

▸ optimize water usage in Syria;

▸ provide predictable and co-ordinated minimum flows of both rivers to Iraq; and

▸ provide predictable and co-ordinated minimum flows of both rivers enabling Iraq to optimize its water usage also.

In addition to this, with a twin-basin approach water quality standards must be developed based on water quality models for both rivers. Below, some principles for an international allocation formula between them are presented.

Principles relevant for determining water use and water allocation *in a twin-basin* model:

▸ Indicative water allocation values must have combined and separate suggestions for both rivers.

▸ To prevent both watercourses being polluted, especially in the dry periods, associated rule curves for the two rivers for the extraction of water for irrigation purposes should be applied. The rule curves shall be revised according to the results of a periodic rule-curve evaluation.

▸ The watercourse countries shall jointly strive to maintain an absolute minimum discharge and expected maximum long term average (m³/s) at the Turkish–Syrian and Syrian–Iraqi borders.

▸ The maximum permissible water quality values at the Turkish–Syrian and Syrian–Iraqi borders must be accepted by the watercourse countries as normal values that do not require specific action to be stated.

▸ If any of the value ranges reported show a total change of a certain percentage over two successive periods, the watercourse countries

Section III

shall investigate the cause of the changes and report on this to a Regional Water Management Organization (RWMO), which may invoke mitigating actions.

■ Photo 36.
Monsul Dam on the Tigris River in Iraq

Based on the findings from the technical study, indicative water allocation and water quality requirements on the borders between the three countries (as outlined at the end of *Annex 5*) should be considered. *However, these figures are illustrations rather than than actual negotiable numbers. More modelling is certainly necessary in order to understand the implications of any chosen formula.*

In addition, likely climate change demands that the countries determine allocation figures on the basis of criteria such as natural rainfall over a certain period – and revise these threshold values on a regular basis.

In summary, as an illustration, approximate water allocation for the Euphrates may be around (with an agreed threshold value): 7 billion m³/year for Turkey, 7 for Syria, and 13 for Iraq.

Approximate yearly values of discharge of the Euphrates River may be around:

▸ an absolute minimum of 450 m³/s at the Turkish–Syrian border, with an expected long-term average of 750 m³/s;

▸ an absolute minimum of 450 m³/s at the Syrian–Iraqi border, with an expected long-term average of 550 m³/s; and

▸ an absolute minimum of 150 m³/s at the convergence point with the Tigris River, with an expected long-term average of 150 m³/s.

The data for the Tigris River is too uncertain to provide illustrative figures at this stage.

Irrespective of whether the twin-basin or separate-basin model is chosen, the water quality of the rivers must be managed in one way or another. The following chapter suggests one way of handling this matter.

Section III

Chapter 6

Mitigating cross-border pollution through a third party compensation mechanism

Raison d'être

The results of the technical study make it quite clear that the water quality aspects – especially for the Euphrates River of today and in the near future – must be given special attention in any basin management strategy, and particularly the impact of Return-flow from irrigation.[V]

In order to avert negative environmental and subsequent humanitarian consequences of a situation that may be described as a crisis[VI], there is a need for concerted measures to reduce the expected adverse impacts of intensified and expanded irrigation.[55]

In order to adequately address these impacts by maintaining a certain water quality level according to agreed standards, a third party compensation mechanism is proposed, in the first stage, at the border of Syria and Iraq. Later, similar plants would be located in the border areas of Turkey and Syria. Such a compensation mechanism demands funds that, realistically speaking, can be raised only by the international community. There are two reasons for this:

1. The amount of funds necessary to mitigate the pollution is so large that only a multi-donor effort can meet the financial requirements.

2. Stakeholders outside the region might consider this compensation mechanism effective in preventing unstable conditions that could stem from such a crisis.

Objective

A compensation mechanism would aim to achieve internationally accepted water quality standards and thereby minimize the negative effects of poor water quality on the sustainable development projects of the watercourse countries. The first priority should be given to the Euphrates River. This would take into account and reconcile four key and potentially conflicting objectives:

▸ Turkey's *planned agricultural use* in the South Anatolia region (GAP);

▸ Syria's demand for expansion of irrigation;

▸ Iraq's long term claim of *access to usable water*; and

▸ the need to sustain the ecological balance of the rivers.

The most effective way of mitigating pollution of the Euphrates, and especially salinity, is to propose that the compensation mechanism

---

V   A primary concern for the management of irrigation is the discharge of salts, pesticides and nutrients tow groundwater and discharge of these pollutants plus sediment to surface water. The goal of mitigating management measures is to reduce the movement of pollutants from land into ground or surface water from the practice of irrigation.

VI Such a crisis would probably first take place in the lower part of the river basin, i.e. affecting Iraq.

compensate Syria for upstream measures to reduce the pollution of the water flowing into Iraq. In addition, and as a next step, the same mechanism could be implemented on the Turkish side at the Turkish–Syrian border in order to achieve acceptable water quality (especially along the drainage areas at the border zone).

An implementation, monitoring and verification system should be an integral part of such a compensation mechanism.

More specifically, third party institutions such as the World Bank or United Nations, or combinations such as the 'Global Environmental Facility' (GEF)[56], Kuwaiti Fund, European Bank for Reconstruction and Development, European Investment Fund, and other countries and groups such as the US, Russia and the EU respectively should offer to cover the incremental costs of a scheme for mitigating pollution in order to achieve agreed-on water quality standards.

Establishment of a desalinization plant

Economic compensation would be used to reduce the negative downstream effects, which could in the first instance include a desalinization plant at the Euphrates River on the Syrian side of the Syrian-Iraqi border.[VII]

Such compensation would also be given to Turkey in the GAP region to undertake measures that aim to reduce the negative pollution effects downstream, through efficient application and

---

VII In order to remove any doubt, it is important to underline that there is neither an explicit nor implicit burden put on Syria regarding pollution of the Euphrates. The location of the plant is solely chosen in order to optimize the water efficiency of such a measure. The establishment of the plant aims to assist all three countries in fulfilling their obligation to maintain a certain water quality.

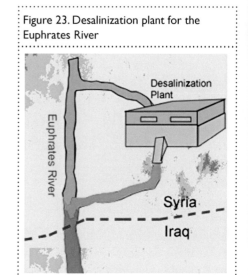

Figure 23. Desalinization plant for the Euphrates River

transport of irrigation water and management of drainage water.

Internationally, there are parallels to such a mechanism, such as the US and Mexico agreement on the Colorado River, where a desalinization plant installed on the US side treats water in order to maintain agreed water quality standards.[57]

Why should the international community fund a compensation mechanism?

One may argue that national water usage for sustainable development should be governed through the respective country's water management legislation. In most cases, however, as in the Euphrates and Tigris basins, national legislations are currently neither harmonized nor reflect international water quality standards.

It is well understood that unrestricted water use upstream would impose environmental and thereby economic burdens on downstream states. At the present time, improving downstream water quality and quantity to minimize adverse

■ Photo 37.
The Murat River close to Lake Van, part of the Euphrates Basin in Eastern Turkey

impacts will place additional cost on upstream users. Over the past decade, this has been internationally recognized, as shown by the establishment of the joint World Bank/UNEP/UNDP Global Environmental Facility. One of its four prime objectives is to cover such additional costs related to international watercourses.[58]

It appears obvious that the challenges to sound management of the two rivers fall within the mandate of the GEF, which is a recognition of the responsibility of the international community to provide additional compensation to upstream countries adopting mitigation measures. Otherwise, the *overall cost* for the concerned national governments, as well as for the international community, is likely to be many times higher in terms of unintended humanitarian, economic, social and environmental consequences as well as potential instability in the region.

In line with such reasoning, the mechanism could be one of the first joint projects under

the new proposed Euphrates and Tigris Basins Initiative.

What kind of costs should the third party compensation mechanism cover?

The mechanism might cover the cost difference between what the national water management practice and legislation would require, and what the internationally accepted water quality standards would require.[59]

These additional costs are calculated as Syria and Turkey's real capital, operation, maintenance and agreed opportunity costs of water resource management that guarantee maintaining a certain *water quality level for uses downstream*. Exactly what incremental costs may be considered should be estimated in a separate study as an input into a negotiated compensation mechanism. The compensation could be used by Syria to build a desalinization plant at the Syrian–Iraqi border as well as to develop programmes to enhance water efficiency and mitigate water pollution, especially from irrigation.

Similarly, the compensation to Turkey should also enhance water efficiency and mitigate its water pollution, especially from irrigation that drains across the border into Syria.

Compensation principles

The compensation mechanism briefly outlined above relies on at least five assumptions:

1. Compensation for foregone water usage should be developed.
2. Agreement on accepted water quality standards at the Syrian–Iraqi border.[VIII]
3. Agreement on accepted water quality standards at particular border areas on the Turkish–Syrian border.[IX]
4. Agreement on the principle that only incremental (additional) costs in Syria and Turkey due to the agreement will be

---

VIII Without agreement on such standards, there is no basis for calculating the incremental costs for the desalinization plant as well as water pollution in general.

IX Similarly, without agreement on such standards there is no basis for calculating the incremental costs of reducing the return-flow from irrigation.

admissible. This implies that compensation for investments in water resource management infrastructure, which is not a consequence of such an agreement, will not be given to either of the Parties.

5. Agreement that actual incremental cost will be calculated using the most cost effective water resource management options available, relative to the agreed standards that guarantee Syrian and Iraqi water resource uses.

As illustrated above, several questions must be answered before such a compensation mechanism can be established, some of which can only be solved through a trilateral negotiated process.

As discussed, one may argue that the three countries should first negotiate a trilateral agreement based on specific principles in terms of water allocation and water quality standards. In order to implement such an agreement, however, a parallel process should deal with the compensation mechanism in order to ensure that any trilateral agreement reached is feasible.

Chapter 7

Establishment of a Euphrates and Tigris Basin initiative

There is a univocal conclusion that co-operative management of the Euphrates and Tigris Rivers must be improved in the future. If this is not achieved, the water resources will not only be insufficient for the countries to provide 'water for the people' in terms of quality and quantity, but equally importantly, they may be irreversibly deteriorated.

This part of the publication has attempted not only to document this conclusion, but also suggest ways of overcoming the problems. Neither is easy.

However, reluctance to deal with these challenges at this early stage among the respective countries and international community will eventually multiply the problems beyond the reach of remedial action.

It is therefore the author's obligation to urge Turkey, Syria and Iraq to take action now. Without action, the problems will continue to grow, with tragic consequences for the people of these countries and possibly for others outside the region.

In addition to sitting around the negotiation table, Turkey, Syria and Iraq should probably take three immediate and concrete steps:

1. Conduct a comprehensive twin-basin modelling and compare it with the so-far studied separate-basin model in order to improve the factual basis for further actions.
2. Begin to develop a third party compensation mechanism.
3. Jointly agree that a Euphrates and Tigris Basins Initiative should be established to address the immediate and long-term water management challenges (see the following description).

This third bold step is required as the first two actions are far from sufficient in the short and long-term. Indeed, complicating political developments may even gridlock co-operation on water.

A new international initiative for the Euphrates and the Tigris River Basins

Regardless of set political changes with geopolitical implications such as in Iraq, it seems obvious that a *new overarching international initiative* must be taken so that the two rivers do not become 'rivers of fire', and instead become a true blessing for the people and lands in the region.

...a new overarching international initiative must be taken so that the two rivers do not become 'rivers of fire',...

The Euphrates and Tigris Basins Initiative (ETI) could be a partnership initiated and led by the riparian states of the two rivers through a Council of Ministers with the full support of the international community, through an international organization such as the Arab development banks and institutions together with, for example, the World Bank (in association with GEF and the UN).

Similarly to the Nile Basin Initiative (NBI)[60], which encompasses nine riparian African states, it could start with a participatory process of dialogue among the riparians that should result in agreeing on a shared vision, for example "achieving sustainable socioeconomic development through the equitable utilization of, and benefit from, the common Euphrates and the Tigris Basins water resources" (cf. the similarity with the NBI). This vision could then be translated into a programme similar to the NBI Strategic Action Program, with concrete activities and projects.[61]

A Strategic Action Programme of the ETI could be made up of two complementary programmes:
1. A basin-wide shared vision programme (SVP) to build confidence and capacity across the basins.
2. Sub-basin subsidiary action programmes (SAPs) to initiate concrete investments separately or jointly for the two rivers.

The two programmes would reinforce each other. Indeed, the SVP focuses on building regional institutions, capacity and trust, laying the foundation for unlocking the development

> ...the notion of 'benefit sharing' has been introduced to international rivers, in the sense that riparian states should share benefits rather than water itself.

potential of the Euphrates and the Tigris basins which can be achieved through the SAPs.

Sharing benefits

It is quite obvious that the potential of co-operation of the Euphrates and the Tigris Rivers is still largely untapped. The abovementioned remedies of curbing pollution and optimizing use of the water flow are significant and urgent, but the potential of enhanced benefits for all countries is huge. More recently, the notion of 'benefit sharing' has been introduced to international rivers, in the sense that riparian states should share benefits rather than water itself.

A gap exists between the academic notion and realities on the ground, but there is of course no doubt that the three countries could have improved the sharing of benefits, such as by:
- optimizing hydropower production in relation to irrigation;
- optimizing the use of water for agricultural purposes – where that should be done in relation to favourable natural conditions;
- optimizing water for agricultural purposes to reduce pollution (i.e., reducing the Return-flow with high salt content, pesticides and fertilizers); and
- developing electricity trading (including hydropower) that could also encompass joint investment in hydropower plants and power infrastructure.

One may argue that such an initiative is unrealistic and even counterproductive, as attention will be taken away from today's pressing problems and precious time lost. Those arguments were also used against the over ten-year-old NBI in Africa. Today, the NBI has achieved remarkable progress, and it is likely that all nine countries will shortly sign a framework water agreement for the Nile Basin. Equally importantly, several concrete water management projects (under SAP) are being prepared and implemented for national and international benefits.

Establishment of an 'ETI Trust Fund'

A Euphrates and Tigris Basins Initiative should be supported by each of the riparian states, but equally importantly, by a number of bilateral and multilateral development partners.

An ETI-Trust Fund (ETI-TF) could be a funding mechanism to help administer and harmonize donor partner support pledged to the ETI. The Arab Banks and/or World Bank could, for example, administer the ETI-TF on behalf of contributing donors in accordance with the ETI-TF Agreement and the Arab Bank/World Bank's Trust Fund Policy and Procedures.

An ETI-TF could support the preparation and implementation of ETI programmes, including the basin-wide shared vision programme (SVP) and sub-basin investment programme, called for example the Euphrates Basin Subsidiary Action Programme (EBSAP) and Tigris Basin Subsidiary Action Programme (TBSAP). At the basin-wide level, the ETI-TF could also support the process of ETI dialogue and engagement as well as efforts to strengthen the capacity of planned ETI institutions. At the sub-basin level, ETI-TF could support the preparation and implementation of joint investment projects.

ETI-TF funds would then be transferred to the ETI, which would have primary responsibility for the implementation of project activities. Almost all of the ETI-TF-financed projects should be recipient-executed. This would help ensure

ownership of ETI activities and contribute to building institutional capacity to implement regional projects. As progress is made in programme implementation and a permanent institutional framework for the ETI is agreed on, the ETI-TF would be transferred to an ETI institution.

As the ETI-TF administrator, the Arab Banks and/or World Bank could be responsible for fiduciary management of pooled multi-donor resources and for preparing and supervising ETI-TF-financed projects in accordance with the Banks' rules and procedures.

In addition, an ETI-TF Committee could be responsible for overseeing the operation of the trust fund and for ensuring that resources used meet ETI programme objectives. This committee would be comprised of representatives from contributing agencies, the ETI and the Arab Banks and/or World Bank.

Concluding remarks

With reference to the water management study of the Euphrates and Tigris Rivers, a univocal conclusion is that co-operative management of the Euphrates and Tigris Rivers must be improved in the future. This part of the publication has attempted to document this conclusion, but even more importantly provide suggested ways out of the problems. Neither of them is easy.

This book is quite adamant on one point: Reluctance to deal with these challenges at this early stage among the respective countries and

Reluctance to deal with these challenges at this early stage among the respective countries and international community will eventually multiply problems beyond the reach of realistic remedial action.

international community will eventually multiply problems beyond the reach of realistic remedial action.

The author strongly urges Turkey, Syria and Iraq to take action now. Without action, the problems will continue to grow, with tragic consequences for the people of these countries and possibly for others outside the region.

Equally importantly, the author notes that the countries, together with the international community, should take the necessary steps to establish a Euphrates and Tigris Basins Initiative that would provide support for *action in the foreseeable future*.

Having had the privilege of knowing many wise key decision makers and knowledgeable experts in the three countries, I am optimistic that they will soon take the necessary steps.

Endnotes

1   See for example *Annex I: Selected international literature regarding the Euphrates and Tigris Rivers.*

2   As stated by Humam Misconi, a Ministry Adviser of Public Works as reported by *Baghdad Mirror*, 2 May 2005 by Rick Jervis (quoted from USA Today).

3   Before the study, one of the very few international scientists that pointed to the international environmental implications of GAP on Syria was Professor Peter Beaumont (Beamont, 1996).

4   Also confirmed by the newly released report on Iraqi living conditions from UNDP (2005).

5   Conveyed by a high official at the Ministry of Irrigation in Iraq to the author in 1999.

6   The establishment (and not the operation) of three stations were funded by the Norwegian Government and implemented by the CESAR Foundation, while the one in Iraq was funded by CESAR itself.

7   Especially related to the relationship between water flow and quality at the Syria-Turkey and Syria-Iraq borders.

8   Also called 'non-evident water': "Invisible or non-evident water is soil water and water embedded in commodities which require water for their production. For example a tonne of grain requires 1000 tonnes (m³) of water to produce it." (Allan, 2002: 336).

9   Such as considering water as an economic good; this may seem contrary to Islamic Law (*Sharia*) for some.

10 See *Annex 1*, and especially a renowned publication by Kolars and Mitchell on *The Euphrates River and the South East Anatolia Development Project* (Kolars and Mitchell, 1991).

11 According to the original documents submitted to the three countries, cf. CESAR (2005) at http://www.cesar.no/

12 As the Chairman of the CESAR Foundation based in Oslo, which carried out the technical studies.

13 A technical study was developed; see CESAR (2005).

14 The Turkish positions are outlined in Turkish Ministry of Foreign Affairs (1996) and SAM (1996). For the specific quotes in the text, see SAM (1996: 18).

15 The only place where the rivers form the borders is the Tigris between Turkey and Syria for a stretch of 62 kilometres, just before it reaches the Turkish, Syrian and Iraqi cross point.

16 Just north of Baghdad – which connects the two rivers.

17 This argument is particularly aimed at Iraq as Turkey argues, "This means that some Iraqi land irrigated from the Euphrates can also be irrigated from the Tigris" (SAM, 1996: 22).

18 By stating, "Therefore, it will not only be uneconomical but will also be inequitable to utilize scarce water resources to irrigate infertile lands at the expense of fertile lands", in Turkish Ministry of Foreign Affairs (1996: 7).

19 The Three Stages Plan consists, among other things, of the following elements:

   •   "Stage 1 – Inventory Studies for Water Resources
       Experts from the riparian States shall exchange full data sets from selected gauging stations in the river basin on:
       -   meteorological data
       -   hydrological information; and
       -   standardisation of measuring techniques

   •   Stage 2 – Inventory Studies for Land Resources
       To exchange information for all projects in operation, planned or under construction, in all the three riparian States on:
       -   soil classifications and conditions
       -   drainage criteria and practices
       -   crop-pattern determined to soil classifications; and irrigation and leaching water requirements.

   •   Stage 3 – Evaluation of Water and Land Resources
       Experts from the three countries will evaluate the following:
       -   Determine irrigation type and system for the planned projects aiming at minimising water losses.
       -   Determine the total water consumption for all the projects in each of the three countries (including evaporation losses, leakages, etc.).
       -   Setting up a simulation model to analyse the demand and supply situation in the river basin ... considering water transfer from the Tigris to the Euphrates River.
       -   Methods and criteria determining economic viability of the planned projects in the three riparian States.
       After the gathering of relevant data, the Joint Technical Committee (JTC) will calculate the water demands for projects under operation, for projects under construction and for planned projects. Determination of these projects will be made separately" (Turkish Ministry of Foreign Affairs, 1996).

20 Specifically stated by several Syrian Government Ministers to the author. See also Daoudy (2005b).

21 Cf. the UN Framework Convention on the Law of Non-Navigational Uses of International Watercourses.

22 Cf. open sources such as http://www.syrianagriculture.org/

23 According to unpublished Syrian documentation from the Ministry of Agriculture as well as from the FAO dating back as far as 1994 (FAO, 1994: 161-167).

24 Communicated to the author by various Syrian Ministers for Irrigation and by the political leadership of the Ministry of Foreign Affairs.

25 As well as upstream of Turkey, just before the Orontes River reaches the Mediterranean Sea in the disputed Alexandretta region (claimed by Syria): This is Syria's argument to counter the abovementioned Turkish statement that the way Syria is utilizing the Orontes has implications for the way Euphrates shall be managed.

26 Cf. the UN Framework Convention on the Law of Non-Navigational Uses of International Watercourses.

27 Communicated repeatedly to the author by various Iraqi Ministers of Irrigation and officials from the Iraqi Ministry of Foreign Affairs. See also Iraq Ministry of Foreign Affairs, 1999.

28 The water quality problems in Iraq are severe, as documented in UNDP's report on Sources of Potable Water (UNDP, 2005):
    • 78% of families are connected to the water network, 88% in the urban areas and 43% in the rural areas.
    • 39% of families in Iraq suffer from instability of supply of potable water.

29 See: http://www.cesar.no/Selected_publication/Selected_publication.htm

30 *Ibid.*

31 *Ibid.*

32 EIE (Elektrik İşleri Etüt). General Directorate of Electrical Power Resources Survey and Development Administration. http://www.eie.gov.tr/

33 See, for example, reports of the British NGO Oxfam and the international Red Cross/Red Crescent.

34 Consultations with Iraqi officials plus documentation provided.

35 As reported in the US State Department's press briefing regarding information on Iraq, *The Madrid Donors' Conference: Helping the Iraqi People Build a New Iraq* (cf. http://www.state.gov/p/nea/ci/c3212.htm) on 6 November 2003. State Department information on Iraq.

36 Personal communication with Iraqi officials from the Ministry of Water Resources in the fall of 2004 and in July 2005.

37 As no national data was made available regarding power tariffs and crop value, a specially designed analytical framework and data set was applied to identify the optimal irrigation strategy, based on economic considerations.

38 The following specific conclusions were drawn in the technical study:
    • "The GAP-region design irrigation volume of approximately 10 billion m³ per year may not be the economically optimal irrigation volume for Turkey. The calculations show a possible optimal irrigation volume of 6-9 billion m³ per year when environmental costs and interests downstream of the Turkish–Syrian border are excluded from the analysis. These numbers will become considerably less when such interests are considered – probably in the range 2-7 billion m³/year.
    • A reduced irrigation volume will reduce possible negative impacts on environment and public health, especially for Syria.
    • The loss of net benefits (to Turkey alone) due to maintaining a minimum flow of the Euphrates at the Turkish–Syrian border, may be considered small compared to the benefits accruing to downstream countries."

39 This section presents some selected data made available by the three countries: data publicly available, and derived data used in the model computations of power production and river discharge.

40 For the model simulations, the period chosen for analysis is 1938–1977 for the following reasons: i) data available for a 40-year period, ii) end of the simulations in a year with approximately the same runoff as the first year of analysis; and iii) inclusion of two dry cycles, 1958–1962 and 1972–1975. The figures over the forty-year period have a high correlation between the various measuring points as well as the different sources (of documentation).

41 These estimates are based on several parameters related to: data on reservoirs and hydropower stations, evaporation, reservoir capacity curves, water demand for irrigation, and assumed natural yearly average model runoff.

42 VANSIMTAP for power production and discharge in Turkey on the Euphrates River and the Tigris River, and MIKE BASIN for river discharge in Syria and into Iraq on the Euphrates River.

43 Council Directive 98/83/EC of 3 November 1998 was applied on the quality of water intended for human consumption (maximum values not to be exceeded). In addition, Council Directive 80/778/EC was applied for recommended guideline values. Many sources were examined regarding standards for water quality for irrigation purposes. Most sources make reference to the Food and Agriculture Organization of the United Nations (FAO) such as FAO (1995) on "Water quality for agriculture". The following sources and stated required water quality for agriculture irrigation in USA, Canada and Australia were also applied: CWOG (1987), NAS/NAE (1973) and Hart (1984).

44 The time of the flow-through of the water.

45 It was revealed that even with a constant conveyance of 200 m^3/s of water from the Tigris with a salinity concentration of 300 mg TDS/l, the concentration in the Euphrates River is reduced by only approximately 20 per cent. In practice, the available long-term average volume of water from the Tigris River will be less than 200 m^3/s and the salinity likely higher than 300 mg TDS/l.

46 Such actions would have to be co-ordinated with all three countries since the proposed water agreement deals with the two rivers separately.

47 It should be noted that the recommended concentration of sodium should not exceed 20 mg Na/l when supplied to hospital patients. In the lower part of the Euphrates River in Syria, all recorded data exceed this limit.

48 A rule-curve means a function that defines the use of water – either for power production or for irrigation.

49 Cf. comments of J.A. Allan on the Study of the Euphrates River and the Tigris River, Water Resource Management, Volume I – Water Resources Analysis (COMPASS, 2005), http://www.compass-org.ch/Selected_literature/selected_literature1.htm

50 Cf. EAWAG: www.eawag.ch

51 COMPASS (2005) requested assistance from EAWAG in the report: "The Euphrates River and The Tigris River – Water Resources Management: Review of Report on Water Resources Analysis, Volume I, II and III" completed in March 2003. EAWAG was truly neutral in relation to the study since it had not been involved in any way. Some other conclusions were that:
- The mass balance approach chosen for the calculation of water and salt balances for the two rivers is very useful to demonstrate and analyse the water quantity and quality problems of the rivers. The "if-then" analyses performed strongly support negotiations as they show the effects of proposed water-use scenarios if the monitored runoff and assumed return-flow regime apply.
- The lack of reliable predictions for input data with respect to Return-flow quantity and quality and changes in climatic conditions introduce uncertainty for the future management regime. Given a prescribed set of water quantity and water quality targets, it is possible to scientifically derive water management rules. However, specification of the exact target values is a matter of social negotiation process with scientific constraints. This means that our current body of knowledge does not allow specification of management rules based on scientific reasoning alone.
- EAWAG approves of the modelling approach and assesses the analyses to follow standard scientific methods. The numbers recommended by the Technical Derivates (Vol. II) report are accepted as starting values, as they in general comply with the current practices. Further river basin data should, however, as proposed in the report, be collected by rigorous monitoring to continuously validate the recommendations."
- See also: http://www.cesar.no/Selected_publication/Selected_publication.htm

52 *Category 1: Explicit Standards:* Four international treaties and two US interstate compacts comprise the first category of water-quality-related treaties. Of the four international treaties, the 1978 Great Lakes Water Quality Agreement is the broadest in scope and provides the greatest detail concerning water quality standards. The 1972 and 1973 agreements between the US and Mexico, while much narrower in scope, contain specific guidelines to reduce the salinity of Colorado waters entering Mexico. The 1994 Convention on the Co-operation for the Sustainable Use of the Danube River, like the Great Lakes Agreement, covers a range of issues related to water quality and its management and outlines a number of co-operative measures to protect the Danube waters. However, rather than defining specific standards, the convention provides a general framework from which the signatories can devise appropriate water quality objectives and criteria. Of the three US interstate compacts included in this first category, the 1941 Interstate Sanitation Commission, one of the oldest compacts addressing water quality, provides the most complete set of effluent standards. The other two compacts, 1938 Rio Grande Compact and 1948 Ohio River Valley Water Sanitation Compact, each set standards related to particular substances (e.g. suspended solids and sodium).

Category 2: General Objectives: The majority of the documents reviewed fall into this second category of agreements, those that reference general objectives or programmes related to water quality. Included in this category are the remaining nine interstate compacts and 31 of the 53 international treaties containing water quality provisions. The dates of these agreements span nearly the entire 20th century and the international treaties relate to basins located in Asia, Africa, the Middle East and Europe. The signatories to these documents agree to certain water quality goals and in many cases broadly describe measures, to be undertaken individually or jointly, to manage the quality of their shared waters. When mentioned, the details of the water quality measures outlined are entrusted to the contracting parties for further negotiations and consultations, often with the assistance of existing or newly created water commissions.

Category 3: Indefinite Commitments: Category 3 includes documents containing only vague references to pollution abatement, prevention and control. While similarities exist between the category two and three agreements, those placed in the latter category are, in general, less specific in nature and do not describe measures to achieve the stated water quality objectives. Included in this category are 16 international water treaties drafted throughout the twentieth century and representing a wide range of geographic regions. Although the references to water quality in the Category 3 agreements are generally brief, many of the treaties, like those in the previous category, include commitments by the respective signatories to further co-ordinate water quality management efforts.

53 Neither Altinbilek nor other Turkish experts and politicians have, however, specified – in terms of a water agreement – what it would mean to look at the two rivers as one basin. This might be developed as the countries choose to co-operate, such as through the more recent technical initiative (ETIC), with Kent State University in the US as the catalyst.

54 Cf. the renowned Swiss water institution, EAWAG, as described above.

55 There are several management measures for irrigation. A primary concern for irrigation water management is the discharge of salts, pesticides, and nutrients to ground water and discharge of these pollutants plus sediment to surface water. The goal of these management measures is to reduce movement of pollutants from land into ground or surface-water from the practice of irrigation. This goal is accomplished through consideration of the following aspects of an irrigation system: 1) irrigation scheduling; 2) efficient application of irrigation water; 3) efficient transport of irrigation water; 4) use of runoff or tail-water; and 5) management of drainage water (cf. EPA, 2000).

56 Global Environmental Facility, a World Bank, UNDP and UNEP arrangement dealing with management of international resources.

57 See "Minutes from the Official Text" (242, Appendix D, Mexico, 30 August 1973) between USA and Mexico signed by their respective Presidents. Regarding the desalination plant, see: Leitz, Frank *et al*, 1978.

58 See GEF: www.gefweb.org

59 Such as the UN WHO's (World Health Organization's) Water Quality Standards as well as EU legislation, especially: Directive 2000/60/EC Establishing a Framework for EU Water Legislation, Directive 76/160/EEC, Directive 80/778/EEC as amended by 98/83/EC (*Drinking Water Quality*), Directive 91/271/EEC, and Directive 91/676/EEC (*Nitrates Directive Concerning Pollution from Agricultural Production*).

60 See, for example, www.nilebasin.org

61 See http://go.worldbank.org/NIYZ0JX6J0

Annexes

Section I, Part 1
Annex 1: Third party compensation mechanism for the Golan Heights

In COMPASS' publication (*Third Party Compensation Arrangements. Water Resources Management of the Golan Heights*, 2005a), some assumptions leading to conservative estimates are assessed in more detail:

- Costs account for expected population growth during the 30-year horizon of the analysis, but assume that income levels remain constant. Water demand and wastewater production could be expected to rise with rising income levels.
- Only Syrian incremental costs of the agreement are calculated. Israel may demand compensation for costs they incur in the passing of the Golan Heights back to Syria (e.g. loss of infrastructure investments on the Golan Heights). Syria may choose to compensate Israel for these investments, but the costs are not considered integral to the costs of guaranteeing water quality and quantity. Incremental costs may in some instances be incurred by Israel (e.g. Israel importing water instead of Syria), in which case they should be subtracted from the total figures given in Table 1 (COMPASS, 2005a).
- Cropping is not assumed to intensify with higher population. Water demand for cropping remains constant. Cropping extensification is assumed unlikely. Lack of data on cropping patterns makes it hard to predict crop switching and crop intensification.
- Industrial water demand is assumed to increase proportionally with population, based on current low levels. With large population resettlement industrial intensification and more than proportional increase in water demand is likely.
- Transportation costs of industrial solid waste have not been included. There was insufficient data to predict the structure of industrial solid waste production.
- Costs of treating agricultural and urban runoff / non-point sources are not included. It is recommended that costs of treating diffuse sources be excluded because technical feasibility of pollution control is highly uncertain.
- Land acquisition costs for water and wastewater infrastructure are not included.
- Infrastructure costs of local water distribution systems on the Golan Heights have not been included. It may be argued that potable water distribution would have to be in place for the resettled Syrian population regardless of where they live. In this sense they do not spring from the guarantees made to Israel. The same could not be argued for wastewater treatment infrastructure.

Assumptions that may inflate estimates:

▸ Water supply costs do not consider the possibility of wastewater reclamation. Reuse may significantly reduce estimates of water demand.

▸ Grazing intensity is assumed to increase proportionally with population. At some point before maximum incremental population, maximum sustainable yield of pasturelands is likely to be reached.

Other main assumptions:

▸ All figures are in US$ for December 2000 unless otherwise stated.

▸ Cost calculations in Table 1 (COMPASS, 2005a) are based on a scenario of maximum incremental population of 433,000.

▸ All infrastructure costs are based on US cost data. These are deflated to Syrian price levels using a correction factor of 0.25.

▸ In selecting sanitation technologies, only technical feasibility has been considered. It has been assumed that other infrastructure is in place (roads, power supply, water supply, administration etc.) and that local resources are available (construction, materials, skilled labour etc.).

▸ Capital costs are all investment costs in year 1 and are consequently not affected by the discount rate. Investment in capital replacement during the analysis horizon is counted as recurrent cost.

▸ All costs are given at market prices. No shadow pricing has been conducted.

Section III
Annex 1: Selected international literature
As part of the CESAR Technical Study (2005b), the following international literature was investigated during 1996-1999.

Allan, J.A. 1981. "Renewable Natural Resources in the Middle East". In: J.I. Clarke and H. Bowen-Jones (Eds.), *Change and Development in the Middle East*. London: Methuen.

Allan, J.A. 1987. "Turkey's Damming of the Euphrates Could Strangle Syria's Agricultural Development". In: *Mideast Mirror Extra*, 20 July 1987, pp. 1-6.

Allan, J.A. 1988. "Water Resources in the Middle East. Economic and Strategic Issues". In: *Oxford Analytica Daily Brief*, June, 1-4.

Allan, J.A. 1992. "Substitutes for Water Being Found in the Middle East and North Africa". In: *GeoJournal, 28*(3), 375-385.

Allan, J.A. 1993. "Overall Perspectives on Countries and Regions". In: P. Rogers and P. Lydon (Eds.), *Water in the Arab World. Perspectives and Prognoses*. Cambridge, MA: Harvard University, Division of Applied Science.

Anderson, E.W. 1988. "Water. The Next Strategic Resource". In: J.R. Starr and D.C. Stoll (Eds.), *The Politics of Scarcity. Water in the Middle East*. Boulder: Westview Press.

Anderson, E.W. 1991. "The Source of Power". In: *Geographical Magazine, 3*, 12-15.

Bagis, A.I. 1994. "Water in the Region. Potential and Prospects. An Overview". In: A.I. Bagis (Ed.), *Water as an Element of Cooperation and Development in the Middle East*. Ankara: Ayna Publications and Friedrich Naumann Foundation.

Bakour, Y. 1992. "Planning and Management of Water Resources in Syria". In: G. Le Moigne *et al.* (Eds.), *Country Experiences with Water Resources Management. Economic, Institutional, Technological and Environmental Issues*. World Bank Technical Paper 175. Washington, DC: World Bank.

Bakour, Y.; J.F. Kolars. 1993 "The Arab Mashrek. Hydrologic History, Problems and Perspectives". In: P. Rogers and P. Lydon (Eds.), *Water in the Arab World. Perspectives and Prognoses*. Cambridge, MA: Harvard University, Division of Applied Science.

Barandat, J. 1993. *Wasser. Ein Neues Pulverfass. Das Internationale Gewassersystem Euphrates und Tigris*. Hamburg: Hamburger Beitrage, Institutt fur Friedensforschung und Sicherheitspolitik.

Beaumont, P. 1978. "The Euphrates River. An International Problem of Water Resources Development". In: *Environmental Conservation*, 5(1), 35-43.

Beaumont, P. 1981 "Water Resources and Their Management in the Middle East". In: Clarke, J.I. and Bowen-Jones, H. (Eds.), *Change and Development in the Middle East*. London: Methuen.

Beaumont, P. 1994. "The Myth of Water Wars and the Future of Irrigated Agriculture in the Middle East". In: *Water Resources Development*, 10(1), 9-19.

Beaumont, P.; Blake, G.H.; Wagstaff, J.M. 1988. *The Middle East. A Geographical Study*. London: David Fulton Publ.

Beschorner, N. 1992/93. *Water and Instability in the Middle East*. Adelphi Paper N° 273. London: Brassey's.

Bilen, Ö. 1994a. "A Technical Perspective on Euphrates-Tigris Basin". In: A.I. Bagis (Ed.), *Water as an Element of Cooperation and Development in the Middle East*. Ankara: Ayna Publications and Friedrich Naumann Foundation.

Bilen, Ö. 1994b. "Prospects for Technical Cooperation in the Euphrates-Tigris Basin". In: A.K. Biswas (Ed.), *International Waters of the Middle East. From Euphrates-Tigris to Nile*. Water Resources Management Series 2. Bombay: Oxford University Press.

Bilen, Ö.; Uskay, S. 1992. "Comprehensive Water Resources Management. An Analysis of Turkish Experience". In: G. Le Moigne *et al.* (Eds.), *Country Experiences with Water Resources Management. Economic, Institutional, Technological and Environmental Issues*. World Bank Technical Paper 175. Washington, DC: World Bank.

Bolukbasi, S. 1993 "Turkey Challenges Iraq and Syria. The Euphrates Dispute". In: *Journal of South Asian and Middle Eastern Studies*, 14(4), 9-32.

Braun, A. 1994 "The Megaproject of Mesopotamia". In: *CERES. FAO Review on Development*, (2), 25-30.

Bulloch, J.; Darwish, A. 1993. *Water Wars. Coming Conflicts in the Middle East*. London: Victor Gollancz.

Caelleigh, A.S. 1983 "Middle East Water. Vital Reource, Conflict and Cooperation". In: J.R. Starr and A.S. Caelleigh (Eds.), *A Shared Destiny. Near East Regional Development and Cooperation*. New York: Praeger.

Chalabi, H.; Majzoub, T. 1995 "Turkey, the Waters of the Euphrates and Public International Law". In: J.A. Allan and C. Mallat (Eds.), *Water in the Middle East. Legal, Political and Commercial Implications*. London: Tauris Academic Studies.

CIA World Factbook. 1995. *Iraq*. (Online document). Retrieved at: http://www.umsl.edu/services/govdocs/wofact96/125.htm

CIA World Factbook. 1995. *Syria*. (Online document). Retrieved at: http://www.umsl.edu/services/govdocs/wofact96/240.htm

CIA World Factbook. 1995. *Turkey*. (Online document). Retrieved at: http://www.umsl.edu/services/govdocs/wofact96/251.htm

Clawson, M.; Landsberg, H.H.; Alexander, L.T. 1971. *The Agricultural Potential of the Middle East*. New York: American Elsevier Publishing Co.

Cohen, J.E. 1991. "International Law and the Water Politics of the Euphrates". In: *International Law and Politics*, *25*(503), 502-556.

Cragg, C. 1996. "Water Resources in the Middle East and North Africa". In: *The Middle East and North Africa*. London: Europa Publications.

del Rio Luelmo, J. 1996. "Water and Regional Conflict. Turkey's Peace Pipeline". In: *European Urban and Regional Studies*, *3*(1), 67-74.

Dellapenna, J.W. 1986. *Water Resources in the Middle East. Impact on Economics and Politics*. Proceedings of the Annual Meeting. Chicago: American Society of International Law.

Dewdney, J.C. 1981. "Agricultural Development in Turkey". In: J.I. Clarke and H. Bowen-Jones (Eds.), *Change and Development in the Middle East*. London: Methuen.

Doluca, K.; Pircher, W. 1971. "Development in the Euphrates River in Basin in Turkey". In: *Water Power. International Development of Hydro-Electric Power*, *23*, 47-55.

DSI in Brief. 1995. Ankara: Ministry of Public Works and Settlement, General Directorate of State Hydraulic Works.

Economist Intelligence Unit (EIU). 1994. *Country Profile. Turkey*. London: Economist Intelligence Unit.

Economist Intelligence Unit (EIU). 1995a. *Country Profile. Iraq. 1995-96*. London: Economist Intelligence Unit.

Economist Intelligence Unit (EIU). 1995b. *Country Profile. Syria. 1995-96*. London: Economist Intelligence Unit.

Economist Intelligence Unit (EIU). 1996a. *Country Report. Iraq*. London: Redhouse Press.

Economist Intelligence Unit (EIU). 1996b. *Country Report. Syria*. London: Redhouse Press.

Embassy of the Republic of Turkey. 1996. (Online document). Retrieved at: http://turkey.org/

Ertan, N. 1995. "Birecik Dam. New Trouble Spot Between Turkey and Syria". In: *Turkish Daily News*, 21 December 1995.

FAOSTAT Statistics Database. 1996. (Online document). Retrieved at: http://apps.fao.org

GAP Main Web Server. 1996. (Online document). Retrieved at: http://www.turkey.org/al_gap.htm

Gould, St. J.B. 1992 "The Troubled Arab Middle East". In: G. Chapman and K. Baker (Eds.), *The Changing Geography of Africa and The Middle East*. London: Routledge.

Hale, W. 1996. "Turkey". In: P. Sluglett and M. Farouk-Sluglett (Eds.), *The Times Guide to the Middle East. The Arab World and its Neighbours*. London: Times Books.

Hellier, C. 1990. "Draining the Rivers Dry". In: *Geographical Magazine*, 7, 32-35.

International Fund for Agricultural Research (IFAR). 1993. *Agriculture in Syria. The Role of International Agricultural Research Centers*. Country Report N° 4. Arlington, VA: International Fund for Agricultural Research.

International Institute for Strategic Studies. 1992. "Water Resources. Scarcity and Conflict". In: *Strategic Survey 1991-1992*. London: Brassey's.

Keenan, J.D. 1992. "Technological Aspects of Water Resources Management. Euphrates and Jordan". In: G. Le Moigne *et al.* (Eds.), *Country Experiences with Water Resources Management. Economic, Institutional, Technological and Environmental Issues*. World Bank Technical Paper 175. Washington, DC: World Bank.

Kemp, P. 1996. "New War of Words over Scarce Water". In: *Middle East Economic Digest (MEED)*, 40, 2-3, 1 March 1996.

Kliot, N. 1994. *Water Resources and Conflict in the Middle East*. London: Routledge.

Kolars, J.F.; Mitchell, W.A. 1991. *The Euphrates River and the Southeast Anatolia Development Project*. (Water. The Middle East Imperative). Carbondale: Southern Illinois University Press.

Kolars, J.F. 1992. "The Future of the Euphrates Basin". In: G. Le Moigne *et al.* (Eds.), *Country Experiences with Water Resources Management. Economic, Institutional, Technological and Environmental Issues*. World Bank Technical Paper 175. Washington, DC: World Bank.

Kolars, J.F. 1994a. "Managing the Impact of Development. The Euphrates and Tigris Rivers and the Ecology of the Arabian Gulf. A Link in Forging Tri-Riparian Cooperation". In: A.I. Bagis (Ed.), *Water as an Element of Cooperation and Development in the Middle East*. Ankara: Ayna Publications; Friedrich Naumann Foundation.

Kolars, J.F. 1994b. "Problems of International River Management. The Case of the Euphrates". In: A.K. Biswas (Ed.), *International Waters of the Middle East. From Euphrates–Tigris to Nile*. Water Resources Management Series 2. Bombay: Oxford University Press.

Lorenz, F.M.; Erickson, E.J. (Eds.), 1999. *Security Implications of the South Anatolia Project, The Euphrates Triangle*. USA: Better World Books.

Meliczek, H. 1987. *Land Settlements in the Euphrates Basin of Syria, in Land Reform. Land Settlement and Co-operatives*. Rome: Food and Agricultural Organization (FAO).

Ministry of Foreign Affairs, Department of Regional and Transboundary Water. 1996. *Water Issues between Turkey Syria and Iraq*. Ankara: Ministry of Foreign Affairs.

Morris, M.E. 1991. "Poisoned Wells. The Politics of Water in the Middle East". In: *Middle East Insight*, 8(2), 35-40.

Morvaridi, B. 1990. *Agrarian Reform and Land Use Policy in Turkey. Implications for the Southeast Anatolia Project*. (Land Use Policy). Butterworth: Heinemann.

Murakami, M. 1995. *Managing Water for Peace in the Middle East*. Tokyo: United Nations University Press.

Musallam, R. 1990. "Water. Source of Conflict in the Middle East in the 1990's". In: *Contemporary Strategic Issues in the Arab Gulf*, 9, 1-22.

Mutlu, S. 1996. "The Southeastern Anatolia Project (GAP) of Turkey; its Context, Objectives and Prospects". In: *Orient* (German Journal for Politics and Economics of the Middle East), 37, 59-86.

Naff, T.; Matson, R.C. (Eds.). 1984. *Water in the Middle East. Conflict or Cooperation?* Boulder: Westview Press.

OECD. 1992. *Environmental Policies in Turkey*. Paris: OECD.

Olcay Ünver, I.H. 1994. "Innovations in Water Resources Development in the Southeastern Anatolia Development Project (GAP) of Turkey". In: A.I. Bagis (Ed.), *Water as an Element of Cooperation and Development in the Middle East* (pp. 27-37). Ankara: Ayna Publications; Friedrich Naumann Foundation.

Olcay Ünver, I.H. 1995. *The Southeastern Anatolia Project (GAP). An Introduction. Seminar. The Southeastern Anatolia Project & Business and Investment Opportunities in Turkey*. Assembly of Turkish American Association, 26-27 October 1995, California, USA.

Özal, K. 1994. "Water and Land Resources Development in Southeastern Turkey". In: M. Ergin, H.D. Altinbilek, and M.R. Zou'bi (Eds.), *Water in the Islamic World. An Imminent Crisis*. Amman: The Islamic Academy of Sciences.

Postel, S. 1993. "The Politics of Water". In: *World Watch, 6*, July/August, 10-18.

Prime Ministry State Institute of Statistics (SIS). 1996. *Republic of Turkey*. (Online document). Retrieved at: http://www.die.gov.tr/ENGLISH/sis-bil.html

Roberts, N. 1991. "Geopolitics and the Euphrates' Water Resources" In: *Geography, 76*(331), 157-159.

Robins, P. 1991. *Turkey and the Middle East*. The Royal Institute of International Affairs (Chatham House Paper). London: Pinter Publ.

Rogers, P. 1993. "The Agenda for the Next Thirty Years". In: P. Rogers and P. Lydon (Eds.), *Water in the Arab World. Perspectives and Prognoses*. Cambridge, MA: Harvard University, Division of Applied Science.

Sabri, A.W.; Rasheed, K.A.; Kassim, T.I. 1993. "Heavy Metals in the Water, Suspended Solids and Sediment of the River Tigris Impoundment at Samarra". In: *Water Resources, 27*(6), 1099-1103.

Sadik, A.-K.; Barghouti, S. 1993. "The Water Problems of the Arab World. Management of Scarce Resources". In: P. Rogers and P. Lydon (Eds.), *Water in the Arab World. Perspectives and Prognoses*. Cambridge, MA: Harvard University, Division of Applied Science.

Saeijs, H.L.F.; van Berkel, M.J. 1995 "Global Water Crisis. The Major Issue of the 21st Century. A Growing and Explosive Problem". In: *European Water Pollution Control, 5*(4), 26-40.

Savage, C. 1991. "Middle East Water". In: *Journal of the Royal Society for Asian Affairs, 22*(1), 3-10.

Scheuman, W. 1993. "New irrigation schemes in Southeast Anatolia and in northern Syria. More competition and conflict over the Euphrates?" In: *Quarterly Journal of International Agriculture, 3*, 240-59.

Schulz, M. 1992. "Turkey, Syria and Iraq. A Hydropolitical Security Complex. The Case of Euphrates and Tigris". In: L. Ohlsson (Ed.), *Regional Case Studies of Water Conflicts*. (Padigru Papers). Gothenburg: Vasastadens Bokbinderi.

Shahin, M. 1989 "Review and Assessment of Water Resources in the Arab Region". In: *Water International, 14*(4), 206-219.

Slim, R.M. 1993. "Turkey, Syria, Iraq. the Euphrates". In: G.O. Faure and J.Z. Rubin (Eds.), *Culture and Negotiation. The Resolution of Water Disputes*. Newbury: Sage.

Sluglett, P.; Farouk-Sluglett, M. 1996a. "Iraq". In: P. Sluglett and M. Farouk-Sluglett (Eds.), *The Times Guide to the Middle East. The Arab World and its Neighbours*. London: Times Books.

Sluglett, P.; Farouk-Sluglett, M. 1996b. "Syria". In: P. Sluglett and M. Farouk-Sluglett (Eds.), *The Times Guide to the Middle East. The Arab World and its Neighbours*. London: Times Books.

Southeastern Anatolia Project Regional Development Administration. 1996. GAP. Project. (Online document). Retrieved at. http://www.turkey.org/al_gap.htm

Starr, J.R. 1990. "Water politics in the Middle East". In: *Middle East Insight*, *7*(2-3), 64-70.

Starr, J.R. 1991. "Water wars". In: *Foreign Policy*, *82*, 17-36.

Starr, J.R.; Stoll, D.C. 1988. "Water for the year 2000". In: J.R. Starr and D.C. Stoll (Eds.), *The Politics of Scarcity. Water in the Middle East*. Boulder: Westview Press.

Stevens, J.H. 1981. "Irrigation in the Arab Countries of the Middle East". In: J.I. Clarke and H. Bowen-Jones (Eds.), *Change and Development in the Middle East*. London: Methuen.

Struck, E. 1994. "Das Sudostanatolien-Project. die Bewasserung und Ihre Folgen". In: *Geographische Rundschau*, *46*(2), 88-120.

Syria Statistical Survey. 1993. *The Middle East and North Africa 1994*. London: Europa Publications Limited.

Tekeli, S.M. 1990. "Turkey Seeks Reconciliation for the Water Issue Induced by the Southeastern Anatolia Project". In: *Water International*, *15*(4), 206-216.

Tekinel, O. *et al*. 1992. *Water Resources, Planning and Development in Turkey*. Workshop on Water Resources Development and Management in the Mediterranean Countries, organized by International Center for Advanced Mediterranean Agronomic Studies. (CIHEAM-TAM/ BARI) University of Cukorova, Faculty of Agriculture (Number 77). 7 September 1992, Adara, Turkey.

Toepfer, H. 1989. "Das Sudostanatolien-Projekt, in Erdkunde". In: *Archiv für Wissenschaftliche Geographie*, *43*(4), 293-299.

Trolldalen [Trondalen], J.M. 1992. *International Environmental Conflict Resolution. The Role of the United Nations*. Geneva; New York: World Foundation for Environment and Development; UNITAR; NIDR; WFED.

Turan, I. 1993. "Turkey and the Middle East. Problems and Solutions". In: *Water International*, *18*(1), 23-29.

Turkish Daily News. 1996. "Turco-Syrian Relations Get Tense over Water". In: *Turkish Daily News*, 1 January 1996.

Turkish Ministry of Foreign Affairs. 1996. *Facts about Euphrates-Tigris Basin*. Ankara: Centre for Strategic Research.

Unver, O.I. 1994. "Innovations in Water Resources Development in the Southeastern Anatolia Development Project (GAP) of Turkey". In: A.I. Bagis (Ed.), *Water as an Element of Cooperation and Development in the Middle East*. Ankara: Ayna Publications; Friedrich Naumann Foundation.

US Army Corps of Engineers. 1991. *Water in the Sand. A Survey of Middle East Water Issues*. Washington, DC: US Army Corps of Engineers.

Vesilind, P.J. 1993. "Water. The Middle East's critical resource". In: *National Geographic*, *183*(5), 43-70.

Wachtel, B. 1994. "The 'Peace Canal' Plan. A New Model for the Distribution and Management of Water Resources and a Catalyst for Co-operation in the Middle East". In: A.I. Bagis (Ed.), *Water as an Element of Cooperation and Development in the Middle East*. Ankara: Ayna Publications; Friedrich Naumann Foundation.

Wakil, M. 1993. "Analysis of future water needs for different sectors in Syria". In: *Water International*, *18*(1), 18-22.

Waterbury, J. 1993. "Transboundary Water and the Challenge of International Cooperation in the Middle East". In: P. Rogers and P. Lydon (Eds.), *Water in the Arab World. Perspectives and Prognoses*. Cambridge, MA: Harvard University, Division of Applied Science.

World Bank. 1994. *From Scarcity to Security. Averting a Water Crisis in the Middle East and North Africa*. Washington, DC: World Bank.

Ya'ar, I. 1994. "Water Disputes as Factors in the Middle East conflicts". In: C. Addis (Ed.), *Seaford House Papers*. London: Royal College of Defense Studies.

Yavuz, H.; Cakmak, E.H. 1996. *Water Policy Reform in Turkey*. Ankara: Bilkent University, Department of Economics.

Annex 2:
Overview of agreements on the Euphrates River and the Tigris River, joint technical meetings, and tripartite ministerial meetings between Turkey, Syria and Iraq.

This list is based on numerous oral and written sources and put together by the CESAR Foundation.

Agreements on the Euphrates and the Tigris Rivers

Dec. 1920

Convention on Certain Points connected with the Mandates for Syria and the Lebanon, Palestine and Mesopotamia [France (Syria), United Kingdom (Iraq)]

- Article 3 recognizes the importance of co-operation on irrigation plans that could diminish to a considerable degree the Euphrates and Tigris waters entering Iraq.

Oct. 1921

Agreement with View to Promoting Peace (Franklin-Boillon) [France (Syria), Turkey]

- Refers to the right of riparian states to share the waters of a transboundary river to give equitable satisfaction to the two Parties.
- Article 12 recognizes a right of the Syrian city of Aleppo to use Euphrates water in Turkish territory to meet its requirements.

July 1923

Lausanne Peace Treaty [Turkey, Allied]

- Article 109 affirms the necessity for agreement between states to manage transboundary waters.
- Includes a provision that Turkey must consult Iraq before undertaking any hydraulic works.

May 1926

Convention of Friendship and Good Neighbourly Relations [France (Syria), Turkey]

- Article 13 asserts Turkey's full co-operation for the purpose of necessary investigations.

May 1930

Final Protocol of the Commission of Delimitation [France (Syria), Turkey]

- Commits the two Parties to co-ordinate any plans to utilize the Euphrates waters.
- Article 2 contains some provisions regarding the Tigris.

March 1946

Ankara Treaty of Friendship and Good Neighbourliness [Turkey, Iraq]

- In Protocol 1 Turkey: obliges itself to report to Iraq on all its plans to utilize the Euphrates and Tigris waters; agrees to install permanent observation stations and ensure their operation and maintenance (costs of operation to be defrayed in equal parts by Iraq and Turkey); and accepts in principle the Iraqi right to construct dams within Turkish territory when necessary to improve Euphrates flow within Iraq.

1964

Turkey pledged to release 350 m³/sec of Euphrates water.

1976

Turkey increased the minimum flow to 450 m³/sec. (during Syria's impoundment of water for the Tabqa Dam).

July 1987

Protocol of Economic Cooperation

Temporary arrangement pending a tripartite agreement [Turkey–Syria]

- In Article 6 Turkey agreed to release a yearly average of more than 500 m³/sec (during filling of Ataturk and until final allocation).
- Article 7 asserts that Turkey and Syria should work together with Iraq to allocate Euphrates and Tigris waters within shortest possible time.
- In Article 9 both states agreed in principle to construct and jointly operate irrigation and HEP projects.

April 1990

Bilateral agreement between Syria and Iraq for sharing Euphrates waters

- Syria would receive 42% and Iraq 58% of annual flows, regardless of quantity.

Joint Technical Meetings on Regional Waters

1962

Syria and Iraq formed a Joint Technical Committee, which had a very limited role as there were no major constructions at this time.

1972-73

Unsuccessful attempts by Syria and Iraq to negotiate an agreement on Euphrates waters.

1980

Protocol of the Turkish-Iraqi Joint Committee for Economic and Technical Cooperation - Creation of a Joint Technical Committee for Regional Waters (JTC)

May 1982

First JTC Meeting in Ankara, with experts from Turkey and Iraq
- Field trip to some Turkish project sites.
- Exchange of information on existing and planned projects.
- Iraq: river basins discussed separately; Turkey: rivers and tributaries as one basin.
- Preparation of detailed hydrology studies for next meeting.
- Iraqi proposal for basic data required (Annex 1).
- Renewed invitation to Syria.

Nov./Dec. 1982

Second JTC Meeting in Baghdad, with experts from Turkey and Iraq
- Continued exchange of information on existing and planned projects.
- Iraq: river basins discussed separately, Turkey: rivers and tributaries as one basin.
- Renewed invitation to Syria.

Sep. 1983

Third JTC Meeting in Ankara, with experts from Turkey, Syria and Iraq
- Syria informed about previous JTC work, which Syria agreed should continue.
- Exchange of available information on regional waters at next meeting.

June 1984

Fourth JTC Meeting in Baghdad, with experts from Turkey, Syria and Iraq
- Field trip to an irrigation project in the Tigris basin.
- Continued exchange of hydrological data.
- Opinions on Iraq's proposal for data required (Annex 1 of First JTC Meeting).

Nov. 1984

Fifth JTC Meeting in Damascus, with experts from Turkey, Syria and Iraq
- Field trip to Yarmouk Irrigation project.
- Discussion of ways to expand and improve exchange of hydrological and meteorological information.
- Turkish proposal (Annex 4) for sub-committees (hydrology, soil, agricultural economy, engineering planning).

June 1985

Sixth JTC Meeting in Ankara, with experts from Turkey, Syria and Iraq
- Field trip to Karakaya Project.

- Discussion of ways to expand and improve exchange of hydrological and meteorological information.
- Views on Turkish proposal for sub-committees (Annex 4 of Fifth JTC Meeting): Turkey insisted on proposal, while Syria and Iraq disagreed.

Jan. 1986

Seventh JTC Meeting in Baghdad, with experts from Turkey, Syria and Iraq
- Field trip to barrages under construction (Kufa and Abbasiya).
- Discussion of ways to expand and improve exchange of hydrological and meteorological information.
- Discussion on previous Turkish and Iraqi propositions.
- Turkey presented amended proposition (Annex 4).
- Turkish statement regarding impoundment of Karakaya reservoir.
- Importance of regional water pollution investigations, exchange of related data.

June 1986

Eighth JTC Meeting in Damascus, with experts from Turkey, Syria and Iraq
- Field trip to sections of the Euphrates Projects near Raqqa and Deirezzor.
- Discussion of ways to expand and improve exchange of hydrological and meteorological information.
- Importance of regional water pollution investigations, exchange of related data.
- Exchanged information on progress in construction of dams.
- Turkey informed on impoundment of Karakaya.
- Iraq informed on impoundment of Kadasiya.
- Proposals by all three countries studied: agreement on hydrological and meteorological items, but not on other items.

Nov. 1986

Ninth JTC Meeting in Ankara, scheduled at the Eight JTC Meeting

Jan. 1988

Tenth JTC Meeting in Baghdad, with experts from Turkey, Syria and Iraq
- Field trip to the new Hindiya Barrage project on The Euphrates River.
- Continued exchange of hydrological and meteorological information.
- Exchanged information on present situation of dam construction and reservoir impoundment.
- Discussed different viewpoints concerning the work of the JTC.
- Turkey submitted modified proposal (Annex 4): agreement reached on hydrological studies but not on soil, agricultural and engineering items.
- Took note on the joint measurements of the Euphrates discharge at Belkiskoy, Jarablus and Kadahyeh, which had been performed by Turkish and Syrian sides for four runs, with the presence of Iraqi observers for the third run.

Nov. 1988

Eleventh JTC Meeting in Damascus, with experts from Turkey, Syria and Iraq
- Discussion of ways to continue and improve exchange of hydrological and meteorological information.

- Exchanged information on progress in construction of dams.
- Discussed different viewpoints concerning the work of the JTC.
- Discussed Turkey's modified proposal (Annex 4 of Tenth JTC Meeting): agreement reached on hydrological studies but not on all other points.
- Wish to intensify meetings to fulfil determined task of the JTC.

March 1989

Twelfth JTC Meeting in Ankara, with experts from Turkey, Syria and Iraq

- Field trip to Ataturk Dam Project.
- Exchanged hydrological data.
- Exchanged information on progress in construction of dams.
- Discussed mechanism for studying water requirements of the three countries: no progress achieved, need to intensify efforts to reach common viewpoint.

April 1989

Thirteenth JTC Meeting in Baghdad, with experts from Turkey, Syria and Iraq

- Field trip to Saddam project on the Tigris River and to pumping station of North Jazira project in Nineva province.
- Exchanged hydrological data: Turkey agreed to provide hydrological and meteorological information for better management during the drought for current water year.
- Exchanged information on progress in construction of dams.
- Iraq informed on Thartar and Main Outfall Drain projects.
- Did not reach common understanding on:
  - whether Euphrates and Tigris should be viewed separately or as one basin;
  - methodology to study and assess factors related to the mandate of JTC.

Nov./Dec. 1989

Fourteenth JTC Meeting in Damascus, with experts from Turkey, Syria and Iraq

- Exchanged hydrological and meteorological data.
- Exchanged information on progress in construction of dams.
- Turkey informed on initiation of impounding of Ataturk reservoir.
- Syria and Iraq asked Turkey to shorten the closure period.
- Turkey: not technically possible, has already been fixed for a minimum range.

March 1990

JTC Meeting in Ankara, with experts from Turkey, Syria and Iraq

- Turkey's proposal for scientific research regarding water use rejected.
- Syria and Iraq insisted on agreement on water distribution instead of more studies.

May 1990

JTC Meeting, with experts from Turkey, Syria and Iraq

- Iraq demanded an increase of the Euphrates flow to 700 m^3/sec

Sep. 1992

JTC Meeting in Damascus, with experts from Turkey, Syria and Iraq

- Syria and Iraq reiterated call for a trilateral agreement.

- Turkey argued that the 1987 quota agreement was equitable and adequate for downstream needs, and that Syria and Iraq should use water more efficiently.

Tripartite Ministerial Meetings on Regional Transboundary Watercourses

Nov. 1988
First Ministerial Meeting

May 1989
Scheduled Ministerial Meeting did not take place.

June 1990
Second Ministerial Meeting in Ankara, with Irrigation Ministers from Turkey, Syria and Iraq
- Turkey defined the Euphrates flow as 'transboundary waters', while Syria and Iraq consider The Euphrates River to be 'international'.
- Turkey's Three-Staged Plan for Optimum, Equitable and Reasonable Utilization of the Transboundary Watercourses of the Tigris-Euphrates Basin.
- Syrian proposal on mission of the committee.
- Iraqi proposal that Turkey will release not less than 700 m^3/sec at the Turkish-Syrian border until a final agreement on water distribution has been reached.

Jan. 2001
Affirmation of the not-public bilateral agreement between Syria and Iraq (from April 1990) for sharing Euphrates waters
Syria would receive 42% and Iraq 58% of annual flows (from Turkey to Syria), regardless of quantity.

Annex 3: Planning structure, data and methods

Illustration of the planning structure of the water resource management analysis for the Euphrates and the Tigris River basin

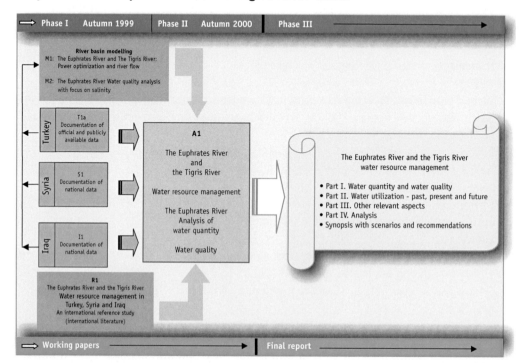

Data and methods

During the process of the study, the data made available by the three countries was considered to be of adequate reliability and validity to be able to draw conclusions with an acceptable degree of accuracy.

The key areas of water management regarding the two rivers are dealt with *in extenso* in the study, including the data, the methods applied, and the technical analyses of the modelling data. In order to fulfil the stated objectives, the following methodological approach was applied:

▸ Adapt and evaluate river basin data authorized by the watercourse countries, as well as publicly available national data.
▸ Perform an assessment of existing water quality data in relation to international guidelines on water quality for different usages, with a focus on drinking water and irrigation.
▸ Perform an assessment of hydro-power production in Turkey (the only country with significant hydro-power production).

- Accomplish sensitivity analysis and appurtenant consequence analysis of different management policies regarding: economical efficiency of the water; water quantity; and water quality.

In the technical study, only the questions asked, the findings, and the reservations regarding the validity of the results are described. The scope of the study is described with respect to the four areas of analysis: optimized power production; economical efficiency; water quantity; and water quality.

One may argue that the emphasis should have been put on other aspects, but during the course of consultations with the three countries, as well as the application of accepted principles of river basin studies, these four areas were emphasized.

Annex 4: Use of terms in the proposed trilateral water agreements

A Trilateral Water Agreement for the *Euphrates River* and the *Tigris River* means (a) water management agreement(s) of the two *watercourses* for the three *watercourse countries;*

Watercourses means in this context the two rivers constituting, by virtue of the relationship between the two, interlinked watersheds;

A watercourse state or country refers to Turkey, Syria or Iraq, as riparian to the two watercourses;

A Regional Water Management Organization means an organization that deals with the implementation of a *Trilateral Water Agreement and the TPCM;*

A Third Party Compensation Mechanism (TPCM) is a fund set up to assist the core states to implement the agreement, especially related to maintaining water quality and improving efficiency.

In addition, the following definitions apply to:

a.	Consumption:	The total long-term average volume of water consumed by all users (including return-flow), e.g., domestic, industrial and agricultural.
b.	Target consumption:	The design value for the consumption.
c.	Actual consumption:	The total volume of water extracted from the sources in a single year
d.	Design return flow:	The planned feedback of water to the sources generated by the target consumption.
e.	Net target consumption:	Target consumption minus the design return flow.
f.	Total yearly runoff:	The total volume of water generated in a watercourse in a year.
g.	Total yearly flow:	The volume of water passing a monitoring station in a year, expressed as m^3/year.
h.	Discharge:	The volume of water passing a monitoring station at any moment of time, expressed as m^3/s.
i.	Average discharge:	Total yearly flow divided by $31,536 \times 10^6$.
j.	Minimum discharge:	The absolute minimum discharge not to be less than the stated value.
k.	Maximum discharge:	The absolute maximum discharge not to be exceeded.
l.	Rule curve:	A function that defines the use of water – either for power production or for irrigation.
m.	Reservoir level:	The water level in a reservoir relative to a defined zero level.
n.	Active reservoir:	The part of the total reservoir volume that may be used in the reservoir management.

Annex 5: Possible common elements in any trilateral water agreement

Reservations: The author does not expect that any trilateral river basin agreement will look exactly like the proposed one. Any agreement is subject to political and technical negotiations, and the technical study does not provide enough scientific underpinning to propose exact figures nor an actual text. It does, however, attempt to illustrate what such an agreement could look like.

Urgency: More importantly, however, the proposed agreement illustrates how the three countries could develop an agreement that includes some important principles for sustainable water management. **Please note:** In case the three countries decide to consider the two rivers as one basin, the allocated water volumes to Turkey and Syria will probably be reduced (since the rule-curves for each river may not be applied). However, if water pollution is more or less going to be ignored, the allocated water volumes to Turkey and Syria may increase.

Part I. CO-OPERATIVE ACTIONS

I.   A Regional Water Management Organization

A Regional Water Management Organization shall implement the Trilateral Water Agreement and the Third Party Compensation Mechanism, and the strategies derived thereof.

The Organization consists of 6 members – 2 from each Core State, appointed by the respective state. In addition, 3 additional extra-regional members will be invited by the Core States that will bring in funding, expertise and additional oversight. The Chair is held by each Core State in turn for a period of 1 year – starting in alphabetical order.

II.   Regional Water Management Organization meetings

Regular Steering Group meetings

The Group meetings are normally held twice a year. The agenda shall include, but not be limited to the following items:

1. Adoption of the draft agenda, and approval of the minutes from the last meeting.
2. Based on the reports from the Technical Group on water quantity and water quality for the previous 6-month period, make a decision on strategy for the next 6 months on water quantity and water quality [as an input into operation of rule-curves].
3. Based on the reports from the Technical Group, make a decision on management of the monitoring and verification mechanism.
4. Based on the reports from the Technical Group, make a management decision for the Third Party Compensation Mechanism.

II.   Regular Technical Group meetings

The Technical Group Meetings are held prior to the Steering Group meetings and give technical recommendations to the Group. The agenda shall include, but not be limited, to the following items:

1. Adoption of the draft agenda and approval of the minutes from the last meeting.
2. Status reports on water quantity and water quality for the previous 6-month period.
3. Recommendation on strategy for the next 6 months on water quantity and water quality [as an input into operation of rule-curves].
4. Discussion and recommendation on monitoring and verification procedures and functionality.
5. Discussion and recommendation on use of funds from the Third Party Compensation Mechanism.

III. Emergency meetings

Any diversion from the stated limiting water quantity or quality value ranges (timeframe defined), emergency meetings may be called for by any of the Core States or one of the 3 extra-regional ones. After notification is given to the Chairman, the meeting shall be held within 2 weeks. The agenda of the emergency meetings are determined by the problem faced, and the purpose of the meeting is to agree on suitable actions.

III. Consecutive model calibration and analysis

The Regional Water Management Organization should work towards managing a regional water management model for the simulation of water quantity and water quality.

The model shall undergo a consecutive calibration based on the 6-month status reports to be able to predict short-term effects and long-term changes under the prevailing conditions.

IV. Verification

All monitoring systems in the watercourse countries related to the .... and .... shall be subject to verification by the Regional Water Management Organization. The watercourse countries shall approve verification procedures before they are put into force.

V. Notification concerning planned measures with possible adverse affects

(The Regional Water Management Organization shall be notified of any planned measure, which may have an adverse effect on the watercourse environment for verification and approval. Such notification shall be accompanied by technical data and information including the results of any environmental impact assessment.)

PART II: GENERAL PRINCIPLES

VI. Equitable and reasonable utilisation and participation[a]

The watercourse countries shall in their respective territories utilize the international watercourses in an equitable and reasonable manner. In particular, the watercourses shall be used and developed by the watercourse countries with a view to attain optimal and sustainable utilization thereof and benefits, therefore, taking into account the interests of the watercourse countries concerned, consistent with adequate protection of the watercourses.

The watercourse countries shall participate in the use, development and protection of the watercourses in an equitable and reasonable manner. Such participation includes both the right to utilize the watercourses and the duty to co-operate in the protection thereof, as provided in an agreement.

VII. Factors relevant to equitable and reasonable utilization[b]

PART III: WATER ALLOCATION PRINCIPLES AND VALUES

VIII. Basis for agreed water allocation and water quality parameters and values:

1. The following water allocation and water quality principles and values must be based on agreed base-line documentation[c] (e.g., over a 2-5 year period) as a co-operative action between the three watercourse countries.

2. Final water allocation and water quality parameters and values must therefore be based on the above-mentioned documentation.

3. It should be noted that the allocation principles and values are based on the prerequisite that a minimum discharge at the point of convergence of the two watercourses should probably not be less than 150 m³/s of the Euphrates River.

4. Based of the data available, the following indicative and preliminary water allocation and water quality parameters and values are suggested:

PART IV: WATER FLOW BALANCE MANAGEMENT

XII. Flow monitoring in the Euphrates River and the Tigris River

The watercourse countries shall establish harmonized river discharge monitoring systems. Monitoring shall be performed according to internationally accepted standards. This shall include, but not be limited to:

- two real-time monitoring stations in each state;

- the number and location of stations shall be agreed upon by the watercourse countries;
- discharge figures are electronically stored once a day;
- flow data shall be reported twice a year for each of the watercourse countries (according to Part I, sub-para. II).

XIII. Monitoring of reservoir volume

Remaining reservoir volume is the basis of the application of rule-curves for power production and irrigation.

As reservoir volume is a function of reservoir level, the reservoir level shall be monitored with an agreed accuracy.

Reservoir level results shall be reported (at least) twice a year with computed data for reservoir volume (according to para. II).

XIV. Watercourse volume of water assessment

Available runoff in the watercourse is a function of precipitation and other climatic conditions.

To meet any unforeseen emergency situations, with respect to water quality, an available runoff assessment system shall be established.

PART V: WATER QUALITY MANAGEMENT

XV. Environment protection and preservation

The watercourse countries shall individually and, where appropriate, jointly:

- protect and preserve the hydrological ecosystems; and
- prevent, reduce and control pollution that may cause significant harm to the environment, including public health and safety of the users of the water of the Euphrates Watercourse and the Tigris Watercourse.

Once a year, a biota classification is performed on one agreed location in each of the watercourse countries on the Euphrates River and the Tigris River.

Paragraph XVI is specified in the two models[c]: *XVI Preliminary maximum permissible values*

XVII. Water quality monitoring system

The watercourse countries shall establish harmonized water quality monitoring systems. Monitoring and water analyses shall be performed according to internationally accepted standards. This shall include, but not be limited to:

- two real-time monitoring stations in each watercourse country;
- the number and location of stations shall be agreed upon by the countries;
- one water sampling station in each country where a 24-hour composite sample is taken once a week.

XVIII. Water transport from or between the watercourses

This section has to be tailored to either single-basin or twin-basin models.

---

a) The text in this section is based on the same article in the UN Framework Convention on the Law of Non-navigational Uses of International Watercourses.

b) The text is subject to development at a later stage since it is interlinked with a final agreement.

c) In the technical study, models for the Euphrates River and the Tigris River are based on a 40-year rainfall/runoff period: 1938-1977 and 1948-1987, respectively.

Paragraphs IX, X, XI and XVI are illustrated at the end of this Annex relating to (IX) Water use and water allocation, (X) Rule-curve for irrigation for the Euphrates watercourse, (XI) Preliminary values of discharge of the Euphrates River, and (XVI) Preliminary maximum permissable values.

INDICATIVE WATER USE AND WATER ALLOCATION IN 'SEPARATE-BASIN MODEL'

IX. Water use and water allocation

The following indicative water allocation values could be further elaborated, with the values for the Euphrates having a stronger technical basis than those for the Tigris.

Approximate water allocation for the Euphrates watercourse[1]

	Target consumption, billion m³/year		
	Turkey	Syria	Iraq
Euphrates	7	7	13

Illustrative water allocation for the Tigris watercourse[2]

	Target consumption, billion m³/year		
	Turkey	Syria	Iraq
Tigris	7	3	x[3]

The two tables reflect the result of the technical study that there is a need of a minimum flow of the Euphrates River at the point of convergence of the two rivers (the exact amount to be determined).

X. Rule-curve for irrigation for the Euphrates watercourse

To prevent the Euphrates watercourse from being polluted – especially during the dry periods – rule-curves for the extraction of water for irrigation purposes should be applied.

The rule-curves shall be revised according to the results of a yearly rule-curve evaluation. It might look like the following:

Approximate rule-curve for irrigation of the Euphrates watercourse

Remaining active reservoir volume	Permissible extraction, % of target consumption		
	Turkey	Syria	Iraq
V > 75%	100	100	100
50% < V < 75%	80	80	80
25% < V < 50%	40	40	40
V < 25%	0	0	0

XI. Preliminary values of discharge of the Euphrates River

Parameters	At Turkish-Syrian border	At Syrian-Iraqi border	At convergence point with Tigris River
Absolute minimum discharge, m³/s	450	270	150
Expected maximum long-term average[4] m³/s	750	550	150

Note: The exact minimum discharge values are subject to negotiations.

XVI. Preliminary maximum permissible values

The maximum permissible values accepted by the watercourse countries as normal values that do not require specific action are given in the table below.

The indicative and preliminary maximum permissible value could be as follows:

Parameter[5]	Salinity: total dissolved solids, TDS/l
Turkish-Syrian border	400[6]
Syrian-Iraqi border	800[7]

For example, if any of the values reported in the half-year report show a total change of +30% over two successive periods, the watercourse countries shall investigate the cause of changes and report to the Regional Water Management Organization (RWMO), which may invoke mitigating actions.

1   The actual consumption may be lower than the target consumption due to climatic variation.
2   The actual consumption may be lower than the target consumption due to climatic variation.
3   No reliable data made available. To be estimated.
4   Conservative estimates from a river modelling perspective (based on the 40-year rainfall/runoff period).
5   It is recommended that additional parameters be included in a water regime framework.
6   Value to be revised according to the base documentation (cf. the study – on drinking water quality parameters).
7   Value to be revised according to the base documentation (cf. the study – on drinking water quality parameters).

Bibliography

Albright, M. 2004. *Madame Secretary*. New York: Random House.

Allan, J.A. 1999a. "Global Systems Ameliorate Local Droughts. Water, Food and Trade". In: *SOAS Occasional Paper N° 10*. London: University of London, School of Oriental and African Studies.

Allan, J.A. 1999b. "Middle Eastern Hydropolitics. Interpreting Constructed Knowledge. A Review Article". In: *SOAS Occasional Paper N° 18*. London: University of London, School of Oriental and African Studies.

Allan, J.A. 2002. *The Middle East Water Question. Hydropolitics and the Global Economy*. (p. 336). London; New York: I.B. Tauris.

Allan, J.A. 2003. "Virtual Water – The Water, Food, and Trade Nexus. Useful Concept or Misleading Metaphor?". In: *IWRA, Water International, 28*(1), 4-11.

Al Masri, A.A. 2003. "An Agreement between the Syrian Arab Republic and the Lebanese Republic for the Sharing of the Great Southern River Basin Water and the Building of a Joint Dam on it". In: *Proceedings from the Water, Energy and Environment in July 2003 at the Water, Energy and Environment Research Centre*. Louaize, Lebanon: Notre Dame University.

Alster, J.P. 1996. "Water in the Peace Process. Israel-Syria-Palestinians". In: *JUSTICE*, No. 10, September 1996.

Altinbilek, D. 2004. "Development and Management of the Euphrates-Tigris basin". In: *Water Resources Development, 20*(1), 15-33.

Amery, H.A. 2000. "A Popular Theory of Water Diversion from Lebanon – Towards Public Participation for Peace". In: H.A. Amery and A.T. Wolf (Eds.), *Water in the Middle East – A Geography of Peace*. Texas: University of Texas Press.

Amery, H.A.; Wolf, A.T. 2000. *Water in the Middle East – A Geography of Peace*. USA: University of Texas Press.

Arad, A.; Bein, A. 1986. "Saline versus Freshwater Contribution to the Thermal Waters of the Northern Jordan Rift Valley". In: *Israeli Journal of Hydrology, 83*, 49-66.

Assaf, K.; al Khatib, N.; Shuval, H.; Kally, E. 1993. *A Proposal for the Development of a Regional Water Master Plan*. Jerusalem: Israel/Palestine Center for Research and Information (IPCRI).

Beaumont, P. 1996. "Agricultural and Environmental Changes in the Upper Euphrates Catchment of Turkey and Syria and their Political and Economic Implications". In: *Applied Geography, 16*(2),137-155.

Bergelson, G.; Nativ, R.; Bein, A. 1998. "Assessment of Hydraulic Parametres in the Aquifers Surrounding and Underlying Sea of Galilee". In: *Ground Water, 36*, 409-417.

Berman, I.; Wihbey, P.M. 1999. "The New Water Politics of the Middle East". In: *Strategic Review*. Available at: http://www.israeleconomy.org/strategic/water12900.thm

Bilen, Ö. 1997. *Turkey and Water Issues in the Middle East*. Ankara: Southeastern Anatolia Project (GAP) Regional Development Administration.

Boisson de Chazournes, L. 2003. "The Role of Diplomatic Means of Solving Water disputes. A Special Emphasis on Institutional Mechanisms". In: Permanent Court of Arbitration (PCA), *Resolution of International Water* Disputes. Peace Palace Papers. New York: Kleuwer Law International.

Boisson de Chazournes, L. 2004. *Changing Perspectives in the Management of International Watercourses. An International Law Perspective*. Geneva: Faculty of Law, University of Geneva.

Broch, E.; Lysne, D. (Eds.). 1992. *Proceedings of the Second International Conference of Hydropower '92*. Rotterdam: Balkema.

Bulloch, J.; Darwish, A. 1993. *Water Wars. Coming Conflicts in the Middle East,* London: Victor Gollancz.

Clawson, P.; Eisenstadt, M. 2000. *The Last Arab-Israeli Battlefield? Implications of an Israeli Withdrawal from Lebanon*. Washington, DC: Washington Institute for Near East Policy.

CESAR. 1996. *A Comparative Study of Water Institutions, Legislation, and Economics between Jordan, PA, and Israel*. Oslo: CESAR.

CESAR. 1999a. *The Euphrates River and the Tigris River, Water Resources Management*. Documentation of National Data on the Euphrates River in Iraq, Draft. Oslo, Norway (unpublished).

CESAR. 1999b. *The Euphrates River and The Tigris River, Water Resources Management*. Documentation of National Data on The Euphrates River in Syria, Draft. Oslo, Norway (unpublished).

CESAR. 2005. *An Independent Technical Study, the Euphrates and Tigris River, Water Resources Management, Water Resources Analysis Methodology*. Oslo, Norway. Published electronically by COMPASS and available at: http://www.compass-org.ch/Selected_literature/selected_literature1.htm

Clark, P.; Magee, S. (Eds.). 2001. *The Iraqi Marshlands – A Human Environmental Study*. London: AMAR Foundation.

Clinton, B.J. 2004. *My Life*. New York: Alfred A. Knopf.

Comair, F. 2003. *Lebanese-Syrian Water Projects on Non-navigational Water Courses – Orontes and Nahel el Kabir*. Proceedings from the seminar on Water, Energy and Environment in July 2003 at the Water, Energy and Environment Research Centre, Notre Dame University, Louaize, Lebanon.

Comair, F. 2004. "Hydro Diplomacy of Middle Eastern Countries along with the UN Convention on Non-Navigational Uses of International Water Courses. Case Study Orontes and Nahr el Kabir". In: ESCWA, BGR, GTZ, *Enhancing Negotiation Skills on International Water Issues in the ESCWA Region*. Beirut: ESCWA.

COMPASS. 2005a. *Third Party Compensation Arrangements. Water Resources Management of the Golan Heights – Concepts for Determining the Costs of Alternative Resettlement Strategies*. Geneva: COMPASS Foundation. Available at: http://www.compass-org.ch/Selected_literature/selected_literature1.htm

COMPASS. 2005b. *An Independent Technical Study, The Euphrates and Tigris Rivers, Water Resources Management, Water Resources Analysis Methodology*. Geneva: COMPASS Foundation. Available at: http://www.compass-org.ch/Selected_literature/selected_literature1.htm

CWOG. 1987. *Canadian Water Quality Guidelines*. Water Quality Branch, Inland Waters Directorate, Environment Canada, Ottawa, Ontario [k1A 0H3].

Daibes-Murad, F. 2005. "A New Legal Framework for Managing the World's Shared Groundwaters – A Case Study from the Middle East". In: *Water Law and Policy Series*. London: IWA Publishing.

Daoudy, M. 1995. "Syrian Water Issues and Relations with Neighboring Countries". In: *Water in the Arab World*. Damascus: Office Arabe de Presse et de Documentation.

Daoudy, M. 1999. *Water, Institutions and Development in Syria. A Downstream Perspective from the Euphrates and Tigris*. Cairo: World Commission of Dams Regional Consultation.

Daoudy, M. 2005a. *Le Partage des Eaux la Syrie, l'Irak et la Turquie Négociation, Sécurité et Asymétrie des Pouvoirs*. Paris: CNRS Éditions.

Daoudy, M. 2005b. "Le Long Chemin de Damas. La Syrie et les Nègociations de Paix avec Israël". In: *Les Etudes du CERI, No. 119*. Paris: CNRS Editions.

Dawood, M. 1995. "Syrian Water Issues and relations with Neighboring Countries". In: *Water in the Arab World*. Damascus: Office Arabe de Presse et de Documentation.

Dolatyar, M.; Gray, T.S. 2000. "The Politics of Water Scarcity in the Middle East". In: *Environmental Politics, 9*(3), 65-88.

Dreizin, Y. 2004. *The Impact of Desalination. Israel and the Palestinian Authority*. [Israeli Water Commissioner Office] Presentation on Stockholm Water Week, SIWI.

de Callières, F. 2002. *De la manière de négocier avec les souverains*. Genève: Librairie Droz.

du Bois, F. 1995. "Water Law in the Economy of Nature". In: J.A. Allan and C. Mallat (Eds.), *Water in the Middle East: Legal and Commercial Issues*. (pp. 111–126). London: Tauris.

Eaton, J.W.; Eaton, D.J. 1995. "Negotiation Strategies in International Disputes". In: K.R. Spillman and G. Bächler (Eds.), *Environmental Crisis. Regional Conflicts and Ways of Cooperation*. Report of the International Conference at Monte Verita, Switzerland, 3–7 October 1994. In: *Occasional Paper no. 14, Environment and Conflict Project* (ENCOP), Zurich.

EAWAG. 2003. "The Euphrates River and The Tigris River – Water Resources Management. Review of Report on Water Resources Analysis, Volume I, II and III" (completed in March 2003). In: COMPASS, 2005: *An Independent Technical Study, the Euphrates and Tigris River, Water Resources Management, Water Resources Analysis Methodology*. Available at: http://www.compass-org.ch/Selected_literature/selected_literature1.htm
http://www.cesar.no/Selected_publication/Selected_publication.htm

Eckstein, Z.; Zakai, D.; Nachtom, Y.; Fishelson, G. 1994. *The Allocation of Water Sources between Israel, the West Bank and Gaza. An Economic Viewpoint*. Tel Aviv: The Pihas Sapir Centre for Development and the Armand Hammer Fund for Economic Co-operation in the Middle East.

EIE (Elektrik İşleri Etüt). *General Directorate of Electrical Power Resources Survey and Development Administration*. Ankara: EIE. Available at: http://www.eie.gov.tr/

El-Ashry, M.T. 1998. "Global Water Facility – Finding solutions to water disputes". In: *Water and Dispute Prevention. South Perspective*. Washington, DC: Centre for Global South.

El-Fadel, M.; Maroun, R.; Semerjian, J.; Harajli, H. 2003. "A Health-Based Socio-Economic Assessment of Drinking Water Quality". In: *Management of Environmental Quality, 14*(3), 353-368.

Elmusa, S.S. 1997. *Water Conflict. Economics, Politics, Law and the Palestinian–Israeli Water Resources*. Washington, DC: Institute for Palestinian Studies.

Enderlin, C. 2003. *Shattered Dreams – The Failure of the Peace Process in the Middle East, 1995-2002*. New York: Other Press.

EPA. 2000. *National Management Measure to Control Non-Point Source Pollution from Agriculture*. Draft. Washington, DC: Office of Water, NSCB, US EPA, 20460.

Erdogan Basmaci, E. (DSI). 1992. "Atatürk Dam and Powerplant". In: E. Broch and D. Lysne (Eds.), *Conference Papers of Hydropower '92*. Rotterdam: Balkema.

EU Directives. Directive 2000/60/EC Establishing a Framework for EU Water Legislation, Directive 76/160/EEC, Directive 80/778/EEC as amended by 98/83/EC (Drinking Water Quality), Directive 91/271/EEC, and Directive 91/676/EEC (Nitrates Directive concerning pollution from agricultural production), and Directive 80/778/EC of 15 July.

EU Rapid Reaction Mechanism. 2004. *End of Programme Report – Lebanon/Israel Wazzani springs dispute*, January 2004. Available at: http://europa.eu.int/comm/external_relations/cpcm/rrm/wazzani.pdf

EU Water Framework Directive. 2000. Directive 2000/60/EC of the European Parliament and of the Council. Available at: http://europa.eu.int/comm/environment/water/water-framework/index_en.html

FAO. 1994. "Nearest and North Africa Regional Overview. Syrian Arab Republic, the State of Food and Agriculture". In: *Water and Agriculture*. (pp. 161-167). Rome: FAO.

FAO. 1995. "Water quality for agriculture". In: *FAO Irrigation and Drainage Paper* 29 Rev.1. Rome: FAO.

Feitelson, E. 2000. "The Ebb and Flow of Arab-Israeli Water Conflicts. Are Past Confrontations Likely to Resurface?". In: *Water Policy, 2*, 343-363.

Feitelson, E. 2002. "Implications of Shifts in the Israeli Water Discourse for Israeli–Palestinian Water Negotiations". In: *Political Geography, 21*(3), 310.

Feitelson, E.; Haddad, M. (Eds.). 2000. *Management of Shared Groundwater Resources. The Israeli-Palestinian Case with and International perspective*. Ottawa: IDRC; Kluwer Academic Publishers.

Fisher, F.; Arlosoroff, S.; Eckstein, Z.; Haddadin, M.; Hamati, S.G.; Huber-Lee, A.; Jarrar, A.; Jayyousi, A Uri Shamir, U.; Wesseling, H., 2002. "Optimal Water Management and Conflict Resolution. The Middle East Project". In: *Water Resources Research, 38*(11), 1243.

Fisher, F.; Huber-Lee, A. *et al.* 2005. *Liquid Assets. An Economic Approach for Water Management and Conflict Resolution in the Middle East and Beyond*. Baltimore: Johns Hopkins University Press.

Fromkin, D. 2001. *A Peace to End All Peace*. New York: First Owl Publications Edition.

GAP. 1996. Main web-server. http://www.turkey.org/al_gap.htm (GAP: Guneydogu Anadolu Projesi),

General Directorate of Energy and Water, 2001. *10 Years Strategic Water Plan for Lebanon (2001 -2010)*. Beirut: Ministry of Hydraulic and Electrical Resources.

Gjessing, J. 2002. "Resource Geography, Conceptual Approaches". In: *Resources and Environmental Geography*, Serie A. No 22. Oslo: Department of Geography, University of Oslo.

Gleick, P, 2004. *World's Water, 2004-2005. The Biennial Report on Freshwater Resources*. Washington, DC: Island Press.

Green Cross International. 2004. "National Sovereignty and International Watercourses Panel". In: F. Curtin and B. Charrier (Eds.), *Water for Peace – Between Conflict and Co-operation. The Role of Civil Society*. Geneva: Green Cross.

Gruen, G.E. 2000. "The Politics of Water and Middle East Peace". In: *American Foreign Policy Interests, 22*(2), 1-21.

GTZ. 1998. *Middle East Regional Water Study on Water Supply and Demand Development*. Under the Multilateral Working Group on Water Resources, with input from and participation of Israel, Jordan and the Palestinian Authority. Eschborn: GTZ; BMZ.

Guttman, J. 2004. *From Oslo to Feshka. Sustainable Utilisation of the Eastern Aquifer*. [Mekorot National Water Corporation]. Presentation in Stockholm Water Week, 2004. SIWI.

Gvirtzman, H. 2002. *Israel Water Resources, Chapters in Hydrology and Environmental Sciences*. Jerusalem: Yad Ben-Zvi Press [in Hebrew].

Habash, M.A. 1995. "Israeli Scheming and Intrusion into Arab Waters". In: *Water in the Arab World – Present and Future*. Damascus: Office Arabe de presse et de documentation.

Haddad, M. 2000. "The Islamic Approach to the Environment and Sustainable Groundwater Management". In: E. Feitelson and M. Haddad (Eds.), *Management of Shared Groundwater Resources. The Israeli-Palestinian Case with and International Perspective*. Ottawa: IDRC and Kluwer Academic Publishers.

Haddadin, M.J. 2001. *Diplomacy on the Jordan. International Conflict and Negotiated Resolution*. USA: Kluwer Academic Publishers.

Hall, J.K. 1996. "Topography and bathymetry of the Dead Sea depression". In: *Tectonophysics, 266*(1-4), 177-185.

Hamner, J.; Wolf, A. 2000. *Water quality aspects in international water treaties (derived from the Transboundary Freshwater Dispute Database)*. Department of Geography, Oregon State University. Unpublished Paper for CESAR Foundation.

Hart, B.T. 1984. "Australian Water Quality Criteria for Heavy Metals". In: Australian Resources Council, *Tech. Pap. No. 74*. Canberra: Department of National Development and Energy, Australian Government Publishing Service.

High Relief Committee; UNDP. 1999. *Regional Socio-Economic Development Programme for South Lebanon, Post-Conflict Socio-Economic Rehabilitation Programme for South Lebanon*. Beirut and New York: High Relief Committee; UNDP.

Hoff, F.C. 2000. "The Water Dimension of Golan Heights negotiations". In: H.A. Amery and A.T. Wolf (Eds.), *Water in the Middle East. A Geography of Peace* (p. 151). Austin: University of Texas Press.

Hydrological Service. 1999. *Hydrological Year Publication of Israel*. Annual Report.

Iraqi Ministry of Foreign Affairs, 1999. *Joint Ministerial Publication. The division of waters in the international laws. FACTS on joint waters with Turkey*. Baghdad: Iraqi MFA; Ministry of Irrigation.

Isaac, J.; Owewi, M. 2000. "The Potential of GIS in water Management and Conflict Resolution". In: E. Feitelson and M. Haddad (Eds.), *Management of Shared Groundwater Resources. The Israeli-Palestinian Case with and International Perspective* (p. 334). Ottawa: IDRC; Kluwer Academic Publishers.

Israel Ministry of National Infrastructure; Water Commissioner. 2002. Tel Aviv: Israel Water Sector, Water Commissioner.

Israeli letter to the UN Security Council. November 21, 2002.

Israeli Water Commissioner. *Various Annual Reports from the Water Commissioner.* Tel Aviv.

Israeli Water Commissioner. 2002. *Israeli Water Sector – Reduce Consumption.* Tel Aviv: Ministry of National Infrastructure and the Water Commissioner.

Israel–Palestinian Interim Agreement on the West Bank and the Gaza Strip. 1995. Available at: http://www.mfa.gov.il/MFA/Peace+Process/Guide+to+the+Peace+Process/The+Israeli-Palestinian+Interim+Agreement+-+Main+P.htm.

Iza, A. 2004. "International Water Governance. Conservation of Freshwater Ecosystems, Vol. 1 International Agreements Compilation and Analysis". In: *IUCN Environmental Policy and Law Paper,* No.55. Available at: http://www.iucn.org/themes/law/pdfdocuments/EPLP55EN.pdf

Jägerskog, A. 2004. *Why States Cooperate over Shared Water Resources. The Water Negotiations in the Jordan Basin:* Linköping: Linköping Studies in Arts and Science.

Kammerud, T.A. 1997. "Geographical Information Systems for International River Basin Management in the Third World". In: *Resource and Environmental Geography.* Serie A, No 17. Oslo: Department of Geography, University of Oslo.

Kantor, M. 2000. "Water in Israel. A View towards the Beginning of 2000". In: D. Zaslavsky (Ed.), *Research Paper N° 9504.* Rehovot: The Center for Agricultural Economic Research.

Kawash, F. 2003. *The Palestinian Water Situation and the Legal Basis for the Palestinian Position on the Question of Palestinian Water Rights.* Interview in *Al-Rai Newspaper, Jordan,* 11 February, 2003 [in Arabic].

Keidar, J.; Kawash, F. 2004. *Joint Presentation of "Regional Cooperation on Water"* at the Stockholm Water Week, SIWI.

Kelly, K.; Homer-Dixon, T. 1995. *Environmental Scarcity and Violent Conflict. The Case of Gaza.* Toronto: American Association for the Advancement of Science and University College, University of Toronto.

Kelman, H.C. 1999. "Experience from 30 Years of Action Research on the Israeli–Palestinian Conflict". In: K.R. Spillman and A. Wenger (Eds.), *Zeitgeschichtliche Hintergründe aktueller Konflikte VII – Vortragsreihe an der ETH Zürich Sommersemester 1999 No 54.* (pp. 173-197). Zürich: Zücher Beiträge zur Sicherheitspolitik und Konfliktforskchung,

Kibaroglu, A.; Ünver, O. 2000. "An Institutional Framework for Facilitating Co-operation in the Euphrates-Tigris Basin". In: *International Negotiation, 5,* 311-330.

Kirmani, S.; Rangeley, R. 1994. *International Inland Water. Concepts for a More Active World Bank Role.* World Bank Technical Paper WTP239. Washington, DC: Available at: http://www-wds.worldbank.org/servlet/WDS_IBank_Servlet?pcont=details&eid=000009265_3970311122714

Klein, M. 1998 "Water balance of the Upper Jordan River Basin". In: *Water International, 23*(4), 244-247.

Klieman, A. S. 1970. *Foundations of British Policy in the Arab World. The Cairo Conference of 1921.* Baltimore; London: Johns Hopkins University Press.

Kliot, N. 1994. *The Geopolitics of Inequality. The Tigris-Euphrates Drainage Basin.* London: Routledge.

Kolars, J.F. 1992. "The Future of the Euphrates bBasin". In: Le Moigne, Guy *et al.* (Eds.), *Country Experiences with Water Resources Management: Economic, Institutional, Technological and Environmental Issues.* World Bank Technical Paper 175. Washington DC: World Bank.

Kolars, J.F.; Mitchell, W.A. 1991. *The Euphrates River and the Southeastern Anatolia Development Project*. Carbondale; Edwardsville: Southern Illinois University Press.

Kristjánsdóttir, E. 2003. "Resolution of Water Disputes: Lessons from the Middle East". In: *Resolution of International disputes*. The Permanent Court of Arbitration/Peace Palace Papers. (pp. 363-368). The Hague: Kluwer Law International.

Lebanese Letter to the UN General Assembly and the Security Council on March 23rd, 2001 and on September 12th, 2002. Available at: http://domino.un.org/unispal.nsf/9a798adbf322aff38 525617b006d88d7/3ceb1a678c9f17b285256c39004f03b7!OpenDocument&Highlight=2,A%2F 57%2F404

Lebanese Ministry of Environment. 1996. "Decision no1/53 related to standards for water, air and soil pollution", and "Decision 8/1 related to standards for wastewater discharges".

Lebanese "Non-Paper" to the UN Security Council, 2002 (not public).

Leitz, F.; Ewoldsen, E.I. 1978. "Design Criteria for the Yuma Desalination Plant". In: *Desalination*, 24(1-3), 321-340.

Lonergan, S. 1997. "Water Resources and Conflict. Examples from the Middle East". In: N.P. Gleditsch (Ed.), *Conflict and Environment, NATO ASI Series 2*. Vol. 33. London: Kluwer Academic.

Lorenz, F. 2001. *Protection of Water Facilities under International Law*. A Research Project by the International Water Academy, Oslo.

Lorenz, F.M.; Erickson, E.J. (with the collaboration of B.R. Shaw, A.T. Wolf and J.F. Kolars). 1999. *The Euphrates Triangle. Security Implications of the Southeastern Anatolia Project*. Washington, DC: National Defense University Press.

Lowi, M.R. 1990. *The Politics of Water under Conditions of Scarcity And Conflicts. The Jordan River and Riparian States*. Unpublished PhD. Princeton, NJ: Politics Department, Princeton University.

Lowi, M.R. 1995. *Water and Power. The Politics of a Scarce Resource in the Jordan River Basin*. Cambridge: Cambridge University press.

Maar'I, T.; Halabi, U. 1992. "Life under Occupation in the Golan Heights". In: *Journal of Palestine Studies, 22*: 78–93

Madrid Donors' Conference, 2003. *Helping the Iraqi People Build a New Iraq* (cf. http://www.state.gov/p/nea/ci/c3212.htm). November 6, 2003.

Mason, S. 2004. *From Conflict to Cooperation in the Nile Basin*, Centre for Security Studies, ETH, Zurich. Available at: http:// www.css.ethz.ch/publications

McCaffrey, S. 1993. "Water, politics and international law". In: Gleick, P. (Ed.), *Water in Crisis. A Guide to the World's Fresh Water Resources*. London; New York: Oxford University Press.

McCaffrey, S. 2001. "The Contribution of the UN Convention on the Law of the Non–Navigational Uses of International Watercourses". In: *International Journal on Global Environmental Issues*, 1(3-4), 250-263.

Mekorot National Water Corporation. 1996. *Background Material for the Peace Talks on Water Issues between Israel and Syria. Situation Assessment and Risk Analysis*. Tel Aviv: Mekorot.

Mekorot National Water Corporation. 2004. *Annual Report*. Tel Aviv: Mekorot.

METAP. 2001. *Mediterranean Environmental Technical Assistance Program, 2001, Lebanon Country Profile*. Available at: http://www.metap.org.files/water%20reports/country/%20Rreport/ LebanonWaterQualityReport%20Report.pdf

Mier, M.B. 1994. "Water Management Policy in Israel. A Comprehensive Approach". In: J, Isaac and H. Shuval (Eds.), *Water and Peace in the Middle East*. Amsterdam: Elsevier.

MOPIC. 1998a. *Regional Plan for the West Bank Governorates – Water and Wastewater Existing Situation*. Ramallah: Ministry of Planning and International Cooperation.

MOPIC. 1998b. *Sensitive Water Resources Recharge Areas in the West Bank Governorates – Emergency Nnatural Resources Protection Plan*. Ramallah: Ministry of Planning and International Cooperation, Directorate for Urban and Rural Planning.

Morris, H.; Smyth, G. 2001. "Israel Talks of 'Water War' with Lebanon". In: *Financial Times*, 16 March 2001.

Mott IV, W. 1997. *The Economic Basis for Peace, Linkages between Economic Growth and International Conflict*. London: Greenwood Press.

Murakami, M. 1995. *Managing Water for Peace in the Middle East: Alternative Strategies*. New York: United Nations University Press.

Muslih, M. 1983. "The Golan. Israel, Syria and Strategic Calculations". In: *Middle East Journal*, 47(4), 611-632.

Naff, D. 1994. "Israel-Syria. Conflict at the Jordan River, 1949-1967". In: *Journal of Palestine Studies*, 23(4), 26-40.

Naff, T.; Matson, R. (Eds.). 1984. *Water in the Middle East. Conflict or Cooperation?*. Boulder, Colorado: Westview Press.

NAS/NAE. 1973. *Water quality criteria. Report of the U.S. Academy of Science and National Academy of Engineering*. EPA-R3-73-033. Washington, D.C.: U.S. Environmental Agency.

ODI; ARACADIS; Euroconsult. 2001. "Transboundary water Management as an International Public Good". In: *Developing Financing 2000*, No 2001:1. Stockholm: Swedish Ministry of Foreign Affairs.

OECD. 1994. *Environmental Indicators*. Paris: OECD.

Omberg Hansen, A. 2004. *Wazzani Spring – Assessment of the Present International Water Conflict between Lebanon and Israel – Concerning the Wazzani Spring and Hasbani River – Seen within an Arab-Israeli Context*, a Cand. Scient Thesis in Resource Geography, Department of Geosciences, University of Oslo (publicly available, but unpublished).

Omberg Hansen, A. 2005. *Chronological Analysis of the Conflict Level between Israel and Lebanon Regarding the Wazzani and Hasbani Dispute*. Oslo: CESAR (upublished).

Oren, B. 2004. *Presentation at the Stockholm Water Week, SIWI, 2004*, Israeli Water Company Mekorot, SIWI, Stockholm.

Palestinian Hydrology Group. 1999. *Assessment of Selected Solid Waste Dumping Sites in the West Bank and Gaza Strip*. Jerusalem: PHG.

Palestinian Water Law enacted 3/2002, Palestinian Water Authority, Ramallah.

Permanent Court of Arbitration (PCA). 2003a. *Resolution of International Water Disputes*. Peace Palace Papers. New York: Kleuwer Law International.

Permanent Court of Arbitration (PCA). 2003b. *Permanent Court of Arbitration (PCA)/Peace Palace Papers. Resolution of International Water Disputes*. New York: Kleuwer Law International.

PWA. 1999. *Strategy for Water Management in Palestine*. Ramallah: PWA.

PWA. 2004a. *The Political Framework of the Water Issues in the Final Status Negotiations between Palestine and Israel*. Paper presented by the Palestinian Water Authority (PWA) at the Special Workshop on Palestinian Water Resources, UNESCWA, Dead Sea, Jordan, 5-6 December 2003.

PWA. 2004b. *The Technical Framework of the Water Issues in the Final Status Negotiations between Palestine and Israel*. Paper presented by the Palestinian Water Authority (PWA) at the Special Workshop on Palestinian Water Resources. UNESCWA, Dead Sea, Jordan, 5-6 December 2003.

Rabinovich, I. 2004. *Waging Peace – Israel and the Arabs 1948–2003*. Princeton; Oxford: Princeton University Press.

Rimmer, A.; Hurwitz, S.; Gvirtzman, H. 1999. "Spatial and Temporal Characteristics of Saline Springs. Sea of Galilee, Israel". In: *Ground Water, 37*(5), 663-673.

Rogers, P.; Peter, L. (Eds.). 1994. *Water in the Arab World: Perspectives and Prognoses*. Cambridge: Harvard University Press.

Ross, D. 2004. *The Missing Peace – The Inside Story of the Fight for Middle East Peace*. New York: Farrar, Straus and Giroux.

Sadoff, C.W.; Grey, D. 2005. "Cooperation of International Rivers - A Continuum for Securing and Sharing Benefits". In: *Water International, 30*(4), December 2005.

Said, E. 2004. *Orientalism* (25th edition). New York: Vintage Books.

Salingar, Y.; Geifman, Y.; Aronwich, M. 1993. "Orthophoshate and Calcium Carbonate Solubilities in the Upper Watershed Basin". In: *Journal of Environmental Quality, 22*(4), 672-677.

SAM. 1996. *Facts about Euphrates-Tigris Basin*. Ankara: Centre for Strategic Research.

Schwarz, Y.; Zohar, A. 1991. *Water in the Middle East. Solutions to Water problems in the Context of Arrangement between Israel and the Arabs*. Tel Aviv, Israel: Jaffee Center for Strategic Studies.

Shapland, G. 1997. *Rivers of Discord. International Water Disputes in the Middle East*. London: Hurst & Company.

Sherman, M. 1999. *The Politics of Water in the Middle East; an Israeli Perspective on the Hydro-political Aspects of the Conflict*. London: Macmillan Press.

Sherman, M. 2001. "Water in Israel. The Dry Facts". In: *Herzliya Papers*. Herzliya, Israel: Institute of Policy and Strategy, Interdisciplinary Center.

Shiff, Z. 1993. *Peace with Security. Israel's Minimal Security Requirements in Negotiations with Syria*. Washington Institute Policy Paper N° 34. Washington, DC: Washington Institute for Near East Policy.

Shoam, Y.; Sarig, O. (Eds.). 1995. *Israel National Water Carrier – from the Sea of Galilee to the Fringe of the Desert*. Tel Aviv: Mekorot National Water Corporation.

Shuval, H.I. 1992. "Approaches to Resolving the Water Conflicts between Israel and her Neighbours – A Regional Water-for-Peace Plan". In: *Water International, 17*, 133-143.

Shuval, H.I. 1994. *Israel and Syria. Peace and Security on the Golan*. Tel Aviv: Tel Aviv University, Jaffee Center for Strategic Studies.

Soffer A. 1994. "The Relevance of the Johnston Plan to the Reality of 1993 and Beyond". In: H. I. Shuval (ed.), *Israel-Palestine Water*. Amsterdam: Elsevier.

Solanes, M. 2000. "Water Rights". In: E. Feitelson and M. Haddad (eds.), *Management of Shared Groundwater Resources: the Israeli-Palestinian Case with an International Perspective*, p. 265. Ottawa: IDRC; Kluwer Academic Publishers.

Starr, J.S. (Ed.), 2001. "Water Crisis in Israel". In: *Proceedings of the Herzliya Forum Conference.* Herzliya, Israel: Interdisciplinary Center Herlziya Lauder School of Government, Diplomacy and Strategy.

Swisher, C.E. 2004. *The Truth about Camp David. New York:* Nation Books.

Tayseer Maar'I, T.; Halabi, U. 1992. "Life under Occupation in the Golan Heights". In: *Journal of Palestine Studies, 22*(1), 78-90.

Tignino, M. 2003. "Water in Times of Armed Conflict". In: *Resolution of International Disputes.* Permanent Court of Arbitration Peace Palace Paper. (pp. 319-349). The Hague: Kluwer Law International.

Tolmach, Y. 1991. *Hydrogeological Atlas of Israel, Coastal Aquifer and Gaza Area*, Hydrological Service of Israel, Jerusalem [in Hebrew].

Toye, P. (Ed.), 1983. *Palestine Boundaries 1833-1947, Vol.3.* Oxford: University of Durham Press.

Trolldalen [Trondalen], J.M. 1992. *International Environmental Conflict Resolution –The Role of the United Nations.* New York; Geneva; Washington, DC; Oslo: UNITAR; NIDR; WFED.

Trolldalen [Trondalen], J.M. 1996. *A Role for the World Bank in International Environmental Conflict Resolution?* Washington, DC: Environment Department, PPU, World Bank [out of print].

Trolldalen [Trondalen], J.M. 1997. "Troubled Waters in the Middle East. The Process towards the First Regional Water Declaration between Jordan, Palestinian Authority, and Israel". In: *Natural Resources Forum – A United Nations Journal, 21*(2), May 1997 Special issue.

Trondalen, J.M.; Munasinghe, M. 1999. *Ethics and Water Resources Conflicts.* UNESCO Working Group on Ethics of the Use of Freshwater Resources, Almeria, Spain (July/August, 1999).

Trondalen, J.M. 2004a. *A Manual on Dispute Resolution of International Watercourses.* Lebanon: ESCWA Beirut.

Trondalen, J.M. 2004b. "Growing Controversy over 'Wise International Water Governance'". In: *Water Science and Technology: Drainage Basin Security – Balancing Production, Trade and Water Use, 49*(7), 61-66 (Plenary Speech at Stockholm Water Symposium, 2003).

Turan, I.; Kut, G. 1997. "Political-Ideological Constraints on Intra-basin Cooperation on Transboundary Waters". In: *Natural Resources Forum – A United Nations Journal, 21*(2), Special issue.

Turkish Department of Information. 1992. *Turkey and the Question of Water in the Middle East.* Ankara: Department of Information.

Turkish Ministry of Foreign Affairs. 1996. *Water Issues between Turkey, Syria and Iraq.* Ankara: Department of Regional and Transboundary Waters, Ministry of Foreign Affairs.

Turton, A. 1997. *The Hydro-politics of Southern Africa. The Case of the Zambezi River Basin as an Area of Potential Co-operation Based on Allan's Concept of "Virtual Water".* Unpublished Master's thesis in international relations, University of South Africa.

UN. 1978. *UN Security Council Resolution 425. Mideast Situation/Lebanon – Establishment of UNIFIL – UN Security Council Resolution 19 March 1978.* Available at: http://domino.un.org/unipal.nsf

UN. 1997. *Framework Convention on Non-Navigational Use of International Watercourses from 1997*. UN DocA/51/869. Retrieved from: www.un.org.law/ilc/texts/nonnav.htm

UNDP. 2005. *Iraqi Living Conditions Survey 2004*. New York: UNDP.

UNECE. 1992. *The UNECE Convention on the Protection and Use of Transboundary Watercourses and International Lakes*. London 17 June 1999. Retrieved from: www.unece.org/env/water/pdf/watercon.pdf

UNECE. 1999. *The Protocol on Water and Health to the 1992 Convention on the Protection and Use of Transboundary watercourses and International Lakes*. London. 17 June 1999. Retrieved from: www.unece.org/env/documents/2000/wat/mp.wat.2000.1.e.pdf

UNEP. 2003a. *Desk Study on the Environment in the Occupied Palestinian Territories*. Geneva: UNEP.

UNEP. 2003b. *Desk Study on the Environment in Iraq*. Nairobi: UNEP.
Retrieved from: http://www.unep.org/pdf/iraq_ds_lowres.pdf.

UNESCWA. 2004. *Enhancing Negotiation Skills on International Water Issues in the ESCWA Region*. UNESCWA/GTZ/BGR, Dead Sea, Jordan, 5-6 December 2003.

UN Framework Convention on Non-Navigational Use of International Watercourses. New York: UN.

Unver, O. 2003. "Southeastern Anatolia Development Project". In: *IEEE Power Engineering Review*, March 2002, 1-3.

Van Baal, T. 2003. *Turkey and the EU*. A MSc-thesis. Oslo: Institute for Geo Science, University of Oslo (unpublished).

Vengosh, A.; Kloppman, W.; Marei, A.; Livshitz, Y.; Guitierrez, A.; Banna, M.; Guerrot, C.; Pankratov, I.; Raanan, H. 2005. "Sources of salinity and boron in the Gaza Strip. Natural contaminant flow in the southern Mediterranean costal aquifer". In: *Water Resource Research*, Vol. 41, W01013, doi:10.1029/2004WR003344

WHO. 1997. *Water Quality Standards*. Geneva: World Health Organization.

Wolf, A. 1995. *Hydropolitics along the Jordan River. Scarce water and its impact on the Arab-Israeli Conflict*. Tokyo: United Nations University Press.

Wolf, A. 2000. "Hydrostrategic Territory in the Jordan Basin". In: Amery, H.A. and A.T. Wolf. (Eds.), *Water in the Middle East – A Geography of Peace*. Texas, USA: University of Texas Press.

Wolf, A.T. (Dir.). 2002. *Atlas of International Freshwater Agreements*. (UNEP/DEWA/DPDL/RS.02-4). Nairobi: UNEP.

Wolf, A.T.; Natharius, J.A.; Danielson, J.J.; Ward, B.S.; Pender, J.K. 1999. "International River Basins of the World". In: *International Journal of Water Resources Development*, 15(4), 387-427.

World Bank. 1996:*Environmental Performance Monitoring and Supervision*. EA Source Publication. Washington, DC: World Bank.

World Bank. 2001a. *Syria. Country Report on Water Quality Management and Possible METAP Interventions*. Washington, DC: World Bank.

World Bank. 2001b. *Syrian Arab Republic – Irrigation Sector Report, Rural Development, Water, and Environment Group, Middle East and North Africa Region*, IBRD. (Report No. 22602-SYR). Washington, DC: World Bank.

Zarour, H.; Isaac, J. 1993. "Nature's Apportionment and the Open Market. A Promising Solution to the Arab-Israeli Water Conflict". In: *Water International*, 18, 40-53.